Translated Texts for Historians
Volume 53

History and Hagiography from the Late Antique Sinai

Including translations of Pseudo-Nilus'
Narrations, **Ammonius'** *Report on the Slaughter*
of the Monks of Sinai and Rhaithou, **and**
Anastasius of Sinai's *Tales of the Sinai Fathers*

DANIEL F. CANER
with contributions by Sebastian Brock, Richard M. Price,
and Kevin van Bladel

Liverpool
University
Press

First published 2010
Liverpool University Press
4 Cambridge Street
Liverpool, L69 7ZU

British Library Cataloguing-in-Publication Data
A British Library CIP Record is available.

ISBN 978-1-84631-216-8 limp

Set in Times by
Koinonia, Manchester
Printed in the European Union by
Bell and Bain Ltd, Glasgow

Translated Texts for Historians

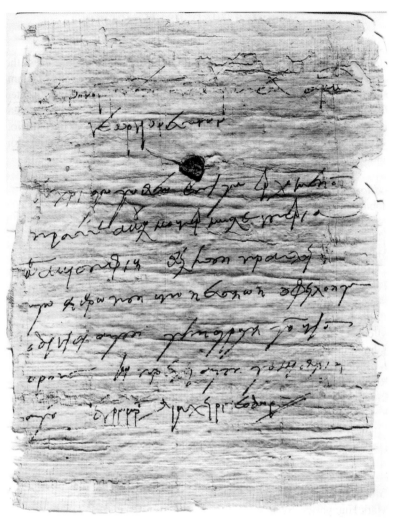

P.Colt 72, 'Order from the Governor for a Guide' to lead pilgrims to Mount Sinai, c. 684 CE.

CONTENTS

Appendix II: Sinai Defences

PREFACE AND ACKNOWLEDGEMENTS

This volume began with a proposal to introduce Pseudo-Nilus' *Narrations*, the last of the ancient novels, to a wider audience. At the suggestion of the TTH editorial board it became a much more ambitious project. With the exception of a few items that have been translated elsewhere or have not yet been sufficiently edited,[1] the present volume brings together all narratives or descriptions written within or about the Sinai peninsula c. 400–700 CE, thereby providing material for a late antique micro-history. Many of these texts, including all the major narratives, are translated into English here for the first time, each with introduction and commentary. The volume also provides a general essay introducing late antique Sinai history and literature. The over-arching theme of that essay, as of the entire volume, is the Christianization of the Sinai and its Old Testament geography.

This volume was conceived with three groups in mind: general readers, advanced students, and professional scholars. For professional historians or classicists it offers detailed commentaries, fresh interpretations, and a compendious bibliography.[2] For students it aims to raise new questions about old texts. For general readers it offers exciting stories set in a remote frontier world.

Some remarks should be made about the arrangement and presentation of the contents. The major Sinai narratives by Pseudo-Nilus, Nilus of Ancyra, Ammonius, and Anastasius of Sinai come first, followed by appendixes comprising pilgrim accounts and other late antique material. Except where stated, the order in which they are presented reflects my estimation of their probable chronological sequence and relationship. In general,

---

1 Excluded are John Climacus' *Ladder of Divine Ascent*, Daniel of Rhaithou's *Life of John Climacus*, stories from John Moschus' *Spiritual Meadow*, various apophthegmata, the *Life of Paul the Bishop and John the Priest*, and a letter by Gregory the Great. Much of this material is either cited or translated in the General Introduction. For full translations or editions, see Bibliography.

2 For comprehensive bibliography to 1998, see Valbelle and Bonnet 1998, 183–90. Sivan 2008 arrived too late for my consideration.

however, I have tried to point out problems rather than resolve them. In particular, I have tried to let the major narratives speak for themselves: my introductory essay is primarily meant to construct a historical background against which those narratives might be read, providing guidance but otherwise allowing readers to relate hagiography to history as they consider best. For my transliterations of modern Hebrew or Arabic proper names I have consulted with Kevin van Bladel and followed the standard used by the *Encyclopaedia of Islam* (3rd edn), along with that of the *Cambridge History of Byzantium*. Greek word searches were made using *Thesaurus linguae graecae* (TLG) version E. Biblical citations reflect arrangements of chapter and verse found in the New Standard Revised (NSR) edition, followed by their Septuagint (LXX) or Vulgate equivalents. Biblical translations derive mainly from NSR; otherwise all translations in this volume are my own except where noted. Here as with all else, I alone am responsible for errors in fact, presentation, interpretation, or judgment.

I come to this project as a historian and classicist whose interest in late antiquity is cultural change, especially as exemplified by early monasticism. I owe much to other specialists, including Mutsuo Kawatoko, Ariel Lewin, and Claudia Rapp. Special thanks goes to Mary Whitby for her hard work and utmost patience as my editor, Averil Cameron for reviewing the manuscript, André Binggeli for providing unpublished editions of Anastasius of Sinai, Sebastian Brock for translations of Syriac and Arabic versions of Ps.-Nilus and Ammonius, Peter Grossmann for providing architectural plans and discussing Justinian's basilica with me, Richard Price for his annotated translation of a letter from Emperor Marcian, and Kevin van Bladel for his annotated translations of Ephraim of Nisibis, Jacob of Serug, and Eutychius of Alexandria. I am especially indebted to Tali Erickson-Gini for hosting me at her house and showing me the Negev by jeep for two days in February of 2007, as well as for giving me a copy of her dissertation on Negev archaeology. I could not have hoped for a more knowledgeable, energetic, or generous guide. Finally, I thank Emma Gilligan for helping me prepare the final draft.

Acknowledgement also goes to Harvard University Press for allowing me to excerpt H. B. Dewing's translation of Procopius of Caesarea's *On Buildings*; to Oxford University Press, for allowing me to excerpt Cyril Mango and Roger Scott's translation of Theophanes Confessor's *Chronographia*, to Peter Grossmann for providing me with plans from Mount Sinai and Rhaithou, to the Israel Antiquities Authority for allowing me to rework maps from Uzi Dahari's *Sinai Settlements in the Byzantine Period*, and to the

Pierpont Morgan Library in New York for providing a photograph of *P.Colt* 72 and permitting its use as the frontispiece.

This volume is dedicated to the memory of my beloved mother, Judith Ann Brentlinger Caner, 19 February 1930–24 November 2009.

ABBREVIATIONS

ACO	*Acta Conciliorum Oecumenicorum*
ACW	Ancient Christian Writers
An. Boll.	*Analecta Bollandiana*
Anast.	Anastasius of Sinai
Apophth. patr.	*Apophthegmata patrum*
Ar.1	MS *Sinaiticus arabus* 542 version of *Report* (Ammonius)
BASOR	*Bulletin of the American Schools of Oriental Research*
BHG	F. Halkin, *Bibliotheca hagiographica graeca* (3rd edn, Brussels 1957); idem, *Novum Auctarium* (Brussels, 1984).
BZ	*Byzantinische Zeitschrift*
CCSL	Corpus Christianorum Series Latina
CI	Cosmas Indicopleustes
CIS	*Corpus inscriptionum Semiticarum*
CPA	Christian Palestinian Aramaic MS version of *Report* (Ammonius)
CS	Cistercian Studies
CSCO	Corpus Scriptorum Christianorum Orientalium
Cyril Scyth.	Cyril of Scythopolis
DOP	*Dumbarton Oaks Papers*
EH	*Ecclesiastical History* (*Historia ecclesiastica*)
ep., epp.	*Letters* (*epistula/ae*)
IEJ	*Israel Exploration Journal*
Itin.	*Itinerarium* (*Travelogue*)
JECS	*Journal of Early Christian Studies*
JESHO	*Journal of the Economic and Social History of the Orient*
John Clim.	John Climacus
John Mosch.	John Moschus
JRS	*Journal of Roman Studies*
L	Syriac MS (British Library Add. 14645) version of *Report* (Ammonius)
Ladder	*Ladder of Divine Ascent* (*Scala paradisa*)
LCL	Loeb Classical Library
LXX	Greek Septuagint version of Hebrew Scriptures
Meadow	*Spiritual Meadow* (*Pratum spirtuale*)
Narr.	*Narrations* (*Narrationes*)

PD	Peter the Deacon
PEQ	*Palestine Exploration Quarterly*
PG	Patrologia graeca
PL	Patrologia latina
PLRE II	See Bibliography, Martindale 1980
PLRE III	See Bibliography, Martindale 1992
PO	Patrologia orientalis
PP	Piacenza Pilgrim
Procop.	Procopius of Caesarea
Rel.	*Relatio* (*Report*)
SC	Sources chrétiennes
SGr 216	MS *Sinaiticus graecus* 216 version of *Report* (Ammonius)
SGr 519	MS *Sinaiticus graecus* 519 version of *Report* (Ammonius)
Top. christ.	*Christian Topography* (*Topographica christiana*)
TTH	Translated Texts for Historians
TU	Texte und Untersuchungen
V	MS *Vaticanus syriacus* 623 version of *Report* (Ammonius)
ZPE	*Zeitschrift für Papyrologie und Epigraphik*

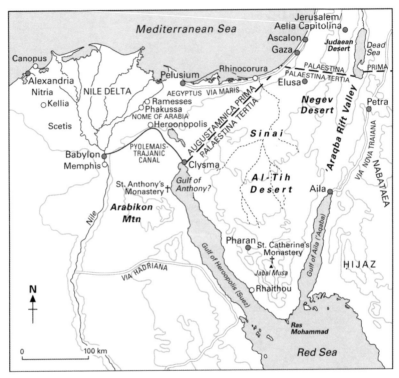

Map 1: Third Palestine and Vicinity

Reworked from Dahari 2000, 13. Courtesy of the Israel Antiquities Authority

INTRODUCTION

The texts assembled in this volume present the interactions and outlook of monks, pilgrims, and bedouins ('Saracens') on the Sinai peninsula from the fourth to the seventh centuries CE. Most have not been translated into English before, and never have they all been made accessible in a single collection. The result is a comprehensive dossier illustrating the ideals and dangers associated with life on a late Roman frontier. That this was the first region of the Roman Empire to be conquered by Arab invaders in the seventh century is just the most obvious indication of its importance. That it inspired the last great work of ancient romance, Pseudo-Nilus' *Narrations*, is another. Indeed, Ps.-Nilus' text exemplifies how closely history is wedded to fiction – or rather, to hagiography, i.e. depictions of holiness and holy people – in late antique Sinai tradition. Our challenge is not just to distinguish the one from the other, but to appreciate why history and hagiography evolved here together at once.

It should be noted that we are dealing with the invention of tradition.[1] In late antiquity the area now called 'the Sinai' was a new and somewhat imaginary frontier. Though long known to Nabataean settlers and bedouin tribes, before the fourth century it was virtually *terra incognita* to Greek, Roman, Jewish, and Christian authors alike.[2] This desolate corner of the Roman Empire only rose to prominence through the shifting military and cultural concerns of late antiquity, 300–700 CE. Wars with Persia, trade, and Red Sea alliances gave the region geopolitical importance from the third century onward, but it took Christian aspirations to put it truly on the

---

1 I.e. the purposeful creation of a meaningful past, reinforced by ceremony (in this case, a martyr cult) that affirmed a particular identity in a particular place (in this case, a Christian identity on the Sinai). For the concept and more recent examples of 'invented' traditions, see Hobsbawm and Ranger 1983.

2 The Hellenistic geographer Agatharchides of Cnidos (c. 110 BCE) learned about Sinai's Red Sea coast from the explorer Ariston, and Pharan was known to the later geographer Ptolemy. Otherwise it is not mentioned before the fourth century: see Solzbacher 1989, 44–74; Abel 1933, 385.

map. Believing that this was where Yahweh had revealed Himself to Moses, Elijah, and the Israelites 'in the wilderness', issuing His 'ten command-ments' and other precepts on righteousness (cf. Exod. 3:2–5,18; 19:16–19; 33:18–21; I [III] Kgs 19:11–12), Christian hermits and pilgrims began to explore the southern Sinai peninsula, assigning a distinct history and religious topography to its features. Imaginary vestiges of Hebrew biblical experiences were detected on rock outcroppings, where Nabataean graffiti was mistaken for Hebrew inscriptions. Indeed, from the late fourth century onward, Christian imaginations transformed the Sinai's terrain into a kind of palimpsest, where zealots of the New Dispensation might glimpse or settle over traces of the Old.[3]

Emperor Justinian's sixth-century church-and-monastic fort complex (now known as the Monastery of St Catherine) remains today the most famous monument of the late antique Sinai. Lesser known are the narratives, travel accounts, and other literary material included in this volume. Apart from archaeology, these must serve as our primary guide for reconstructing this period in Sinai history. They focus mainly on the three major Christian centres of the southern peninsula: the monastic settlements surrounding 'God's Mountain', i.e. Mount Sinai itself (Jabal Musa); the central southern oasis town of Pharan (Wadi Feiran); and the settlement founded along Sinai's south-west coast, at an area known as Rhaithou (Wadi al-Tur/Ras Raya).

This Sinai literature was written by or for late antique Christians, its purpose being to edify as much as to inform. Despite that original narrow purpose, it can still be used to explore broader regional issues, e.g. questions of political, military, economic, and cultural development. Though commonly regarded as the southernmost extension of the late antique holy land, the Sinai peninsula was, from an administrative perspective, officially part of a late Roman province known as 'Third Palestine' (*Palaestina tertia*). Probably created in the late fourth century, this sprawling provincial unit had its principal civilian headquarters at Elusa (Halutza/Khalasa), a city located about 60 km (37 miles) south-east of Gaza in an area now known as the Negev desert. Though historically overshadowed by its southern Sinai

---

3 See below, Egeria, *Itin.* I.1–5.12 and CI, *Top. christ.* V.53. Cf. Rothenberg 1970, 19, discussing the graffiti and other carvings – including five Jewish candelabra – on the Aila-Pharan pilgrimage route: 'for many generations a sort of *Kulturkampf* or a "War of Symbols" was fought out on these rocks … The "War of Symbols" was particularly in evidence between the Nabataeans and the Christian-Byzantines. Numerous Byzantine crosses of various types were demonstratively carved next to or on top of Nabataean and Hebrew inscriptions.' See also Leyerle 1996.

hinterland, this more northerly Negev area is recognized today as one of
the great success stories of late antiquity. Like rural northern Syria, it flourished in this period as never before or (until recently) since. Like northern
Syria, its landscape is dotted with ruins of farmsteads, terraces, churches,
and ghost towns attesting former agricultural prosperity. However, unlike
rural Syria, the Negev was – and still is – extremely dry land (the meaning of
'Negev' in Hebrew).[4] While Sinai pilgrimage traffic cannot fully account for
this late antique desert bloom, the sources collected in this volume nonetheless suggest close connections between the northern and southern regions
of Third Palestine in terms of pilgrimage and prosperity.

Yet these developments did not make the region any less dangerous for
its inhabitants. Justinian's Sinai complex, simply known as 'the Fort' in
the seventh century,[5] bears witness to the hazards of living or travelling in
remote areas of Third Palestine. It is, in fact, on matters of frontier security
that the Sinai literature has primarily attracted scholarly interest. As one
fourth-century pilgrim observed, this was 'Saracen country'.[6] Scattered
remnants of ancient rock structures or shrines called *nawāmīs* remind us
that the Sinai peninsula had been home to native communities and their
gods long before Christian settlers claimed it for their own.[7] Even in the
late sixth century, pilgrims could see an idol being tended by a 'Saracen'
priest right on the very slopes of Mount Horeb.[8] Historians dispute whether,
or to what degree, such pagan 'barbarians' actually posed a threat, but their
presence clearly shaped both the reality and the imaginations of contemporary monks and pilgrims. Indeed, their sporadic but devastating raids gave
rise to a Sinai martyr tradition, and inspired three of the narratives translated
here – Ps.-Nilus' *Narrations* (also called *On the Slaughter of the Monks of
Sinai and the Captivity of Theodulus*), Nilus of Ancyra's *Letter to Heliodorus*, and Ammonius' *Report concerning the Slaughter of the Monks of
Sinai and Rhaithou* – as well as one of Anastasius of Sinai's edifying tales.

These narratives describe, in unusual detail, not only the conditions of
early monastic life on the peninsula, but also the practices of local bedouin
tribes and the arrangements that isolated communities sometimes had to

4 Foss 1995 conveniently surveys the two regions together. Comparisons have also been
drawn between the Negev and developments in Roman Libya's north-west hinterland: see
Barker 2002.

5 See below, n. 224.

6 Egeria, *Itin.* VII.6.

7 Cf. Negev 1977b; Rothenberg 1970; Moritz 1916.

8 PP, *Itin.* 38.

make in order to secure from them peace or protection. The texts have therefore been used to illuminate a diverse number of subjects, ranging from monasticism and imperial defence, to Arab religion and Roman–Arab relations in pre-Islamic times. Yet these narratives were primarily written as works of literature or edification, meaning that their value as history (if read for that purpose) cannot be taken for granted. Recent scholarship has identified many of the problems involved, but it must be emphasized again that we are dealing with the invention of tradition, intent on establishing a Christian identity on the Sinai peninsula. How that effort affects the evidentiary or 'historical' value of each narrative needs to be carefully assessed. The following three sections of this introduction survey the Negev–Sinai milieu in which most of these narratives were probably written, based as far as possible on sources other than those in question. With that as our framework, we shall return to the narratives themselves, in order to discuss their possible dates, provenance, and the traditions they reflect.

1. THE FORMATION AND HISTORY OF THIRD PALESTINE

Roman Third Palestine comprised a geographical region now divided among the modern states of Israel, Egypt, and Jordan. Shaped somewhat like a huge extracted molar, it included not only the central Negev plateau and the Sinai peninsula, but also a vast area extending to the Gulf of Eilat/'Aqaba (the ancient Gulf of Aila) and the Transjordanian highlands (biblical Edom) to the east, as well as to the Dead Sea and its tributary wadis to the north. Though defined north and south by coastal waters of the Dead Sea and Red Sea, its western and eastern limits were formed by seemingly impenetrable desert buffers, like the Halutza sand dunes that separated Third Palestine from Gaza and the Mediterranean coast.[9] Much of the interior is scored by badlands and depressions. One such depression, the 'Araba rift valley, runs all the way down from the Dead Sea to the Gulf of Eilat/'Aqaba, effectively cutting Third Palestine in half.

The Sinai peninsula itself, wedged between Egypt, Palestine, and Arabia, is roughly the size of Ireland or West Virginia,[10] and may be divided into

9 We do not know how far east the province extended. Geologically, the terrain was formed 30 million years ago by seismic activity along the Syrian–African rift. Jabal Musa was once a volcano; Jabal Sufsafa was created by its molten run-off.

10 61,000 sq. km/23,550 sq. miles: see below, Map 2; also Dahari 2000, 3–6; Hobbs 1995, 5–8; Gatier 1989, 499–502; Abel 1933, 385–96; and Weill 1908.

five distinct zones: the Mediterranean coast, which in Roman times was not part of Third Palestine but split between the provinces of *Augustamnica prima* (in Egypt) and *Palaestina prima*; the Red Sea coasts that run along the Gulf of Suez on the west and Gulf of Eilat/'Aqaba on the east, meeting at Ras Muḥammad, Sinai's southernmost promontory; then, moving inland, the Negev desert, sometimes identified as the northern Sinai; further south, the central al-Tih plateau, an area comprising most of the Sinai below the Negev and traditionally identified with the deserts of Shur and Cades (Exod. 15:12; Ps. 28[29]:8); and finally, the southern Sinai proper, a 1,300 sq. km (500 sq. mile) massif that includes Jabal Musa ('Mount Moses', i.e. Mount Sinai) near its centre. This was the core area of Christian settlement and pilgrimage in late antiquity.

The setting is dramatic. The southern third of the Sinai peninsula is a geologically distinct, red and grey granite triangle defined by Wadi Feiran and Wadi al-Sheikh to the north and gulfs of Suez and Eilat/'Aqaba on either side. The centre of this triangle is a swirling mass of jagged mountains formed ten million years ago by volcanic action. With elevations ranging between 1,500 and 2,642 metres (4,900–8,600 feet), this mass features several high peaks, but none higher or more central than the cluster that includes Jabal Musa (2,286 m/7,500 feet) and Jabal Katharina (2,642 m/8,668 feet). Together with subsidiary peaks Jabal Sufsafa (2168 m/7,113 feet, traditionally identified with Mount Horeb of 1 Kgs 19:9) and Jabal al-Dayr (2065 m/6,775 feet), these stand amid a series of high plains and ravines (Wadi al-Raya, Wadi al-Dayr, Wadi Leja/al-Arba'in) in relative isolation from other prominent mountains to the south (Jabal Umm Shomer, 2590 m/8,500 feet) and west (Jabal Serbal, 2070 m/6,790 feet).[11] Generally speaking, it is aptly described as a 'country of stern desolation'.[12] The main oasis is a good two days away (49 km/35 miles) at Wadi Feiran. Yet that was a major oasis, extending 6.5 km (4 miles) in the nineteenth century. The mountains of the southern Sinai catch Mediterranean rainfalls and snows that can be collected in cisterns, and water percolates below the sandstone

11 Covering about 5.6 sq. km/2.2 sq. miles, the Jabal Musa-Sufsafa massif is separated from Jabal al-Dayr to the north-east by Wadi al-Dayr and from Jabal Katharina to the south-west by Wadi Leja/al-Arba'in. Jabal Sufsafa is essentially a ridge of Jabal Musa that juts off its north-west side. It includes about 25 smaller peaks, and is the first mountain of the cluster to be seen from the al-Raya plain. Jabal Katharina rises south-west of the Musa-Sufsafa massif, appearing behind it when looking from Raya. Though Jabal Katharina is the highest mountain on the peninsula, no settlements or stories became associated with it in antiquity (its connection to St Catherine is medieval), and we do not know its late antique name. See Dahari 2000, 25.

12 Eckenstein 1921, 5.

even in summer. As a result, the area around Jabal Musa and other peaks is not as inhospitable as one might think. It may have once been wooded, and can still be cultivated: date palms, fruit trees, and tamarisks producing 'manna' are grown there today.[13]

The other major oasis in the southern Sinai is located on the south-west coast. This area, known as Rhaithou, not only has several springs, but also the only good harbour to be found anywhere on the peninsula. For this reason it became not only a prominent monastic centre but also an important entry depot, supplying Pharan and other settlements of the Sinai interior.[14] Here one could find boats crossing to Egypt or coming up from Ethiopia, Arabia, and India to unload ivory and other goods at the Roman port at Clysma (Suez/Kum al-Qulzum). Otherwise the southern Sinai peninsula was cut off from the rest of civilization by the al-Tih desert. This was a waterless waste indeed: it takes ten days of walking north-west from Wadi Feiran to reach Clysma on the Gulf of Suez, or eight days north-east to reach the port city of Aila on the Gulf of Eilat/'Aqaba, or six days north to cross the Tih plateau itself, before reaching any of the springs – 'Ain Qusayma, 'Ain Muwayla, 'Ain Qadais, 'Ain al-Qudayrat (the last two are both often identified with biblical Cadesh Barnea) – located on the southern outskirts of the Negev.[15]

At first it may be hard to see why the Romans decided to turn such disparate terrain into the provincial unity that was Third Palestine. From a historical and administrative perspective, however, consolidating it made sense. Originally this territory belonged to the Nabataeans, an Arab people who rose to power in the second century BCE by taking control of the trade in frankincense and myrrh that passed from Arabia overland to Gaza and elsewhere. Besides adorning their spectacular capital at Petra in the Transjordanian highlands, Nabataean rulers used their profits to build roads (notably, the Petra–Gaza road) and fortify nearby promontories in order to facilitate trade across the Negev desert: indeed, most of the Negev towns

---

13 Manna is excreted by insects attracted to the tamarisk's sap. For this and other aspects of Sinai flora, fauna, climate, agricultural potential or deforestation (which implies a greater availability of fuel in late antiquity), see Perevolotsky 1981; Hobbs 1995, 1–31, 48, 178–88; and Eckenstein 1921, 6–7. Although the annual precipitation only averages 65 mm, Sinai's elevations make it more favourable to human settlement than other desert areas such as Scetis in Egypt.

14 See below, pp. 35–36. The precise area designated by the name Rhaithou is unknown, but most probably it referred to a wide swath of terrain extending about 12 km (7.5 miles) from Bir Abū Suwayra down to Ras Raya, rather to a single location within that terrain (cf. the area of Scetis in Egypt): see Solzbacher 1989, 400–04.

15 See Mayerson 1963, 43–44 and 1982, 53–54.

known to late antiquity (Elusa, Betomolachon, Nessana, Sobata, Oboda) were originally Nabataean military outposts or caravanserais.[16] They may have been the first to cut passable tracks across the Sinai peninsula, such as the one leading from Aila (Umm Rashrash, near 'Aqaba) to the Feiran oasis. By the late first century, at any rate, Nabataean groups seem to have penetrated the southern Sinai, as indicated by the coins and the wealth of graffiti, later interpreted by Christians as Hebrew inscriptions, left in Wadi Mukattab ('Valley of Writings') and other Sinai locations.[17] Presumably these Nabataeans came to the Sinai to mine copper and turquoise, as had Egyptians long before them; perhaps they also found it convenient for evading Roman port taxes on luxury goods being brought up the Red Sea. For reasons unknown, Nabataean graffiti stopped being written on the Sinai after the third century. Perhaps those responsible had settled down with local inhabitants of a hilltop settlement overlooking the Feiran oasis at Tall Mahrad.[18] Later known as the 'city' of Pharan, this citadel was the only interior settlement on the Sinai known to Greek or Roman geographers. In late antiquity its churches and mudbrick houses covered about eight hectares (20 acres), all of which was surrounded by a gated circuit wall, 2 m (6.5 feet) thick.[19]

Having lasted nearly four hundred years, the Nabataean kingdom provided a virtual template for the later Roman province. When Emperor Trajan annexed it in 106 CE, he followed the example of the last Nabataean king and centred the capital of his new province, *Arabia*, farther north at Bostra (Busra al-Shom, Syria).[20] Only with the empire's reorganization at

16 Erickson-Gini 2004, 122–26. For Nabataeans in general, see Bowersock 1983 and Millar 1993, 400–08.

17 About 3,000 Nabataean inscriptions or graffiti have been published; all date between the second and third centuries CE. It has been conjectured that their Nabataean writers (if they were Nabataeans: see next note) went to the Sinai to escape Roman rule. See Solzbacher 1989, 53–59; Dahari 2000, 7.

18 Most evidence for Nabataean activity comes from the northern Sinai. In fact, there may never have been any Nabataeans in the southern Sinai, only locals who had learned to write in Nabataean script. Nevertheless the disappearance of their graffiti is curious. See Rosenberg 1970, 18–21; Teixidor 1998; Dahari 2000, 6–9; and Erickson-Gini 2004, 121.

19 Pottery suggests that Pharan was first settled in the first–second centuries CE, and then resettled in the fourth or fifth century: Dahari 2000, 17–16, and Grossmann 1996.

20 Inscriptions indicate that Nabataean settlements in the Negev and elsewhere in the area were incorporated into Trajan's *Provincia Arabia*: e.g. Negev 1977a, n. 643. The region prospered under Trajan, who replaced the old King's Highway with his *Via nova Traiana* connecting Petra and the port at Aila with Bostra and other eastern cities. It may have been built to supply troops along the eastern frontier: see Bowersock 1983, 76–89; Millar 1993, 90–96.

the end of the third century did the region begin to acquire its late Roman infrastructure and shape. Petra and the Negev had evidently suffered like everywhere else during the crises of the third century, when all traces of fine pottery along the Petra–Gaza road disappear.[21] But in the 290s, Emperor Diocletian broke up the Trajanic province and assigned its areas south of the Dead Sea to a new province that encompassed much of Syria and Palestine.[22] He also transferred the Roman infantry legion *X Fretensis* from Jerusalem down to Aila and stationed another at Beer Sheva, thereby placing two major military camps in the region, one to the north and one to the south. For the next century or more, these camps would serve as headquarters for the fortresses and strongholds that secured the roads connecting the central Negev to the Gulf of Aila.[23] Later in the fourth century, Diocletian's province was divided into three smaller units constituting the three Palestines. As a result, by 409, the entire region below the Dead Sea from Transjordan to the Sinai became known as 'Salutary Palestine' (*Palaestina salutaris*), or more prosaically, Third Palestine.[24]

It has been observed that Diocletian's arrangements showed 'exceptional understanding of the geographical necessities of the region', since his plan recognized that the areas south of the Dead Sea were most naturally bound by the Petra–Gaza road crossing the Negev.[25] The fact that Petra was officially designated the metropolis (provincial capital) of Third Palestine indicates that the Roman government expected her to regain centrality in the region. Yet Petra never did. Instead, when the region revived after the third-century collapse, its network of roads remained the same, but its major commodity became wine instead of unguents, and its administrative centre

21 Erickson-Gini 2004, 166–80.

22 The name of the new province is debated. The Verona list (c. 312–314) and a papyrus dated c. 314–318 may be interpreted to designate it as 'New Arabia'; hence modern maps often identify it as such: see Mayerson 1983 and Tsafrir 1986.

23 On the Beer Sheva camp, see Fabian 1995. The transfer of *X Fretensis* to Aila is attested in Eusebius of Caesarea's late third-century *Onomasticon*: 'Aila: on the borders [of Palestine], lying next to the southern desert and the Red Sea which is next to it, sailed by both those crossing from Egypt and those from India. Stationed there is the tenth legion of the Romans. It is now called Aila.' See Millar 1993, 175–76, and 387. Also attested in the *Notitia Dignitatum Or.* XXXIV.30.

24 Attested by *Theodosian Code* VII.4.30, promulgated in 409. The exact date and rationale for creating these new provinces are debated: see Mayerson 1987a and 1988. *Palaestina prima* was in the centre of the three; it included Jerusalem and the Judaean desert, and its capital was at Caesarea. *Palaestina secunda* was the northernmost of the three, and its capital was Scythopolis.

25 Bowersock 1983, 143.

shifted westwards, to Elusa, 20 km (12 miles) south of Beer Sheva in the central Negev – a city located, as a sixth-century pilgrim observed, 'at the head of the desert that leads to the Sinai'.[26]

When European explorers first entered the central Negev desert in the nineteenth century, they were astonished at what they saw: besides massive irrigation systems, farmsteads, watch towers, and wine presses were the ruins of six large, well-built villages or towns. All are situated within a day's walk of each other on an arid plateau rising 60 km (37 miles) south-east of Gaza (see appendix, Map 2). Most are exceptionally well preserved, owing to their construction in a place so seemingly forlorn that 'the careless traveller who piles up four stones in a heap by the roadside here erects an eternal monument to himself'.[27]

Identified as Elusa (Halutza/Khalasa), Betomolachon (Rehovot-in-the-Negev/Ruhayba), Nessana (Nitzana/Auja al-Hafir), Sobata (Shivta/Isbayta), Mampsis (Mamshit/Kurnub), and Oboda (Abda/Avdat),[28] these ghost towns have been subjected to study and speculation ever since. Often described as 'urban settlements' in modern literature, it is clear that they experienced major development in late antiquity: while most of them in the Nabataean era consisted of no more than 20–30 domestic, temple, or caravan structures, Sobata alone in late antiquity had at least 170 and perhaps even 240–340 such buildings, including three large basilica churches.[29] At their peak in the sixth and seventh centuries, their populations ranged from 500–2000 at Mampsis, Oboda, and Sobata, to about 10,500 at Elusa, despite scant

26 PP, *Itin.* 34. The Nessana papyri (see below) classify Elusa as a *polis* that received taxes from the other Negev sites, all of which (except perhaps Mampsis) were regarded as large villages (*kōmai*) or towns. Elusa's importance may have originated when the earthquake of 363 devastated Petra: see Gutwein 1981, 10–14; Dan 1982; and Erickson-Gini 2004, 161–65, 178.

27 Woolley and Lawrence 1936, 36. The westernmost sites (Elusa, Betomolachon, and Nessana) were all but obliterated by Ottoman quarriers in the early twentieth century: visitors in 1919 were still able to see a bathhouse at Betomolachon and a whole lower town, featuring two colonnaded streets, at Nessana.

28 Listed in geographical order, moving south-west from Elusa, and excluding smaller clusters that may have been hamlets (e.g. Saadi – ancient Soudanon? – 9 km/5.6 miles south-west of Elusa). The entire Negev region and its sites can be inspected via Google Earth: e.g. for Shivta, Pointer 30° 52'.52.10" N, 34° 37'51.30" E. For general surveys, see Foss 1995; Shereshevski 1991; and Gutwein 1981; but Kraemer 1958 is unsurpassed for both introduction and commentary.

29 All the more remarkable because Sobata apparently had no permanent structures before late antiquity: see Negev 1976, 132; Segal 1983. Estimates vary depending on how one defines domestic dwellings; the low estimate is from Hirschfeld 2003, the high from Shereshevski 1991.

rainfall and the difficulty of tapping groundwater (Sobata had no wells at all).[30] Obviously their existence depended greatly on techniques of dry farming and water conservation still visible today in the ancient terracing and architecture (the streets and roofs at Sobata, for example, were designed to channel rainfall into cisterns).[31] But this all required considerable initial investment, and does not explain the number of basilicas, bathhouses, and other amenities found at each. What accounts for their late antique expansion and prosperity?

While much remains to be explored, it is now fairly clear that the 'urban' transformation of the region was not the result of any direct government policy initiated for that purpose. Many have assumed that it was, given the scale of the hydraulic installations and investment presumably involved;[32] it has even been argued that the region's dams and terraces were part of an imperial programme to settle southern Palestine's nomadic population.[33] But no evidence for such an imperial policy or outside initiative exists. Instead, scholarship now tends to emphasize the independent ability of local inhabitants to take advantage of needs created elsewhere by the late Roman government. It has recently been proposed, for example, that Diocletian's military build-up in the region (his stationing of legions at Beer Sheva and Aila, as well as his placement of forts and troops in the Negev and Transjordan) not only brought security to the region but also stimulated its agricultural development, prompting locals to adopt Nabataean hydromechanics to supply a new market.[34] This in turn laid ground for viticulture, which spread in the late fourth and fifth centuries to such an extent that it seems to have become the area's cash crop, perhaps capitalizing on demands created by the government's distribution of free wine at Constantinople.[35] If, as seems

30 These are conservative estimates, based on structures and acreage, with Elusa covering 35 ha (86 acres), Betomolachon 12 ha (30 acres), Nessana 15–18 ha (37–44 acres), Sobata 11.5 ha (28.5 acres), and Mampsis 4 ha (10 acres). Betomolachon and Nessana probably had 3,000–3,500 inhabitants. The region as a whole (including farmsteads and hamlets, but not the monastic or nomadic population) had some 30,000. See Shereshevski 1991, 200–14, and Mayerson 1994b, 235.

31 The region receives an average of 100–150 mm of rainfall, less than the 200 mm usually required for dry farming. On Sobata's architecture, see Gutwein 1981, 165–67; Segal 1983; Hirschfeld 2003.

32 E.g. Woolley and Lawrence 1936, 48; Haiman 1995, 32.

33 Nevo 1991; reviewed in Foss 1995, 231–34.

34 Erickson-Gini 2004, 424–26; Parker 1987, 39; Schaefer 1979, 28; Kraemer 1958, 17.

35 Thus Lewin 2002, 361–68, arguing that viticulture was adopted from Nabataean practices in use at Petra and elsewhere, rather than introduced by outside monks, as often claimed. For a similar argument regarding Roman Libya, see Barker 2002.

likely, much of the Gazan wine being sold and served across the Mediterranean in late antiquity was actually produced in Negev vineyards,[36] then we might well regard its inhabitants as some of the most successful entrepreneurs of the age.

These initiatives linked the peripheral Negev to a wider world, enabling it to flourish culturally as well as economically. From an architectural perspective, this desert region remained plainly unclassical: Negev towns follow no grid plan, but were made for circuitous camel traffic. Elusa, however, by the middle of the fourth century had become a regional centre of late antique Hellenism. We learn from the letters of Libanius, the great orator of Antioch (314–393), that in his day this small city not only had its own rhetorical school with resident sophist on imperial stipend, but had even once been home to his old teacher, Zenobius.[37] Appropriately, one of the few archaeological discoveries made at the site (sadly devastated by Ottoman builders) is that of a modest odeon or theatre, whose floor in 454 was repaved for further re-use by a certain 'Zenobius, son of Abraham' – perhaps a descendant of Libanius' own teacher.[38] Provincials would have used the building to display their attainments in traditional Greco-Roman *paideia*. Indeed, by the late fourth century Greek had largely displaced Nabataean in Negev inscriptions, attesting the emergence of a Hellenized elite throughout the region.[39]

Subsequent developments in the Negev are revealed by the papyri archives found in 1935 by the Colt Archaeological Expedition at Nessana, located about 32 km (20 miles) south of Elusa. Written in the sixth and seventh centuries, these 195 Greek, Syriac, and Arabic documents enable us to study this provincial community with a degree of detail unparalleled outside Egypt.[40] They demonstrate that Nessana's citadel in the fifth century became the fort camp (*kastron*) for a mobile camel corps consisting of about 200 soldiers, all apparently local recruits. Called 'The Very Loyal Theodosians', this camel corps represents a classic example of Roman *limitanei* – frontier guards or border militia – who received land in return for a heredi-

---

36 On the Gazan wine trade, see Glucker 1987, 93–94, and Mayerson 1985.

37 Libanius, *epp.* 100–01, 532; see Mayerson 1983, 249.

38 Negev 1977a, 92–93; 1981, 73–76. According to Erickson-Gini 2004, 138, it was originally built in the second century, when several Arab sophists were known by name: Bowersock 1983, 135.

39 Lewin 2002, 355; cf. R. Rubin 1996.

40 Published in exemplary fashion in Casson-Hettich 1950 and Kraemer 1958, the papyri (often incorrectly cited as *P.Ness*) are now in the Pierpont Morgan Library collection in New York.

tary obligation to serve in defence of the empire.[41] Indeed, the papyri show that the land around 'Camp Nessana' (as contemporaries called it) was owned by these soldiers and other local farmers, producing yields comparable to those usually only found in more northerly climes.[42] But residents had other sources of income. Nessana was located at a major crossroads, and several papyri deal with the sale or transport of fish and other imports, demonstrating the vitality of regional trade.[43] Such trade, however, does not suffice to account for Nessana's two caravanserais, one of which, the 'House of Abū Joseph Son of Doubabos' located below the citadel, is described as having an upper storey furnished with 96 bed mats.[44] That seems an extraordinary level of accommodation for a relatively small town. The question is, what might account for it.

One obvious answer, besides the surrounding wine trade, was Christian pilgrimage.[45] By the sixth century, three pilgrimage routes connected Jerusalem to Mount Sinai.[46] The longest, called the 'western route', is described in great detail by the pilgrim Egeria in her fourth-century *Travelogue* (translated below, pp. 212–31). It took 22–25 days, passing down the Mediterranean coast and crossing into Egypt before turning south at Pelusium (Tall al-Farama) and continuing down Sinai's west side. A shorter way, the 'eastern route', took 18 days, passing from Elusa to Oboda or Nessana and then on down to Aila, whence it entered the eastern Sinai peninsula, turning 240 km (150 miles) further inland to reach Mount Sinai. Numerous inscriptions along this route shows that it was by far the most popular pilgrimage route in late antiquity. A third, even shorter but more hazardous 'central route' passed straight through the al-Tih desert.

41 Kraemer 1958, 13, 21–22, 110–17. Some have contended that the title 'Very Loyal Theodosians' ([ἀριθμὸς] τῶν καθοσιωμ[ένων] Θεοδοσιαῶν) mentioned in *P.Colt* 15.3 applies to a regiment stationed at Rhinocorura (Al-Arish) rather than Nessana, but the fact that *P.Colt* 16.7 refers to a soldier who received land at Nessana as 'the very loyal' Zunayn (τῷ καθ[ωσιωμένῳ] Ζοναινῳ), supports Nessana's claim.

42 Mayerson 1962, 211–12 and 224.

43 Cf. *P.Colt* 47 and 90, elucidated by Schaefer 1979, 28–36.

44 *P.Colt* 31.34 and 40, discussed by Kraemer 1958, 27–28.

45 Mayerson 1987b argues that had commerce and road systems alone dictated development in the region, we might expect more of it in eastern Third Palestine along the Trajanic highway; that such is not the case suggests that pilgrim traffic was decisive. But the Negev's proximity to Gaza, and thus its ability to transport wine to the coast, would seem equally pertinent.

46 For more on the routes, see Dahari 2000, 9–15; Solzbacher 1989, 153–63; and Mayerson 1982.

According to the Piacenza PilgrimTimes sixth-century *Travelogue* (translated below, pp. 253–62), it included a stop at an inn located in a fort beyond Elusa, probably at Nessana.[47] Thus, two of the three late antique routes to the Sinai traversed the Negev; indeed, seventh-century papyri (*P.Colt* 72 and 73, translated below, p. 270) show that Nessana remained an embarkation point for Sinai pilgrims after the Arab conquests. Names written in chalk by a variety of hands in different groups on Nessana's north church walls attest the presence of several different companies of Egyptian pilgrims who passed through the area in the fifth or sixth centuries.[48]

Whether such pilgrims were responsible for introducing Christianity to the region is open to speculation. We know from church council records that Christian communities already by 325–347 existed in cities such as Aila, Petra, and Gaza on the outskirts of the Negev.[49] Since Elusa was officially a city and administrative centre, it may have had a bishop as early as that. But the best-known account of Christianity's entry to the Negev depicts it as being brought not by pilgrims or imperial administrators, but by monks from nearby Gaza. In his *Life of Hilarion*, the monastic author Jerome (c. 347–420) tells how Hilarion († 371), a Gaza native, used to visit monks in the vicinity.

> On his way to the desert of Cades to visit one of his disciples, he arrived at Elusa together with a great number of monks. It happened to be the day on which the whole population of that town had gathered in the temple of Venus for the annual celebrations. They worshipped her on account of Lucifer, to whose cult the Saracen people are devoted. But in fact the town itself is to a large extent semi-barbarous on account of its situation.
>
> When they heard that the holy man Hilarion was passing through, crowds of them went out to meet him, together with their wives and children, for he had often cured many Saracens possessed by demons. They bowed their heads and shouted, '*Barech*', a Syriac word meaning, 'bless'. Hilarion received them in a friendly, humble manner, and entreated them to worship God rather than stones... They would not allow him to depart until he had marked out the

47 PP, *Itin.* 39, makes plain that he had come through the desert, *contra* Dahari's (2000, 11) claim that his route was identical with the eastern route. The identification of the fort and inn outside Elusa with Nessana is disputed: see below, PP, *Itin.* 35 and notes *ad loc.*

48 Nessana inscription no. 30, ed. and trans. Kirk and Welles 1962, 146–48, discussed in Kraemer 1958, 15–16.

49 Bishops from Eleutheropolis, Gaza, and Aila attended the Council of Nicaea in 325, and one from Petra attended the Council of Serdica in 347: Solzbacher 1989, 168–69. Fourth-century Christian inscriptions have been found along Sinai's Mediterranean coast: Lifshitz 1971.

foundations of the future church and until their priest, garlanded as he was, had been marked by the sign of Christ.[50]

This episode is usually dated c. 350. Whatever the truth behind it, Jerome's story suggests a more complete and early conversion of the area than the evidence otherwise admits. In fact, no Christian monument or inscription has yet been found in the Negev that can be dated before 415/435,[51] and we have no clear evidence that Elusa itself became an episcopal see until 431, when a certain 'Ampellas-Theodulus [i.e. 'Abd Allah, 'Slave of God'], Bishop of Elusa', signed the Acts of the Council of Ephesus.[52] The general impression is that Christianity took root rather slowly in the Negev. When the Syrian monk Barṣawma passed through on his way to Mount Sinai in the early fifth century (c. 419–422), 'pagans' were said to be still noticeably strong there: 'They were the masters of the country and towns of this region. They closed the gates of the towns before him.'[53] A fifth-century dedication to Dushara, consort of al-'Uzza (i.e. Venus/Aphrodite), recently discovered at Oboda, corroborates that report, showing that traditional cults continued to be openly practised in that town well after the fourth century.[54] In fact it is impossible to tell how thoroughly the region was ever converted, as we shall see.

By the sixth century, however, Christianity had certainly become conspicuous in the area. Negev towns evidently competed in building

50 Jerome, *Life of Hilarion* 25 (PL 23.41AC) trans. White, 102–03, slightly adapted. Jerome wrote this story c. 390 and may have heard it from Epiphanius of Salamis. Noting the lack of Semitic names among the martyr shrine inscriptions at Nessana, Kraemer 1958, 16, notes 'It appears that Christianity came to Nessana by way of monks or missionaries, or both, settling in the desert among the Nabataean natives and gradually infecting them with the new spirit'. For discussion, see Shahid 1984, 288–95.

51 Date of an inscription from the southern church at Sobata according to Negev 1982, 10, making the church the earliest Christian monument in the region. The earliest Christian inscription found at Elusa dates to 530/1; at Beer Sheva, 516; Oboda, 541; at Nessana, 464; all are epitaphs.

52 Mayerson 1963, 168. As Solzbacher 1989, 168, observes, there is no reason to doubt that Elusa did not have a bishop in the early fourth century. That does not also mean it had a large Christian population, since late antique cities usually received bishops as an administrative procedure.

53 *Life of Barṣawma* 26; summarized in Nau 1913, 382. The *Life* purports to have been written by one of Barṣawma's disciples.

54 'Pagan Inscriptions greatly outnumber Christian until the beginning of the sixth century': thus Kraemer 1958, 15. For the Oboda inscription, see Erickson-Gini 2004, 223–24; cf. Epiphanius of Salamis, *Panarion* LI.52, written c. 375 (on pagan worship at Elusa and Petra) and PP, *Itin.* 38.

churches. Each had at least two; Nessana had five; the four found at Sobata are remarkably large, especially considering the town's size (Betomolachon also had four).[55] Each also had a monastic community established within or nearby. These seem to have been fully integrated into the daily life of the town: Patrick son of Sergius, leader of St Sergius' monastery at Nessana, was one of Nessana's major landowners in the late sixth century.[56] As far as ecclesiastical administration was concerned, all of the Christian communities in Third Palestine were subject to the Patriarch of Jerusalem following the Council of Chalcedon in 451 (the situation earlier is not clear).[57] Elusa remained the Negev's only episcopal see. It probably also held jurisdiction over Sinai until Pharan received a bishop of its own some time in the early fifth century. We hear little about this first bishop, a monk named Netras, or any of his successors, but Pharan remained the centre of ecclesiastical, civilian, and military authority on the Sinai until the Arab conquests.[58] Then it vanishes from record.[59]

The impact of the seventh-century Persian and Arab invasions in Third

---

55 Mayerson 1987b, 5; Negev 1982. Some of the construction was funded by pilgrims: cf. the church mosaic inscription (Nessana Inscription no. 94, ed. and trans. Kirk and Welles 1962, 173–74) recording donation by a family from Emesa (modern Homs, Lebanon) in 601, and *P.Colt* 89, recording 270.5 *solidi* being handed over by the Mt Sinai monastery, a sum that must have come from donations. But as Foss 1995, 222, notes with regard to northern Syria, local surplus wealth was often invested in religious buildings (there being few other options in pre-capitalist times), the return being both salvation and prestige. Negev churches may have responded to such local needs.

56 Kraemer 1958, 6–8; for a survey of monasticism and monastic ruins in the Negev, see Figueras 1995.

57 Solzbacher 1989, 171–98; Dahari 2000, 19–20.

58 Our knowledge of Netras, a disciple of Abba Silvanus, comes solely from *Apophth. patr.* Netras 1 (PG 65.511–12). According to Shahid 1984, 303, his name suggests Arab background. For more on Sinai bishops, see below, p. 32. St Catherine's has several copies of a *chrysoboulon* or 'bull' that purports to have been issued by Emperor Justinian, granting the monastery independence from Pharan and other privileges (PG 86:1149–1152). It is a late Byzantine forgery, probably dating to the sixteenth century: see Solzbacher 1989, 258. John Mosch., *Meadow* 127 (PG 87[3].2992B), clearly presents the Mt Sinai monastery's *hēgoumen* as being subordinate to the bishop of Pharan. The first known 'bishop of Mt Sinai' is a certain Constantine who attended the synod of Constantinople in 869.

59 Since it is not mentioned by Anastasius of Sinai, some have thought that it was destroyed during the Arab conquests: e.g. Mayerson 1964, 197; Solzbacher 1989, 285. Peter Grossmann, however, informs me that no destruction layer has been found to substantiate such a violent end. Its last known bishop was a certain Theodore of Pharan, perhaps to be identified with Theodore of Rhaithou, leader of the Alexandrian 'Union' of 633: see Elert 1951 and Solzbacher 1989, 287. Anastasius mentions a bishop of Aila (*Narr.* I.27), but as Mayerson notes, Aila seems to have made special terms with the Arab invaders early on.

Palestine is hard to determine. Both the Negev and Sinai reached their peak of prosperity in the late sixth and early seventh centuries.[60] Nessana's camel corps had been disbanded long before then, as had the legionary regiments at Beer Sheva and Aila, a consequence of Emperor Justinian's decision, c. 546, to entrust Rome's eastern frontier defences to various Arab phylarchs instead of the *limitanei* troops.[61] Eventually the Romans, under financial duress, stopped paying these too. Persian forces seem to have skirted Third Palestine on their way to Egypt in 618/19, but Arab warriors advancing out of the Ḥijaz brought the region under their control c. 630–633/34, taking Aila and other strongholds before moving on to Gaza (635–639).[62] Our knowledge of these events and their consequences is incomplete, and comes mainly from the narratives of Theophanes Confessor († 818) and Anastasius of Sinai († c. 700/1), both translated below. Aila capitulated in 630 on condition of paying annual tribute; presumably all Christians in the area, including monks, made similar arrangements. Papyri show that by 674, the former Roman province of Third Palestine had been absorbed into a new, larger Umayyad province, the *Jund Filastin*, and was locally taxed and governed by an *amīr* at Gaza.[63] From then on, no new structures of any note were built in the region. Nonetheless, the sleepy Negev towns seem to have continued to prosper, with most remaining inhabited until the ninth century.[64] Christian pilgrims continued to pass through *en route* to the Sinai peninsula for the next few centuries, aided by the fact that Muslims regarded Mount Sinai to

60 Thus Kraemer 1958, 23, based on the quantity of glass and coins found at Nessana, most of which date from the reign of Justin I (518–527) to Maurice (582–602); cf. Gutwein 1981, 100–02.

61 The key evidence is the so-called Beer Sheva edict, which seems to reflect a disbandment of the *limitanei*: see Di Segni 2004. On Justinian's policy more generally, see Parker 2000, 380–83; Mayerson 1988; and Gutwein 1981, 353.

62 Mayerson 1964, 169–77; Mouton 1998, 177. Mayerson's argument that Muslim warriors sacked Pharan has been widely rejected, but Solzbacher 1989, 283, defends it, based on his interpretation of an allusive passage from Sebeos' Armenian *History*, ch. 42. Persian forces may have destroyed Oboda, but there is no sign of their having occupied the region.

63 For provincial arrangements in Umayyad times, see Kraemer 1958, 32–33; on terms imposed on Aila, Mayerson 1964, 176; cf. the 270.5 *solidi* handed over by the Mt Sinai monastery in *P.Colt* 89 (see below, p. 268). St Catherine's has a famous 'letter of Muhammad', allegedly signed by his hand print, granting the monastery protection from Muslim exactions. Like the bull attributed to Emperor Justinian (see above, n. 58), it is surely bogus. It follows a similar letter created in an Iranian monastery point-by-point; it may have been created c. 1009, when the Fatmid Caliph al-Hakin ordered the destruction of churches and monasteries in his empire: see Mouton 1998, 177–78.

64 Magness 2003, 178–215.

be sacred as well.[65] But religious identity, always contested in late antiquity, exacerbated local tensions after the Arab conquest, with antagonisms now emerging along ethnic lines.[66] By the eighth century Christian settlement on the Sinai had largely receded to the area around the 'fort' in Wadi al-Dayr, surviving under far more insular conditions and reduced circumstances than had marked its previous four hundred years, the period of Christianity's ascendancy on the peninsula.

2. THE CHRISTIAN DEVELOPMENT OF THE SINAI PENINSULA

We have no information about who the first Christians who came to the Sinai were apart from later legends.[67] It does not seem to have been known, or its relevance to Judeo-Christian tradition established, until well into the fourth century.[68] But then things changed. Our earliest eyewitness report comes from Egeria, an aristocratic pilgrim from Gaul or Spain who visited in 383. Her *Travelogue*, a quintessential source for the study of early Christian pilgrim practices and pilgrimage sites, tells us much about Sinai's development at that time, and a full translation of it has been included in

65 Solzbacher 1989, 277–98.

66 Solzbacher 1989, 284–85; cf. Anast., *Narr.* II.8. The oldest of the 21 mosques that exist or are known to have existed on the Sinai were built c. 900–1171.

67 Medieval legends include a report that Helena, Emperor Constantine's mother, visited and built a tower dedicated to the Theotokos at the site of the Burning Bush (first attested in Eutychius' tenth-century *Annals*), and that a Christian couple named Galaction and Episteme took refuge in Sinai monasteries during the Decian persecution of 250 (first attested in the tenth-century *Menologion* of Basil). See Devreesse 1940a. A third-century letter by Bishop Dionysius of Alexandria (*ap.* Eusebius of Caesarea, *EH* VI.42.3–4) is often cited as evidence that Christians fled to the Sinai during the Decian persecution: 'Chaeremon was an elderly bishop of the city called Neila. He fled with his spouse to the Arabian Mountain and never came back...' However, this *Arabikon oros* was not on the Sinai, but in the region of Egypt that went by that name on the north-east bank of the Nile: cf. above, Map 1; Talbert 2000, pl. 75, and Moritz 1916, 58 n. 2.

Sinai's connection with the fourth-century Christian martyr Catherine of Alexandria may date as early as the ninth century, but is not clearly attested until the eleventh and will not be discussed here: see Skrobucha 1966, 67–68, and Braun 1973, 28.

68 It is important to note that Eusebius of Caesarea does not include Mt Sinai in his *Onomasticon* in 330 CE, although he does note the location of Rephidim/Pharan. At the same time (333) the so-called Bourdeaux pilgrim did not include the Sinai among his Holy Land visits. These silences suggest that Mt Sinai's identity had still not been established or publicized at that time. Also see discussion below, n. 72.

this volume. It shows that, by 383, numerous features of Sinai topography had already been identified with biblical sites, churches had been placed on top of Jabal Musa and Jabal Sufsafa (also down at the 'the Bush' in Wadi al-Dayr), and extensive monastic colonies had sprung up below Mount Sinai and at Pharan.[69] Indeed, the construction of Jabal Musa's summit chapel some twenty years earlier by a Syrian monk named Julian Saba († 367), the first known Sinai pilgrim, is celebrated in two Syriac hymns attributed to Ephraim, Deacon of Edessa (363–373). The hymns celebrate the earliest known Christian event to have occurred on 'God's Mountain', and may in fact represent our earliest texts regarding the late antique Sinai.[70]

These accounts show how vigorously Christians had appropriated and developed the southern peninsula by the last decades of the fourth century. They also indicate that this effort was being driven mainly by monks: unlike other sites of the new Christian Holy Land, there is no evidence for the initial involvement here of either church officials or imperial patrons.[71] Presumably monks were the first to identify the peninsula with the biblical 'Sina', and Jabal Musa-Sufsafa with Mount Sinai-Horeb in particular, possibly because this was the only mountain in the area that featured both a cave on top and a tree and spring at its base.[72] Certainly monks led the effort to make

69 Egeria, *Itin.*, PD/Y 15, III.1, 3, IV.1, 7 (*ecclesiae*); III.1, 7, IV.6 (*monasteria*).

70 See below, pp. 204–10 [Syriac hymns] and pp. 233–36 [Theodoret, *Religious History*]. Saba is often presented as the first Christian to have identified Mt Sinai with Jabal Musa; there is no way of telling if that is true.

71 On the importance of bishops and imperial families elsewhere in the Christian Holy Land see Hunt 1982 and Wilken 1992, 82–100.

72 Sivan 1990, 84-85, emphasizes the role of monks. Presumably they were guided by certain biblical 'clues': Deut. 1:2 says Mt Horeb was 11 days from Cadesh Barnea, while Gal. 4:25 places Mt Sinai in Arabia ('Now Hagar is Mount Sinai, in Arabia'). Perhaps more influential was the publication of Eusebius' *Onomasticon*. Although, as already noted (n. 68), this work does not include Mt Sinai, it does locate Pharan; perhaps that detail provided crucial orientation. Over the centuries many alternatives to Jabal Musa have been proposed for the site of the ancient Hebrew experience: see Bordreuil 1998, 117, and Hobbs 1995, 46–72. Cosmas Indicopleustes' description has been interpreted (erroneously, in my view) as a late antique example: see below, pp. 246–48. It is clear that some Sina identifications were unstable: e.g. Wadi Gharandula and Rhaithou were both identified as the biblical Elim in the sixth century (cf. CI, *Top. christ.* V.14 vs. PP, *Itin.* 41).

The LXX spelling 'Sina' (probably derived from 'desert of Sin', Exod. 16:1) for 'Sinai' remained conventional among late antique Christians, and is used in my translations of their texts. Hebrew scripture refers to both Horeb and Sinai as God's Mountain due to the fusion of two different traditions. Jerome identified them as one and the same, but Eusebius considered them to be different; Sinai monks solved the problem by making Horeb subsidiary to Sinai. See Maraval 1985, 138.

this a Christian setting. Besides planting churches around Jabal Musa and colonizing its base, they personally guided pilgrims around Sinai's rock formations, showing them the exact locations where events of Exodus and Numbers had occurred, and how to heighten their experience by offering a prayer or eucharist service as appropriate at each. In this way the monks mapped out the area's Old Testament history while 'Christianizing' it through Christian rites.[73]

The Syriac hymns on Julian Saba alert us to the significance associated with such monastic efforts at the time:

> The circumcised [Jews] boast of Mount Sinai
> but you humiliated them down to the ground.
> This proclamation is great
> for now the church of the Son is on the Father's mountain.

The hymn proclaims reclamation and triumph. By putting a church on Sinai's summit, Saba had restored God's domain to its proper heirs: Christianity now reigned all the way from Golgotha to Mount Sinai, with 'both covenants', in effect, 'completed' (*Hymn* 19.13, 16–17).[74] That might have struck contemporary Jews as an empty boast, since no Jew in antiquity seems to have cared either to locate Mount Sinai or claim it for their own. But the idea that monks had transcended Hebrew piety and were fulfilling God's plan by persevering in the Sinai wilderness voluntarily, without complaint or 'murmuring' like Old Testament Jews (e.g. Exod. 15:22–16:36, Num. 11), continued to be expressed into the sixth century. Jacob of Serug († 521) represented Sinai monks as nothing less than 'the disciples of Moses and the ministers of the Old [Testament]', i.e. the true Israel, through whom the mysteries that God had once revealed to Moses were being revealed again (see his *Letter to the Sinai Monks*, translated in the appendix below).

Clearly this distant setting, the consummate site of Old Testament revelation, raised high expectations. We have numerous references to monks travelling here to pray, some fasting all the way *en route*. One is said to have kneeled an entire week 'at that very spot where Moses was privileged to see God', refusing to eat or drink anything until he finally heard a voice 'revealing to him his Master's favour'.[75] Despite the denials of fourth- and

---

73 On this method of cultural appropriation during Egeria's visit, see Jacobs 2004, 120–21, 135–38.

74 See Solzbacher 1989, 114–19.

75 Theodoret, *Religious History* VI.12; cf. Egeria, *Itin.* I.2; *Life of Barṣawma* 26; Philoxenus of Mabbug, *Letter to Patricius* 51; John Mosch., *Meadow* 100 and 170; Tsafrir 1993.

fifth-century theologians that God was located in any physical place,[76] such anecdotes indicate that early pilgrims came to the Sinai with the assumption that here, on 'God's Mountain', they might hope to experience, like Moses and Elijah, God's actual presence.

Such hopes eventually were given theological support in the early eighth century, when John of Damascus (c. 676–749) put Mount Sinai on top of his list of sites, relics, and other physical objects deemed worthy of veneration as 'receptacles of divine energy'.[77] Long before then, however, small apsidal niches had been fixed along Mount Sinai's ascent routes, all facing the mountain, apparently to help pilgrims focus their prayers on its peak.[78] So too had Emperor Justinian (527–565) built his famous basilica beside the Burning Bush, below the Sinai summit. This church seems to have been designed to accommodate large numbers of pilgrims,[79] and the theme chosen to adorn its central mosaic – Matt. 17:2, the Transfiguration – suggests a contemporary's understanding of why they came. Here they would see Christ hovering in radiant gold above Moses and Elijah, his Old Testament Sinai forebears. This was the consummate moment of New Testament revelation, one that explained and subsumed at once the Old Testament theophanies revealed to Moses and Elijah on the Sinai. Surely when viewed here, in this Old Testament setting, its representation was meant to convey a sense of Christian triumph.[80] Like Saba's summit church, its display within Justinian's church may have been considered a means of 'Christianizing' the mountain. But its radiant image also affirmed expectations that God's 'energy' could still be experienced here, on Mount Sinai, as it had been in Old Testament times.

Such expectations were no doubt both heightened and safeguarded by a custom, or rule, attested from the fourth to seventh centuries, that no

76 E.g. Gregory of Nyssa, *ep.* II and Theodoret of Cyrrhus, *Religious History* VI.8; see Bitton-Ashkelony 2005.

77 *Against Detractors of the Worship of Icons (Contra imaginum calumniatores)* III.34. On the relevance to Sinai pilgrimage, see Maraval 1985, 146–47.

78 The structures are roughly 1.5 m (4 feet) high by 2 m (6 feet) wide and their niches, all oriented towards Jabal Musa's peak, differentiate them from other ruins: see Finkelstein 1981, 86. But the method of dating such structures is unclear.

79 Forsyth 1985, 51.

80 The mosaic is the centrepiece of a complex scheme, and scholars debate its significance, date (550–551 or 565–566) and relation to patristic thought. Gregory of Nyssa and Ps.-Dionysius the Areopagite considered the Burning Bush to be a 'type' for Jesus' incarnation, and Moses/Elijah's experiences on Mt Sinai/Horeb as a type for Jesus' own theophany. My interpretation largely follows Elsner 1995, 99–116; see also Andreopoulos 2002; Solzbacher 1989, 262–68.

one could spend a night on the Sinai summit (cf. Exod. 19:20–25).[81] This custom seems to be reflected in monastic settlement patterns: for while more monastic dwellings have been found on the ridges of Jabal Sufsafa (i.e. 'Mount Horeb', just below Jabal Musa) than anywhere else on the entire Sinai, none at all has been found on Jabal Musa's summit itself.[82]

Not everyone chose to settle within sight of that mountain, however. Ruins of hermitages have been found all over the southern peninsula, and early Sinai literature preserves the names of several colonies at places called Thōla, Malōcha, Arselaiou, Bētrambē, etc. It is impossible to match most such names to modern sites with certainty.[83] Nonetheless, apart from the Jabal Musa-Sufsafa area (where 41 separate hermit colonies have been counted in all), there were four other distinct settlement areas on the peninsula. Besides Pharan, 56 km (35 miles) west of Jabal Musa,[84] there was the area of Wadi Sigilliya, about 10 km (6 miles) south-west of Pharan on the slopes of Jabal Serbal. This area, perhaps ancient Malōcha, had two separate colonies.[85] The next settlement area was in the wadi valleys below Jabal Umm Shomer, about 28 km (17 miles) south-west of Jabal Musa. Perhaps to be identified with ancient Arselaiou, it had at least nine colonies.[86] Finally, there was Rhaithou, the second most important area of monastic settlement on the Sinai, discussed further below. Travel between Rhaithou and other settlements of the Sinai interior passed through Wadi Isla and the Umm Shomer

---

81 Egeria, *Itin.* III.5; PP, *Itin.* 37; Procop., *Buildings* V.viii.7; Anast., *Narr* I.3 and I.5, which alludes to the demise of this tradition after the summit had been 'defiled'.

82 See Dahari 1998, 152, and 2000, 37–48. A hermit cell found 250 m (800 feet) below Musa's summit may have housed the monk responsible for maintaining its chapel.

83 The only inscription to identify a site by name was found in Wadi Sigilliya and refers to the site as Singis, a name otherwise unknown: see Dahari 2000, 156–57. Modern monks have their own suggestions for the identity of these sites, but their connection to ancient usage is unclear. The Jabal Musa-Sufsafa cluster and, indeed, the entire southern Sinai can now be explored via Google Earth (e.g. for St Catherine's, Pointer 28° 33'.18.27" N, 33° 58'34.11" E); viewers will still be able to see many ancient remains despite the modern development.

84 On Pharan's monastic ruins, see Dahari 2000, 132–37, and Grossmann 1996 and 1999–2000.

85 Anast., *Narr*. I.21, says Malōcha is set in inaccessible ravines 64 km/40 miles from Jabal Musa, a description that fits here: Dahari 2000, 114–32; Solzbacher 1989, 405, and appendix, Map 3.

86 See Dahari 2000, 94–112; Solzbacher 1989, 402–03, and appendix, Map 3. Dahari considers it a sub-centre of Jabal Musa; he and Solzbacher identify Arselaiou more specifically as Wadi Rimhan, a tributary valley of Wadi Isla. This seems plausible, since a ninth-century MS of Anastasius of Sinai identifies the site with Wadi Isla. Dahari 2000, 156, also associates the Umm Shomer area with Anastasius' Metmōr, which is possible, but no specific detail supports it.

massif, which rose 10 km (6 miles) east of Wadi al-Tur (see appendix, Map 3). The journey from Rhaithou to Pharan took three days.[87]

The monastic ruins found in these areas usually consist of three or four separate, single-storey domiciles or 'cells' (*monasteria*), each equipped with one or two rooms built out of granite slabs or set beneath boulders, about 4–5 sq. m (44–54 sq. feet) in total size. Most are perched high up on slopes out of sight of the next, but all were originally connected to some central chapel, workhouse, or garden located below on nearby wadi floors.[88] Such ruins conform to the monastic arrangement known as a *lavra*, by which small groups of hermits (technically called *anchorites*, meaning 'recluses' or 'solitaries') maintained individual seclusion while sharing a common pathway (*lavra*) that led to a communal building or garden. The earliest such ruin on the Sinai has been dated to the fifth century, but Egeria saw similar arrangements during her visit in 383. Indeed, such *lavrae* arrangements always prevailed on the late antique Sinai, even after Justinian's fort and *coenobium* (a more formal monastic community regulated by an *hēgoumen*, a 'leader' or abbot) came to dominate Wadi al-Dayr.

This anchoretic emphasis on the Sinai meant that monastic communities there were always fairly autonomous and open to movement. One key to achieving both self-sufficiency ('autarchy') and stability in such circumstances was the communal cultivation of an orchard or garden.[89] Indeed, monks may have been the first to introduce agriculture to the Sinai.[90] Archaeology shows that those living in its mountains subsisted mainly on fruit, wine, and vegetables cultivated on wadi floors, where plots of land averaged about 323 sq. m (386 sq. yards) in size. Such large plots were necessary in this arid climate to obtain any reliable yield at all, but the labour also provided a welcome break in a monk's meditative routine.[91] Pottery from Palestine and Egypt suggests that many settlements had economic ties

87 Wadi Isla was the main route from Rhaithou to Jabal Musa until modern times: see Kawatoko 1998, 75–78.

88 See Dahari 2000, 152–67: ceramics and carbon-14 analysis suggests that most were established in the fifth century, flourished in the sixth and seventh, and remained inhabited until the tenth.

89 See Flusin 1998, 135.

90 Thus Dahari 2000, 147 and 159–62. No pre-Byzantine pottery or Nabataean inscriptions have been found in Sinai orchards. Pits and seeds provide evidence for the consumption and possible cultivation of peaches, apricots, grapes, almonds, prunes, plums, pomegranates, pears, dates (mainly at Rhaithou) and (near Jabal Musa) olives.

91 *Apophth. patr.* Silvanus 8 (PG 65.412AB) warns against cultivating a garden to the neglect of one's soul.

with those regions; however, all the pottery found in Wadi Sigilliya is local, indicating that few imports arrived there from the outside world.[92] Interestingly, no coin has been found at any anchoretic site on the peninsula. This may mean that barter was the predominant form of economic exchange in the monastic colonies.

These arrangements resemble those known on a larger scale from the most early famous monastic sites of Egypt, namely Kellia and Scetis. Indeed, while it is apparent that many early monks came down to the Sinai peninsula from Syria and Palestine on pilgrimage (e.g. Julian Saba, Symeon the Elder, Barṣauma), most of our early evidence for monastic settlement on the Sinai comes from the literature associated with the Egyptian desert fathers, namely the *apophthegmata patrum*, i.e. stories and 'sayings of the fathers', most of which were written down in fifth-century Palestine.[93] Several such stories focus on monks who moved to the Sinai after many years in Egypt.[94] Not surprisingly, all of the Sinai locations they name – Clysma, Rhaithou, Pharan – were situated on the western side of the peninsula, suggesting ease of travel between there and Egypt. Most of these stories focus on a particular group that came over from Scetis early in the fifth century, following an elder named Silvanus. Having settled somewhere 'on the mountain of Sinai', this group toiled together in a fenced orchard: interestingly, most of the stories associated with them illustrate the virtues of manual labour. Silvanus eventually continued on to Syria, but some of his disciples remained. One, named Netras or Nethyra, became the first known bishop of Pharan.[95]

Such groups were said to be practising a 'philosophy' that aimed at repentance as well as communion with God. Two factors besides asceticism and prayer were considered crucial to their success: guidance by a spiritual master, and the attainment of unperturbed tranquillity, known as *hēsychia*. The Sinai environment generally offered ample opportunities for both. Of course, one of its main attractions was that it had been home to

---

92 Dahari 2000, 164, 183–231.

93 Good introductions are Chitty 1966 and Harmless 2004, 167–273.

94 Clysma: *Apophth. patr.* (alph. series) Pistus 1, Sisoes 21, 26, Tithoes (anon. series) XV.43; Pharan: Nicon 1; Rhaithou: Matoes 9, Nisterius 6, Peter the Pionite 3, VII.16, XV.28; Mt Sinai: Cronius 5, Mark 4, Megethius 2, Xoius 2, Silvanus 4, 5 X.36, 69, XI.28,. XII.14. The incidents reported in this literature are notoriously difficult to date and perhaps unreliable as historical evidence; but it is possible that the relocation of monks to Sinai occurred after devastating nomadic raids on Kellia and Scetis in the early fifth century caused a monastic diaspora, on which see Gould 1993, 3–16.

95 *Apophth. patr.* Netras 1 (PG 65.312A) , assuming that this Netras was appointed earlier than the Bishop Macarius addressed by Emperor Marcian in 453 (see below, pp. 237–41).

Moses and Elijah, both considered monastic prototypes.[96] But monks also were said to have travelled here simply to 'visit the holy ones', in hope of gaining advice from experts.[97] Much of what Sinai offered in this regard is preserved in the *Ladder of Divine Ascent* by John Climacus, the famous sixth- or seventh-century *hēgoumen* (i.e. leader or abbot) of the Mount Sinai monastery. Climacus wrote this guidebook for his counterpart John, *hēgoumen* of the community at Rhaithou, so as to help cenobites become anchorites; its thirty-step approach to conquering demonic impulses reveals a profound psychology, based in part on his own years of 'wrestling' (i.e. ascetic practice) as an anchorite in the Sinai desert.[98] But most of all, the Sinai offered almost unparalleled opportunities for obtaining the solitude essential to *hēsychia*. At the height of its settlement, it is estimated that the southern peninsula had no more than 500 to 1000 monks, giving each a potential 2–4 sq. km (0.75–1.5 sq. miles) of land, making it more sparsely settled than any other monastic landscape in late antiquity.[99]

Indeed, by the mid-sixth century, the southern Sinai ranked beside Palestine's Judaean desert and Egypt's Thebaid as the premier centre for anchoretic monasticism in the Roman Empire. This is generally considered Christianity's golden age on the peninsula, due in no small part to imperial patronage. While it is possible that Emperor Anastasius (491–518) was responsible for building the fortifications whose ruins may still be seen

96 Solzbacher 1989, 109.

97 Cf. John Eph., 'The Spurious Life of James', PO 19.257. For visiting saints as a pilgrimage goal, see Frank 2000.

98 John Climacus refers to his own struggles in *Ladder* 7 (PG 88.720A). For introduction to this work, see Ware 1982 and Chryssavgis 2004; for translation, see Bibliography. When Climacus lived and died are a matter of debate. He does not make any reference in his *Ladder* to the Persian or Arab invasions, and since Byzantine menologia state that he died in 603, his lifespan has traditionally been set c. 525–600. However, scholars have argued for dates c. 579–669, based in no small part upon Anastasius of Sinai's stories, many of which deal with Climacus: for review of the arguments, see Chryssavgis 2004, 42–44. (Daniel of Rhaithou's *Life of Climacus*, written in the ninth century, is of little historical value, being based almost entirely upon Anastasius' stories: see Müller 2002). The later dates for Climacus' death have generally gained acceptance, but Müller 2006, 21–56, has vigorously defended the traditional dates. I am sympathetic to his view, since it might make sense of all the Johns attested on the Sinai in the second half of the sixth century. However, the case is not yet closed: for further discussion, see below; Anast., *Narr* I.11, 16; and notes *ad loc.*

99 Dahari 2000, 150–52, prefers a population around 500. Such estimates are extrapolated from architectural remains and thus remain highly conjectural. Palladius in the early fifth century gives 500 for the number of monks inhabiting the much smaller area of Kellia in Egypt (*Lausiac History* 7.2) and 5,000 as the number for Nitria (*Dialogue on the Life of John Chrysostom* 17).

along the coast at Rhaithou (discussed below), Justinian (527–565) was the first (and apparently only) Roman emperor to do so at Mount Sinai itself. But it is not exactly clear when, where, or why he built in the area. The reason for this is that the epigraphical evidence is not as precise as one might hope,[100] and because archaeologists have not been able to excavate below the existing structures. Moreover, our two literary accounts describing Justinian's constructions – one by Procopius of Caesarea († c. 565), the other by Eutychius (Sa'īd ibn Bitrīq), a tenth-century Patriarch of Alexandria – differ in their explanations of his motives, and are difficult to interpret on their own (see the introductions to their texts below). Nevertheless, it is certain that Justinian was responsible for building the basilica church and surrounding walls that are visible at the site of the Burning Bush in Wadi al-Dayr today.

These walls retain much of the same form as when Justinian built them. Made of local granite blocks, they vary considerably in height, giving the structure a somewhat lopsided appearance (see appendix, Plan 1). This was not due to haphazard planning: the walls were positioned this way in Wadi al-Dayr in order to surround the Burning Bush while avoiding flash floods that wash down the wadi's floor.[101] Best preserved is the south-west wall, facing Jabal Musa's slope and decorated with cross reliefs; at 2.75 m (9 feet) thick, it is a thicker by a third than the others, no doubt to withstand rocks rolling down from Musa's summit. The adjacent north-west wall faced the Raha plain and served as the monastery's main façade. In its centre was a monumental entryway (now sealed) 3 m (10 feet) high by 2 m (6.5 feet) wide, surmounted by a massive, ornamented lintel. It featured the inscription:

> This is the gate of the Lord: Let the Righteous Pass through It [Ps. 118(117):20].
> In the age of Justinian, Sole Ruler, Who Loves Building Buildings.[102]

100 Out of 70–200 monastery inscriptions, only 14–16 date before 700 CE: see Ševčenko 1966.

101 The south-west wall (furthest up Jabal Musa's slope) is actually the lowest at 8 m (26 feet), the north-east wall the highest at 35 m (114 feet); lengths range from 80.5 m (264 feet) and 87.5 m (287 feet) (the south-west wall and the north-west wall) to 73.5 m (241 feet) and 74.8 m (245 feet) (the south-east and north-west walls). This north-east wall is the least well preserved, having been severely damaged in an earthquake in 1312; much of it reflects French restorations made in the early nineteenth century. To add strength, towers were added to the four corners and south-west, south-east, and north-east walls; another in the south-east wall served as a latrine. Altogether, the walls enclosed 6,030 sq. m (1.5 acres). See Forsyth 1968, 5–7; Tsafrir 1978m 228–29; Dahari 2000, 57.

102 Sinai Monastery inscription no. 1, ed. Ševčenko 1966, 262. The psalm verse of this inscription was also used for the basilica entry: Sinai Monastery inscription 2.2, ed. Ševčenko 1966, 262. Ševčenko publishes Justinian's epithet as *philoktistēs* ('Lover of Foundations'), but

Above the entryway was a *machicoulis*, a device for pouring boiling oil or water on enemies below. Entry could also be made through a simpler postern gate.[103]

This is what the Piacenza Pilgrim would have seen when he visited the '*monasterium* surrounded by fortified walls', probably some time in the 550s.[104] At that time it may not have been possible to see much else. Archaeologists think that the space enclosed by Justinian's walls initially contained little more than storage rooms, hermit cells, a kitchen or refectory, all set against the walls as casements to provide more strength (see appendix, Plan 1).[105] Soon, however, Justinian's church was added towards the northeast side, its apse oriented towards an outside tree identified as the Burning Bush. Its entryway was inscribed:

> And the Lord Spoke to Moses in this Place, saying 'I Am the God of Your Fathers, the God of Abraham, of Isaac, and of Jacob. I Am Who I Am' [cf. Exod. 3:14–15].[106]

Despite some later accretions (the Russian Campanile, leaden roof, narthex, and two chapels beside the altar), the present structure is more or less Justinianic, built in the basilica style (37 m/120 feet long by 20 m/66 feet wide) typical of late antique pilgrim churches in Palestine (see appendix, Plan 2).[107] After passing through its towering wooden doors, one entered the central nave. Its floor is paved with ornamental marble; ancient ostrich eggs still hang from a ceiling, which like the doors is carved with trees, birds, and hares, all painted gold, suggestive of paradise. Two rows of columns divide the central space, while separate side aisles led to the Burning Bush that grew in a courtyard directly behind the basilica's apse wall.

Illustrated on the mosaic of that wall above the altar is not only the Transfiguration scene described above, but a complex programme of Old Testament, New Testament, and imperial motifs. Its uppermost frames depict

---

also proposes that it be read as *philochristos* ('Lover of Christ'). The imperial title used here, *Autokrator*, differs from the title *Basileus* (lit. 'King'; Greek for 'Emperor') found in the roof beam noted below, p. 27: does this use of different titles have chronological implications? An inspection of Justinian's *Novels* and the inventory of inscriptions from his reign (including these) provided in Feissel 2000 might provide an answer.

103 On the gate, see Forsyth 1968, 7–8; Tsafrir 1978, 223; and Dahari 2000, 5.

104 PP, *Itin.* 37; for the dates of his visit, see below, p. 252.

105 Grossmann 1988, 544–45, accepted by Dahari 2000, 57; a structure near the church identified as a *xenodocheion* by Forsyth 1970 may also date to this period.

106 Sinai Inscription no. 2.1, Ševčenko 1966, 262.

107 See Forsyth 1968, 16–18, and 1988, 553–58.

Moses in his two great moments of revelation on the Sinai: in one, Moses loosens his sandal at the Burning Bush (Exod. 3:5); in the other, he receives the Law on the Sinai summit (Exod. 24:12). Directly below are a pair of winged angels, flying inwards to present cross-inscribed globes to an image of the Lamb of God, set at the centre of the arch above the Transfiguration scene. Medallion portraits of the Theotokos (i.e. Mary, 'Mother of God') and John the Baptist appear in gold below the angels' feet; then, bordering the apse mosaic itself, is a blue ribbon of medallions depicting the faces of prophets and apostles, as well as those of a Sinai *hēgoumen* named Longinus and a deacon named John. The centremost medallion, placed directly below Christ's feet, is a portrait of King David that bears striking resemblance to contemporary portraits of Emperor Justinian himself.[108] It was through such doublings of Old and New that the mosaic connected past to present.

The dates of the basilica and of its art are controversial. An inscription carved in one of the ceiling rafters informs us that the basilica was constructed by 'Stephen, Son of Martyrius, Deacon and Builder from Aila', requesting salvation for himself and repose for his children, Georgia and Nonna.[109] Two other rafters are inscribed, 'For the Salvation of Our Pious Emperor Justinian', and, 'For Memory and Repose of Our Late Empress Theodora'.[110] These inscriptions make plain that Theodora († 548) was dead and Justinian still alive at the time when they were carved; hence, the roof frame and basilica superstructure must have been completed some time around 548–565. Controversy arises as to how to make that date more precise. An important clue is found in the reference to a specific indiction, or tax cycle, in the mosaic inscription that runs along the bottom of the apse Transfiguration scene:

> In the name of the Father and Son and Holy Spirit: All this work was done for the salvation of the ones who provided the fruits in the time of the most holy priest and *hēgoumen* Longinus, by zeal of Theodore, priest and *deuterarius* [i.e. 'second in command'], indiction fourteen.[111]

108 On this and other works of Sinai art, see Forsyth and Weitzmann 1970, 392–405; plates no. ciii–cxxviii in Forsyth and Weitzmann 1973; essays in Weitzmann 1982; and Elsner 1995. On the David–Justinian medallion (Forsyth and Weitzmann 1973, pl. cxix), see Solzbacher 1989, 267, and Andreopoulos 2002, who compares it to Justinian's San Vitale portrait (Ravenna), dated c. 547; for its possible significance as for Justinian and the Sinai, see Müller 2006, 133–39.

109 Sinai inscription no. 3, ed. and trans. Ševčenko 1966, 262; see also below, n. 118.

110 Sinai inscriptions no. 5 (Justinian) and 4 (Theodora) on beams no. 8 and 7, ed. and trans. Ševčenko 1966, 262.

111 Sinai inscription no. 7, Ševčenko 1966, 263. Indictions were fifteen-year periods, with

The tax cycle year specified (the fourteenth indiction) would have fallen during Justinian's reign in 535/6, 550/1, or 565/6. Unfortunately the dates of Longinus' tenure are unknown, but we do know that another Mount Sinai *hēgoumen* named George (the earliest whose date is known to us) died in 551/2,[112] making 550/1 improbable (though not impossible) for Longinus. It is notable, however, that the Piacenza Pilgrim does not report seeing a church within Justinian's complex (although he does mention seeing churches within other Sinai forts) when he visited the mountain in the early 550s.[113] These considerations make 565/6 preferable for the church mosaic's date and Longinus' tenure (535/6 falls before Theodora's death and is therefore excluded).[114] Certainly the church must have been built before the mosaic was set into it, but the question remains, when?

Following the French scholar Robert Devreesse, we may consider one other clue, though one of dubious merit. Above the present entryway to Saint Catherine's are marble inscriptions in Greek and Arabic that date the monastery's building with casual precision. The Greek text states:

> This holy monastery of Mount Sinai, where God spoke to Moses, was erected by the humble Justinian, Emperor of the Romans, for unceasing remembrance of him and his consort Theodora; it was finished after the thirtieth year of his reign, and he established in it an *hēgoumen* named Doulas, in the year 6021 after Adam, or 527 after Christ.

The Arabic inscription is longer, and runs:

> The monastery of Tur Sina together with the church was erected on the mountain of the Dialogue, by the pious king, poor in God's sight but expecting His forgiveness, Justinian, of the Greek religion, in memory of himself and his consort Theodora, for all time, until that day when God, the best of heirs, takes possession of the earth and all upon it. The building thereof was completed in the

---

each year reckoned beginning in September and ending in August. Note that we are in a period before the adoption of the universal Christian reckoning systems (AD/BC or CE/BCE) used today.

112 John Mosch., *Meadow* 127 (PG 87[3].2989C) pegs the date of his death to that of Peter of Jerusalem (524–552): 'within six months, the old man [i.e. George] and the patriarch died'. Moschus reports that George had been living at Mt Sinai for the previous seventy years, but does not specify how long he was *hēgoumen*.

113 A date c. 570 is often given for his visit, but is surely erroneous. See Introduction to PP, *Itin.*, below, p. 252, n.1. Of course, his silence does not prove that no church existed within Justinian's walls at the time of his visit. Nonetheless, the fact that he does mention churches when visible within similar complexes (e.g. *Itin.* 41) gives weight to his silence here.

114 Devreesse 1940a, 213, believes the mosaic was completed in 565–566, based on his 557 date for the monastery.

thirtieth year of his reign. He appointed to it as abbot a man named Doulas. This took place in the year 6021 after Adam, which corresponds to the 527th year of our Lord the Messiah.[115]

Believing these inscriptions to have been based on early records, Devreesse used them to date the foundation of the monastery and its walls to 557, i.e. 'thirty years' after 527, which he considered a garbled reference to the beginning of Justinian's reign.[116] Their later editor, Ihor Ševčenko, dismissed the two inscriptions as historically worthless, noting that the Greek merely translates the Arabic text, both probably dating to the eighteenth century.[117] Ševčenko, however, also left open the possibility that the Arabic inscription was based on earlier records, and its reference to completion in the thirtieth year of Justinian's reign, i.e. 557, is sufficiently odd to require explanation. Although a date c. 550 is possible for the building of the church (perhaps built to honour Theodora after her death?), the 557 date fits within all known parameters, and may in fact be correct.[118]

Finally, there is the question of the church's dedication. According to Procopius, *On Buildings* V.viii.5–6, Justinian dedicated a church to the Theotokos (i.e. Mary, 'Mother of God') somewhere below the Sinai summit. Most scholars have assumed that this refers to Justinian's basilica beside the Bush, which was certainly associated with Mary later in the Middle Ages.[119] But others think Procopius was mistaken: noting that no inscription refers to the Theotokos, they maintain that Justinian meant it to commemorate the Transfiguration instead, partly because that would seem a more appropriate

115 The Greek text is Sinai Inscription no. 17, ed. and trans. Ševčenko 1966, 255–56; the Arabic text is trans. G. Hunt in Skrobucha 1966, 32.

116 Devreesse 1940a, 213 n. 2; see now also Müller 2006, 70–76.

117 Ševčenko 1966, 258–59 n. 14, attributing them to Cyril of Crete, Archbishop of Sinai 1759–1798.

118 Also important is the date of Procopius of Caesarea's *On Buildings*, which notes Justinian's construction of the church; many believe Procopius finished this work in 554, but others have plausibly argued for c. 560 (see below, p. 273, n. 1). A 554 date would require that Longinus' tenure as Mt Sinai *hēgoumen* be dated to 550/1, which is possible, but seems improbable given the indication for the Mt Sinai *hēgoumen* George's death in 551/2 (above, n. 112). Reference is sometimes also made to an epitaph found at Beer Sheva: 'Here lies the blessed Nonna, child of Stephen from Aila. She died in the sixth indiction', Alt 1921, 23, no. 36. This may be the same Nonna commemorated in Sinai inscription no. 3; 'sixth indiction' could mean 532, 547 or 562. Its relevance to the dating of the Sinai church is intriguing but perhaps misconstrued, as argued by Ševčenko 1966, 257 n. 7, and Solzbacher 1989, 252–62.

119 E.g. on 6 August 1218, Pope Honorius III confirmed the possessions of the 'Monastery of St Mary' on the Sinai: see Skrobucha 1966, 65, and Braun 1973, 9, 227.

theme for the Sinai.[120] It should be remembered, however, that the Burning Bush was considered a prefiguration of the Theotokos (and the Theotokos a typology for the Bush, both being a 'type' for the Incarnation) in fourth- and fifth-century patristic thought.[121] Moreover, two of the seventh-century stories of Anastasius the Sinaite (*Narr.* I.13, 17) refer to the Theotokos as 'Our Mistress', where it is fairly clear that the setting is Justinian's monastery. We may therefore be confident that the Wadi al-Dayr basilica is the Theotokos church to which Procopius refers.[122]

These constructions brought an imperial monumentality to the Mount Sinai area that had not been there before, and must have provided an added attraction for pilgrims. Indeed, most of our evidence for Sinai pilgrimage in late antiquity dates to the late sixth and seventh centuries, when we find references to mass tour groups (Anastasius describes 800 Armenian pilgrims visiting the summit at once) as well as smaller parties of Roman aristocrats.[123] From then on there was a steady growth of facilities at Wadi al-Dayr; by the early seventh century, visitors would have found the monastery equipped with a two-story guesthouse and a fifteen-bed infirmary, fitted out with sheets and blankets donated by the Roman pope, Gregory the Great.[124] According to the Piacenza Pilgrim (*Itin.* 37), it also was staffed with three multilingual elders, as well as individuals who spoke Latin, Syriac, Coptic,

120 Forsyth 1973, 52; Dahari 2000, 29. The view appears as early as the sixteenth century: see Braun 1973, 9, 226.

121 Solzbacher 1989, 264–65, argues that both, as symbols of the Incarnation, would have been also regarded as symbols of Chalcedonian orthodoxy.

122 Readers should be aware that Dahari 2000, 28–36 and 1998a, proposes an altogether different identification, arguing that Justinian's Theotokos church was not the one beside the Burning Bush (which he believes was dedicated to the Transfiguration), but a smaller church on the Sinai summit, which, he claims, Justinian also built. Little remains of that summit building (the present summit chapel incorporates ashlar stones from an earlier church, but dates to 1934). Nonetheless, Dahari finds substantiation in the fact that Eutychius specifies that Justinian built a church on the Sinai summit, while Procopius does not exactly state that Justinian built his Theotokos church within his Sinai fort; moreover, numerous architectural fragments have been found on the summit that bear the letters ΘΚ, a late antique abbreviation for 'Theotokos'. Dahari reports finding over 20 other stones marked with these letters, which he considers to be mason's marks. It should be noted, however, that the Piacenza Pilgrim only saw a 'small oratory' during his visit to the summit (PP, *Itin.* 37) and that Anastasius never mentions the Theotokos when referring to its church (which he consistently calls the 'Holy Summit'). Dahari reports finding several of the ΘΚ fragments down at St Catherine's. It may be that such pieces, originally cut to build or repair the Sinai monastery or its basilica, were later brought up to make repairs on the summit during the Middle Ages.

123 E.g. Anast., *Narr.* I.4 and 12, Gregory the Great, *Letter* IV.44; cf. *P.Colt* 72 and 73.

124 Gregory I, *Letter* XI.2; Anast., *Narr.* II.8.

or other languages. Other sources make clear that its monks represented a confluence of backgrounds: we read of some from Rome, Cilicia, and Cappadocia conversing together in one story alone.[125] Indeed, another story reports that so many monks were travelling back and forth from Jerusalem to Sinai that even the demons were being driven to distraction.[126] Obviously, that implies criticism. So we might ask: was Sinai monastic life significantly changed by Justinian's patronage and the later pilgrimage traffic?

In certain respects it must have been. The influx of pilgrims created a need for monks skilled not only in communications but in other mundane services as well, such as economics. Anastasius describes the monastery catering to 500 pilgrims at a single meal (*Narr.* I.12), indicating the scale of provisions it would have needed to acquire and keep in stock. Fortunately pilgrims brought gifts as well. No doubt many of the famous sixth- or seventh-century icons that belong to the monastery today originated as gifts left by pilgrims or sent by donors.[127] More illustrative, however, of the wealth the monastery received in post-Justinianic times is the record kept by a group of traders who visited Mount Sinai some time in the late sixth or seventh century (*P.Colt* 89, 'Account of a Trading Company', included in appendix below). Not only did the traders give 17 gold coin *solidi* to the monastery (or its church) as a donation from people of the Negev, but also, 'after praying', they left one such 'blessing' themselves. Then they received 270.5 *solidi* from a Sinai elder. These are remarkable sums. Nuns living in Rome at the time received no more than two *solidi* each as an annual pension, while some Italian oratories were endowed with only six.[128] The

125 John Mosch., *Meadow* 127. Ševčenko 1966, 258, remarks that inscriptions reflect a Palestinian, Syrian, and Egyptian milieu, cosmopolitan but not sophisticated.

126 *Apophth. patr*, Syriac collection no. 420; trans. Budge, II.239:

There was a certain holy man who used to see visions, and he told the following story, saying, 'Once when I was standing in prayer I heard a devil complain in the presence of his companion, saying, "I am [suffering] great labour and trouble." And when the other devil asked him … the cause of his trouble, he said to him, "This is the work which hath been handed over to me. When I have carried these monks, who are in Jerusalem and its neighborhood, to Mount Sinai, I have to bring those who are in Mount Sinai to Jerusalem, and I have no rest whatsoever."'

This story is only preserved in the Syriac apophthegmata collection, which was compiled some time in the seventh century.

127 Twenty-four of the monastery's 2,048 icons date to the sixth and seventh century (perhaps one to the fifth). Based on their style and quality, Weitzmann 1976, 13–56, believes most of these were made in Constantinople, but there is no direct evidence and not all would agree.

128 Gregory the Great, *epp.* VII.2, IX.72, and XIII.21.

papyrus does not reveal why the Sinai elder entrusted so much to these traders, but it does show how much the Sinai monastery had on hand, and suggests how much it could profit from pilgrimage.

With pilgrim traffic also came the need to appoint monks to guide guests, maintain shrines, run the infirmary and guesthouse, or serve as stewards. This entailed, or presumed, the existence of a centralized, administrative hierarchy at Wadi al-Dayr, especially the emergence of an *hēgoumen*, i.e. an officially recognized 'leader' or abbot.[129] The lack of historical documents clearly datable between the late fourth and early sixth centuries prevents us from tracing the inception of this office on the Sinai with certainty. However, the fact that a letter sent by the Roman Emperor Marcian to the Sinai community in 453 is only addressed to 'Macarius, the most pious Bishop, and the archimandrites and all monks' of Mount Sinai implies that no single, central authority existed there yet, and that several archimandrites ('leaders of a flock'), representing different anchoretic colonies, shared leadership instead.[130] No *hēgoumen* is reliably attested on the Sinai until the middle of the sixth century.[131]

Sinai tradition maintained that Justinian himself established the monastery's first abbot, named Doulas.[132] Indeed, although someone was probably made responsible for pilgrims and logistics at the Sinai before the mid-sixth century, it is possible that the office of *hēgoumen* itself was introduced here by the emperor himself. Justinian was keen on standardizing monasticism throughout the Roman Empire. In the years 535 and 539 he issued laws dictating how coenobitic monasteries were to be built (each must have strong walls, with only one or two entrances) and their *hēgoumens* elected. We may assume that he would have wanted these laws to be applied to the Sinai as well.[133] But we may go farther than that. The fact that his successor

129 As Flusin 1998, 136, notes, pilgrimage traffic may have necessitated someone to coordinate resources; such circumstances are reflected in Ammonius *Rel.* 2. In 536 CE a Sinai representative served at Constantinople as 'Theonas the priest by God's mercy of the Holy Mountain of Sinai, and *apocrisarius* [representative] of the Sinai Mountain and the Church of Pharan and the Lavra of Rhaithou'. This indicates that there was already enough organization by 536 to keep a permanent representative in Constantinople. See ACO III.I.1.146 ('Collectio sabbaitica'), no. 82, and Solzbacher 1989, 194.

130 See Emperor Marcian, *Letter to Bishop Macarius and the Monks of Sinai*, below, p. 283, n. 3.

131 I.e. George, who died in 551/2: see above, n. 112.

132 Cf. Sinai inscription no. 17, translated above, pp. 28–29. This or some other 'Doulas' (perhaps an abbreviation for Theodulus or Ab'd Allah, 'Slave of God') appears in other sources of dubious historicity: see Ammonius, *Rel.* 3, 9, and 40; Eutychius, *Annals* (below, p. 281).

133 Justinian, *Nov.* V.9 (535), CXXXIII.1 (539); see Granić 1929 and Müller 2006, 111–27.

Justin II (565–578) personally appointed a new *hēgoumen* to the Mount Sinai monastery at the beginning of his reign suggests not only that the Sinai monastery was regarded as an imperial foundation legally passed from one emperor to the next, but that its builder, Justinian, had also been the one who had legally founded it as a formal institution.[134] While it is usually assumed that his walls simply provided housing for a coenobitic community that already existed at Mount Sinai, there is in fact no evidence that such a formal community existed there before his time. It is therefore plausible that the emperor himself ordered the creation of the Sinai *coenobium*, perhaps to serve at his basilica below the mountain.

If this is correct, then Justinian's legacy on the Sinai includes not only the physical structures still visible in Wadi al-Dayr, but also the coenobitic institution that survives today as St Catherine's (the military protection he also provided is discussed below). Besides receiving pilgrims, this institution provided monastic training: after receiving a tonsure on Mount Sinai's summit, novices completed a two-year diaconate (i.e. 'service', aimed at instilling humility) at the *coenobium* before being allowed to dwell closer to their ascetic 'supervisors' (i.e. the anchorites who served as their spiritual masters).[135] As this arrangement indicates, coenobitic monasticism never eclipsed traditional anchoretic life in this period. Indeed, one may have facilitated the other, inasmuch as the *coenobium* apparently provided affiliated anchorites with supplemental bread rations, delivered by mule.[136] Yet such solitaries were now formally subject to the Sinai monastery's *hēgoumen*.[137] Did this or any other aspect of Sinai organization cause complaint? Protest against change of some sort is certainly expressed in a story about Abba Orentius, an anchorite of the late sixth century:

134 Evagrius, *EH* V.6; trans. Whitby, 262: '[Gregory] was leader of the monastery of the Byzantines … and on orders of Justin also that of Mount Sinai.' Founders of religious institutions and their heirs were entitled to appoint their *hēgoumen*s: see Thomas 1987, 54–55, noting in this case, '[Justin] surely inherited his rights with respect to St Catherine's from his predecessor Justinian, who founded it in the 550s'. Flusin 1998, 133, emphasizes that the creation of the *coenobium* at Mt Sinai was not the result of a simple evolutionary process from anchoretism to coenobitism (however, he does not believe the monastery followed Justinianic convention: see Flusin 2006, 202).

135 Anast., *Narr.* I.10–13 and 39; for the process, see Flusin 1998, 138 and 2006.

136 John Mosch., *Meadow* 125 (PG 87[3].2988AB). Dahari 2000, 94, estimates that the ratio of Sinai anchorites to coenobites would have been about 5:1, with 100 monks living in the *coenobium*.

137 John Mosch., *Meadow* 124 (PG 87[3].2988A) tells how three anchorites were sent to serve in Egyptian churches at the *hēgoumen*'s command.

One Sunday he came to church with his smock turned inside out, so that the hair was on the outside. When he went to stand in the choir, those who administered the place said to him, 'Good Old Man, why have you come in like this? Are you going to make a scene in front of our guests?' The old man said to them, 'You've turned Sina inside out, and no one has said anything to you. Now that I've turned my smock around, are you going to call me to account? Go on your way, and I'll straighten out what I've turned around.

An enigmatic gesture, a riddling rebuke: did it decry an excessive concern for outside guests, or more fundamentally the fact that 'administrators' were now running the place?[138]

Otherwise there is no sign that Sinai tranquillity was disturbed by internal dissent. Its monks seem to have been spared any serious involvement in the doctrinal disputes dividing Christian communities elsewhere in the empire at the time, especially in nearby Egypt. True, some early opponents of the Council of Chalcedon (451 CE) took refuge here. This prompted Emperor Marcian to write to the Sinai monastic communities in 453 CE, forbidding them to shelter Theodosius, a monk who had fled to Mount Sinai 'with his comrades' after his rebellion against Chalcedonian authorities in Jerusalem had collapsed.[139] Later an anti-Chalcedonian priest was reportedly given lodging among monks at Rhaithou and Mount Sinai.[140] Whatever that implies, the peninsula had become firmly 'orthodox' (i.e. Chalcedonian) by 536, when a representative at the Synod of Constantinople signed on behalf of the 'Sinai and the Church of Pharan and the Lavra of Rhaithou' in support of the imperial position.[141] Thereafter all evidence shows close allegiance

---

138 John Mosch., *Meadow* 126 (PG 87[3].2988BC), interpreted by Solzbacher 1989, 272, as criticism that *coenobium* administrators (οἱ τὸν τόπον οἰκοῦντες) had lost sight of priorities by doting on pilgrims (Anast., *Narr.* I.7 also alludes to administrators at the mountain, τοὺς τὸν ἅγιον τόπον διοικοῦντας, probably the same group mentioned here). Müller 2006, 57–69, cites this anecdote as evidence that Justinian's coenobitic foundation resulted in a monastic hierarchy that upset older anchorites, creating a 'clash of monastic civilizations' (p. 430) on the Sinai that Climacus tried to mitigate with the vision of coenobitic–anchoretic cooperation put forth in his *Ladder*.

139 See Emperor Marcian, *Letter to Bishop Macarius and the Monks of Sinai*, below, p. 240; also Theophanes, *Chronographia* A.M. 5945. On the improbability of anti-Chalcedonianism at Sinai, see Solzbacher 1989, 184–93.

140 John Rufus of Maïouma, 'Vision of Priest Zosimus', *Plerophoriae* 30 (PO 8.72), written c. 512–518.

141 See above, n. 129; signatories also included bishops of Aila, Petra, and Iotabē. Despite the assertion of Trimingham 1979, 257, that 'various synods had regularly excommunicated groups of monks in Sinai as heretics', Sinai's only recorded home-grown heretic is Theodore of Rhaithou, whose treatise on the incarnation was condemned as 'monothelite' in 649 at Rome

with Constantinople and Jerusalem. Indeed, the close relations expected between Mount Sinai *hēgoumens* and Jerusalem patriarchs is illustrated by a sixth-century story in which one Patriarch of Jerusalem asks the Bishop of Pharan to send him the Sinai *hēgoumen*, in the mistaken belief that this *hēgoumen* had snubbed an earlier invitation to dine with him.[142] Jerusalem patriarchs probably also supported the monastery financially: one at any rate is said to have constructed a 'reservoir' (*lakka*) somewhere on the Sinai, perhaps the two-tiered cistern that may still be seen today below the Jabal Musa summit.[143]

Our impression of this era in Sinai history comes largely from the writings of John Moschus (c. 550–634), a Palestinian monk who visited the region some time in the late sixth or early seventh centuries, and became sufficiently attached to the place to request that his bones be brought there from Rome for burial after his death.[144] Several stories in his *Spiritual Meadow* are about monks of Rhaithou. Although Christian memory of this coastal settlement faded in the West during the later Middle Ages – by which time it had become a transit point for pilgrims heading to Mecca as much as to Mount Sinai – it continued as a monastic centre until the eleventh century at least, and was well known in late antiquity. It seems to have comprised a broad swathe of land, centred on Wadi al-Tur but ranging 8 km (5 miles) north to Bir Abū Suwayra and 10 km (6 miles) south to Ras Raya ('Point Rhaithou').[145] By the sixth century, this area featured two imperial forts,

---

and 680/1 at Constantinople. Sinai monks were appointed to episcopal sees in problem areas such as Antioch and Egypt, indicating that they were considered dependably Chalcedonian. Solzbacher 1989, 268, explains Sinai orthodoxy by reference to its diversity, noting that monks here (unlike those in Egypt or Syria) came from many different areas, i.e. from no single region or ethnic background. Sinai's proximity to Jerusalem–Palestine no doubt also helped (Flusin 1992, vol. 1, 43–45, sees it as a virtual extension of the Judaean desert). A cynic might suggest that imperial patronage was intended to keep them in the emperor's camp; this would have been financially helpful to the monks, whose support in turn would have lent weight in turn to the emperor's doctrinal efforts.

142 John Mosch., *Meadow* 127.

143 John Mosch., *Meadow* 134 (PG 87[3].2997C); Dahari 2000, 37.

144 See Solzbacher 1989, 270–75, and Flusin 1992, vol. 1, 16 n. 2, arguing that the transferral of Moschus' bones to Sinai was impeded not by the Persian invasion of 619 but by the Arab invasion of 634. There is no modern edition of Moschus' stories and the MSS show many variants. For a full but imperfect translation, see Wortley under John Moschus in Bibliography.

145 Cf. Solzbacher 1989, 400. No inscription has been found to identify the ancient site. Mayerson 1980, 146, restricts it to Bir Abū Suwayra. Dahari 2000, 140–41, prefers Ras Raya, based on ruins of a fort there (see next note) and his belief that the modern name locates the site. Similar ruins at Wadi al-Tur reportedly date to the sixth century: see Kawatoko 1995,

one at Wadi al-Tur and another at Ras Raya. Each was built on the same scale and essentially the same pattern as Justinian's constructions at Wadi al-Dayr; each similarly had an apsidal church (see appendix, Plan 3).[146] No doubt Rhaithou received such attention because of its harbours: as noted above, these made Rhaithou the principal commercial depot on the peninsula, exposing it to both dangers and profits. Local Pharanites apparently kept a permanent base somewhere in the area (probably at Wadi al-Tur or Ras Raya) for fishing, trade, and importing supplies.[147]

One of these church-and-fort complexes may have turned the 'Lavra of Rhaithou', first attested as such in 536, into a coenobitic monastery; otherwise Rhaithou, like the rest of Sinai, remained predominately anchoretic.[148] Did proximity to the coast make the monastic experience here any different than in the Sinai interior? Moschus' stories mainly focus on solitaries who died of thirst on coastal islands. Beside these seaside examples of ascetic heroism there are, however, hints of more worldly connections. Most intriguing are the utterances attributed to John the Cilician, a sixth-century *hēgoumen* at the lavra. Aside from platitudes bemoaning increased luxury (e.g. 'As we fled the world, so let us flee the desires of the flesh'; 'Let us imitate our Fathers, who settled here in such hardship and tranquillity') are two remarks particularly suited to Rhaithou: 'This is a place for ascetics, not for merchants', and, 'Children, let us not defile this place which our Fathers cleansed of demons'.[149] The first would seem to warn against involvement

---

844, 847–48. However, the reasons for assigning them that date are nowhere explained, and it would be nice to know if they dated earlier (e.g. to Anastasius' reign, 491–518) in the sixth century rather than later.

Wadi al-Tur's topography appears to conform to the description of the area in Ammonius, *Rel.* 10. The Tur and Raya sites can both be inspected via Google Earth (Wadi al-Tur: Pointer 28° 16'28.94" N, 33° 36'41.33" E; Ras Raya: Pointer 28°, 10'02.45" N, 33° 39'53.24" E)

146 No final excavation report for these sites has been published; for preliminary discussion and sketches, see Kawatoko 1998; 2004; 2005; and Grossmann 2002, 358–61. The name al-Tur, 'the Mountain', derives from the fact that pilgrims used the site to approach Mt Sinai on the way to Mecca.

147 Mentioned by Ammonius in *Rel.* 19.

148 The discovery of four lavra clusters and a small rectangular encampment at Bir Abū Suwayra make it a plausible candidate for the 'Lavra of Rhaithou' site: see Dahari 2000, 141–45, summarizing an unpublished survey by Y. Tsafrir and A. Goren. Its late antique date is surmised from similarities between its ruins and those found at Kellia in Egypt, as well as a description in Ammonius, *Rel.* 11. It is, however, possible that the ruins date to the later Middle Ages.

149 John Mosch., *Meadow* 115 (PG 87[3].2980BC). John the Cilician may be John of Rhaithou.

in the business opportunities that passed through Rhaithou's harbour, while the second may allude to the fact that its 'Palm Groves' once featured two sizeable altars, one dedicated to Poseidon, the other to an unknown, native god.[150]

Spiritual connections between Rhaithou and the Sinai interior were evidently close, at least in the time of John Climacus. As noted above, his masterpiece, the *Ladder of Divine Ascent*, was written for Rhaithou monks at the request of their *hēgoumen*, John of Rhaithou. Scholars are now beginning to recognize the sophistication of Climacus' rhetorical craftsmanship.[151] Indeed, it is clear that the Sinaite world was not only literate but literary: besides Climacus' *Ladder*, Anastasius' *Tales of the Sinai Fathers* and *Edifying Tales* as well as Daniel of Rhaithou's ninth-century *Life of Climacus* exemplify the hagiographical nature of some of the literature being produced both at Mount Sinai and Rhaithou. We cannot tell what proportion of Sinai monks were literate or how widely such writings circulated among them. To judge from Moschus' stories from the Jordanian desert, however, it was not unusual to find books in hermit cells.[152] The early history of St Catherine's famous library is unknown, but there are indications that it was operating in the eighth century;[153] one might assume that it began earlier.

The sayings and stories in Moschus' *Spiritual Meadow* commemorate Christianity's heyday on the Sina. He recorded them some time before his death c. 634, having lived to see the Persian and Arab invasions and the loss of the peninsula from the Roman domain. Anastasius of Sinai's stories, written a generation later, show Sinai monks trying to cope with the new situation. At the time, however, they may not have thought that it would last. Other invaders had come and gone. According to the chronicler John of Nikiu, one attack had occurred during the reign of Emperor Anastasius (491–518), apparently against monks at Rhaithou.

> In the reign of this God-living emperor impious barbarians, who eat human flesh and drank [*sic*] blood, arose in the quarter of Arabia, and approaching the borders of the Red Sea, they seized the monks of Arâitê, and they put them to sword or led them away captive and plundered their possessions; for they hated

---

150 Agatharchides of Cnidos, *ap.* Diodorus Siculus 85; Solzbacher 1989, 45, locates the altars in the al-Tur–Suwayra area.

151 Duffy 1999; Johnsén 2007. John of Rhaithou may be John the Cilician.

152 John Mosch., *Spiritual Meadow* 46, 134. For the practice of reading and existence of books in late antique monasteries see Kotsifou 2007 and Rapp 2007.

153 On the library, see Géhin 1998; for early Syriac evidence, see Binggeli 2005, 168.

the saints, and were themselves like in their devices to idolaters and pagans... When the emperor was informed of this event he had strong forts constructed as a defence to the dwellings of the monks.[154]

Assuming that 'Arâitê' is a garbled form of Rhaithou, this is the first report of an assault on the Sinai by outside marauders, and may explain the forts placed at Wadi al-Tur and Ras Raya.[155]

But we should not let such reports distract us from the more persistent source of Sinai danger. When Arab invaders arrived in the seventh century, they tipped a balance that had long held between monastic settlers and Sinai's native Arab or 'Saracen' population. That balance, or peace, was always unsteady. According to the sixth-century historian Evagrius, 'Scenite barbarians' – i.e. Arab nomads – had besieged Mount Sinai's monastery while George of Antioch was serving as its *hēgoumen* c. 566–570, exposing him to 'very great' danger. Eventually he restored 'great peace' to the place.[156] How George did so we are not told; but presumably he was helped by the 80 or more soldiers that Justinian had installed, apparently at Pharan. Like the 'Very Loyal Theodosians' garrisoned at Nessana, these were native recruits; they rode Arabian horses and received pay, fodder, and uniforms from Roman officials in Egypt. The Piacenza Pilgrim says that their patrols were meant to serve as a 'guard for the monasteries and hermits, on account of attacks by Saracens'.[157] But the Pilgrim was not impressed. The gates of Pharan, he notes, had to be locked 'on account of attacks by Saracens' whenever the soldiers went out on patrol; as for their patrols, they did not make the Saracens in question 'tremble in fear'.[158]

Such notices indicate more tensions and troubles on the peninsula than

154 John of Nikiu, *Chronicle* LXXXIX.33–34; trans. Charles 1916, 125. John was bishop of Nikiu (upper Egypt) and wrote c. 690 in Greek. His *Chronicle* is only preserved in Ethiopic.

155 This would make the fortresses Anastasian rather than Justinianic. Dahari 2000, 141, argues that John of Nikiu was swayed by anti-Chalcedonian prejudice to attribute these constructions falsely to Emperor Anastasius, rather than Justinian; that seems both far-fetched and unnecessary, since we know that Anastasius provided defences for other 'Chalcedonian' monks (cf. Cyril Scyth., *Life of Abraamius* 1). Eutychius' attribution of them to Justinian cannot be taken as confirmation, since it may simply reflect later monastic tradition. Geopolitical strategy made Persians and Romans more active in the Red Sea from Anastasius onward (see Fowden 1993); it could be that the forts were needed to protect merchant commerce from Ethiopia and Yemen from attack from raiders or Persian allies.

156 Evagrius Schol., *EH* V.6; trans. Whitby, 262.

157 PP, *Itin.* 40, and note *ad loc.*; Procop., *Buildings* V.viii.9, attributes a garrison to Justinian without specifying where they were stationed; probably it was at Pharan, whose defensive circuit walls also apparently date to the second half of the sixth century.

158 PP, *Itin.* 40.

Sinai's reputation for tranquillity would otherwise suggest. Indeed, they reveal conditions not unlike those depicted in the Sinai martyr narratives discussed below. Before turning to those narratives, however, we should consider what other sources reveal about the Saracen situation in the region.

3. ASSESSING THE SARACEN MENACE ON THE SINAI FRONTIER

Who were 'the Saracens'? The word conjures images of scimitar-waving horsemen swarming over desert hills. The earliest version of that stereotype comes from the fourth-century historian Ammianus Marcellinus, who notes how, during a Persian attack upon the Roman Empire in 354, the *Saraceni* had, by 'ranging up and down the country … laid waste to whatever they could find like rapacious kites, which, whenever they catch sight of any prey on high, seize it with a swift swoop, and … make off'. As he further explains,

> Among those tribes, whose original abode extends from the Assyrians to the cataracts of the Nile and confines of the Blemmyes, all alike are warriors of equal rank, half-nude, clad in dyed cloaks as far as the loins, ranging widely with the help of swift horses and slender camels in times of peace or of disorder. No man ever grasps a plough-handle or cultivates a tree, none seeks a living by tilling the soil, but they rove continually over wide and extensive tracts without a home, without fixed abodes or laws … I have seen many who were wholly unacquainted with grain and wine. So much for this dangerous tribe.[159]

Ammianus' sketch, though vivid, broadly replicates classical stereotypes of 'barbarian' fringe groups in general and nomadic groups in particu-lar.[160] Modern historians have long recognized the need for a more nuanced understanding of the late antique Saracen phenomenon, if not simply to understand Roman military arrangements along the eastern frontier before

---

159 Ammianus Marcellinus XIV.4.1, 3–7, trans. Roelfle vol. 1, 27–29, slightly adapted.

160 Viz., in its unhistorical approach, its failure to differentiate between tribal or ethnic groups, and its equation of nomadism with lawlessness, ignorance of cultivation or cultivated foods, and wild beasts: on such representations in Greco-Roman sources, see Shaw 1982–83; cf. Ammianus' description of the Huns, XXXI.2.1–12 and Procop., *Wars* I.19.8–16, which differentiates tribal groups in the Arabian peninsula according to their proximity to the Roman Empire: most distant are 'the man-eating Saracens'. Christian ethnography claimed that Saracens had descended from Ishmael and Hagar (hence the names 'Ishmaelites', 'Hagarites'); it also assimilated them to Jews: see Sozomen, *EH* VI.37, Shahid 1984, 560–64; 1989, 167–78; 1995, 331–37; Jeffreys 1986; and Hoyland 1997, 24.

the seventh-century Arab conquests.[161] Elsewhere Ammianus reports that by his day, the term 'Saracen' was being used instead of the older phrase 'Scenite ['Tent-Camp'] Arabs' to designate Arab nomads in general: in other words, 'Saracen' had become the late antique equivalent of the modern term, 'bedouin' (derived from the Arabic word *badawī/badw*, 'desert-dweller').[162] While it is important to distinguish 'Saracen' supergroups such as the Arab Ghassanids or Lakhmids from smaller groups of regional bedouin, it appears that there were sometimes connections between the activities of such different groups, and an attempt will be made here to survey possible links between them. Our main concern, however, is to clarify what circumstances may have contributed to the amelioration or exacerbation of 'Saracen'– settler relations within the Negev–Sinai region. Indeed, the sources from Third Palestine allow us to study the late antique Saracen phenomenon and associated threat with unparalleled detail.

   Certainly it appears that Diocletian believed the Saracen threat along his empire's south-eastern border to have been sufficient to warrant posting two Roman legions there, as noted above. Later sources claim that Arab groups began migrating north from the Arabian peninsula in the second century, and Diocletian's build-up probably responded to the consequences.[163] Whether on horseback or camelback, 'Saracen' warriors were considered an unusual

---

161 The purpose of the Roman military presence along that frontier remains debated, largely between those who see it chiefly as one of border control against infiltration by external enemies (e.g. Parker 1986; 1987; and 2000, based primarily on archaeology of legionary camps) and those who see it as one of policing against internal enemies (e.g. Isaac 1984; 1990; and 1995, based primarily on the literary evidence presented in this volume). Mayerson 1989b strikes middle ground with a macro-micro approach that has inspired my own presentation.

162 Ammianus Marcellinus XXII.15.1; cf. Shahid 1984, 296, 'the Saracens were nomadic Arabs and the Arabs were sedentary Arabs'. Etymological explanations of the origin of the term 'Saracen' have been inconclusive. An attractive solution once seemed to lie in *shirkat*, an Arabic term for 'confederation', proposed by Graf and O'Connor 1977. But this proposal was forcefully challenged by MacDonald 1995, arguing that the word more likely derived from a specific tribal name: cf. 'Tayites', which became the generic Aramaic term for nomadic Arabs but was originally the name of a specific group, the *Tayyiye*: see Segal 1984, 89–101, and Hoyland 2001, 235. Others have sought origins in Arabic words such as *sarqiyyin* ('easterner') or *sharaqa* ('bandits'), but these are based on perceived phonetic similarities and stereotypes; we might equally propose its origin in the Latin word *sareca*, used to describe Saracen blankets by PP, *Itin.* 36.

163 Diocletian fought Saracens somewhere in 290 and dedicated an arms factory at Damascus against their incursions. Ammianus implies that the Roman Empire had been dealing with Saracen groups since the reign of Marcus Aurelius (161–180): see Graf 1978; Parker 1986; 1987, 46–48; Erickson-Gini 2004, 184. On the Arab tradition, see Hoyland 2001, 231–36.

foe, being highly mobile and adept at hit-and-run tactics.[164] But the challenge facing Rome involved nomadic leadership structures as well as military tactics. Local sheikhs had always depended on launching raids or *razzias* to enforce obedience, procure gifts, or provide their pastoral communities with sufficient resources to survive: such raids, in other words, were considered essential to maintaining tribal leadership, unless replaced by other sources of funds.[165] But tribal leadership structures became more complex during the third century. Regional branches continued to be led by local sheikhs. By the later third century, however, most local tribes and their sheikhs had come under control of dynasts who called themselves 'kings' (Arabic *malik*; Greek *basileus*). Born out of third-century wars between Rome and Persia, such dynasts represented their tribal confederations as regional overlords along the Roman–Persian frontier, offering allegiance to either power for a price. Rome officially designated such leaders as 'phylarchs' ('tribal rulers'). Their responsibilities transcended political borders, requiring them not only to aid Rome against Persia but to prevent local sheikhs from raiding Roman towns. Rome made alliances with at least three tribal confederations in the fourth century, each responsible for limited territory. In the sixth century, however, Justinian decided to pay a single supergroup, the Ghassanids, to provide security along the entire eastern frontier.[166]

Such arrangements were made because they seemed mutually advantageous. But the subsequent history of Roman dealings with the Arab confederations and phylarchs bears comparison to the Roman–Germanic or Roman–Gothic situation farther north. With tribal networks transcending imperial boundaries and answering to regional kings, each Arab confederation constituted, like their northern counterparts, 'a powerful autonomous group allied to Rome in a tenuous relationship that at times benefited the empire, and at others hurt it gravely'.[167] An example of the latter case – one that affected Third Palestine – is the Mavia revolt that occurred in 377/78. According to the church historians Rufinus, Socrates, and Sozomen, it was triggered by the death of Mavia's husband, who had been 'king' (i.e.

---

164 *ad furta bellorum appositi*: Ammianus Marcellinus XXIII.3.8; cf. Evagrius Schol., *EH* V.20, trans. Whitby, 282–83.

165 Whittow 1996, 32–36; Shahid 1995, 310.

166 The arrangement lasted from 546 to 585. See Graf 1978 and 1989; Donner 1981, 43–49; Shahid 1984; 1995 *passim*; Isaac 1990, 235–49; Millar 1993, 431–35. Shahid believes that in the fifth century, each Roman duke (i.e. provincial military commander) was paired with a phylarch from the Salih confederation.

167 Lenski 2002, 203, referring to Saracens. On the transformation of Germanic and Gothic groups under overlords and subsequent relations with Rome, see Heather 2006, 85–94.

phylarch) of Rome's Saracen allies: this precipitated a crisis in which Mavia turned against Rome.[168] Rufinus reports that her troops laid waste to cities and towns in Palestine, while Sozomen specifies that they went 'as far as the regions of Egypt lying to the left of those who sail towards the source of the Nile, which are generally denominated Arabia'.[169] The attack overwhelmed local *limitanei* as well as the field troops of the East, forcing Rome to seek terms. Mavia agreed, but only on condition (church sources report) that her troops be given, as a bishop, a Nicene monk named Moses who lived 'in a nearby desert', 'on the borderlands of Egypt and Palestine'.[170] Once ordained outside Alexandria, Moses is said to have converted many of her Saracens to Christianity, thereby reconciling them to Rome. Meanwhile, her daughter was wedded to a Roman general to consolidate the alliance.[171] As a result, Saracen troops helped save Constantinople after the Battle of Hadrianople in 378, and Mavia was celebrated long afterwards in Arabic song.[172]

We know more about Mavia's revolt than about any other Saracen incident before the seventh-century Arab invasions. An apparently comparable disturbance arose in 411, when Jerome says an attack 'overran the frontiers of Egypt, Palestine, Phoenicia and Syria'.[173] Another happened c. 500, when 'Scenite Arabs made a raid against the Roman realm and ravaged ... both Phoenicias and the Palestines'.[174] These are, however, the only major Saracen problems recorded on the south-eastern frontier before the Arab conquests. For some, this proves that Diocletian's border camps were effective in keeping enemies out.[175] But by the late fifth century, most

168 Lenski 2002, 203–09, believes it was triggered by a Roman levy on allied Saracens to fight the Goths in Thrace. But the sources do not mention such a levy, and Mavia may have initiated the action to prove herself a warrior and maintain power after her husband's death. Bowersock 1980 clarifies the source tradition, favouring Rufinus *EH* XI.6, Socrates, *EH* IV.36, and Sozomen *EH* VI.38, over Theodoret *EH* IV.23 and later sources.

169 Rufinus, *EH* XI.6; Sozomen *EH* VI.38.1, ed. Bidez–Hansen, 297. Cf. also Map 1.

170 ἐν τῇ πέλας ἐρήμῳ, Sozomen, *EH* VI.38.5 (ed. Bidez–Hansen, 298); Rufinus, *EH* XI.6; cf. Theodoret, *EH* IV.23.1 (ed. Parmentier–Hansen, 261): ἐν μεθορίῳ τῆς Αἰγύπτου καὶ Παλαιστίνης ἐσκηνημένον. According to Socrates *EH* IV.36.11 (ed. Hansen, 271), Moses was ordained 'on the mountain' (πρὸς τὸ ὄρος), which Rubin 1990, 185, believes to be a reference to Mt Sinai.

171 Sozomen, *EH* VI.38.6; Lenski 2002, 208.

172 Sozomen, *EH* VI.38.4; on possible remembrances of her in Arabic tradition, see Bowersock 1980, 490–92.

173 Jerome, *ep.* CXXVI.2 (PL 22.1086), dated by its reference to the sack of Rome in 410; for discussion, Shahid 1989, 22–25.

174 Evagrius Schol., *EH* III.36, trans. Whitby, 181. Probably to be identified with an attack mentioned by Theophanes, *Chron.* 5990. See Shahid 1989, 121–27.

175 E.g. Parker 2000; cf. Isaac 1984, 193.

of the action in Rome's struggles with Persia had shifted either to the Syro-Mesopotamian frontier farther north, or to Ethiopia and Himyar (Yemen) farther south. Moreover, the Saracen threat that did exist in this area in this period seems to have been mainly one of small-scale raids, as when monks at Teqoa were killed by 'roving Saracen bandits' in the Judaean desert in the early fifth century.[176] Such references, however, are numerous, and point to a more low-level, indigenous problem than Roman troops in their legionary camps could easily handle or remove.

The fact is that Rome already had a volatile Saracen presence nestled deep within its south-eastern frontier.[177] When the term 'Saracen' first appears in Ptolemy's *Geography* (c. 150 CE), it is used to designate two tribes, one dwelling in the northern Arabian Ḥijaz, the other along Egypt's eastern border, including north-western Sinai.[178] We know nothing about these Saracens, whether they were sedentary, nomadic, or related to each other. But Ptolemy's notice helps explain later references to Saracen problems in north-eastern Egypt and the north-western Sinai peninsula. For example, Dionysius, a third-century bishop of Alexandria, describes a raid by 'Saracen barbarians' against towns in north-eastern Egypt, c. 251.[179] It was also here, near 'the border of Egypt and Palestine', that church historians place Mavia's reception of Roman ambassadors and their request for the local monk Moses: evidently this was the site of her base camp.[180] That the area continued to be considered a dangerous Saracen domain is attested in the later fourth century by Egeria, who places Mount Sinai within the 'lands

176 John Cassian, *Conference* VI.1.1, ed. Petschenig–Kreutz, 153. This event has often been associated with the 411 attack reported by Jerome. For Rome's involvement with Persia in the Red Sea under Anastasius, see Z. Rubin 1989; more generally, Fowden 1993, 109–21.

177 It should be pointed out that Romans conceived of their frontier (*limes*) as a zone assigned to a duke for military defence, not as a fortified line bordering enemy terrain: see Isaac 1998 and Mayerson 1989a. Thus, as Mayerson argues, the appropriate frontier analogy for Third Palestine may be the nineteenth-century American West, a sparsely settled expanse where raids by indigenous 'Indian' tribes – the Saracens of the American experience – had to be kept in check by a combination of forts, cavalry, and self-help: thus Mayerson 1986, 39; 1989a, 290; 1990, 267–70.

178 Claudius Ptolemaeus, *Geographia* V.17.3 (Sinai) and VI.7.21 (Ḥijaz), followed by Graf 2000 and so identified as 'Sarakene' in Talbert 2000, pl. 76 ('Sinai') and below, Map 2.

179 See above, n. 67, describing an incident that took place during the Decian persecution, when Christians sought refuge from Roman officials in the Nile's desert fringe. It was here that the Egyptian Saracens attacked.

180 See above, nn. 169, 170; also Millar 1993, 388; Lenski 2002, 205 n. 287, and 208 n. 305, *contra* Shahid 1984, 142–50. Many have assumed that Mavia's revolt was launched from outside the empire; but that is nowhere stated and the assumption is unwarranted.

of the Saracens', and reports receiving a military escort on her way from Clysma (which was fortified against Saracen raids) past the Bitter Lakes until she reached the main Roman highway.[181]

Of course, it is easy for scholars from a distance to overstate the case. To estimate what threat such Saracens actually posed to settled inhabitants of Third Palestine, we might look again to the Negev. Located some distance south-east of major Roman defences, this area could hardly have prospered as it did in late antiquity were it perpetually being menaced or under attack.[182] Indeed, few Negev towns felt the need to build defensive walls. At Elusa, Betomolachon, and Sobata, residential houses provided the only defences, being built side-by-side to form a circuit wall.[183] Security seems to have been left to a 'Peace Warden' (*Irenarch*) at Elusa and the *limitanei* scattered in the towns. Apparently here, as in other outlying areas, trouble was handled on an *ad hoc* basis by mustering such troops in 'sufficient force'.[184]

No doubt one reason that conditions in the Negev remained fairly stable in late antiquity was that its Arab population was for the most part sedentary, and had long been assimilated into the imperial domain. Nessana, as we have seen, had a camel corps stationed for much of the period in its citadel fort. The names of its recruits reveal at once the area's native colour and Roman veneer: 'Flavius Aws', 'Flavius Zunayn son of Abraham, Flavius al-Ubayy son of Elias', etc.[185] The Roman army had always provided a mechanism for co-opting occupied peoples: upon dissolving their kingdom,

---

181 Egeria, *Itin.* VII.2 and 6; cf. III.8 and PD/Y 6. Z. Rubin 1990, 177–82, argues that her escort served as a precaution against bandits in general. Bardaisan refers to Saracens as living between the Tayites and Libya: *Book of the Laws of Countries*, ed. Drijvers, 50–51; later, the Governor of First Palestine, Stephen (c. 535–540), was praised for checking attacks by 'Saracens of Egypt': see Choricius of Gaza, *In Praise of Aratius and Stephen* 33, ed. Foerster and Richtsteig, 57–58.

182 Cf. Lewin 1989, 163–65; 2002; Mayerson 1986b, 38; Isaac 1998, 152–53. Parker, however, argues that such prosperity began with, and depended upon, Roman border defences.

183 Mampsis had a perimeter wall of modest height (1.3–1.6 m/4–5 feet).

184 Mayerson 1986b, 40–41, citing Choricius of Gaza's *In Praise of Aratius and Stephen* 34, which applauds the Governor for having 'gathered together a sufficient force' (δύναμιν… ἀποχρῶσαν ἀγείρας) to defeat Saracens marauding from Egypt. This strategy was necessitated by Justinian's withdrawal of legionary troops from the area. Even after security had been entrusted to Ghassanid client kings, groups of *limitanei* presumably continued to operate in the Negev or remain in service near vulnerable targets such as Sabas' monastery in the Judaean desert (see below) or Pharan in the Sinai. See Shahid 1989, 282–89; 1995, 95–143, 183–85; Parker 2000, 381–82. On the *Irenarch*, Lewin 1989, 167–71.

185 *P.Colt* 15, 16, 18, 25.

for example, Trajan drafted Nabataeans into his army and posted them around the Roman East.[186] Culture provided another mechanism. We have already noted that traditional Greco-Roman *paideia* had been established in Elusa by the fourth century; more surprising are papyri scraps that show that some Greek-speaking citizens of Nessana still passed their time in the late sixth century by trying to read the Latin of Vergil's *Aeneid*.[187] But by then, religion and religious conversion had provided an additional, equally effective bond.[188] Just as Mavia's Saracens were reportedly reconciled to the Romans through their conversion by the monk Moses, so too are other Palestinian monks said to have turned Saracen 'wolves of Arabia' into a 'rational flock of Christ', thereby rendering them at once both Christian and amenable to Rome.[189] Interestingly, most of the names of the fathers of the Nessana recruits are biblical.[190]

The impression is one of a fully 'Romanized' and Christianized community on the Negev plateau. Yet it would be wrong to assume the Nessana papyri give a full picture of all the religious or social bonds at play in Third Palestine. South of the Negev, reaching 70 km (44 miles) into the al-Tih desert, archaeologists have found hundreds of stone livestock pens with single-room structures nearby. They consider these to have been temporary nomadic encampments, dated by pottery from the fourth to eighth centuries. One striking feature that many such encampments share are the so-called *masseboth*, clusters of smooth-faced stones fixed in the ground. Archaeologists tend to associate them with 'pagan' ritual.[191] In fact the worship of stones believed to have dropped from the sky (*baetyls*) was basic to the cult of Dushara and his consort, al-'Uzza (i.e. Venus/Aphrodite, also identified with the Morning Star). These two celestial deities were the chief deities of the Nabataean kingdom, and remained widely venerated from Transjordan to the Sinai and northern Ḥijaz in pre-Islamic times.[192]

Interpreting such stones as religious idols or cult objects is a notoriously risky business. Nonetheless, if accurate, we have evidence here of a pagan,

186 Graf 1989, 296, 299, and 305.

187 Casson and Hettich 1950, 7–78.

188 R. Rubin 1996, 55–58; see also Fowden 1993, esp. 109–21 on Roman efforts to ensure dominance by converting peoples of the Red Sea coast to Christianity.

189 Cyril Scyth., *Life of Euthymius* 15, ed. Schwartz, 24, 20–23.

190 Negev 1981, 84–88, notes the predominance of biblical over Semitic names in the papyri and sixth-century inscriptions.

191 Haiman 1995, 31–33; Avni 1996; Magness 2003, 131–70. The *nawāmīs* of southern Sinai are similar in many respects, and some may have also been nomadic structures.

192 Fahd 1968, 18–24, 111–20, 163–82; Hoyland 2001, 142, 183–86.

nomadic presence entrenched within the al-Tih desert throughout late antiquity. That is, however, exactly what we might expect, given epigraphic testimony for a cult of al-'Uzza in southern Sinai and the Piacenza Pilgrim's report of seeing a marble stone being tended by a Saracen priest right on the slopes of Mount Horeb in the middle of the sixth century.[193] The Pilgrim even offers a figure for the number of Saracens in the Tih desert: 12,000.[194] What ordinarily typified relations between such nomads and their sedentary neighbours? Anthropologists tend to favour a symbiotic model, with both groups providing complementary services.[195] The poverty of the Sinai encampments and their proximity to Negev farmsteads suggest that Sinai bedouin depended on them and nearby towns to provide odd jobs and markets.[196] One Nessana papyrus mentions a Saracen who served as a courier between Aila and Nessana, while another ('Account of a Trading Company', translated below) records how travellers purchased camels, horses, and donkeys while *en route* to Mount Sinai, presumably from bedouin of the Tih desert.[197] However, the same document also records the theft on that trip of a camel by Saracens of the Banū l-Udayyid tribe, and may allude to another Saracen's extortion of payment from the traders in return for safe passage.[198] As the editor of these papyri remarks, 'the general impression is of Bedouins controlling the area in southern Sinai'.[199]

What would that have meant for the monks living there? Here we may consider the experience of those who settled in the Judaean desert, as represented by Cyril of Scythopolis and John Moschus in the late sixth and

193 *CIS* II.1.611 and II.1236; Moritz 1916, 30 n. 3 and 59; Zayadine 1990, 164 (these seem to be of Nabataean date, i.e. second–third century), PP, *Itin.* 38.

194 PP, *Itin.* 36, 38, 39 and notes *ad loc.*; also Negev 1977. His figure apparently goes back to the number of Israelite warriors conscripted in Num. 31:4, but Avni 1996, 71–73, defends a similar estimate.

195 Barth 1961; Rowton 1974; Mohammed 1978; Lewis 1987; Donner 1989; for the Third Palestine region, Banning 1986 and Rosen 1987.

196 Haiman 1995, 34; Avni 1996, 83–85; cf. Gutwein 1981, 259, referring to Ps.-Nilus, *Narr.* VII.10: 'To the pastoral mind, Byzantine Subeita is a market town for the disposal of booty, livestock, and other commodities, much as Gaza was to be in the Arab period.'

197 *P.Colt* 51 (cf. Anast., *Narr.* 1.20) and 89, as noted in Mayerson 1989b, 73.

198 *P.Colt* 89.35 and 22, as interpreted by Mayerson 1989c, 284: 'The likelihood is that the Saracen was not a passing nomad but the sheikh of a tribe who demanded the money so that the caravan would travel under his protection and be free from harassment, or worse, by his tribesmen.' The Banū l-Udayyid are otherwise unattested, but Anast., *Narr.* I.39, and *P.Colt* 93, both of late seventh-century date (apparently later than *P.Colt* 89), indicate the presence on the Sinai of the Banū Judham, a well-known tribe of the northern Arabian peninsula. *P.Colt* 28 refers to the Banū Zamzam.

199 Kraemer 1958, 146 n. 2.

early seventh centuries. According to Cyril, monks in this area would hire 'Saracen' camel drivers to transport grain up to their monastery from the Dead Sea.[200] Descendants of the 'Christian Saracens' whom Abba Euthymius had converted built a permanent camp beside his monastery and served its monks for more than a century afterwards. Cyril was himself on hand in the sixth century when one delivered up a 'pagan Saracen' who, 'most barbarically excited', had broken down the monastery cistern's door in order to water his camels.[201] Thus, we have clear signs of symbiosis. But otherwise the picture is negative. Cyril and Moschus present numerous stories about Saracens sneaking into caves to steal from anchorites.[202] Moschus emphasizes atrocities. In one story, a Saracen cuts off the head of a hermit who passed him by on the Red Sea shore.[203] In another, a Saracen confesses that he had intended to rob and kill a monk found reading on a mountainside.[204] Several describe miraculous escapes from such marauders, as in one case when a monk sought to save a young man being led off by a band of Saracens for sacrifice:

> Concerning Abba Nicholas, Abba Jordanes told us that the old man had said that, 'In the reign of our most faithful Emperor Maurice [582–602], when the Saracen phylarch Nu'man was making his depredations [against the Romans c. 582], I was travelling near Arnōn and Aidon, when I saw three Saracens holding captive a very handsome-looking young man, about twenty years old ... I implored the Saracens to release him. One of the Saracens said to me in Greek, "We'll not release him". So I said, "Take me and release him, for he cannot [endure to] be distressed". The Saracen told me, "We will not". Then I asked for a third time, "Do you not intend to release him because you want a ransom? Let him go with me, and I'll bring whatever you want." The same one replied, "We cannot give him to you, because we already arranged with our priest that if we captured anything beautiful, we would offer it to him, so he might lay it up for sacrifice. Now get lost, or we'll smash your head on the ground."'

So Nicholas prayed and the Saracens became possessed by demons: 'they unsheathed their swords and cut each other to pieces'.[205]

200 Cyril Scyth., *Life of Saba* 81, ed. Schwartz 186.15.

201 Cyril Scyth., *Life of Euthymius* 15 and 51, ed. Schwartz 75.18. On relations between Judaean monks and Saracens of the *parembolē* ('encampment'), see Shahid 1989, 185–213.

202 Cyril Scyth., *Life of Saba* 14 and 15; John Mosch., *Meadow* 99 and 133. For their depictions, see Shahid 1995, 597–602; Solzbacher 1989, 267; and Hoyland 1997, 61–67.

203 John Mosch., *Meadow* 21 (PG 87[3].2868BC); cf. *Meadow* 99.

204 John Mosch., *Meadow* 133 (PG 87[3].2996D–2997A).

205 John Mosch., *Meadow* 155 (PG 87[3].3024BC). Shahid 1995, 597–98, locates the setting east of the Dead Sea, in Wadi al-Mujib and Seil Heidan.

It is hard to know what to make of such desert horror stories, especially those concerning human sacrifice. Its practice by 'barbarian' bandits of the eastern Egyptian desert is prominent in Achilles Tatius' second- or third-century novel, *Leucippe and Clitophon*.[206] It is also featured in the sixth-century *Life of Paul the Bishop and the Priest John*, in an episode that takes place on the Sinai peninsula: just as they are about to reach Mount Sinai, the two clerical pilgrims are captured by a group of Saracens and taken to their king's camp, apparently somewhere in the Ḥijaz, so that he might sacrifice them to the camp's god, an especially tall palm tree.[207] Such stories reflect deeply rooted antipathies toward Arab nomads – 'barbarous in character, malicious in intent', 'carried away by evil temper' – that show little change from earlier Roman attitudes.[208] It would seem prudent to treat them as fantasies conjured for urban audiences, rather than as accurate descriptions of Arabs or Arab religious practices.[209] Yet human sacrifice is attributed to a Lakhmid Arab phylarch by the usually sober historian Procopius of Caesarea,[210] and certain details indicate that the situations described in these stories, however exaggerated they may be, were not totally random or without cause, and reflected genuine concerns.

Indeed, such stories usually indicate that the incidents they depict coincided with major hostilities that had arisen either between Rome and Persia, or between phylarchs allied to Rome. Apparently some bedouin seized such occasions as opportunities to commit various low-level 'blasphemies'

---

206 See below, p. 70.

207 See Brock 2003, 104–05, based on the Syriac MS. British Library *Add.* 14597, dated 569 CE; an edition of this and two other Syriac MSS is being prepared by Hans Arneson, Christine Luckritz-Marquis and Kyle Smith. Thanks to Sebastian Brock and Kyle Smith for providing this information on this fascinating text. A later Greek version (BHG 1476) is also available, but with many lacunae: see Bibliography, below.

208 Cyril Scyth., *Life of Euthymius* 14, ed. Schwartz, 97.8–9; cf. *CIG* III no. 4668 (Berlin 1853, p. 277), the inscription written by a Roman soldier on the eastern Sinai in the late second century, apparently referring to local bedouin as an 'Evil Race': Solzbacher 1989, 67.

209 Henninger 1955, 103–04, dismisses the depiction of human sacrifice in Ps.-Nilus' *Narrations* as a romantic motif, otherwise unattested in late antique sources. John Mosch., *Meadow* 155, shows that the latter contention is false; see also Christides 1973, 49–50. But literary attestations do not add up to fact, especially given Greco-Roman expectations of extreme barbarism among nomads (cf. Shaw 1982–1983). Such reports may simply be rumours – like modern urban myths, they are often attributed to second- or third-hand informants. Hence the importance of Arabic sources cited by Hoyland 2001, 163. However, Hoyland does not assess their credibility. Whether or not Arabs practised human sacrifice in pre-Islamic times will probably only be resolved by archaeology.

210 See below, n. 216.

(as monks called them), such as breaking into the cistern at Euthymius' monastery – an event that happened, Cyril notes, at a time when Rome's allied sheikhs were feuding.[211] Other actions seem to have been linked to broader disturbances, as when the invasion of Persia's phylarch al-Mundhir caused barbarians to 'spread over the desert'.[212] The people captured on such occasions were normally held for ransom, dispensed among tribes, sold as slaves, or used as bargaining chips.[213] But Greek, Syriac, and Arabic sources (and not all of them Roman or Christian) agree that such captives were also sometimes sacrificed to celebrate triumphs or to exact revenge.[214] The phylarch Nu'man mentioned in Moschus' story above is elsewhere reported to have responded to Rome's imprisonment of his father by 'sacrificing humans to his demons with his own hand'.[215] Procopius reports that the Persian phylarch al-Mundhir sacrificed a Roman phylarch's son to Aphrodite (i.e. al-'Uzza); this same al-Mundhir is also alleged to have sacrificed to al-'Uzza 400 virgins, taken from a church at Emesa (Homs, Lebanon), in just one day.[216] It thus might be that the Saracens of Moschus' Nicholas story – or others like them – made money by supplying sacrificial victims to such distant overlords.

Historians dispute whether such actions represent the rebellion of unassimilated Arab peoples against their occupiers,[217] or simply the opportunism of local Arab bandits to intimidate and profit.[218] Whatever the case, Cyril and Moschus indicate that another factor was involved. Both depict Saracens as being driven by hunger to seek out caves of hermits, hoping to be provided with food as hospitality. Cyril, however, also describes an incident where nomads tried to extort payments by repeatedly grazing flocks

---

211 Cyril Scyth., *Life of Euthymius* 51; ed. Schwartz, 75.9–11. Cyril remarks that this outbreak was 'well known', indicating a major event. Lee 1993 argues that Persian, German and Gothic raids on the Roman Empire in late antiquity were often based on knowledge of, and coincided with, disruptions that occurred elsewhere.

212 Cyril Scyth., *Life of John the Hesychast* 13, ed. Schwartz 211.15–23. For context, see Procop., *Wars* I.17.41–42, 45–47.

213 Mayerson 1989b, 77, collects and translates the sources.

214 Hoyland 2001, 163.

215 Evagrius Schol., *EH* VI.22, trans. Whitby, 314. For context, see Shahid 1995, 464–71.

216 Procop., *Wars* II.28.13; Ps.-Zacharius, *Chronicle* VIII.5; for references in Syriac sources describing atrocities during the fifth-century sack of Beth-Hira, see Segal 1984, 106–13.

217 Graf 1989 and Isaac 1990, rejected by Parker 2000, 376, on grounds that there is no evidence for such rebellion (i.e. no Saracen action is described as such in our sources).

218 E.g. it has been proposed that the bandit attack on Teqoa noted above coincided with the more widespread incursion mentioned by Jerome. Such linkage would modify the view put forth in Isaac 1984, 192, that all such events were merely 'local' in scope.

on monastery land.[219] Such stories show not only that economic disparity existed, but also that it occasionally caused tensions between monks and bedouin living in the same marginal, and thus impoverished, areas.[220] Monastic settlers may well have been considered to be encroaching on bedouin territory. The *Life of Theognis*, written by a seventh-century monk at Elusa, describes how one Saracen threatened a monk, not to obtain money or food, but merely to intimidate and drive him out of the cave he was occupying. Since it is common for bedouin to use caves to pen their sheep, perhaps this story reflects a shepherd's effort to reclaim such a pen from a monastic squatter.[221] Regardless, robbing hermits and raiding monasteries – at least those thought to have treasure or ample store rooms – must have been constantly tempting as a means to exact tribute, alleviate poverty, or redress perceived wrongs.

The preceding may help us judge the situation on the late antique Sinai itself. Here, by any estimate, native bedouin far outnumbered monastic settlers. The fact that so many hermitages in the southern Sinai were built without walls or towers suggests that here, as in the Negev, the two groups normally lived in peace. Indeed, Anastasius shows that by the seventh century, Christianized Saracens had pitched a camp beside the Mount Sinai monastery in Wadi al-Dayr, just as had Saracen converts beside Judaean monasteries (*Narr.* II.8); he also indicates that they sometimes served anchorites as couriers, as Saracens had for Negev villagers (*Narr.* I.22). These are signs of mutual dependency rather than threat. Nonetheless, the Piacenza Pilgrim implies that Sinai's Tih desert was really not safe to travel once Saracen festivals were over (PP, *Itin.* 39 with note *ad loc.*), and distant disturbances also had repercussions here: Saracen robbers reportedly terrorized the roads leading to Rhaithou during the Persian invasion of Egypt in 618/19, as well as during the Arab invasion of 633/34.[222] The simplest way to prepare for such events was to build a secure refuge: for Saracens, it was said, 'though most skillful of all at plundering', were nevertheless 'incapable by nature

219 Cyril Scyth., *Life of Sabas* 59, ed. Schwartz 160.16–18: 'impudently demanding ἀναλώματα, not letting us be in tranquillity'. (Saracen shepherds were also attached to Euthymius' monastery: *Life of Euthymius* 53.)
220 On the chronic poverty of the local bedouin, see PP, *Itin.* 36; Mayerson 1989b, 74; Haiman 1995, 31.
221 Paul of Elusa, *Life of Theognis* II.9. Isaac 1990, 216, and Parker 2000, 379, propose that Negev farming, or the placement of military camps in grazing zones, caused friction with local nomads.
222 Antony of Choziba, *Life of George of Choziba* VIII.32; Solzbacher 1989, 277.

of storming a wall'.[223] Certainly all the Sinai monastic centres and pilgrim stations had been fortified by the time of the Piacenza Pilgrim's visit in the middle of the sixth century.[224] Indeed, defensive measures seem to have been taken below Mount Sinai well before then. Near the entrance to Justinian's basilica within St Catherine's in Wadi al-Dayr, archaeologists have discovered what appears to be the foundations of a two-storey tower, not unlike the defensive towers found at monastic settlements in the Egyptian and Judaean deserts. Although the date and purpose of these Sinai ruins are not absolutely clear,[225] it would appear that anchorites felt the need to build a rudimentary refuge below Mount Sinai long before Justinian's time. What circumstances might have called for its construction or use?

4. THE SINAI MARTYR TRADITION

Within Justinian's basilica at St Catherine's, just to the right of the central apse, is a small, rectangular side chamber. Originally intended as a *pastophorion*, or sacristy, it now serves as 'the Chapel of the Holy Fathers Slaughtered at Sinai and Rhaithou'. Set into its south wall is a small (0.91 x 0.25 m, 36 x 10 in.) marble slab. Much of its space is filled by three iron crosses, but along the top runs a formal inscription. Consisting of two lines of Greek text framed by small incised crosses, it reads:

[✝] Τῆς δ δεκάδος τὴν διὰ τοῦ αἵματος κολυμβήθραν ζηλώσαντες οἱ ἰσάριθμοι ὅσοι π(ατέ)ρ(ε)ς // ἐνθάδε κατάκεινται, ὧν ἡ εὐφροσύνη ἡ βάτος ἡ ἀληθινὴ ὑπάρχει · δι' ὧν ὁ θ(εὸ)ς σῶσον ἡμᾶς [✝]

[✝] Having emulated the baptism by blood of the 4 [and] ten, the equal-in-number Holy Fathers // lie in this place. Theirs is the joyous and true Bush. Through them, may God save us [✝]

Although the letterforms suggest the inscription is late antique, its actual date is not known,[226] and though perfectly legible, its original meaning is not

223 Procop., *Wars* II.19.12, a comment that probably simply meant they brought no siege engines on their raids.

224 Cf. PP, *Itin.* 37, 40, 41. John Climacus and Anastasius in the seventh century both refer to Justinian's monastery simply as 'the Fort': *Ladder* 7 (PG 88.812B); *Narr.* II.8.

225 The structure is 12 x 12 m (33 x 33 feet) wide, 1.2 m (4 feet) thick, with evidence of an upper storey. Its thickness suggests that its original purpose was defensive: see Grossmann 1988, 556–58. Judging by its stonework, Dahari 2000, 59, believes it to be pre-Justinianic, but cautions that its date is uncertain.

226 Ed. with measurements Rabino 1935, 83 (inscription no. 27) and Ševčenko 1966, 263

clear. It relates one group of martyrs to another, but what martyrs are meant in either case? The groups are related numerically, but what was intended by the odd numerical abbreviation, Τῆς δ δεκάδος, 'of the 4 [and] ten', that defines the earlier group? The room's current dedication to martyrs of Sinai and Rhaithou may be accurate, but it might also be a much later guess.

Connected to these questions are two lengthy texts translated in this volume: Ps.-Nilus' *Narrations* (BHG 1301–1397b) and the Ammonius *Report* (BHG 1300–1300b). Both describe the slaughter of Sinai monks by nomadic pagan barbarians at different times in late antiquity. Both were written to edify readers, and after the Arab conquest (perhaps as early as the eighth century) were placed side by side (along with Anastasius' *Tales of the Sinai Fathers*) in a hagiographical collection assembled at the Mount Sinai monastery in an historical effort to document early examples of Christian holiness on the peninsula.[227] By the tenth century they were also being consulted at Constantinople for historical data regarding the slaughtered Sinai monks whose relics had been brought to the capital during the reign of Emperor Justin II (565–578), and whose martyr cult was being celebrated there and elsewhere on 14 January.[228] Thus, the two texts came to be read in medieval times not merely as sources of edification but as sources of historical information. Modern historians have also valued them as sources of information, albeit more for information about nomadic 'barbarians' (Saracens or Blemmyes) and their relations with settled inhabitants of Third Palestine than about Sinai monks and their depictions of holiness. Both texts undoubtedly offer useful historical data, but those who read them for that purpose must proceed with caution: much of the misinformation found in popular accounts of Sinai history derives from uncritical readings of these narratives.[229] Detailed discussion of each is provided in the prefatory introduction attached to its translation below. The following is simply meant to highlight problems that both share, and to propose a chronological framework for both.

(no. 6.1). Ševčenko asserts a late sixth-century date without explanation, but the forms appear similar to those used in the basilica ceiling beam inscriptions (see Forsyth–Weitzmann 1973, pl. lxxx.b–c = inscription no. 4–5). However, Gatier 1989, 518 n. 64, thinks the forms reflect a later date. Besides smaller crosses and some later graffiti, it features three monograms that seem contemporaneous with the commemorative inscription, two of which seem to mean 'Priest John' (see Ševčenko 1966, 263, inscription no. 6.2, a–b).

227 MS *Vaticanus syriacus* 623, a ninth-century collection based on earlier Greek exempla: see Binggeli 2005, 168.

228 Cf. 14 January, notice no.1, *Synaxarium ecclesiae Constantinopolitanae*, ed. Delehaye, col. 391; also Conca 1983a, v–xxiv, and Heussi 1917.

229 E.g. Hobbs 1995; Skrobucha 1966; Eckenstein 1921.

First, a plot summary is in order. Ps.-Nilus' *Narrations* tells the adventures of a father (the unnamed narrator) and his son, Theodulus. On 14 January, as the two are visiting monks at Mount Sinai a week after Epiphany, unnamed barbarian nomads attack. After killing many monks, they seize Theodulus, intending to sacrifice him to their god, the Morning Star, at dawn. The father escapes to nearby Pharan, where he describes what happened, and then explains how the barbarians' customs differ from those of Sinai monks; there ensues a discussion of why God failed to act in the monks' defence. The rest of the tale tells how father and son reunite. The Pharanites send the father on a journey north to seek help from a barbarian 'king' named Ammanes with whom they have a treaty. Meanwhile Theodulus' captors, having missed the time of sacrifice by sleeping past dawn, decide to sell him as a slave. Having failed to do so in the town of Sbeita (i.e. Sobata in the Negev), they sell him off to the bishop of Elusa. There the father eventually finds him and obtains his release. The story ends with both returning home to fulfil vows of asceticism; as stated in its coda, both live happily ever after.

To turn from the *Narrations* to the *Report* is to turn from a sophisticated novella to what seems a simple pilgrim's account, remarkable only for its detail and drama. Its narrator, Ammonius, after describing his visit to monks at Mount Sinai, tells how Saracen raiders suddenly attacked, explaining that they did so because a Saracen king 'who had held the phylarchy' had died. Eventually the Sinai summit burst into flame and scared them off, but not before they had killed 39 monks in four separate places around the mountain; later, as the survivors gathered the dead, a wounded monk prayed for death and died, raising the total number of Mount Sinai martyrs to 40. Ammonius then relates what another unnamed character says had just happened at Rhaithou, where, on the same day, 40 monks had also been slaughtered, this time by barbarian raiders called 'Blemmyes'. He describes the Rhaithou setting, its monks, their relations with Sinai's Pharanites, the Blemmyes' invasion by sea, their slaughter of the monks and subsequent destruction by Pharanite archers, who bury the martyred dead in a tomb nearby. The *Report* ends with a note explaining that the Mount Sinai and Rhaithou martyrs died and were commemorated on 28 December, and that Ammonius' writings had been found and translated from Coptic into Greek by a priest named John.[230]

---

230 Although some MSS differ on this point, 28 December was clearly the date of martyrdom originally recorded in the text: see below, p. 142.

These narratives add considerable colour and tension to the early history of the Sinai, providing dramatic examples not only of late antique pilgrimage, monasticism, and martyrdoms, but also of relations between settled groups (Sinai monks, Pharanite Arabs, inhabitants of Sobata and Elusa) and nomadic groups in Third Palestine more broadly. It is no wonder that historians have taken interest in them, given the paucity of sources illustrating such a regional or 'frontier' perspective. Indeed, both offer 'a reasonable picture of how isolated communities in the deserts of Sinai and Palestine dealt with the problem of security'.[231] Moreover, both refer to fairly obscure local toponyms (e.g. Sbeita, probably a clipped version of Sobata in the Negev; also the 'place of the Pharanites' at Rhaithou) and use names appropriate to the region (e.g. Ps.-Nilus' 'Ammanes' recalls *Ammaye*, an Arab priest's name attested at a shrine in southern Sinai, while 'Theodulus' possibly renders 'Abd Allah, 'Slave of God'; cf. the name of the bishop of Elusa recorded at the Council of Ephesus, above, p. 14). This suggests their authors were familiar with the region.[232] But who were these authors? Or rather, when and where did they write? And in what sense should their narrative descriptions be considered historical?

Critical analysis of the two narratives began in the twentieth century with Karl Heussi's research on the *Narrations* and its supposed author, the early fifth-century monk Nilus of Ancyra.[233] Noting that many of its features were typical of ancient romance, and that Nilus of Ancyra otherwise showed no knowledge of the Sinai region, Heussi declared the *Narrations* to be a Christian fiction written in the romance tradition by an unknown author, probably in the fourth century (see discussion in the introduction to the text below). Heussi's studies generated scepticism about the historical merits, not only of the *Narrations*, but also of Ammonius' *Report*. In 1940, in the first comprehensive review of early Sinai history and literature, Robert Devreesse declared the *Report* to be not a late fourth-century document, as formerly assumed, but a sixth-century fabrication based on fourth- and fifth-century sources. Devreesse regarded its claim to have been discovered and translated from Coptic into Greek to be a blatant sign of forgery; in

---

231 Mayerson 1963, 162; cf. Isaac 1984, 194: 'a vivid picture of incursions and banditry in Sinai and the Negev … and of agreements made by small communities with bedouin sheikhs for protection'.

232 Thus Mayerson 1963, 168; Negev 1977b; cf. Kraemer 1958, 333–34; Shahid 1984, 301–02; 1989, 137. Solzbacher 1989, 213, however, believes all such details came from maps or word lists.

233 Heussi 1916; 1917.

particular, he believed its portions concerning a monk named Moses who converted a number of Pharanites (*Rel.* 12–14), and its reference to the death of a Saracen phylarch as the cause of the Mount Sinai raid (*Rel.* 3), were both inspired by Sozomen's account of the Mavia revolt (see above, p. 42). In his view, both the *Report* and the *Narrations* were written at Justinian's monastery some time in the late sixth century: for only then, he believed, would monks capable of producing such literature have been present on the Sinai.[234]

Defenders have dismissed such assertions as purely speculative, pointing out that neither narrative contains any obvious anachronism that proves it to be a forgery, and that both contain details congruent with what we otherwise know about Sinai conditions from other demonstrably early sources, such as Egeria's late fourth-century *Travelogue*. In their view, whatever historical problems are posed by the narratives may be explained by the fact that they were written by pious outsiders: as Philip Mayerson puts it, 'the Ammonius narrative and the *Narrationes* should, like so many [pilgrimage accounts], be taken as reports coming from travelers who were strangers to the Sinai'.[235]

Certainly it would be easier to read both narratives literally, treating them as efforts to depict reality as it actually was. But such an approach is hard to accept for either text. Anyone who has read ancient works of fiction such as *Leucippe and Clitophon* or Fourth Maccabees will recognize that the *Narrations* is a romance that borrows basic features of plot and presentation from both. Likewise, anyone who reads the Ammonius *Report* with an eye to its narrative structure will note that the portion allegedly reflecting Ammonius' own experience of the raid on Mount Sinai is far shorter and less detailed than the portion he supposedly heard second-hand about Rhaithou, exactly the opposite of what one might expect from a record of a narrator's own personal experience. For this reason, Pierre-Louis Gatier has argued that the Ammonius *Report* was written by a sixth-century monk of Rhaithou.[236] Indeed, the Mount Sinai portion includes a curious detail – the request of a monk to die so as to round off the number of Sinai martyrs to forty, so that he might be included in 'the list of the holy Fathers' (καταλόγ[ος] τῶν ἁγίων πατέρων, *Rel.* 7). This parallels a similar request made in the legend

234 Devreesse 1940a, 216–22, followed by Solzbacher 1989, 210–13; cf. Devreesse 1940b.

235 Mayerson 1980, 136; cf. 148: 'It must be recognized ... that experiences in the desert *are* dramatic, and very often read like fiction. These adventures are sometimes difficult for scholarly critics to appreciate or evaluate.'

236 Gatier 1989, 510–17. Gatier follows Devreesse in assuming that the *Narrations* was written by Sinai monks in the late sixth century.

of the Forty Martyrs of Sebaste. It also indicates the probable source of this portion of the *Report*: an original Mount Sinai liturgical 'list', or record, of the monastic 'fathers' who had died there during a raid.

Such narratological observations challenge the presumption that these narratives reflect actual experience. What, then, is their historical value? Devreesse, Mayerson, and others assume that a work of fiction *ipso facto* lacks merit as historical evidence. That stance is debatable, and has been addressed for the *Narrations* in particular by Vassilios Christides: Christides notes that to achieve verisimilitude, a historical romance (as he classified the *Narrations*) must reflect real circumstances and possibilities.[237] Yet, the problem remains of how exactly to define, identify, or delimit the so-called 'historical kernel' of such a narrative. This is a problem familiar to historians who wish to use the *Acts of the Apostles* or Apuleius' *Golden Ass* to cast light on provincial life under the Roman principate, or hagiography to do the same in a later period.[238] We might wish to trust the 'realistic' details or circumstances described in such texts, but our estimation of their realism – i.e., what details are realistic – is often highly subjective, or presupposes the reality in question; there is also the likelihood that many details were added simply to lend realism to an edifying story or to advance its plot.[239] An example of the latter might be Ps.-Nilus' reference to the Pharanite treaty with the 'barbarian' sheikh Ammanes, a detail that provides a rationale for the narrator's travel towards Elusa and the subsequent resolution of the story.

It is the historian's task to decide which narrative features seem specific to a particular time, place, and literary genre, and which do not. There are no easy guidelines: as I have argued elsewhere, the safest course may be to use early Sinai history to understand the *Narrations* and the *Report*, rather than the other way around.[240] Besides the fact that any search for anachronisms or congruencies runs the risk of mistaking apparent congruencies for true, rather than contrived, congruencies (as would be intended by good historical fiction writers or forgers), there is also the problem that we know so little

237 Christides 1972; cf. Rapp 1998.

238 See e.g. Millar 1981, 66, 75, and Morgan 1993.

239 Plausibility, not truth, being the chief aim of *diēgēsis* or *diēgēma*, as both of our narratives and almost all hagiographies are called: see especially Rapp 1998, 442–44, and Flusin 1991, 381. Solzbacher 1989, 223–30, dismisses the historical merit of both narratives because all their details could have been lifted from prior sources; he considers the *Narrations* a composite of three sources assembled in the fifth century (see below, p. 75).

240 Caner 2004.

about early Sinai history. It must be remembered that after Egeria's visit in the late fourth century, we have virtually no detailed information – apart, perhaps, from these narratives – about life on the Sinai until about the middle of the sixth century. That amounts to nearly 150 years of silence, a long gap by any standard. Much may have happened in those years that slipped off record, to be filled in by later invention. Take, for example, the brief, tantalizing reference to an embassy of ten Sinai monks sent to Constantinople on account of some 'need' found in the Greek alphabetical version of the *apophthegmata patrum*. Like many tales in that collection, this one probably dates to around 350–450.[241] But we cannot be more precise than that. We might speculate that the embassy was sent (if actually sent at all) to petition for imperial aid regarding monastic security, quite possibly in response to a Saracen raid. After all, Cyril of Scythopolis describes an embassy of Palestinian monks going to ask Emperor Justinian to build a fort to serve as a refuge for monks against Saracen raids in the Judaean desert. But Cyril also describes an earlier monastic embassy that was sent to Emperor Anastasius simply to request financial aid, and that may have been the purpose of the Sinai mission as well: we cannot tell.[242]

Obviously much depends on the questions being asked and degree of factual specificity being sought from these narratives, as well as on the date or context of their composition. What do we know about the dates of the *Narrations* and the Ammonius *Report*? Both offer certain chronological clues. The *Report* informs us not only that its Sinai and Rhaithou martyrs died on 28 December (*Rel.* 7), but also that its action occurred during the persecution of an Alexandrian bishop named Peter (*Rel.* 1). As for the monks whose martyrdoms the *Narrations* describes, Ps.-Nilus distinguishes them from an earlier set of Sinai martyrs:

> They died in perfection on the eighth day after Epiphany, on the fourteenth of January ... But others were also slain, many years earlier [πρὸ πλειόνων ἐτῶν]. Their commemoration is celebrated on the same day, due to the length of the journey and number of people who attend. (*Narr.* IV.14)

Thus Ps.-Nilus posits two sets of martyrs commemorated on 14 January, one

241 *Apophth. patr.*, alphabetical series, Cronius 5 (PG 65.249B): 'Once when the Fathers had some need, ten brothers were sent to the emperor on account of [the] need'. This serves to contextualize a story, told by Joseph of Pelusium to Abba Cronius († c. 386), about a monk's attempt to hide his aristocratic origins when sent on the embassy to the imperial court. On the date associated with the collection, see Solzbacher 1989, 88–92.

242 Embassy to Emperor Justinian: Cyril Scyth., *Life of Saba* 72; embassy to Emperor Anastasius: *Life of Saba* 50–54. On the former, see below, p. 278.

earlier, one later.[243] Who were the earlier martyrs? Probably those Mount Sinai martyrs described in the Ammonius *Report*. Evidently these died some time in the 370s: for if, as argued above (pp. 55–56), the Mount Sinai portion of the *Report* goes back to an early martyr record, then we may assume that that record provided the original date on which the Mount Sinai martyrdoms were thought to have occurred: viz., 28 December, in the time of an Alexandrian bishop named Peter. Most likely that meant Peter II of Alexandria, the Nicene bishop whose persecution lasted from 373–378,[244] giving about five years in the 370s for the narrative setting of the *Report* and the December 28th martyrdoms it describes. These would be the earliest attested martyrs on the Sinai in late antiquity (those of Rhaithou being another question), and so it is reasonable to assume that these are also the ones to whom Ps.-Nilus refers as having been slain 'many years earlier' than the martyrs of his own account.[245] Consequently, although we cannot say with any certainty when the Ammonius *Report* was written (it may have been written immediately after, or long after, the 370s), we may at least conclude that Ps.-Nilus wrote his *Narrations* 'many years' after the 370s.

It may be possible to refine that further. Noting that Ps.-Nilus has his barbarian raid occur after the Sinai monks had congregated to sing their 'sacred hymns', Peter Grossmann infers that the raid must have occurred on a Sunday, since Ps.-Nilus states elsewhere that Sinai anchorites only congregated on Sundays (*Narr.* III.12 and IV.3). We know that 14 January fell on a Sunday on the following years in the late fourth and early fifth centuries: 367, 378, 389, 395, 423, and so on. Therefore, if Ps.-Nilus' event occurred in the fourth or early fifth centuries, then it may have occurred in one of those years.[246]

Beyond that, we can only speculate, guided by archaeological evidence or documents that can be independently and securely dated. As should now be apparent, evidence and documents of that sort for the Sinai are in scant

243 Mayerson 1975 argues that Ps.-Nilus' notice regarding the earlier martyrs is an interpolation, but it is found in all the MSS: see below, p. 76, n. 11.

244 Two other Alexandrian bishops, Peter I (300–311) and Peter III 'Mongus' (477–489), though both subjected to persecution, are far less likely: see Introduction to Ammonius below, p. 148, n. 27.

245 The fact that Byzantine redactors of the *Report* replaced its martyrs' original December 28th commemoration date with the January 14th commemoration date indicates that they at least believe these to have been the earlier martyrs to whom Ps. Nilus refers.

246 Grossmann 1999, 461, based on the calculations of Leitzmann–Aland 1956, 22–24. As explained below, Grossmann himself believes the attack occurred in 367; for additional dates based on Leitzmann–Aland, see below, p. 76.

supply. There is, however, the letter from Emperor Marcian (translated below, pp. 238–41). Securely and independently dated to 453, it is addressed to a group of archimandrites (as well as a bishop) at Mount Sinai.[247] As Bernard Flusin observes, the collective nature of that address suggests that no single monastic superior had yet been recognized at Mount Sinai in 453, as would later be the case in the sixth century. That is important, because whereas Ammonius presumes the existence of such a superior (*Rel.* 2), Ps.-Nilus does not. For this reason, Bernard Flusin believes the *Report* to be a sixth-century text that reflects sixth-century developments.[248] For the same reason, the *Narrations* would be earlier, since the only figure it depicts in a leadership position on the Sinai is a monastic priest (*Narr.* IV.2).

To summarize, both the *Narrations* and the *Report* seem to have been written between the late fourth and the late sixth centuries. The *Narrations* appears to be the earlier of the two, reflecting fourth- or fifth-century leadership arrangements on the Sinai, and the *Report* appears to be the later, reflecting leadership assumptions of the (later fifth?), sixth, or seventh centuries. That would concur with the chronology proposed by Richard Solzbacher, who believes that a 'Saracen' raid took place at Mount Sinai some time in the late fourth century, forming the basis for the Mount Sinai portion of the Ammonius *Report*. He believes that Ps.-Nilus wrote his *Narrations* some time in the fifth century, after another raid had produced a separate set of Sinai martyrs. He argues that yet another raid occurred during Emperor Anastasius' reign (491–518) on the Sinai coast, providing the basis for the *Report*'s account of the Blemmyes' raid on Rhaithou. Thus Solzbacher posits three different raids, spread over a hundred years; as for the *Report* itself, he proposes that it was composed c. 500–650.[249]

This chronological framework would take into account most of the historical and literary problems detected by Heussi, Devreesse, Gatier, Flusin, and even Mayerson (at least as far as the *Narrations* is concerned), and it seems most plausible to me. Of course, not all will agree with it, and it may in fact be wrong. Peter Grossmann, for example, has taken an entirely different approach to the chronological problem, albeit one that assumes both texts reflect real events, and depends on discounting the reference to earlier martyrs in the *Narrations* as a later interpolation. Noting that Ammonius refers to a tower below Mount Sinai (*Rel.* 5) but that Ps.-Nilus does not, Grossmann contends that Ps.-Nilus must be depicting an even earlier raid,

247 See below, p. 238, n. 3.
248 Flusin 1998, 134.
249 See Solzbacher 1989, 222–42.

which he believes occurred before such a tower existed. Presuming that the *Report* reflects events surrounding the Mavia revolt in the 370s, Grossmann believes this earlier raid must have occurred before the 370s, creating martyrs and prompting survivors to build the tower mentioned in the *Report*. He therefore proposes that Ps.-Nilus' raid occurred in the year 367, when 14 January fell on a Sunday.[250] Grossmann has in fact discovered what may be the remains of a pre-Justinianic tower inside the St Catherine's compound, as noted above (p. 51). The reference to such a tower in the Ammonius *Report* suggests that its author was writing some time before Justinian's constructions, i.e. before the middle of the sixth century.[251]

Another question is how these narratives might clarify the Sinai martyr inscription with which we began. Who were 'the 4 [and] ten' who suffered 'baptism by blood'? Who the 'equal-in-number Holy Fathers' who 'emulated' (or perhaps 'rivalled') them? Diverse explanations have turned on the unusual phrase, δ δεκάδος, '4 [and] ten.' In Greek, the letter δ is conventionally used to represent the number four, and the noun ἡ δέκας-αδος for 'ten' or 'group of ten'; what is odd is their singular combination in this inscription. Ihor Ševčenko believed it meant '[Group of] Forty', referring to either the 'Forty Martyrs of Sebaste' or the 'Forty Martyrs of Rhaithou': in his opinion, the inscription's 'equal-in-number Holy Fathers' who emulated them were Ammonius' forty Mount Sinai martyrs, making these the ones being commemorated by the inscription.[252] Mayerson however countered that '4-ten' was an abbreviation for 'fourteenth', and proposes the translation, 'The Holy Fathers lie here, equal in number to those who were killed on the 14th [viz., of January], and imitating them through a baptism of blood'. In his view, 'those who were killed on the fourteenth' refers to those monks whose deaths on 14 January Ps.-Nilus describes, but Mayerson leaves open the identity of the 'Holy Fathers' who imitated them (indeed, he maintains that the referent to the phrase, 'equal in number', was left intentionally vague, due to uncertainty as to how many had actually died on 14 January). Mayerson concludes that the inscription commemorated an unspecified number of Mount Sinai monks who were martyred 'at a later

250 Grossmann 1999 (for an English version, see Grossmann 2001, 178–82).

251 Unless some remembrance of it was found in the Mt Sinai martyr record, or its foundations remained visible: a 'Tower of St Helena' was pointed out to Burckhardt in the nineteenth century, which he described as being older than the monastery: see Braun 1973, 5.

252 Ševčenko 1966, 258, preferring the 40 Rhaithou martyrs to those of Sebaste because the former died by sword, whereas the latter froze to death. But the phrase 'baptism by blood' was a common metaphor for martyrdom.

date (sixth century?)' than Ps.-Nilus' group.[253] Pierre-Louis Gatier, on the other hand, notes that there is no attestation for the use of the phrase '4 [and] ten' to abbreviate a date.[254] Like Ševčenko, he believes that it must mean 'forty'; however, he considers it sufficiently odd to have further significance. He therefore proposes that it refers to the number of Mount Sinai monks whom the Ammonius *Report* specifies as having died at four different sites around the mountain ('Gethrambi', 'Horeb', 'Kodar', and 'Mount Sinai' environs; *Rel.* 4). He believes that the 'equal-in-number Holy Fathers' who emulated them must refer to the later monks whose deaths Ps.-Nilus describes: 'Having zealously sought the baptism of blood of the four-fold ten [viz., Ammonius' Mount Sinai martyrs], equal in number, the Holy Fathers [Ps.-Nilus' Sinai martyrs] rest here...'[255]

To reprise, the inscription commemorates either Ammonius' Mount Sinai martyrs, who emulated the Forty Martyrs of Sebaste or Rhaithou (Ševčenko), or some unknown number of later Mount Sinai martyrs, who emulated Ps.-Nilus' 14 January martyrs (Mayerson), or Ps.-Nilus' martyrs, who emulated Ammonius' Forty Martyrs of Mount Sinai and environs (Gatier).

It seems simplest to assume that the phrase '4 [and] ten' means 'forty' and was simply chosen as an abbreviation in order to fit all the words into two lines. It would also be simplest to agree with Ševčenko (and later Sinai monastic tradition, as indicated by the name of the chapel at St Catherine's) that the groups in question were the Mount Sinai and the Rhaithou martyrs described in the Ammonius *Report*. That said, the inscription presents another curious feature that might help further clarify the identity of the commemorated martyrs. The feature is this: although the inscription emphatically states that the martyrs it commemorates 'lie here', there is no sign that anything lies, or ever lay, below the floor of the room in which it is placed. Indeed, investigations undertaken in 1996 found nothing in the wall behind the inscribed plaque itself.[256] Thus, it appears that no martyrs' relics were ever interred in the room, despite what the inscription says.

253 Mayerson 1976, 375–79, accepted by Solzbacher 1989, 215–16, and Shahid 1984, 317–18.

254 One would expect an abbreviation of the ordinal τέταρτεσκαιδεκάτης, sc. ἡμέρας.

255 Gatier 1989, 518–19.

256 Grossmann, personal communication, in which he also suggests that this absence of relics confirms that the Ammonius *Report* was written before the veneration of relics came into vogue, i.e. early in the fourth century. Alterations to the room were made, apparently in the tenth century, to direct pilgrim traffic; but there is still no sign that anything existed before then: see Grossmann 2001, 191–93. However, those alterations may have included the placement of the plaque. Grossmann has suggested to me that it may have once decorated a door lintel.

It may be that the relics were transferred to Constantinople when Justin II became the monastery's patron in the late sixth century, since the tenth-century *Synaxarion* of Constantinople implies that he bestowed Sinai martyr relics upon the Church of the Apostles Peter and Paul that he constructed within his orphanage, the Orphanotropheion.[257] Yet a different explanation arises if we consider the possibility that the plaque might have originally come from Rhaithou (it must have come from somewhere else, since it is made of marble, a material not naturally found on the peninsula), where it might have originally marked the tomb where Ammonius reports the forty martyrs of Rhaithou to have been interred, across from the Rhaithou fort (*Rel.* 38). We may further conjecture that the plaque was discovered and installed in the Sinai monastery after the abandonment of Rhaithou, some time in the Muslim era. By this hypothesis, the subject of the inscription's commemoration would not be the Mount Sinai martyrs (as often assumed), but those of Rhaithou, who, 'equal in number', emulated the 'fourfold-ten' of Mount Sinai. This would make sense of both the wording of the inscription and the makeshift nature of the chapel in which it is now placed. The relics of these forty Rhaithou martyrs have long disappeared; perhaps Mount Sinai's martyr relics are still drying in St Catherine's ossuary, or somewhere in the ground below Jabal Musa.[258]

Of course, this assumes that such discrete sets of martyrs ever existed. Indeed, about the only thing on which all scholars agree is the improbability that a perfect sum of forty martyrs died at either Mount Sinai or Rhaithou, let alone at both simultaneously. Here we are clearly dealing with the inventions of a Sinai martyr tradition. It has already been noted that the portion of the Ammonius *Report* dealing with the Forty Martyrs of Mount Sinai

257 Cf. the notice to 12 November in *Synaxarium ecclesiae Constantinopolitanae* col. 217 and 14 January (coll. 389–94) with Theophanes, AM 6064, Solzbacher 1989, 225–26, and Gatier 1989, 520–21. According to Theophanes, Justin began constructing his Apostoleion in 571/2, the same year in which he sent an embassy to Ethiopia. Perhaps Sinai relics were collected *en route*.

258 Climacus locates Mount Sinai's ancient cemetery 'near the Fort', *Ladder* 6 (PG 88.797A). On the ossuary, see Dahari 2000, 63. There is also the 'Monastery of the Forty Martyrs' (Dayr al-Arba'in) located in Wadi Leja/al-Arba'in. When or why it acquired this name is not known, but it was reported in the fourteenth century that it housed many remains: see Mayerson 1976, 377; Shahid 1984, 318 n. 132; and Dahari 2000, 66. If this in fact was where Mt Sinai's martyrs were originally interred, then the plaque might have come from there; in which case I would agree with Ševčenko that the inscription's subject (i.e. those who 'lie here') would be Mt Sinai martyrs, and that '4-ten' would refer to the Forty Martyrs of Sebaste, given that Ammonius, *Rel.* 7 implies an early association between these two groups.

was modelled after the story of the Forty Martyrs of Sebaste. That story itself was a legend that probably originated in the need for a collective set of martyrs to fortify Christians during the forty days of Lent: as Severus of Antioch explained to his congregations in the sixth century, 'they are the offspring of these forty days of fasting, [and] each day has brought forth for us an athlete and martyr'.[259] Thus we find a Christian tradition being moulded around death to answer an ascetic need. Gatier supposes that the Rhaithou martyr tradition arose out of that community's sense of rivalry with the prestigious Mount Sinai monastery,[260] but it undoubtedly also served that community's religious needs, providing its monks with their own set of intercessors and exemplars. Yet the focus on death is so emphatic in late antique Sinai literature that it warrants further explanation itself. I therefore conclude by considering other ways in which the Sinai martyr tradition may have bolstered the late antique Christian experience on the Sinai peninsula.

5. DEATH AND THE MOUNTAIN

How did Christians first come to identify and make places 'holy'? The development is not attested until the fourth century and, as noted above (pp. 19–20), was by no means accepted or taken for granted by all Christians even then. However, in most early instances where it occurred, the Christian 'sanctification of place' was closely connected to the establishment of local martyr cults. Historians have emphasized that such cults not only made intercession more accessible, but also helped late antique communities reclaim and relive the heroic age of the martyrs, creating a network that helped unify their now Christian Roman Empire in a dramatic, new historical narrative.[261]

In the case of 'God's Mountain', however, such explanations may seem unnecessary, and the establishment of a martyr cult superfluous: fourth-century monks or pilgrims undoubtedly sought out Mount Sinai already

---

259 Severus of Antioch, *Homily* 18 ['On the Holy Martyrs'] 6, trans. Allen–Hayward 2004, 120. Another martyr group whose number was increased to 40 over time was the 'Forty Martyrs of Palestine': while there are 39 martyrs in the short recension of Eusebius of Caesarea's *History of the Martyrs of Palestine*, these become 40 in the long recension (section XIII.10: BHG 1193). Of course, 'forty' was a numerical trope for the years of the Hebrews' wanderings in the wilderness: e.g. Num 33:38, Amos 5:25.

260 See below, pp. 147–48.

261 See MacCormack 1990; Markus 1994; Bitton–Ashkelony 2005.

assured of its sanctity by Scripture. The question becomes more interesting, I believe, when recast in terms of 'Christianization': how did Christians make this Old Testament site their own? Here too I concede that the question itself may seem unnecessary or odd. Yet the Ephraimic hymns on Julian Saba and the letter of Jacob of Serug, even when celebrating the achievement of reclaiming the site, imply a sense of need: e.g. it took Saba's construction of a church upon Mount Sinai's summit to fulfil God's will and make the mountain Christian. I propose that establishment of the Mount Sinai (and Rhaithou) martyr cult and tradition fulfilled a comparable purpose of completing a process of Christianization. If obedience, suffering, and triumph were considered essential components of the Christian ascetic spirit (and of Christ) in the late antique East, then we should not be surprised that monks would want to infuse Mount Sinai with a similar spirit by establishing a cult of martyrs there. It also fortified them with ascetic exemplars who managed to 'keep the faith' despite the stern desolation and spiritual misgivings that assuredly plagued them in this barren frontier.

We must remember that Mount Sinai differed from other sites of the new Christian Holy Land, set apart by both distance and biblical associations. This was, above all, the domain of God in His Old Testament aspect, the place where 'God's majesty descended' (Exod. 19:18). It inspired late antique authors to write differently than they did about sites more firmly connected to Jesus's life farther north. Their mode of description, which emphasized the physical isolation of the setting, its grandeur, as well as its potential impact on human visitors, might be called romantic.[262] Procopius of Caesarea, for example, described Mount Sinai as a 'precipitous and terribly wild mountain' looming over the Red Sea. No one could pass a night on its peak, he explained, 'since constant crashes of thunder and other terrifying manifestations of divine power are heard at night, striking terror into a man's body and soul' (*Buildings* V.viii.1, 8). Written in far off Constantinople, his description captures the numinous sublimity and expected revelations that the Sinai conjured in the imaginations of his Christian contemporaries.

The solitary was the absolute hero of this distant desert landscape. True, the monastic movement had already developed a mythology of its own about

---

262 Romantic in the eighteenth-century sense of an encounter with a crushing natural sublime. Egeria's sections on Mt Sinai markedly differ from her presentation of other sites, which forego geographical descriptions. For survey and discussion, see Leyerle 1996. It may be pertinent that late antique Sinai descriptions were written at exactly the time (late fourth–early sixth centuries) when nature metaphors were adopted by patristic authors to convey God's profundity: see Lane 1995, 52–53.

long-haired hermits who haunted remote Egyptian oases, beyond all worldly interference or concerns.[263] But after the destruction of Scetis and environs in the early fifth century, such figures seem to have been relocated to the Sinai wilderness, their wondrous isolation matching that of its peak. The following vignette was supposedly reported by a pilgrim from Gaul. It represents an early fifth-century effort to romanticize the Sinai frontier:

> I saw the Red Sea and the ridge of Mount Sinai, whose peak almost touches heaven, and which no one can approach. Within its recesses was said to be a certain anchorite, whom I was unable to see, despite much time and effort. Having been removed from human intercourse for nearly fifty years, he wears no clothes, but by divine grace is oblivious to his own nakedness, since he is covered by the hairs of his body. Whenever pious men wished to approach him, he would evade human contact by disappearing in the pathless wilderness.
>
> It is said that he allowed himself to be seen by one man only, about five years ago, who was deemed worthy to do so, I believe, because of his power of faith. They discussed many things, including the question of why he evaded humans at all costs. He replied that he who is visited by men cannot be visited by angels. Hence the rumour was spread and has been accepted by most folk – not without reason – that the holy man is visited by angels.[264]

Such figures embodied the mysteries of 'God's Mountain', and are almost always described as being just on the verge of vanishing: in John Moschus and Anastasius' seventh-century stories (probably written to edify coenobitic monks safe within their fortified compounds), to catch a mere glimpse of a Sinai anchorite constitutes a spiritual revelation in itself.[265] Such figures were also said to have been discovered with hands raised

---

263 For the motif, see Reizenstein 1916, 172–80.

264 Sulpicius Severus, *Dialogue* I.17, ed. Halm, 169–70, attributing the report to a monk named Postumianus. Solzbacher 1989, 119–20, is surely correct that it is fictional. On the expectation of marvels in ancient literature on far-off places, as well as strategies used by Christian writers to help readers envision exotic lands, see Frank 2000, 45–61.

265 Anast., *Narr.* I.2, 30, 31, 33, 35, 36; cf. John Mosch., *Meadow* 122, trans. Wortley, 100: When I was at Mt Sinai some years ago, I was in church … When the holy sacrifice was being offered and all the fathers were present, I looked and saw two anchorites enter the church. They were naked, yet none of the fathers perceived that they were naked except for me. When they had received the communion of the body and blood of the Lord, they left the church and went away. I went out with them and … prostrated myself before them, saying, 'Of your charity, take me with you', for they knew that I had perceived that they were naked. They said to me, 'You are well installed here – stay where you are.' Again I asked them … Then they said to me, 'It is not possible for you to be with us – stay here – this is the place for you.' They offered a prayer on my behalf and then, before my very eyes, went onto the waters of the Red Sea on foot, and departed across the sea.

in prayer, kneeling completely still, dead in their caves. Among the most famous of these was the hermit Onophrius. During the Middle Ages his 'cave of penance' was located at Mount Sinai, in Wadi Leja/al-Arba'in, near the Monastery of the Forty Martyrs.[266] The original rationale behind the identification or placement of these sites is unknown. We may assume, however, that Onophrius, found frozen in prayer to the end, was thought to be akin to the Martyrs and to embody similar virtues: above all, fortitude (καρτερία/*karteria*) and perseverance (ὑπομονή/*hypomonē*) in devotion to God, tested and proven unto death.

Though considered essential monastic virtues everywhere, fortitude and perseverance appear to receive special emphasis in our Sinai sources (cf. Ps.-Nilus, *Narr.* III.18, Climacus, *Ladder* 27, and Anastasius, *Narr.* I.29),[267] perhaps for good reason. Procopius of Caesarea told readers that Mount Sinai was populated by monks 'whose life is a kind of "careful rehearsal of death"' (*Buildings* V.viii.4). His description has been criticized on the grounds that it borrows from Plato's *Phaedo* and could have been said of monks anywhere. Be that as it may, a perusal of Climacus' *Ladder of Divine Ascent* shows that Procopius certainly captured the spirit of the place. Here, preparing for death through 'studious, true repentance' or 'penance' (μετάνοια μεμεριμνημένη) is presented as a crucial, transformative aim of ascetic practice. To this end, the remembrance of death was considered 'the most essential of all works', since it made monks mindful of priorities, keeping coenobites focused on their 'labours and meditations', while liberating anchorites from daily worries and energizing their prayers.[268] Ideally, it offered a foretaste of their state in the world to come. Climacus knew a Sinai anchorite at Thōla who 'experienced ecstasy' at the very thought of death. 'Whenever the brothers found him they had to raise him up and carry him, scarcely breathing, like someone who had fainted or suffered an epileptic fit.'[269]

Such an experience could transform even the most negligent monk: 'nobody', says Climacus, 'who acquires the remembrance of death will ever be able to sin'.[270] The experience often brought with it terrifying visions of judgment. Seventh-century monastic literature tended to focus on deathbed

---

266 The Egyptian Onophrius was conflated with Sulpitius Severus' Sinai hermit some time in the Middle Ages. See Skrobucha 1966, 20. On his 'cave', Dahari 2000, 66–67.

267 For their origin in Stoic thought, see Shaw 1996.

268 John Clim., *Ladder* 6 (PG 88.793C), trans. Luibheid–Russell, 132.

269 *Ibid.*, PG 88.796C, trans. Luibheid–Russell, 134, slightly adapted.

270 *Ibid.*, PG 88.797A, trans. Luibheid–Russell, 134.

scenes, highlighting a moment when monks watched to find out whether their practices or leaders were effective or not.[271] Such an occasion inspired one of the most vivid passages in Climacus' *Ladder*. 'Listen', he writes, 'to a story that is sad but beneficial to the soul.' An elder solitary named Stephen, having gained a reputation for holiness 'on the side of the mountain where the holy prophet and seer of God Elijah once lived', i.e. Mount Horeb/Jabal Sufsafa, decided to practise a 'much more effective, strict, and hard form of repentance'. So he moved to Siddim, 'an abode of anchorites' located 110 km (70 miles) away, a place that 'lacked every comfort and was rarely visited'. There he was said to have tamed a leopard and attained the gift of tears. Eventually he returned to his cell on Mount Horeb, aware that he was about to die. As John describes the scene,

> On the day before his death, he went into ecstasy and began to look to the right and to the left of his bed. He seemed to be rendering an account to someone. While all the [monks] standing by [his bed] were listening, he said, 'Yes, true, of course – but that's why I fasted for so many years!', or else, 'No, you're all lying, I didn't do that!', or 'Yes, that's true. But I wept and did my duties', or, 'No! A false accusation!' Or sometimes, 'Quite right. I have no excuse. But God is merciful.'

Despite having trained as an anchorite for over forty years, Stephen now lay charged with sins he never knew he had, and for which he had no defence. This 'truly frightful and terrifying spectacle' left its observers thoroughly dismayed at the uncertainty of the final judgment.[272]

Thus Procopius was correct in reporting that Sinai monks made a careful study of death. He reveals his distance from the monks' reality, however, by insisting that they also enjoyed their solitude there 'without fear' (V.viii.4). Stephen's story demonstrated that the need for vigilance, prayer, and mourning was constant, lest one be taken to task too late. What made it 'truly frightful', though, was that it signalled the possible failure of even extraordinary efforts.[273] Indeed, Climacus was aware of the misgivings that tempted desert solitaries to give up on their ascetic enterprise before ever reaching the end. There was, first, the sense of futility that plagued all desert monks:

271 Constas 2000; Brown 1999.

272 John Clim., *Ladder* 7 (PG 88.793C), trans. Luibheid–Russell, 141–42, adapted.

273 Müller 2006, 202, makes the important point that this fear of judgment was mitigated by the system of spiritual direction that made ascetic masters responsible for the sins and punishments of their disciples. Stephen, an old anchorite, does not seem to have had a spiritual director who could stand for him at judgment: hence his fate would have been especially unclear.

Climacus deals with this demon of despondency, 'the solitary's constant companion', early in the *Ladder*.[274] Listed higher in his concerns, just below vainglory and pride, was a demonic passion that afflicted anchorites living in 'more solitary' places, namely the demon of 'unmanly cowardice' (ἄνανδρος δειλία). Climacus argues that this passion arose from 'barrenness of the soul, rather than the darkness or desolation' of a solitary's surroundings.[275] But isolation certainly compounded the problem. Evagrius Ponticus, the fourth-century theorist of Egyptian desert monasticism, says that it typically involved imagining wild animals approaching, or people being pursued by invading Ethiopians.[276] But Cyril of Scythopolis and Paul of Elusa, both Palestinian hagiographers, relate it more specifically to a fear of Saracen marauders. In one such case, the monk Saba reportedly prayed so hard that earth devoured his demonic Saracen attacker, after which Saba 'received the divine grace of never being driven to panic again due to barbarian plots'.[277]

Such were the powers of a saint; the letters of Barsanuphius of Gaza († c. 540) suggest that ordinary monks had a harder time in the desert mastering their fears of sudden attacks. When such attacks occurred, divine power must have seemed conspicuously absent. Nonetheless the proper response, insisted Barsanuphius, was to trust in God, who allowed such things to happen precisely 'in order to prove the faith of those who place their hope entirely' in him.[278] Both Climacus and Anastasius agreed. Indeed, among his edifying tales of Christian heroism during the Arab invasions, Anastasius includes a story about a Christian Saracen who decided to throw himself off the Mount Sinai summit rather than renounce his faith to Arab warriors who had laid siege. Later, gathered around his deathbed, Sinai elders imagined him being greeted and led off to heaven by the earlier Sinai martyrs. This, they affirmed, was his reward for having 'demonstrated to God a love and faith that exceeded the Righteous Ones of old' (*Narr.* II.8).

Historical or not, the martyrs of Sinai tradition represented a group of monastic exemplars whose Christian faith had been thoroughly tested and

274 John Clim., *Ladder* 13 (PG 88.860A), trans. Luibheid–Russell, 162.

275 John Clim., *Ladder* 21 (PG 88.945BD).

276 Evagrius Ponticus, *Eight Thoughts* VIII.10, *On Thoughts* XXIII; trans. Sinkewicz, 87, 169.

277 Cyril Scyth., *Life of Saba* 14, ed. Schwartz, 97.23; cf. *Life of John the Hesychast* 13, Paul of Elusa, *Life of Theognis* II.9. The identification of Saracens as demons is prominent in late sixth- and seventh-century literature, and becomes an important means of explaining Arab activities in many of the stories found in Anastasius of Sinai's Collection II: see Flusin 1991.

278 Barsanuphius, *Letters* 182 (cf. 386, 390, 391); trans. Chryssavgis, 1.190.

proven against all imaginable onslaughts. Not only did their deaths set the benchmark of fortitude and perseverance for later monastic settlers. To the extent that the Sinai martyrs embodied precisely those virtues – fortitude and perseverance – deemed necessary to transcend the Hebrew experience on the Sinai peninsula (cf. Ps.-Nilus, *Narr.* III.18), they embodied precisely the power necessary to endure, and thereby Christianize, this remote Old Testament frontier.

MAJOR SINAI NARRATIVES

Introductions, Translations, Commentaries

PSEUDO-NILUS' *NARRATIONS*:
INTRODUCTION AND TRANSLATION

The first and longest piece in our collection, conventionally called the *Narrations*,[1] is at once the most sophisticated and the most extraordinary. Most sophisticated, because it artfully blends Greco-Roman and Judeo-Christian literary genres (romance, philosophical diatribe, ethnography; martyr narrative, hagiography) to create an original Christian narrative that also represents the last great example of the ancient novel. Most extraordinary, because, although it may be described as a Christian monastic tale or martyr narrative, it avoids using such common terminology as 'monk', 'martyr', or 'Christian', and draws almost exclusively from the Old Testament for its scriptural allusions. It also presents us with a literary and historical puzzle, because we do not know when, where, or by whom it was written – its traditional attribution notwithstanding.

The earliest Greek manuscripts attribute the work to a certain 'Nilus the monk', 'Nilus who was a monk', or 'Nilus the Desert Monk'.[2] From at least the tenth century if not earlier, that Nilus has been identified with Nilus of Ancyra (modern Ankara, Turkey), a learned monk who lived in the late fourth and early fifth centuries († c. 430). Indeed, the *Narrations* tells a remarkably similar tale to that which Nilus of Ancyra himself tells in his *Letter to Heliodorus the Silentiary* (introduced and translated separately below): in both, a father and son visit Mount Sinai and are separated during a 'barbarian' raid; the son is led away captive, but the two eventually reunite through divine intervention. The fact that both have similar plots that are unparalleled by other Sinai stories, and that both are written in a similar style of elevated Greek, suggest that both issued from the same pen. Moreover, it seems likely that the *Narrations*, like the *Letter to Heliodorus*, was written outside the Sinai, some time in the early fifth century. It is no wonder, then, that the *Narrations*, written as a first-person narrative, has

---

1 Latin: *Narrationes*. According to the MSS, its traditional title was 'Narrative [*diēgēma*] by Nilus the Monk of the Slaughter of the Monks of Mount Sinai and of the Captivity of his Son, Theodulus'. It is not known if that was actually its original title.

2 See the critical apparatus in Conca's 1983 edition, p. 1.

traditionally been regarded as Nilus of Ancyra's autobiography, explaining how he converted to monasticism after surviving a harrowing experience in the Sinai desert.

Most scholars, however, now reject that traditional attribution.[3] Research has revealed Nilus of Ancyra to be something of a cipher, to whom much has been ascribed, but about whom little is really known. Although most of the works ascribed to him have not yet been edited, it is nonetheless clear that he did not write them all himself (e.g. several treatises preserved under his name are now known to have been written by the more controversial monk, Evagrius of Pontus). There are reasons to suspect that Nilus of Ancyra did not write the *Narrations* either, despite its similarities to his *Letter to Heliodorus*. Upon scrutiny, the two narratives differ considerably in vocabulary, imagery, and plot. For example, while the *Narrations* focuses on the execution of several monks, no monk at all dies in the *Letter*; in the former, the father mounts an expedition to save his son; in the latter, he merely prays for help in a cave; in the former, there is much speculation about the nature of Providence, and no miracle resolves the crisis; in the latter, an Ancyran saint suddenly arrives and saves the day. The praise for anchoretic monasticism found in the *Narrations* also seems inconsistent with the preference for coenobitic monasticism expressed in another letter attributed to Nilus of Ancyra.[4]

It is therefore now generally agreed that the *Narrations* should not be attributed to Nilus of Ancyra (hence 'Ps.-Nilus', used here). How, then, did the work pass into his literary corpus? It is probable that later scribes, upon finding the 'Nilus' name on *Narrations* manuscripts, simply assumed it referred to Nilus of Ancyra, especially if they knew that Nilus of Ancyra

---

3 Exceptions are Conca 1983b, 343–60, and Ringshausen 1967, 25–32, 59–66. Ringshausen believes the verbal and thematic similarities between the *Narrations* and Nilus of Ancyra's *Commentary on the Song of Songs* (the only work securely attributed to Nilus of Ancyra that has received a modern edition) are sufficient to establish common authorship, arguing that any differences between them, or between the *Narrations* and any other of Nilus' works, can be explained by differences in genre or time of composition. Unfortunately Ringshausen never published his supporting research. His conclusions and method are critiqued by Link 2005, 16–21, who argues that Heussi's methodology, which assumes that sentiments expressed in a single author's works should generally cohere, is preferable to Ringhausen's focus on stylistic parallels (as Link points out, Ringhausen's approach might result in the attribution of innumerable works of this period to Nilus of Ancyra).

4 Nilus of Ancyra, *ep.* III.72 (PG 79.421C), noted by Heussi 1917, 156, and Link 2005, 6. However, this letter is quite brief, and it is not certain that Nilus wrote all of the letters attributed to him. See Alan Cameron 1976.

had told a similar tale in his *Letter to Heliodorus*.[5] This may have occurred in the eighth century, when the *Letter* was presented as evidence during the Iconoclast controversies (see its introduction below). As for the similarities between the two works, scholars have hypothesized the existence of yet a third narrative – a Sinai romance, now lost – that both authors reworked, it is argued, for different purposes.[6]

Such arguments now carry the field. Nonetheless, the case for Nilus of Ancyra ought not be considered completely closed. Rather than posit another source now lost, it would be simpler to assume that Nilus of Ancyra reworked his own material at some point for a different purpose or audience. Certainly we can reject one primary objection to his authorship, namely that a monk known for writing ascetic treatises and stern letters of admonishment would have trifled with romance novels. After all, his elder contemporary, the monk Jerome, wrote three.[7] It is true that Nilus of Ancyra shows no familiarity with the Sinai-Negev region in the other works attributed to him. Then again, Nilus reveals little about himself in those works at all. While the traditional attribution of the *Narrations* to Nilus of Ancyra cannot be assumed, it cannot be discounted until his literary corpus has been more fully edited and studied.

If, however, his authorship is rejected, then the date and provenance of the *Narrations* become open to speculation. All we know for certain is that it was written before 886, when a brief excerpt of it written in Syriac (and translated separately below) appears in a Sinai manuscript of that date, directly following a Syriac translation of the Ammonius *Report*.[8]

---

5 Derived from the Nile river, 'Nilus' was in fact a common name in the late Roman East, amply attested in the north-east Delta as well as the Negev in late Roman times: e.g. several early fifth-century letters of Isidore of Pelusium discussing literary matters are addressed to a certain Nilus: see Évieux 1995, 401–02; Negev 1981, 69–71; and Mayerson 1975, 53–54. Nilus of Ancyra is the only patristic author known to have had this name. There is a curious narrative that purports to be told by 'Abba Sophronius and Abba John', apparently referring to Sophronius of Jerusalem and John Moschus, which describes a colloquy over the night vigil between them, a certain Nilus, and two of his disciples one night on the Sinai summit: see Longo 1965–1966. It is undoubtably a later Byzantine text; in any case the colloquy takes place during a vigil held atop Mt Sinai, which does not appear to have been permitted until the seventh century at earliest.

6 Link 2005, 12; Solzbacher 1989, 213–15, 227–29; Thümmel 1978, 20.

7 *Contra* Link 2005, 20; for the novelistic aspects of Jerome's *Life of Paul the Hermit, Life of Hilarion*, and *Life of Malchus*, see Weingarten 2005.

8 MS *Vatican syr.* 623. The earliest Greek attestation of the *Narrations* is found in the tenth-century *Synaxarion* of Constantinople (ed. Delehaye, p. 217), whose authors mined the *Narrations* for information for their entry on Nilus of Ancyra, commemorated on 12 November. See Heussi 1917, 16–22.

Some believe the Greek original must have been written while the Sinai monastery was flourishing in the late sixth century.[9] But a date in the fifth century seems preferable: on the one hand, the work lacks references to coenobitic monasticism on the Sinai, to fortifications below Mount Sinai, or to church leadership at Pharan, all of which we know existed by the late sixth century.[10] On the other hand, its narrator alludes to an attack on Sinai monks that had occurred 'many years earlier' and to their subsequent commemoration (*Narr.* IV.14). Most likely that corresponds to the attack on Mount Sinai monks described in the Ammonius *Report*, which presumably occurred in the 370s. A fifth-century date for the *Narrations* would allow for the establishment of this Sinai martyr cult.[11] Finally, if the attack Ps.-Nilus describes took place on a 14 January that corresponded to the eighth day after Epiphany (*Narr.* IV.14), and if that day was also a Sunday (cf. IV.1), we might narrow the historical date of that attack to the years 406, 412, 417, 423, 434, 440, 445, 451, 462, 468, 473, 479, 490, or 496.[12] Otherwise, no detail enables us to date the *Narrations* with any certainty. It is worth noting, however, that Ps.-Nilus does not try (in contrast to the author of the Ammonius *Report*) to assure us that he is recording events of a particular period or era. Accordingly, if his narrative seems to reflect early conditions, we may at least be confident that he was not trying to mislead us.

Also unknown is the provenance of the text. However, Ps.-Nilus gives accurate details regarding obscure features of Sinai-Negev topography: e.g. the distance for travel from Pharan to Elusa through the Tih desert (*Narr.* VI.12, 17, 22), the location of large springs towards the end of that route (VI.12), and the identity and approximate location of the Negev town of

9 Devreesse 1940, 220–22, assuming that the *Narrations* was written by monks inspired by Nilus of Ancyra's *Letter to Heliodorus*; his late sixth-century date is accepted by Gatier 1989, 518.

10 See General Introduction, above, pp. 15 n.58, 25–33.

11 Mayerson 1975, 55, considers the notice concerning the earlier martyrs to be a later interpolation, but it is accepted by both Conca and Link and conforms stylistically to the rest of the narrative. If later scribes had interpolated this clarifying detail, it would be odd that they did not also add other information (e.g. year of martyrdom) that might further clarify the passage. Finding no anachronism that would require a date later than the fifth century, Heussi 1917, 147, 154 n. 4, believes the work was based on the Saracen raid recorded for 411 mentioned above, General Introduction, p. 43.

12 Cf. Grossmann 1999, 461, based on Leitzmann–Aland 1956, 22–29. Fourth-century possibilities include 367, 378, 389, and 395; sixth-century possibilities would be 501, 507, 518, 524, 529, 535, 546, 552, 557, 563, 574, 580, 585, 591, and 596. As noted in the General Introduction, Grossmann believes the attack occurred on 14 January 367.

Sobata (VII.10, where it is called Subaïta). Unless these details came from some local map,[13] we may conclude that Ps.-Nilus truly was familiar with the region he describes. It is unlikely, however, that he was writing at Mount Sinai itself, or for monks there, inasmuch as these would have not have needed the extensive information he provides in his ethnographic sections (III.4–18) regarding Sinai monastic customs.[14] It seems more plausible that he was writing in the Negev city of Elusa, or had lived there for some time.[15] Not only does he end his story in Elusa, but his awareness of the Morning Star cult, as well as the ornamentation of this prose, reveal an author familiar with the kind of religious cult and rhetorical training we know could be found in Elusa in the late fourth and early fifth centuries.

So much for the possible historical circumstances behind the *Narrations*. Clearer are its literary antecedents. As Karl Heussi observed long ago, its narrative structure (e.g. use of first-person narration, dreams, and flashbacks), plot situations (e.g. bandit raids, captivity, sacrifice of a virgin, separation and reunification of loved ones in exotic lands), emphasis on preserving chastity, and musings about Fate, Necessity, and Providence (*Narr.* VI.24), are basic features of Greco-Roman romance.[16] This literary aspect of the *Narrations* must be recognized by historians and classicists alike; indeed, Heussi's observations beckon a fuller exploration of the literary complexities and historical significance of this fascinating text.

Whatever lost Sinai narrative may possibly have lain behind the *Narrations*, it is clear that Ps.-Nilus used at least two earlier works of fiction to craft his narrative. One of these was Achilles Tatius' *Leucippe and Clitophon*. This quintessential Greek romance was written in the second or third century. Papyri fragments attest its popularity during that period, and indeed its popularity continued well into Byzantine times.[17] The parallels

13 Solzbacher 1989, 228, believes that Ps.-Nilus got his information from a map.

14 As argued by Link 2005. Given the acceptance of panegyric in late antique society, the point should not be stressed; however, the only internal evidence that Ps.-Nilus was writing on the Sinai is his use in III.17 of a demonstrative adjective when referring to Elijah's cave (τοῦτο … τὸ σπήλαιον), suggesting it was close at hand; but Ps.-Nilus' diction is generally loose, and does not allow for certainty on this point.

15 Thus Heussi 1917, 152 n. 1; Solzbacher 1989, 248; Caner 2004, 138. Another candidate might be Gaza, which featured literate ascetic communities from the mid-fifth century onwards and might fit the *Narrations*' description of its narrator's homeland as a land that was 'everywhere peaceful' (*Narr.* VI.23). An origin in either Gaza or Elusa would not prevent attributing the work to Nilus of Ancyra, since his origins are unknown.

16 Heussi 1917, 144–50; Conca 1983, 252–53; Link 2005, 8–11.

17 Achilles Tatius' popularity was due in part to the fact that for some reason he became

between the two authors come mainly in those sections of the *Narrations* that depict nomadic 'barbarians' and their sacrificial rites. As others have noted, Ps.-Nilus uses words and phrases in these sections that are also found in the first half of the third book of *Leucippe and Clitophon*.[18] By themselves, these verbal correspondences are too slight to prove that Ps.-Nilus took them from Tatius. However, these words and phrases in *Leucippe and Clitophon* also come precisely in those passages where Tatius describes how his own two protagonists become separated during a raid by Egyptian bandits (simply called barbarians) who decide to sacrifice the captive virgin Leucippe to their gods in a rite that includes, among other things, eviscerating their victim.

These points are also prominent in the *Narrations*, indicating that its correspondences with the first half of Achilles Tatius' third book extend beyond mere diction to the level of plot and narration.[19] It is also notable that Ps.-Nilus shares Tatius' habit of breaking up his narrative with detailed digressions on how passions affect a person's body, thereby 'killing the action by analytic asides that dissect the physiology of emotions'.[20] Indeed, in no other ancient authors is this stylistic tic so prominent. But more to the point, each example of it in Ps.-Nilus' work (*Narr.* I.6, III.2, VI.2) finds its parallel precisely in the first half of Tatius' third book where the other linguistic and narrative parallels are found. Taken together, these correspondences prove that Ps.-Nilus had carefully read *Leucippe and Clitophon* before writing his *Narrations*. Achilles Tatius' romance novel not only helped him describe the sacrificial rites of his own barbarian bandits, but also to explain the impact of emotions on his characters.

That is not all. Besides *Leucippe and Clitophon*, Ps.-Nilus also read a Jewish novel known as Fourth Maccabees. Written in Greek and probably in the late first century CE,[21] Fourth Maccabees celebrates the resistance

identified as a Christian: see Plepelits 1996, 411 (cf. the case of Heliodorus, author of the *Aethiopica*, presented as a Christian by Sozomen, *EH* V.22). A copy of his *Leucippe and Clitophon* is preserved in St Catherine's library (MS *Sinaiticus gr.* 1197).

18 Detected by Henrichs 1972, 51–56; instances are signalled in the *Narrations* footnotes.

19 Having read Heussi, Henninger 1955 dismissed anything in the *Narrations* that was not documented elsewhere; in particular, he maintained that Ps.-Nilus' description of bedouin religious practices was purely fictional. The parallels with Achilles Tatius suggest he was correct, but Ps.-Nilus adds some details that may (or may not) reflect genuine practice: see notes *ad loc.*

20 For this and other aspects of Achilles Tatius' style, see Winkler 1989a, 170–75 (quoted here from p. 174). Correspondences between his work and the *Narrations* are signalled in the footnotes below; the translation of Achilles Tatius cited there is Winkler 1989b.

21 Preserved only in the Septuagint and Syriac versions of the Old Testament. For introduction, see van Henten 1997, 58–82.

and martyrdoms of the elderly Jewish priest Eleazar, the seven Maccabean brothers and their mother under Seleucid-Greek domination in 167 BCE. As Brent Shaw points out, it dramatically illustrates the change that occurred, under the pressures of autocracy and imperialism, to ancient notions of what constituted heroism. By presenting suffering and patience as aristocratic virtues, Fourth Maccabees valorizes a new set of heroes whose nobility and autonomy are conveyed through sheer corporeal endurance (*hypomenē*) of violence perpetrated by unjust force. In this narrative, a hero's passivity itself becomes a spectacle that demonstrates his or her manly virtue (*andreia*). The work has been described as a philosophical novel, and often reads like a philosophical treatise, featuring diatribes that extol the sovereignty of pious reason over the tyranny of emotions (*pathē*). As Shaw explains,

> The main point is that one can be 'Master of Oneself' (*autodespotos*) by using mind and logical powers to control the body. In short, a sort of Stoic philosophy written small for everyone ... the message is reiterated repeatedly in the rhetoric of Fourth Maccabees: knowledge and logic enable one to control the body's driving forces, so that one does not become subject to the body – a slave to one's passions, and so to others.[22]

Such themes dominate the *Narrations* as well; Ps. Nilus uses similar diction to illustrate the stoic heroism that Sinai monks displayed against unrighteous violence, inflicted by 'passions' and passion-mad barbarians alike.[23] Otherwise his debt to Fourth Maccabees is evident mainly at the level of patterning. For example, Ps.-Nilus' account of the death of the elderly priest Theodulus and several other anonymous monks (almost all described as youths) recalls the martyrdoms of the elderly Jewish priest Eleazar and the anonymous Maccabean youths; while the prominence he gives to the unnamed, noble mother of one of the martyred monks is clearly patterned after that given to the anonymous mother of the Maccabean youths (IV Macc. 14:11–17:1).[24]

This should not be too surprising: by the late fourth century, the Maccabees were being venerated as proto-Christian martyrs in the Roman East.[25] For preachers such as Gregory of Nazianzus (c. 330–390) and John

---

22 Shaw 1996, quoted at 277. Shaw notes a similar emphasis in Achilles Tatius' work.

23 Examples signalled in footnotes. However, Ps.-Nilus nowhere uses the phrase 'devout reason' (εὐσεβὴς λογισμός). This is the most prominent concept in IV Macc.: see van Henten 1997.

24 IV Macc. and the *Narrations* leave most of the martyrs they describe anonymous. That is not usually the case in Christian martyr narratives: see Rajak 1997, 57–68.

25 Rutgers 1998; Schatkin 1974.

Chrysostom (c. 347–407), they exemplified the fortitude that Christians should emulate in their own commitment to virtue. In particular, Gregory and Chrysostom used the magnanimous mother in Fourth Maccabees to chasten members of their own congregations, male and female alike. For example, in his homily, 'On the Maccabees and Their Mother', Gregory portrays the Maccabean mother delivering a funeral oration explaining how 'philosophy' kept her from exhibiting emotions as 'women of the flesh' usually did at funerals by wailing, disfiguring their faces or singing dirges for the dead.[26] Ps.-Nilus likewise composes a funeral oration, delivered by a martyred monk's Pharanite mother, in which such behaviour is similarly repudiated (*Narr.* VI.3–7), in one instance actually using the same words ('women of the flesh', VI.5) found in Gregory's homily. Thus it appears that Ps.-Nilus had also read Gregory's homily before writing his *Narrations*.

This use of Greco-Roman, Jewish, and patristic Christian templates calls into question any attempt to interpret the *Narrations* literally as history. That does not mean the work lacks historical value. Like other writers of the period, Ps.-Nilus integrated pre-existing works into his own to embellish its effect. While Achilles Tatius, Fourth Maccabees, Gregory of Nazianzus, and perhaps others provided descriptive phrases and patterns to adorn and package his narrative, they did not necessarily dictate his content. Moreover, as noted above, his depiction of conditions or locations in the Sinai-Negev region correspond to what we otherwise know from other literary sources or archaeology. We may therefore assume that the details he offers about things for which we have no other report reflect an honest effort to approximate reality.[27] For example, we might credit his work with historical accuracy regarding the existence of a bedouin overlord on the Sinai, the location of his camp, and his relations with Pharan (*Narr.* VI.11–17) at the probable time of its composition, the early fifth century.

Nonetheless, it is clear from his choice of literary models that Ps.-Nilus was neither writing history nor regarded his work as such. It is difficult to classify the *Narrations* according to conventional genre categories. Certainly it should be regarded as an example of ancient romance – indeed, it appears to be the last ancient exemplar of that genre (a distinction usually given to Heliodorus' *Ethiopian Tale* (*Aethiopica*), since the *Narrations* has hitherto gone unnoticed). On the other hand, it has a theological seriousness that is

26 Gregory of Nazianzus, *or.* XV.9 (PG 35.925C–928D). On the Christian use of the Maccabean mother 'to teach an old Stoic lesson', see Samellas 2002, 98.

27 Thus Mayerson 1963 and Christides 1973, noting late antique testimony regarding Arab religious practices that Henninger 1955 missed.

alien to that genre. Yet it is no typical martyr narrative or monastic hagiography either. No other martyrology or hagiography of the period presents martyrdom or monasticism within such a complex, romantic and didactic framework.[28] Moreover, as noted at the outset, the *Narrations* is an unusual Christian text in its near complete avoidance, not only of familiar Christian terminology, but also of references to New Testament Scripture. Instead it is packed with paraphrases and allusions from the Old Testament. Some have suggested that this Old Testament emphasis reflects a Judaizing orientation in Ps.-Nilus' circle or background.[29] But we should probably seek a literary explanation: if not just a taste for archaism that was common to authors of his era, then a sense that Old Testament Scripture was particularly appropriate to his Sinai setting and drama. According to Numbers, it was due to their grumbling that God decided to decimate the Hebrews in the Sinai wilderness (Num. 14:27–35). In his *Narrations*, Ps.-Nilus raises the question of how Christians might fare when tested in that same Old Testament setting.

Ps.-Nilus' main theme is, in fact, theodicy and the operation of divine Providence on the Sinai: for this reason Richard Solzbacher calls it a 'theological romance'.[30] At the same time it celebrates the willingness of Sinai monks to endure hardships unto death: hence it has also been called an 'ascetic romance', a 'philosophical romance', and a 'martyr romance'.[31] Evidently Ps.-Nilus considered it a kind of doxology, i.e. a work meant to praise or thank God: 'I know you mean to make my salvation the theme of your doxology, as it is your habit to sing God's hymns for the benefaction He grants you', the narrator is told towards the end of the story (*Narr.* VII.1). Viewed as such, the *Narrations* bears comparison to Paulinus of Pella's early fifth-century *Eucharisticus*, a semi-autobiographical narrative written in Latin in which Paulinus thanks God for restoring his fortunes after harrowing encounters with barbarians in Gaul.[32] Ps.-Nilus' treatment of the theme differs, however, from Paulinus', inasmuch as it directly deals with the challenges of failed expectations and doubt. Pagan barbarians had

---

28 Solzbacher 1989, 220, argues that the *Narrations* is no different from Palladius' *Lausiac History* or the *History of the Monks of Egypt*, both of which combine hagiography with descriptions of travel and monastic life. In my opinion, the only Christian narrative of comparable complexity is the third-century Ps.-Clementine *Recognitions*, on which see Robins 2000.

29 Mayerson 1975. About half of the Old Testament paraphrases or allusions come from Genesis, Exodus, III and IV Kings, with Gen. 22 (Abraham's sacrifice of Isaac) being the most prominent.

30 Solzbacher 1989, 220–21; cf. Caner 2004, 145–46.

31 Caner 2004; Mayerson 1975; Link 2005.

32 On Paulinus and his work, see McLynn 1995.

butchered God's 'holy ones' below Mount Sinai with impunity: how, asks the narrator, could Providence let 'lawless hands' fall so easily upon 'holy bodies'? Why had Mount Sinai's 'avenging power' not acted as Scripture says it had, so dramatically, in the past (*Narr.* IV.7-8; cf. II.7–10)?

The answer is a kind of *Bildungsroman* that ends with father and son vowing to assume the 'harsh servitude of ascetic life' (δουλείαν ἐγκρατείας ... σκλῆραν, VII.13). They do so partly because their trials had exposed them to monks who had managed to maintain both their nobility and their resolve unto death. As one martyred monk explains, alluding to 1 Cor. 2:9, 'no eye has seen, nor ear heard, nor heart conceived, what God has prepared for those who struggle in His behalf' (*Narr.* IV.12). This is one of the very few New Testament allusions found anywhere in the *Narrations*. Significantly, however, Ps.-Nilus has changed Paul's sentence: instead of Paul's 'for those who love Him' (τοῖς ἀγαπῶσιν αὐτὸν), he has substituted, 'for those who struggle on His behalf' (τοῖς ὑπὲρ αὐτοῦ ἠγωνισμένοις). Elsewhere Ps.-Nilus uses the expressions 'those who struggle' and 'struggle' to describe monks and their ascetic efforts below Mount Sinai (*Narr.* II.2; cf. III.12–13, IV.7, 12, VI.4). He also describes these monks as 'instrument[s] of grace in action' (ὄργανον τῆς ἐνεργούσης χάριτος, *Narr.* III.9) – an interesting phrase, given classical descriptions of slave as instruments (*organa*), and Christian associations of divine *energeia* with Mount Sinai itself.[33]

Such remarks suggest that, in Ps.-Nilus' view, divine power was no longer made manifest on Mount Sinai through Old Testament thunderbolts and other dramatic miracles, but through the voluntary struggles of Christian monks who served God below. Through their steadfast fortitude and perseverance, his monastic heroes transcend both the false fatalism associated with heroes of Hellenistic romance (cf. *Narr.* VI.24) and the reluctant submission associated with Hebrews of earlier Sinai experience (cf. III.18). At the same time, the monks of the *Narrations* recall and replicate the heroism of the Maccabees, whose heirs Ps.-Nilus clearly deemed them to be. Such appropriations make the *Narrations* an outstanding example of the 'totalizing discourse' by which late antique Christian authors sought to subsume and transcend all prior literary traditions.[34] With his *Narrations*, Ps.-Nilus turned Mount Sinai's Old Testament setting into a romantic framework that enabled him to highlight the attainments of Christian heroism and culture. Therein, perhaps, lies its ultimate historical significance.

---

33 Maraval 1985, 146–47.
34 Cf. Averil Cameron 1991, 123, 220–21.

The following translation is based on Fabrizio Conca's 1983 edition.[35] Its seventeenth-century editor, Pierre Poussin, divided the text into seven different 'narratives', which Conca further organized by numbering the paragraphs in each narrative section: though somewhat arbitrary, these divisions remain convenient and are indicated in the translation by Roman and Arabic numerals.[36] Regarding the translation itself, Ps.-Nilus presents the greatest challenge of any text in this collection. Truly a baroque masterpiece, his *Narrations* is a highly stylized flow of words, written in densely packed sentences that often extend a page or more. Assonance and alliteration are his favourite devices, and in several instances it is clear that Ps.-Nilus wrote his words simply to put them on display.[37] His diction tends to be archaic, abstract, and vexingly vague; his syntax, like that of Nilus of Ancyra, abounds in impersonal periphrastic constructions. I have tried to approximate the rhythm and stilted style of his prose without making it too tortuous for the modern reader. Above all, I have tried not to mislead readers by making it any more precise or less dream-like than is found in the original Greek.[38] Bracketed words and footnotes offer clarifications, especially of the many biblical allusions that inform the narrative.

35 Conca 1983a, v–xxiii. Conca identifies two main recensions and based his edition primarily on four tenth–fourteenth-century MSS (drawn from menologia or collected works of Nilus of Ancyra). Link's recent edition differs little from Conca's; I note where it does in the footnotes to the text.

36 Pierre Poussin, *Nili opera quaedam nondum edita* (Paris 1636 and 1658), 1–126. His edition was based on a tenth-century menologion (see Conca 1983a, viii) and is reprinted in PG 79.589A–649B. Conca 1983b, 349–50, suggests that the text originally consisted of four narrative sections.

37 See Conca 1983a, xxi, and Conca 1983b, 354–55. The style is also quite similar to IV Macc..

38 I have checked my translation with the German translation in Link 2005 and the modern Greek translation in Tsames–Katsanes 1989.

TRANSLATION

Narrations
by
Nilus the Monk
of the Slaughter of the Monks on Mount Sina
and the Captivity of His Son, Theodulus

[Narrative I: Threnody for Theodulus]

[I.1] Wandering after the Barbarians' attack, I came to Pharan.[39] As some men passed by, I heard them extolling the life of desert solitude, each adding many points to the others' praises of it: how full of serenity it is, how free from all disturbance, and how its tranquillity increases a soul's capacity to contemplate visible things, and to advance thereby on a path that leads close to knowledge of God, which all wise men since time began have, with one accord, acclaimed to be the ultimate object of desire[40] and supreme blessedness. Since I was listening intently to them with tear-soaked eyes and most grievous lamentations, they soon decided to speak to me. I was sitting, you see, in great dismay because of the appalling things that had happened, and my face still bore a visible account of the calamity. So they turned off the road and sat down around me. After hesitating a little when they noticed my quiet sighing, they asked with interest and sympathy the cause of my dismay.

[I.2] At this request I began to lament more pathetically still. Their question stirred my memory, which had become a bit becalmed, back to

---

39 Pharan (modern Feiran), the only *polis* on the Sinai, was located about 49 km/31 miles west of Mt Sinai. The narrator apparently reached it about five days after the attack (see below, section VI.10). The story's action takes place within 18–20 days over all (see sections VI.12, 22, VII.18). Like Heliodorus' *Ethiopian Tale*, the *Narrations* begins *in medias res*; like Achilles Tatius' *Leucippe and Clitophon*, it begins with an encounter that leads to a first-person recapitulation of prior events. It is often inferred that the men whom the narrator encounters at Pharan are supposed to be monks, but only their praise of desert solitude supports that inference.

40 γνώσεως ... Θεοῦ, ἣν εσχατον ὀρεκτὸν. Both Basil of Caesarea (c. 330–379), *Homily on Psalm 114*.1 (PG 29.484C) and Gregory of Nazianzus (329–389), *Discourse* 32.2 (PG 36.1084B) describe God as the 'ultimate object of our desires' (ἔσχατον τῶν ὀρεκτῶν). That description, as well as the notion of the soul's progress from visible things to things invisible, ultimately derives from Plato's theory of knowledge (cf. *Symposium* 209e–212e). On the practical importance of 'tranquillity' (ἡσυχία/*hēsychia*), see below, *Narr.*III.11; the identification of monasticism as a philosophic pursuit was common among fourth- and fifth-century monastic writers: cf. Theodoret of Cyrrhus, *Religious History* VI.7 and 13.

its state of suffering. Recounting the drama compelled me to see the events reenacted in thought as if they were happening right in front of me, refiguring in my mind those things which the experience had exposed to the perception of my senses. 'Good Sir',[41] they said, 'has something that we've spoken given you grief on the grounds that it is false? Do you sit here lamenting some erroneous opinion of ours? Or has our discussion caused some kindred suffering to take hold of you, so that this you bewail, being struck unawares by its memory? For your gloomy expression betrays no small sorrow, and your tears bear witness to the grief that is ravaging you within.'

[**I.3**] Gradually their exhortations released my tongue from its fetters. 'What can I say?' I replied. 'What answer can I give you, when a cloud of despair prevents me from seeing the truth clearly? For I am of the same opinion as you, and have known the benefits of desert solitude. So much, in fact, did I admire it, that I felt forced to abandon everything – house, homeland, kith, kin, family, possessions – once I succumbed to my yearning for it. But it has destroyed what was dearest of all to me,[42] and has left me alone, as you see, bereft of consolation. My emotions of suffering will not let me praise it. The terror of the event has overthrown my tyrannical passion for it [i.e. desert solitude]. For when one passion overpowers another, it will yield no ground to the one it has vanquished; it wants to reign uncontested, and rejects any appeal for partnership as something hostile.'[43]

[**I.4**] 'But oh! how foolish of me, to prefer to philosophize and neglect the lament for my boy. My power of reason had found some respite, having never [previously] permitted me to ponder anything other than Theodulus' execution.[44] Its image is with me constantly: sometimes I picture the slaughter this way, sometimes that, in various twists of death. I imagine I hear the sound of his voice crying out in pain, and think I see him rolling on

---

41 πρεσβῦτα, literally 'old man', a title of respect; also the Greek word for 'priest'.

42 A manuscript scholion clarifies, 'Nilus refers to his son Theodulus who was taken to Barbarian lands'.

43 In Stoic and Christian treatises, as well as in IV Macc., human *pathē* – variously translated here as 'passions', 'feelings', 'emotions', 'sufferings' – were often presented as forces (e.g. 'yearning' in the previous sentence) that actively 'tyrannize' a person if not controlled by reason. Hence one finds in such treatises a subtle analysis of the various modes of passion aimed at educating the reader to recognize or predict them in advance. The foremost passions were those of desire and grief: Ps.-Andronicus of Rhodes enumerated 24 types of the latter. See Samellas 2002, 93–99.

44 To describe the murder of Theodulus and the Sinai holy men, Ps.-Nilus mainly uses σφαγή, a word that may imply sacrificial murder (cf. below, II.15, III.1, VII.2, 8). Otherwise the words used for sacrifice/sacrificial victim are θυσία, ἱερεῖον, or their cognates.

the ground after the blow, imagining things in my mind that being present I would have probably learned by sight.

[I.5] 'Alas,[45] my child, so pitiful, whether still alive or dead! Oh, for your bitter slavery, if you have escaped death! Oh, for your tombless tomb, if a Barbarian's sword has cut you down! How shall I lament your slavery? How shall I weep your death?

'For if you've been enslaved and are still alive – something too unlikely to consider, for when has the Barbarian's hand not been prompt to slaughter, serving a wrath that always thirsts for human blood? – then under what conditions is your lot? Forever daily lashings, callous demands, merciless threats. Yours shall be a bestial way of life that shall drain the blood out of you with most grievous toils beyond your strength. Prison without escape, freedom without hope, with daily fear of death, the sword always near – for this the Barbarian uses to mete out his torments, not the customary whip or rod to strike his blows. One thing alone does he know for infractions large or small: death at all times, even when no wrong has been done, once he goes mad with drink or gives way to brute impulse. Habit has taught him to play casually with the destruction of others.

[I.6] 'But if you are dead, then where on your body did you receive the executioner's blow? From what part did your blood stream forth? Bespattered with gore, in what ways did you gasp and twitch your poor little feet, performing your dance of death? How did you supplicate your Barbaric slayer? With what pitiful gestures did you hope to soften his hard heart? For neither of you would have understood the other's speech, which, when proffering prayers in right-sounding tones, can assuage an angry spirit and bend it towards mercy.[46]

---

45 Here begins the first formal threnody or song of lament. By the first century CE, rhetorical training usually included the composition of threnodies, partly as an exercise in *ēthopoiia* (fictional character development). They became regular features of Greek romance; cf. Charicles' father's lament for his son in Achilles Tatius I.13.2–6. Ps.-Nilus' threnody follows convention by opening with an address to the deceased expressing uncertainty on how to lament and prominently featuring antitheses (living–dead, freedom–slavery, tombless–tomb). Also conventional are its quick transitions from thought to thought (i.e. asyndeton), assonance, and relatively simple syntax. See Birchall 1996 and, in general, Alexiou 2002, 151–52. The narrator's threnody is not merely a set-piece: like his second threnody in IV.7–9, it sets up points of contrast with the Pharanite mother's 'anti-threnody' in VI.3–7.

46 Cf. Achilles Tatius, III.10.2–3 (Clitophon is speaking after his capture by Egyptian bandits): 'A Greek bandit would respond to our speech, and his hard heart might melt at our prayers. Speech often succeeds in its mission of mercy. The tongue as go-between serves the

'Where was [the place] that received your fall? What the beasts that tore at your limbs? What the birds that feasted on your flesh? Which luminous star now knows the secrets of your stomach, having risen to view your vitals spilled out in the air?[47] Did anything survive the beasts' savage teeth? Did anything remain, too tough to be consumed, once they had had their fill? If so, it lies out in the open, exposed to the sun, deprived the dignity of a hallowed burial, this being the desert.

[I.7] 'If someone had gathered that remnant and conveyed it to me, or if I were brought out beside it, then at least I would have had some small consolation for my suffering, since I could have addressed whatever remnant remained as if it were alive and sentient, be it bone, flesh, or hair. For those who suffer only moderate misfortune amid disasters can take much relief – indeed, truly revel with renewed delight – by passing their time in tending the sick: for they take lasting solace from seeing the sick, from sitting beside their last breath, from hearing their last words, from following the body being carried out on a bier, from seeing the final seal being placed on the tomb. The procession, the burial, the sympathy of friends: each of these elements brings deep and substantial solace to a person in sorrow, and helps to dispel his despair.

[I.8] 'But as for me, which of these shall I use to soothe me in my suffering? I know not how he died, and have no picture of how his corpse looked in its final moment imprinted on my imagination. Without being etched in memory through the faculty of sight, their forms remain vague and unstable; they take different shape at different times, in shifting apparitions that deceive and trouble my mind.

[I.9] 'Oh, evils unseen and calamities unresolved! I know not what to weep for, know not what to grieve for. Shall I mourn him alive or dead? Bound or slaughtered? Reduced to bitter slavery, or raised for painful sacrifice?

'Captives must accept every insult with alacrity, bearing their torments whether they want to or not, since their master's will is now lord of their

---

beleaguered soul, conveys its point of view to the listener, and mollifies his angry spirit. But now in what language will we frame our requests? What solemn oaths can we offer? If I were as persuasive as a Siren, still the butchers would not listen. I can only communicate my cause by expressive gestures, display my desires in sign language.' Trans. Winkler 1989b, 213–14.

47 Cf. Achilles Tatius, III.16.3 (Clitophon laments Leucippe's apparent sacrifice by bandits): 'they took communion of the secrets of your stomach and left what was left of you on an abject altar and bier. Your body is laid out here, but where will I find your vitals?' Trans. Winkler 1989b, 217.

own. Oh, my partner of everything else in life until now! You alone have been given this trial of captivity – you alone, who joined me on the long emigration, who shared my adversity in a foreign land, who shouldered the desert's hardships, emulating Isaac's obedience to what his father thought best.[48] So why now did this utmost disaster single you out to undergo captivity's evils alone? For what was I humanely spared? Why did I escape experiencing the sword? Why did that murderous hand not add my body to the rest of the corpses? Or was I spared for a trial of evils still worse? Was I begrudged a quick release so that I could reap the long and bitter fruit of mourning for you?

[I.10] 'Since I see that you sympathize with me', said I, 'and are no less disposed than the sufferer himself – for so your straining ears and unremitting outcries attest – I shall go over my whole story, bit by bit. I shall not speak at length, but as long as you have leisure to listen and nothing compels you to answer needs of your own. For when one's soul is distracted and preoccupied with care, telling a story is harder than hearing one.'[49]

[I.11] But the expression on their face and sound of their voice displayed displeasure at my remark. 'What more worthy way to pass the time', they said, 'than to nurse a broken heart and relieve an unhappy soul of its grief? A cloud loses its gloom by discharging drops of rain; the darkness clears, little by little, by releasing its tinge of water. So too a saddened soul can be unburdened by recounting its tragic reversals, and have its despair dispersed by describing its grievances. But if stifled by silence, a passion may well swell up like moisture in a festering wound that constantly throbs and cannot be drained of pus.'

Since what they said seemed reasonable, I began my account as follows.

[Narrative II: Departure to Sinai, Debate over Providence]

[II.1] 'Two children, my friends, were born to me: the one whom I now sit lamenting, and another who remains with his mother.[50] After having these I gave up marital intercourse with my wife, reasoning that they would

---

48 Cf. Gen. 22:1. For further allusions to the distance travelled by narrator and son from home, cf. VI.24 and VII.18.

49 Link conjectures that this sentence originally read, 'hearing [a story] is harder than telling [one]'.

50 Throughout the *Narrations* the narrator uses the generic term παῖς, 'child', for Theodulus and his other child. Although masculine endings are used here and below for both children, later tradition held that the second child was a daughter.

suffice to perpetuate our race and nurse our old age. For I decided that it was inappropriate for any rational being to either revel in pleasure or abuse nature by overindulging in the license of the law. One should cease once one has served the purpose of Him Who created us, Who ordained marriage for the increase of our race, and not as a comfort for our passions.[51] If not, then later, as one's potency wanes and appetites slacken with the cessations that inevitably accompany old age, one's accomplishment of self-control will be ascribed to force of age rather than an honourable resolve. [II.2] For no one can raise a trophy who does not fight a battle, and no athlete can vaunt of victory if his contest has been cancelled, there being no risk of taking a tumble if no one is wrestling.[52] Glory comes when a contestant, while still in the prime of youth with desires hot and passions inflamed, uses reason to curb his desire and to restrain his impulsive appetite for marital intercourse, even if lawful. Doing so bears witness to his possession of the power of self-governance.[53]

'But I was seized by a great desire for the places in which I have now been ruined. So swept up was I by the thought of tranquillity that I was unable to see or think about anything else. [II.3] For when ardour for anything takes hold of a soul, it is forcibly torn from everything else, even from those of greatest import, and is unabashedly borne towards its object of yearning, giving no thought for pain, trouble, or disgrace. For all are wont to become slaves to desire; wilfully tyrannized, they gladly submit to a yoke of compulsion that is voluntary and self-imposed.

[II.4] 'And so, since this [desire] demanded my departure from home with tyrannical commands that allowed no refusal, I took my young children and brought them both to their mother. To her I gave one, but the other I kept for myself by my side. I told her my decision and firmly maintained that I could not be persuaded against it. She already had been trained not to refuse

---

51 Perhaps referring to Gen. 1:28 and the command, 'be fruitful and multiply'. These scruples concerning sexual intercourse are also Stoic: see Brown 1988, 21–22.

52 Athletic imagery was common in Stoic texts and hence also in Christian ascetic texts: see Stewart 1984. In IV Macc., however, it is used to show how the tortured hero defeats a tyrant by enduring physical pain in view of a large audience: see Shaw 1996, 278.

53 λογισμὸς κρατῶν ἐπιθυμίας … τὴν αὐτοκρατορικὴν μαρτυρῶν αὐτῷ ἐξουσίαν. The Greek used here echoes language found in Stoic and Christian texts, as well as IV Macc. Cf. 1 Cor. 7:37, where readers are exhorted to chastity by gaining 'control' (ἐξουσία) over their will, and IV Macc. 1:7, which expresses the author's intention 'to show that reason is sovereign over emotions' (αὐτοκράτωρ ἐστὶν τῶν παθῶν ὁ λογισμός). See also the concern of the young martyr in V.15. Note that the narrator commends avoiding not only pre-marital sex, but also marital sex (as often in Christian apocryphal acts, e.g. the *Acts of Paul and Thecla*).

me, and she could see from my face that I would hear no appeal. Although she could not stand the constraint nor hold back her tears, she consented to my journey, ceding to necessity more than agreeing by choice. While she knew that our separation would cause sorrow, when she saw that my resolve was firm, she decided to disregard her grief and to look instead to what would please me, preferring to be defeated where she knew she could not prevail even if she wanted to.

[**II.5**] 'Do you have any idea how painful parting is for a couple that has been united once and for all by the lawful conjunction of marriage, having become a single body through the mysterious arrangement of Him Who paired them? The pain that a knife makes when it cuts through a body – such is the pain of parting for those who have become "one flesh".[54] But at the time I was astounded by the power of my desire, seeing how it could conquer both nature and a relationship many years old. Its potency is proved by the fact that it broke unbreakable bonds that are only wont to be dissolved by death, which offers the absence of grief through the absence of sensation. For sensation makes pain unbearable for those who are still living by prompting recollections of intimate affections, unless desire for some greater good blunts the pricks of what we desired in the past.

[**II.6**] 'This [desire] made me ardent for tranquillity. It drove me to the desert solitude for which I had yearned, enabling me to live happily and enjoy great serenity for a considerable time.[55] With a favourable breeze I sailed straight towards my goal, until that gale burst upon us. How or whence it came I know not. The storm it raised buffeted those great vessels of ocean transport, namely the bodies of holy men.[56] It buffeted them, but did not sink them; it battered them, but did not destroy their cargo. For when their pilots turned the prows of their ships heavenward from the sea, they took with them all their cargo and merchandise, leaving only broken planks behind for the pirates.'[57]

[**II.7**] 'But what explanation', they asked, 'can you give for their slaughter? Why were those who blamelessly served God handed over to impious men for their destruction, to become playthings in the Barbarian's

54 Cf. Gen. 2:28, 'a man leaves his father and his mother and clings to his wife, and they become one flesh'; also Mt. 19:5, Eph. 5:31.

55 I.e. the narrator and son had been at Mt Sinai for some time before the raid.

56 Literally, 'the thousand-ton merchant freighters of the holy bodies'.

57 I.e. they were killed by the barbarian bandits, but their souls were preserved for recovery in heaven.

hand?[58] Why was nothing done by the power of Providence? Why did it stay silent as the drama unfolded? Why not prevent the attack when it could? Why not strike the savages with blindness?[59] Why not wither the hands being lawlessly raised against those saintly ones,[60] as Scripture declares to have happened so often in the time of the blessed ones?[61]

[**II.8**] 'When, for example, the Babylonians marched on Hezekiah unjustly, they were rendered powerless, and were repulsed. Not only could they do no harm to the men they were harassing, but they even lost most of their own force when everyone in the army fell asleep. By morning only few were left alive: one hundred and eighty-five thousand had been slaughtered, but no one could tell how or who did the slaughter.[62] For this massacre, though so great, had happened in silence, the work of a single angel in a single night. Indeed, the soldiers looked as if they were sleeping, but in fact they were dead, their armoured corpses having been stripped of their souls without being struck by a sword. They bore no trace of slaughter, leaving their comrades long at a loss as to what had occurred. For as each survivor awoke from sleep, he nudged his neighbour, who did not move. When spoken to, he lay mute; when his body was examined, no wound was found; when his nostrils were probed, there was no breath. So it went, until the brilliance of the dawning sun cast light on their condition, revealing signs of death in the slain men's pallor.

[**II.9**] 'Furthermore, when the Assyrians attacked Elisha and tried to kill that holy man,[63] or when the Sodomites confronted Lot about the angels in his house, they were struck blind, and became objects of sport and mockery to those they had tried to harm. For once blinded, Lot's enemies needed to grope to find the door,[64] while Elisha's enemies were led round in circles without being told where they were going. Although they had come so close

58 Achilles Tatius, III.16, refers to the 'barbarian' act of sacrificing Leucippe as turning her into a 'plaything' (παίγνιον).

59 Cf. Gen. 19:11, where angels blind the Sodomites attacking Lot's house.

60 Cf. 1 [III] Kgs 13:4, where the apostate priest Jeroboam's hand withers when he ordered the seizure of a holy man of Judah.

61 I.e. in the age of the Hebrew judges and prophets; as Link notes, μακάριος ('blessed one') is often used in LXX for Old Testament prophets.

62 Cf. 2 [IV] Kgs 19:35, where the Assyrian army besieging Jerusalem is attacked by an angel at night, leaving 185,000 dead. A similar assimilation of 'Babylonians' with Assyrians is found in Judith; Ps.-Nilus has considerably embellished the brief scriptural account.

63 Cf. 2 [IV] Kgs 6:18–22, where God blinds a Syrian army (the Arameans, not the Assyrians, as Ps.-Nilus states) at Elisha's request; Elisha then leads them in a column to Samaria.

64 Cf. Gen. 19:11, where Lot's attackers are blinded in the doorway and find no way out.

to the one they had sought, they nonetheless did not know it; they stumbled around as though sick and maimed, lying prostrate, their panoplies idle. It was as if they had lost their limbs or capacity for hostile action, since the eyesight that had commanded them in the field had either fallen dead or into sleep. The enemy's vast multitude followed a single unarmed man into captivity. They could have easily vanished off cliffs or in the ravines, had their guide wanted that. They were only saved because the prophet's solicitude restored their eyesight: then they could see the road that led back to their homeland.

[**II.10**] 'Another time, when an impious king became wroth with a prophet for criticizing his law-breaking, he raised his right hand against [the prophet], holding up a sword with bloody intent. But that hand withered up and stayed suspended, like the hand of a statue that cannot be moved to any other position than that in which the artist originally cast it.[65] This happened so that the prophet's body would not suffer what that unjust hand was about to do in the service of law-breaking rage.

So why did those who died this time die so helplessly? How could their attackers have accomplished this so easily, without meeting any opposition from anywhere?'

[**II.11**] 'What good is it now', said I, 'to debate over Providence? Who sufficiently understands God's judgments so as to defend the justice of our Master's dispensations in such dire situations? For all human reason falls short when applied to such inquiry. Defeated by its lack of comprehension, it fails to offer plausible explanations for what has happened.

[**II.12**] 'There have been many examples in the past of wicked people and their plots achieving their goal while Justice kept silent, without repulsing or punishing the perpetrators. By all means, Judgment will bring them their reckoning. For how [else] did Cain in his jealousy kill Abel, whose piety had been acknowledged by God?[66] How could he have brought such grief upon his parents, who never yet had seen a corpse or known anything about death? He riled God by perpetrating murder, the first ever; he diminished our race at the dawn of creation, just as it was beginning to increase; he took no pity on his brother who shared in his own birth and nurture, not wanting him as a comfort in the face of solitude, preferring to live alone with his parents on

---

65 Cf. 1 [III] Kgs 13:4, where Jeroboam, the Israelite king, threatens a prophet for opposing his erection of an altar for Baal; the sword and the comparison to the statue are Ps.-Nilus' additions.

66 Cf. Gen. 4:8.

earth's wide plain, when people were few and not yet able to console each other by their numbers.

[II.13] How could that law-breaker Jezebel have ordered Naboth to be killed by stoning because he had not given her his vineyard?[67] How could Doeg have caused sixty of those three hundred priests to fall with a single blow?[68] Or what about those countless righteous ones in Jerusalem whom conquering armies have slaughtered and left to be eaten by wild beasts and birds, about whom the Melodist laments when he says,

"They have given your slaves' bodies to the
birds of the air for food, the flesh of your saints
   to the beasts of the earth.
They have poured out their blood like water
all around Jerusalem, and there was no one
   to bury them'"?[69]

[II.14] 'How could the many choirs of prophets and apostles have died as victims of plots, vivisections, executions, and ruthless stonings at the hands of law-breakers?[70] Nothing they had done was deserving of death; indeed, they had always been benefactors to the very ones who slew them.

Need I mention those infants who were innocent of all evil? How could those of Pharaoh's day have been drowned in the river's waters, condemned to death for fear that some youth would be raised as Pharaoh's rival?[71] How could those in Herod's day have been mercilessly cut down with a sword? They learned death's pain before they ever tasted life's pleasures, so that the suspected king might not be secretly reared.[72] In all these cases the Judge kept silent and let foul murderers have their way unopposed. But He has set a day of reckoning, when all will receive retribution for the things they

67 Cf. 1 [III] Kgs 21:1–29, Jezebel plots to have Naboth stoned to death after he refused to give his ancestral vineyard to Ahab.

68 1 Sam. [I Kgs] 22:18; Saul orders Doeg to kill David's priests when all the other guards refuse. The Hebrew text gives 85 dead priests; LXX gives 305. It is not clear why Ps.-Nilus has 60 (no manuscript offers an alternative number).

69 Ps. 79[78]:2–3. The 'Melodist' refers to King David, traditionally regarded as the author of the Psalms.

70 Cf. Heb. 11:37, 'They were stoned to death, sawn in two, killed by the sword...' Paul cites several prophets by name; 'apostles' is Ps.-Nilus' addition. The word χορός ('choir') was often used to refer to philosophic circles in late antique Greek.

71 Alluding to Moses and Exod. 1:22.

72 ὁ ὑπονοούμενος βασιλεύς – 'the suspected king' – an oblique allusion to Jesus and Mt. 2:16 ('Slaughter of the Innocents').

have done. Meanwhile He patiently forebears the transgression of His laws, saving His chastisements for that date.

[**II.15**] 'But as I was previously saying, now is not the right moment, nor do I have power to propound lessons that require much time and eloquence to explain with consistency, as is appropriate to God's righteousness. But I shall tell you now what suffering impels me to say, hoping that I might feel better if I unload some of my unbearable pain.

'For I can't bear the memory of the deed I have seen. I do not know how I survived the experience, the recollection of which produces such pain as to make me recoil. I almost curse my own eyes, as if these were to blame for the images I'm forced to see over and over again. Constant are my pangs of suffering: in dreams at night or in thoughts by day, I slip into sorrow most bitter. I cannot sleep untroubled as most people do, losing their diurnal cares in the oblivion of sleep. I am agitated by apparitions of those who have died, and by images of a recent sacrifice gasping and quivering as if fresh in its suffering. Then my agony is again renewed.[73]

[**II.16**] 'But at this point I must take the opportunity my narrative affords to describe how the holy ones in those places formerly lived, and to tell how the Barbarians who attacked them exist, so that the substance of my story might achieve a harmonious balance. I will omit nothing that ought to come to the attention of anyone keen to know, for I know how upsetting it can be when something that interests a person is passed over in silence. Until the matter is made known to full satisfaction, the neglect of what is wanted causes endless frustration.

[Narrative III: Ethnographic Excursus on Barbarians and Monks]

[**III.1**] 'The aforesaid nation [of Barbarians] inhabits the desert extending from Arabia to Egypt's Red Sea and the River Jordan.[74] They practise no craft, trade, or agriculture at all, but use the dagger alone as their means of subsistence. They live by hunting desert animals and devouring their flesh, or else get what they need by robbing people on roads that they watch in ambush. If neither is possible and their provisions run out, then they consume pack animals – they use camels called dromedaries – for food. Theirs is a bestial and bloodthirsty way of life. Killing one camel per clan or cluster of tents, they soften its flesh with heat from a fire only insofar as

---

73 Ps.-Nilus heightens the drama with poetic diction: e.g. ἀνία ('sorrow'), ἄλγος ('agony').

74 Cf. Egeria, *Itin.* VII.6, on the *terrae Saracenorum* ('Saracen territory'); also Ammianus Marcellinus XIV.4.3 and Shahid 1984, 294.

it makes it yield to their teeth without having to be too forcefully torn. In a word, they eat like dogs.

'They know no god abstractly conceived or materially hand-crafted, but bow down instead to the Morning Star.[75] When it appears on the horizon they offer to it the best of their spoils, if anything suitable for sacrifice falls into their hands from their bandit raids.

[III.2] 'They especially like to offer children distinguished by beauty and the bloom of youth.[76] These they sacrifice on piles of stones at dawn.[77] What troubles and worries me so, my friends, is that my boy's comeliness might be appetizing to the lawless ones for their accustomed impieties, seeming serviceable for their purpose. I fear lest his pure soul's body be offered up as a sacrificial victim to abominable demons on behalf of unclean people, to be, as they believe, their atonement and cleansing.[78] Habituated as they are to performing human sacrifice without reservation, they feel no pity for the children whom they slaughter, even if the suppliants sing their laments as seductively as Sirens.[79]

[III.3] 'But if no children are available, they make a camel that is white

---

75 Θεὸν οὐκ εἰδότες οὐ νοητὸν οὐ χειρότευκτον, ἄστρῳ δὲ τῷ πρωινῷ προσκυνοῦντες. The star is described as 'the one named for the passion of sexual lust' and 'the Dawn-Bringer' below, sections VII.5 and 7. For its identification with the Greek goddess Aphrodite, see Jerome, *Life of Hilarion* 25 and John of Damascus, *On Heresies* 101 (PG 94.764), referring to Saracen practices of idolatry before Muhammad. For its identification with the Arab goddess al-'Uzza, see Fahd 1968, 163–68.

The historicity of this description of bedouin/'Saracen' cult has been disputed, since much of its testimony is unique and bears similarity to the description of human sacrifice in Achilles Tatius III.15. The main sceptic (followed by Link) is Henninger 1955, its main defender Christides 1973. For human sacrifice as a narrative device in ancient Greek romance, see Winkler 1980.

76 παῖδας, probably male children. John Mosch., *Meadow* 155, describes Saracens leading a handsome young male captive to their priest for sacrifice.

77 This is the only attestation for Arab sacrifices either occurring at dawn or being performed on a makeshift altar: see Henninger 1955, 104–05. Achilles Tatius III.15.1 locates Leucippe's sacrifice on an improvised mud altar.

78 The Greek, ἀγνῆς σῶμα ψυχῆς … ἱερεῖον δαίμοσι, λύτρον αὐτοῖς καὶ καθαρσίον, finds close linguistic and conceptual parallel in Achilles Tatius, III.12.1, trans. Winkler 1989b, 214: 'if there be any virgin among the captives … take her away for the god, to be a cleansing sacrifice' (ἱερεῖον ἐσομένην καὶ καθαρσίον). Sacrifice by Arabs for the purpose of expiation or atonement is nowhere else attested.

79 Cf. Achilles Tatius III.10.4: 'even if I were as seductive as a Siren, the murderers would not listen', and IV Macc. 15:21, 'Neither did the melodies of Sirens nor the songs of swans attract the attention of their hearers as did the voices of the children in torture crying to their mother.'

and free from blemishes[80] bend down on its knees. Then they circle around it three times in a procession that is drawn out by the multitude of participants involved.[81] The person who leads in the procession and in singing a hymn they compose for the star[82] is either one of their kings or one of their priests distinguished by old age.[83] After the third circuit, but before the throng has finished its hymn, while the last refrain is still carrying on their tongues, this man draws a sword and vigorously strikes at the victim's sinews. Eagerly, he is the first to have a taste of the blood.[84] Then the rest run up with daggers drawn. Some cut off just a small patch of hide and hair, others seize whatever flesh they see and hack away, while others go straight for the innards and entrails. No part of the sacrifice is left unconsumed, so that nothing remains to be seen when the sun appears. They do not even refrain from eating bone and marrow, gradually overcoming its hardness and toughness through perseverance.

[III.4] 'Such is the traditional way of life and cult among the Barbarians. In this way they subsist in the desert, moving from place to place, making encampments wherever they find easy pasturage for their flocks and plenty of water.

'But those who pursue the solitary way of life select a few places in

---

80 Ps.-Nilus' use of feminine adjectives implies the chosen camel was female: see Henninger 1955, 116–22. The Arab practice of sacrificing camels to Aphrodite (i.e. al-'Uzza) is noted by Theodoret, *Religious History* XXVI.13; cf. Qur'an, V.103.

81 Such circular processions are known in pre-Islamic Arab cult, of which the triple procession around the Ka'ba at Mecca may be reminiscent: Henninger 1955, 122. See, however, next note.

82 No such hymn is attested in pre-Islamic Arab literature, and Henrichs 1972, 55, believes Ps.-Nilus derived this entire scene from Achilles Tatius III.15.3–4, which is set in Egypt: 'They had improvised an altar of earth and near it a coffin. Two of them were leading a girl to the altar with her hands tied behind her back ... They poured a libation over her head and led her around the altar to the accompaniment of a flute and a priest intoning what I guessed was an Egyptian hymn ... Then at a signal they all moved far away from the altar. One of the attendants laid her on her back ... He next raised a sword and plunged it into her heart and then sawed all the way down to her abdomen. Her viscera leaped out. The attendants pulled out her entrails and carried them in their hands over to the altar. When it was well done they carved the whole lot up, and all the bandits shared the meal.' Trans. Winkler 1989b, 216.

83 Henninger 1955, 119–22, suggest that the 'priests distinguished in age' (τῶν ἡλικίᾳ γήρους σεμνυνομένον ἱερέων) refer to *kāhine* who were in charge of sacrifices. Two inscriptions record the presence of a *kāhin* of al-'Uzza on the Sinai peninsula: see *Corpus inscriptionum semiticarum* II.611 and II.1236; cf. PP, *Itin.* 38.

84 Although Conca and Link's μετὰ σπουδῆς, 'eagerly', is found in all manuscripts, Henninger 1955, 109, would read here μετὰ σπουδάς, 'after libations [of blood]', in the belief that the scene describes a ritual blood libation; cf. VII.4 below.

the desert for themselves where water suffices to meet the needs of their bodies. Some build huts, while others inhabit caves or grottoes for their entire existence.[85] Few have bread in their diet, only those whose diligence forces the barren desert to yield up grain. With a small trowel they work a wretchedly small and solid piece of earth, only as much as needed to just barely survive. Most observe a diet of raw fruits and vegetables. They prefer their meals plain and simple, having bid farewell long ago to chores of cooking and baking, lest by spending too much time on needs of their bodies they neglect the more important object of their care. And so they attend the cult of the divine with pure and sober minds, because they neither load down their thoughts by gorging on meats, nor do they stimulate their stomachs with rich aromas of fatty sauces.

[**III.5**] 'For such is the insatiable force of gluttony today that people feel compelled to minister to their desire with sights, aromas, and tastes, inflaming their sense of pleasure with a blend of juices that is embellished by an ever-changing variety of scents, colours, and textures. For gluttons cannot be satiated by mere changes in flavour or by a succession of savoury dishes. Though they feast their eyes on a sauce's red, white, or liquescent dark shades before tasting it on their tongues, no mere variation of colour can satisfy their appetite's desire. [**III.6**] No, to please their sense of smell they must stir their sauces into a bouquet of aromas; to delight their mouths, there must be a pleasant blend of sweet and sour flavours, combined with coarse and pliant textures. Of course their eyes must have a share in the fun: and so they season their food with a succulent flow of safflowers, rices, saffrons, nuts, or countless other varieties of colouration, mixed together as by a painter. All this they do so that their mistress, their stomach, might receive an exact consistency of dressings and give her assent to things already tested in advance by the aforesaid senses, as if persuaded by discerning experts.

[**III.7**] 'The dietary regimen of the aforesaid [monks] tends not towards such delicacies. Not only have they renounced those pleasures of quality, deriding a superfluous sense of need as foolish and irrational, but they also strive, as a matter of competitive honour, to abstain from excess with respect to quantity. They eat only as much as they must, so as not to die against the

---

85 'solitary way of life' translates τὸν μοναχικὸν ... βίον. Some 175 hermit cells have been found in the Sinai peninsula. Most were two to three room lavra structures accommodating masters and disciples: see Beaux and Boutros 1998. The use of such laurae (as opposed to monks living together in a single monastery) was common in late antiquity. For general discussion, see Patrich 1995.

will of their Creator,[86] and lose thereby all recompense for the good works they did in life. Some touch food only on the Lord's Day [i.e. Sunday] after seven days without it. Others cut that time in half by having meals twice a week, while others eat every other day. The latter demonstrate that they cherish austerity and abstemiousness, but still obey nature's laws and yield reluctantly to the body's necessity, stooping to this need only when they perceive that their physical capacity has utterly expired and can no longer sustain their labours virtuously. Each of them is suffused with such fervour for angelic conduct that he tries to mimic the austerities [of the other monks] by being content with little, striving to transcend his innate deficiencies with an abundance of zeal.

[III.8] 'Caesar's coinage has no currency among them,[87] since they know neither buying nor selling. Each freely offers the other what he needs and takes back whatever remains. Vegetables, fruits, an occasional loaf of bread – such is generosity among them, using anything at hand to represent tokens of charity. Such love is demonstrated, not by the cost of the materials involved, but by the magnanimity of the outlay; thus a wealth of intention becomes conspicuously clear even in gifts that are small.

[III.9] 'Never does envy, which is especially wont to accompany advancements, ever gain ground there, nor does the pre-eminent brilliance of one arouse slander in another whose reputation for good [works] is lesser, since there is no conceit to cause one to puff up against another, deluding him into thinking his accomplishments great. For whoever achieves pre-eminence in virtue readily ascribes his attainments to God's power, rather than to his own effort, modestly recognizing that he is not the author of his good [works], but rather an instrument of grace in action.[88] Even one who, perhaps because of his body's infirmity, fails in his efforts and humbles himself reluctantly – even he attributes his disability to a slackened resolve, and not to an infirmity of nature.

[III.10] 'One is more modest than another, and all more so than everyone else: in this way each strives for pre-eminence, not in his pretensions, but in the brilliance of his way of life. For this reason they have fled the inhabited world[89] and made their home in the desert, in order to demonstrate their virtues to God, from Whom they hope to receive requital as workers for

---

86 I.e. commit suicide by eating so little.

87 Cf. Mt. 22:19–21.

88 ὄργανον τῆς ἐνεργούσης χάριτος, an interesting phrase suggesting the monks represent the 'tools' of God's will on earth.

89 τὴν οἰκουμένην, perhaps 'civilization'.

their toils, and so that their acts for God may not be displayed to humans.[90] For human praise naturally nullifies [a monk's] zeal and reward: the one it slackens through negligent vanity, the other it reduces through deceptive prestige. For whoever seeks human glory for what he does will receive the reward that he seeks, only to lose his real reward.[91] No longer will he believe there is another [reward that] he might reasonably request, by which he might profit, for which he has wearily toiled. Unable to resist human glory, he deprives himself of the true, eternal glory.

[**III.11**] 'They do not dwell near each other, but keep a considerable distance between their dwellings, some twenty stades[92] or so apart from one another. This they do not because they live like beasts or hate all humanity – for how could that be so, when they treat each other as I have described? Rather, it is because they seek complete tranquillity, as they tutor themselves in what pleases God and continually strive to hold discourse with the divine – something hard or impossible to achieve amid crowds and confusion.[93] For the clamour of neighbours distracts the mind from concentrating on its goal, causing it to wander. Accustomed by long force of habit, it is borne away by what brings it delight rather than by what benefits it.

[**III.12**] 'But on the Lord's Day [i.e. Sunday] they go to church, where they gather and commune with each other every week,[94] coming together so that the common bonds of concord might not be broken over time by total separation, and they forget, little by little, their obligations towards each other. For prolonged isolation can make dispositions fearsome and cause one to forget what once was known about the convivial and gregarious nature of charity.[95]

'And so they partake in the Divine Mysteries[96] and entertain themselves with exercises in edifying discourse, rubbing each other with the oils of moral exhortation.[97] For the life dedicated to virtue especially needs these

90 Cf. Mt. 23:5, where Jesus says that the scribes and Pharisees 'do all their deeds to be seen by humans'.

91 Cf. Mt. 6:5.

92 About 4 km/2.5 miles or an hour's walk. This is a reasonable estimate of the distances between the hermit colonies found around Mt Sinai: see Dahari 2000, 25–112.

93 In sections VII.5 and 14, ὁμιλία (translated here as 'discourse') refers to a vow made to God.

94 Ps.-Nilus does not say that they gather on Saturdays for the night-time office before Sunday communion, as described by Ammonius, *Rel.* 2.

95 On this concern, see Donahue 1959, and Gould 1993, 139–50.

96 I.e. the Eucharist.

97 From here on Ps.-Nilus uses wrestling metaphors to describe ascetic training, as was common in Stoic and Christian discourse. Examples of the edification mentioned here are

exhortations to triumph in its contests. They reveal secret moves so that no one will be caught by their opponent through ignorance of his wrestling technique. In these contests that involve no actual substance, a sin may be slow to take effect; but since the entire struggle takes place in the mind, death can move in easily and take up position, unnoticed by those who look only for external moves, undetected amid concessions we make in our resolve.

'That is why men who have trained long for the contest coach those who are inexperienced and have only recently taken up wrestling by advising them to stand obstinate through abstinence against the passion of gluttony. For in its forays against the soul, gluttony stimulates the mad frenzy of lust.[98] It jabs at a wrestler's gut while he is still in the sand box, so as to see if he will still remain standing when struck in the loins in the wrestling ring, or else be easily tackled and quickly give way to his opponent. [III.13] For whoever indulges the pleasure of eating reveals how easily he will be brought down by passions that strike below the belt: defeated by this smaller challenge, he is bound to take an even bigger fall.[99]

'Such is the advice given to young contestants by experts who have advanced far in the competition through time and ascetic training. They know and can clearly see how to break free of their opponents' grips. Those who are most accomplished fend off vainglory and pride, both in themselves and in others.[100] They exhort each other to guard against these like rocks below the surface of a harbour, lest after much toil and battling of waves in their ships, after avoiding shipwreck under passion's high swells or squalls of impure thoughts, they should be dashed upon this last mortal danger.[101]

[III.14] For [advanced monks] are like those who weather the clashing waves and driving winds of the open sea. Constant fear of imminent danger makes them stay alert and keep control; yet as they approach the harbour, placid though it seems, they run aground on hidden shoals. Having become

---

found among the *apophthegmata patrum*; cf. those in the alphabetical collection concerning the fifth-century Sinai anchorites Silvanus and Netra (PG 65.312 and 408–412).

98 This reflects the ascetic theory of sins and their antidotes developed in Egypt by Evagrius Ponticus († 399) and later known in the West as the 'seven deadly sins'. According to Evagrius, Gluttony (γαστριμαργία) was the first of eight passions or thoughts (Gluttony, Lust, Greed, Anger, Grief, Despondency, Vainglory, Pride) to attack a monk. Novices must especially guard against it through abstinence (ἐγκρατεία). If not, it will give rise to the next, more severe passion of sexual lust (πορνεία; here, λαγνεία).

99 Cf. Isidore of Pelusium, *ep*. I.29 (PG 78.228D).

100 Vainglory (κενοδοξία) and pride (ὑπερηφανία) are the most dangerous passions in Evagrian theory, since even expert monks might be unaware of their presence.

101 Similar imagery is used to describe vainglory and pride in Ps-Basil's *Ascetic Rules* X.1–2 (PG 31.1372B).

free from care,[102] they relax, grow inattentive, and suddenly, right at the harbour entrance, lose all the merchandise they had kept safe amid storms of the sea.

'So too it can happen with those who have withstood temptations' onslaughts and have made progress without harm because of their ascetic training and fortitude. Victorious, they often become emboldened by their attainments, or vaunt with a little vanity against those who seem more negligent than they. They are like athletes who stumble and cannot recover when just within reach of wreaths and prizes, or like sailors who dump all their cargo at the end of a long, terrible voyage. In one untimely moment, not only do they lose all the wealth they had accumulated little by little with great trouble, but they also get blamed for negligence on account of the loss.

[III.15] 'Vainglory not only deprives workers of their wages but also makes the labour itself unprofitable for those who toil. Pride, on the other hand, brings not only that loss, but also great danger in the form of self-absorption.[103] It makes a person ascribe to himself his ability to attain virtue and deny God His due. Concerning the effects of vainglory, the Prophet says, "He who earned his wages has put them in a bag full of holes."[104] Not yet lost, but already pouring out, they linger not in the bag, but swiftly pass through its mesh, since the hole through which they exit is bigger than that through which they enter. Such is vainglory: with any profit comes loss, since the profit vanishes in the work itself through clumsy execution. But concerning pride and its effects, the Proverbist says, "My Lord scorns the proud."[105] Denied His due, He becomes hostile towards those who deny Him His due.[106]

[III.16] 'For this reason they bear in mind the [earlier] citizens of that desert, Moses and Elijah. In their asceticism they practise the modesty of those residents of that land, considering it righteous to imitate their virtue. For the magnitude of Moses' command did not inflate him with conceit,[107] and Elijah's miracle of the burnt offering did not render him senseless.[108] Both maintained the same disposition, ever preserving it on every occasion: neither changed his outlook when his circumstances changed.

102 Freedom from care (ἀμεριμνία) was one of the goals of Christian asceticism.

103 περιαυτία, attested only here in *TLG*.

104 Hag. 1:6.

105 Prov. 3:34.

106 An example of Ps.-Nilus' amplifying a point simply for the sake of euphony.

107 Cf. Num. 12:3: 'Now the man Moses was very humble, more so than anyone else on the face of the earth.'

108 Cf. 1 [III] Kgs 18:37–39, where God responds to Elijah's request to send fire to consume his offering, so that he might triumph over the priests of Baal (a miracle that occurs before Elijah retreats to Mt Horeb).

'In this place Moses escaped the Egyptians' treachery, tended Jothor's sheep,[109] and observed that miraculous sight, when he learned that a dry bush could be more resilient than all-consuming fire, and saw that green growth could blossom in the midst of flames.[110] Later, after leading his flock to it, he was appointed Lawgiver on this mountain, at that time for the Jews alone,[111] but now for every nation, since grace has spread through natural kinship to the entire [human] race.[112] For his ordinances on conduct[113] have shone forth from the lampstand on which they were placed, although once they were hidden under a bushel-basket of verbiage before they became clear.[114]

[III.17] 'Elijah came hither when he fled Jezebel. In this land he slept and rose to find a bread cake and a flask of water;[115] this is the cave he inhabited, having wrapped his body in a sheepskin mantle, the ancient garb of his ancestors.[116] Here he knew God in a soft breeze and heard a voice proclaiming His decrees.[117]

[III.18] 'But the first and final proof of the fortitude and perseverance of the men [i.e. of the monks][118] is this: they pass their entire lives in that same wilderness which caused the Israelites to grumble when they were just

---

109 Exod. 2:15–16.

110 Exod. 3:2.

111 Cf. Exod. 20–32.

112 κατὰ συγγένειαν τῆς φύσεως εἰς ὅλον τὸ γένος διελθούσης τῆς χάριτος, an unusual explanation for the success of Christianity.

113 οἱ θεσμοὶ τῆς πολιτείας. Perhaps 'ordinances of the community' i.e. 'constitution', in keeping with the description of Moses and Elijah as 'citizens' (πολῖται) at the beginning of this section.

114 Cf. Mt. 5:15: 'No one after lighting a lamp puts it under the bushel basket, but on the lampstand'; Mk 4:21, 'Is a lamp brought in to be put under the bushel basket, or under the bed, and not on the lampstand? For there is nothing hidden, except to be disclosed; nor is anything secret, except to come to life'; also Lk. 8:16–18 and 11:33. By 'hidden under a bushel-basket of verbiage' (ὑπὸ τῷ μοδίῳ τῆς λέξεως κεκρυμμένοι), Ps.-Nilus may mean Greek philosophy, which was often criticized by Christians as being wordy nonsense; otherwise he may be referring to the details of Hebrew Law presented in the books of Leviticus, Deuteronomy, and Numbers.

115 Cf. 1 [III] Kgs 19:6, where Elijah, having fled to Mt Horeb after offending Jezebel, is fed by an angel.

116 Cf. 1 [III] Kgs 19:9.

117 Cf. 1 [III] Kgs 19:13.

118 καρτερίας καὶ ὑπομονῆς τῶν ἀνδρῶν, 'fortitude and perseverance of the men': In Stoic and Christian discourse καρτερία and ὑπομονή became chief indicators of manly valour (ἀνδρεία): see Shaw 1996, 310. All three are identified with the mother of the Maccabees in IV Macc. 15:30. In Christian ascetic thought καρτερία and ὑπομονή were considered foundational virtues or 'weapons of Philosophy'. Cf. Anast., Narr. I.29.

passing through.[119] The Israelites cursed their tables when dined on ambrosial nourishment prepared in heaven.[120] They could not bear the absence of their overseer for forty days, nor did they know how to properly manage the freedom of choice that came with their liberty, for soon they rebelled and misused that license for the sake of impiety.[121] But these men [i.e. monks], though bereft of necessities, spend all their time philosophizing in the desert, being their own teachers of piety.'

[Narrative IV: Barbarian Raid and Slaughter of Monks]

[IV.1] 'It was against men of such character and so attentive to the divine that the phalanx of Barbarians fell so suddenly and unexpectedly, like a squall out of nowhere. The lawless ones attacked at break of dawn, just when the reverent ones had finished their sacred hymns. I happened to be there too with my boy, having come down from the Holy Mountain to visit the holy ones in [the church of] "the Bush",[122] as long had been my habit. They ran at us howling like mad dogs, shouting incomprehensibly as they plundered. They seized the food that had been gathered for the winter – for [the monks] set aside to dry whatever fruit can be preserved for that purpose – making us collect it and carry it ourselves.[123] Then they led us out of the church. After stripping off our ragged cloaks,[124] they ordered the oldest among us to line up, naked, for execution.

[IV.2] 'Next, some Barbarians nearby drew their swords, utterly enraged, eyes ablaze and glancing from side to side. They ordered the celebrant of the holy place[125] to stretch out his neck first. The two men [standing] beside

119 Initially the Israelites were just passing through the Sinai, then God condemned them to wander in its wilderness for forty years in punishment for their grumbling: Num. 14:20–35.

120 Cf. Num. 11:4–35, when the Israelites murmur about eating manna instead of meat.

121 Cf. Exod. 24:18 and 32:1–6, when the Israelites erect golden idols while Moses was away on Mt Sinai for forty days.

122 Egeria, *Itin.* IV.6–7, mentions seeing this church during her visit in 383, the earliest reference to it. Presumably the narrator had been at dawn prayers on the summit. By the late sixth century, monks performed a service there every morning (PP, *Itin.* 37).

123 Apparently the church was used at this time as a common storehouse for winter supplies, another indication that the text reflects early conditions: see Flusin 1998, 136–37.

124 κεντώνια, from Latin *cento*, a patchwork overcoat. For this and other forms of monastic garb, see Patrich 1995, 210–21.

125 The word ἱερεύς ('celebrant'), was an elevated term used for priests and bishops; here it refers to a priest (named Theodulus: see IV.14), and may have beeen meant to recall the title (ἱερεύς) of the Jewish martyr Eleazar of IV Macc. 5–6, on which this passage seems to have been based.

him did not strike at once, but took turns hacking away at his upper back from either side. The victim did not cry in pain, twist his face, or show any sign of anguish. All he said, as he sealed himself,[126] was "Blessed be the Lord", with a whisper from his mouth.[127] The first blow cut from his upper back to his jaw and ear; the second came down from his shoulder to his chest. After gently swaying, the blessed one fell with decorous poise: neither in being slain nor in being naked did he present any unsightliness, since his body glowed with a certain grace that covered the unseemliness of his nakedness.[128]

'Indeed, the holy one had nearly prophesied all this the previous evening both in word and deed. For he greeted with more than his usual welcome those who had gathered at dinner, saying, "Who knows if we shall all meet together again at one hearth and table before we die?"'

[**IV.3**] 'Next they slew the man who lived with that elder. He was also quite old, and had worn himself down by rather excessive labours of ascetic training. Then they killed the boy who attended them[129] in the following way.

'One of the Barbarians ordered him to pick up some fruit that had spilled to the ground. To please the one who had given this command, the boy quickly bent down and stretched out his hands to gather the scattered fruits as ordered. He showed the same eagerness to please as he always did in his ministrations, believing that he might be able to gain his life by appearing to be eager. But he gained nothing. He failed to soften their barbaric cruelty or coax them to be kinder – something far from likely. Another Barbarian standing behind him secretly pulled his sword from its sheath. Either sensing that a sword had been drawn or expecting his slaughter, the boy turned back his head in terror as if startled by a sound. While the one standing over him filled him with fright through his twisted

---

126 σφαγισάμενον, probably meaning that the monk made a cross on himself; it could also be translated 'as he received the seal', i.e. the seal of baptism (in this case, baptism by blood).

127 Cf. Ps. [123]:6, 'Blessed be the Lord, Who has not given us as prey to their teeth', cited by Climacus as uttered by dying monks whose penance made them hopeful of God's mercy, *Ladder* 5 (PG 88.773A). Cf. Ammonius, *Rel.* 29.

128 Cf. IV Macc. 6:2: 'First they stripped the old man, though he remained adorned with the seemliness of his piety.' This is the first of three subtle miracles found in Ps.-Nilus' narrative: the others are the preservation of the dead monks' bodies for five days (VI.10) and – if it be counted as a miracle – the saving of Theodulus (VII.3–9).

129 Such attendants were usually disciples who lived with and ministered to elder monks in exchange for spiritual training. Numerous Sinai structures with two or three rooms may reflect this arrangement: see Dahari 2000, 155. In some cases they were local laymen or even slaves, as attested in Egypt and perhaps implied here by the word παῖς: see Wipszycka 1996a, 358–59.

look and barbaric cry, the other, leaning down upon [the boy's] collar bone, thrust his sword most forcefully straight up, from [the boy's] diaphragm to his chest.[130] The boy rolled over dead before it was even pulled out. Either he died ahead of time through fright or died at the moment of the blow: either way, he was not aware that death would soon oust his soul from his corporeal cavities, instantly releasing it from the bonds that had so firmly constrained it in its mesh.

[**IV.4**] 'The rest of us they let go, though I do not know why. They ordered us to flee with a gesture of their hands, which were still clenching bloody swords. The others [i.e. the monks] ran through the ravines in a hurry to reach the mountain – for they [i.e. the Barbarians] do not approach it, in the belief that God once stood upon it and uttered commandments to His people[131] – but I remained where I was, completely still and transfixed, with my mouth open, unable to do anything. I could not leave my lad; his very vitals bound me to him. Held as I was by nature's bonds, I felt no urge to save myself, till the child signalled me to leave, gesturing with his eyes, gradually persuading me to go.

[**IV.5**] 'And so my feet moved forward, and somehow my whole body was borne and followed them. But my heart refused to budge: it constantly kept me turning to face the boy. I could not keep my eyes to myself; instead of looking straight forward where my feet were going, they kept piteously turning back. Finally, following those who had gone ahead, I proceeded towards the mountain.

'As I looked down I could see the poor boy being led away. Although he was not free to look around, he shot a glance towards me with his eyes without his captors knowing. And so it is with nature's bond: physical separation cannot sever it, but only make it stronger. For if a soul cannot be near its object of longing, it becomes vexed and distracted in the extreme, devoting all of its memory to what it wants, having no other means at hand

---

130 'Diaphragm' = literally, 'muscle from which the liver hangs' (ἀπὸ τοῦ ἡπατικοῦ κρεμαστῆρος). A sexual *double entendre* may be intended here: cf. Shaw 1996, 305. If so, it would add a subtext to the dangers threatening the magnanimous lad of V.14–17.

131 The lack of specific subjects for the verbs in this sentence (οὐ προσβαίνουσι γὰρ ἐκείνῳ δόξῃ τοῦ τὸν θεὸν ἐπ' αὐτῷ στῆναι καὶ χρηματίσαι ποτὲ τῷ λαῷ) makes unclear exactly which group refrains from approaching Mt Sinai because of their beliefs. Link contends that Ps.-Nilus refers to monks, arguing that it is unlikely that he would ascribe knowledge of Judeo-Christian tradition to barbarians; Link believes that the passage is based on Exod. 19:24, 'Let neither the priests nor the people come up to the Lord, otherwise he will break out against them.' This seems implausible, since it is clear in both this and the next section that the monks are the ones trying to reach Mt Sinai to escape danger.

to fulfil its desire. **[IV.6]** Only those who have experienced such separation can know how deep its anguish is, but those who have not experienced it can learn from the example of brute animals.[132] Animals are naturally endowed with an instinctive and dominant sympathy for their young, as are the young for their parents. Evidence of their affection is obvious in the clear signs of suffering they make at their parting. When, for example, a cow is led away from her calf, she begins to bellow incessantly with grief. She repeatedly looks back for her calf, declaring the enormity of her grief through the expression of her eyes. Since nature has not given brutes any other organs to express the passion that grips them, they rely on their eyes alone to attest their grief; with a clear clamour these bespeak, as it were, a condition that cannot be otherwise expressed. As for the calf, it can be separated only with difficulty, and will not submit to being led away by force: either it flees for protection to its mother's udders, as if to some sacred sanctuary, grasping for that asylum with its mouth, since it has no hands; or else it runs around in a circle, proclaiming its need by stomping its hooves, since it has not the power of speech to articulate its pain.

[IV.7] 'How I reached the mountain's peak I do not know. My mind was not moving in the same direction as my body; turning back to the boy, it kept following him as he was led away, contemplating his misfortune. Finally I could no longer see him, for a great expanse now hid him from view. Accordingly, since in all likelihood he was gone for good, I began to address God with words that expressed grief for my son's captivity and sadness for the holy ones slain:

> "O blessed and thrice-blessed men", said I, "Where now are your toils of abstinence? Where your feats of fortitude? Is this the victory you received for your great struggle?[133] Are these the prizes for your blessed contest?[134] Did you run the race for righteousness in vain? Is there no point in labouring for virtue? For divine Providence left you helpless just as you were about to be slaughtered. Justice did not oppose your killers. No, lawless hands prevailed against your saintly bodies; impiety can vaunt of victory over piety, as if it had vanquished truth itself.

---

132 IV Macc. 14:14–18 also draws on analogies from brute or 'unreasoning' animals (birds and bees) to explain the sympathy (συμπάθεια) and affection (στοργή) felt by human parents for children and vice-versa. Basil of Caesarea, *Homily on the Martyr Julissa* 4 (PG 31.248B) and Gregory of Nazianzus, *or.* XLIII.24 (PG 36.529B) also use the example of cows and calves to illustrate the pain of separation.

133 Cf. 1 Cor. 9:25, 'Those who contend, using every form of abstinence, will receive a victory wreath that perishes, but you will receive one that will not perish.'

134 Link proposes μακράς ('long [contest]') for Conca's μακαρίας ('blessed [contest]').

[IV.8] "Why didn't the Burning Bush burst into flame, as in the days of old?[135] Why didn't it burn the accursed ones with fireballs as they approached? Why didn't the earth split open and swallow them up, as it had once consumed all of Korah's band, together with its tents and kin?[136] Why did Mount Sinai keep its terrifying prodigies silent? It could have stunned the law-breakers with bursts of thunder, clouds of darkness, or brilliant flashes of lightning.[137] Instead the Avenging Power did nothing. Neither did it punish the unrighteous ones with thunderbolts or violent whirlwinds, nor did it shield with its strong hand the righteous ones who suffered, so that they too might experience a miracle and learn the incredible force of Invincible Power.[138] Instead, the pious ones fell helpless beside the very Bush itself and the mountain where the Law was given, just like sacrificial brutes.

"Where, then, was that Power which swept the Egyptians into the sea and quickly made its depths their tomb?[139] Where that Power that once granted its own flock an easy victory without bloodshed by pummelling that foreign tribe with hailstones as it made war upon the Israelites?[140] Where that Power that another time drove those men mad who were attacking the holy land and turned them against each other? Cast into darkness, they did not realize they were killing each other, or that those being slaughtered were their own.[141]

[IV.9] "When did that Power ever fail to show its promptness to lend aid or protect people in danger? Why, if once it quelled the rage of wild lions against those who were cast in their teeth and checked the overwhelming force of fire, so as to make the boys' piety known far and wide, as a reward for their venerable conduct[142] – why did it let these

---

135 Cf. Exod. 3:2.

136 Cf. Num. 16:31–33, when the Levite Korah and his followers revolted against Moses at Cadesh Barnea.

137 Cf. Exod. 19:16.

138 Cf. Dan. 6:15–25; 3:46–50; Heb. 11:33–34.

139 Cf. Exod. 14:27–28.

140 Cf. Josh. 10:11, where God aids Joshua against the Amorites: 'the Lord threw stones from heaven on them as far as Azekah, and they died. More died because of the hailstones than the Israelites killed with the sword.'

141 Reference unclear. Conca and Tzames–Katsanes cite Josh. 10:12–14, but there God makes the sun shine all day; Mayerson 1975, 63, cites 2 [IV] Kgs 6:18, but there God blinds Elisha's enemies, and they do not kill each other.

142 Cf. Dan. 6:16–22 (Daniel in the lions' den) and 3:19–29 (Shadrach, Meshach, and Abednego in the fiery furnace).

righteous ones be attacked on every side, left alone and utterly helpless, letting them be thought unworthy of concern?"

'But all of this was spoken in grief and rage, which can drive even those who strive for self-control to utter blasphemies in the face of misfortunes.[143] In such cases, emotion dominates judgment, prompting a grieving person to make many pronouncements that he does not want to say, perhaps because he is overwhelmed by the enormity of his circumstances. In fact, righteous men have often been left helpless and delivered to tyrants to be tortured with elaborate torments and unsanctified slaughter. That happens so that the fame and manly valour of those who contend might be made known, and so that the luminous power of their radiant faith might shine forth; for since their outspoken boldness remains unflagging unto death, they utterly vanquish in their suffering the madness of their tormentors.[144]

[IV.10] 'Even those who survived [the Barbarian's attack] did not want to withdraw from the desert, preferring death to the indifferent way of life [found] in the cities. Similarly, those who were slaughtered preferred to die instead of enduring the evils that are currently found in the inhabited world. They knew that the death of the soul was worse than physical death, and that death through sin is more perilous than dying by a sword. While the one brings slight and temporary pain, the other brings long, continuous punishment.

[IV.11] 'Eventually the Barbarians moved away, slaughtering and plundering many others in the desert. Nightfall enabled us to emerge. After descending from the mountain we turned to the task of burying the bodies. Those we found had been dead for a long time, but one holy man was still breathing and could still slightly speak.[145] We sat down beside him and lamented what had happened, keeping watch with him through the night.

[IV.12] 'The old man asked us to not be surprised by his hardship. "Satan is wont", he explained, "to request that God give him people to be tested. Consider how many of Job's own people he slew, some by fire, some by sword, others by collapsing their houses.[146] What happened should not trouble you", he continued, "because the Master of the Contest knows the stakes involved when He hands over athletes to the Opponent. Shining

---

143 Evagrius and others considered grief (λύπη) to be one of the most serious passions (or sins) to afflict a Christian.

144 This might be alluding to the Maccabees; cf. IV Macc. 10:5, 11:24–27, and Shaw 1996.

145 Literally 'the holy one', referring to the priest Theodulus who was killed in IV.2–3: see below, IV.14.

146 Job 1:16–19.

trophies and prizes He has set up for those who take their blows with a positive attitude, such as the great Job displayed – despite the fact that he received twice as many blows as might have been expected to kill him, far more, indeed, than anyone else has received.[147] For 'What no eye has seen, nor ear has heard, nor human heart has conceived, these God has prepared' for those who struggle in His behalf prizes for piety, things surpassing thought and perception.[148] It befits our munificent God to exceed our labours in the rewards that He gives, to surpass our struggles with the wreaths that He grants, and to offer His athletes things beyond their hopes or expectations. In this way, He not only pays out whatever wages are deserved, but also adds His grace as a reward of exceeding value.'

[IV.13] 'Thus spoke the old man, who embraced us with kisses while he had power to speak and move his tongue. Then he died. We put him in the ground with the rest and wept.

[IV.14] 'Then I came to you here [in Pharan] while it was still dark, which kept my arrival unseen.' Of those who were killed, two were named Paul and John, and the priest was Theodulus.[149] They died in perfection on the eighth day after Epiphany, on the fourteenth of January. For pious men are always interested in learning the names and date because they want to participate in the remembrance of holy ones. But others were also slain, many years earlier. Their commemoration is celebrated on the same day,[150] due to the length of the journey and number of people who attend.

[Narrative V: The Escaped Slave's Story]

[V.1] While we were speaking it was reported that someone had escaped from the [Barbarians'] camp. Soon he was with us. He showed the tracks of fear on his face, unable to control the turmoil within him. Greatly agitated,

---

147 Cf. Job 42:10, where God restored to Job 'twice as much as he had before'.

148 Isa. 64:4 and 52:15; quoted in 1 Cor. 2:9. Ps.-Nilus has substituted τοῖς ὑπὲρ αὐτοῦ ἠγωνισμένοις ('for those who have struggled in His behalf') for the scriptural τοῖς ἀγαπῶσιν αὐτόν ('for those who love Him'). TLG searches have found no parallel for this version.

149 Tsames–Katsanes maintain that πρεσβύτερος, here translated 'priest', simply means 'elder', and is used to distinguish the slain monk from the narrator's son. But surely these are the same three killed in IV.2–3. The preceding four sections (IV.11–14) together with sections below VI.11–12 are summarized in the ninth-century MS *Vaticanus syr.* 623 and translated below, pp. 136–37.

150 ἀνῃρέθησαν δὲ καὶ ἄλλοι πρὸ πλειόνων: These 'others' (ἄλλοι) must refer either to the martyrs recorded in the Sinai martyr inscription (see General Introduction, pp. 60–61), to those described in the Ammonius *Report*, or to both.

he was still panting heavily after his long run and ordeal: he was behaving as though his pursuers were close, and might at any moment catch up and kill him. **[V.2]** When asked how he had made his escape, this was what he said:

'Conversing over dinner, [the Barbarians] disclosed that they would sacrifice your child and me at daybreak to their star. They built an altar and put wood beside it, without us knowing why. Then a fellow captive who knew their language and secretly had overheard them told me what was going on. I informed your son about the Barbarians' plan, saying that unless we ran off to save ourselves, neither of us would be alive by sunrise, nor would our eyes see its rays.

'Although he feared to be left behind, nevertheless he chose to remain, saying that he could nowhere escape what God thought best, even if he hid in the most inaccessible places.

[V.3] 'So I waited for dark, until I saw that all had succumbed to sleep, for I knew they had imbibed deeply in drink. Then I moved slowly, crawling low on the ground at first so that my body would not cast a shadow that someone upon waking might see. After I had gone some distance from their camp, I ran straight here to my goal, carried fast on swift wings of fear. I reckoned that by running I would either escape or, if captured, would suffer no more than the death they intended for me, since they had already decided to execute me.

'In any case I preferred hope's uncertainty over something avowedly evil. **[V.4]** For while it was impossible to escape the danger of death by staying still, there was a chance to escape by entrusting salvation to the assistance of the feet. I knew that many had received more help from their feet than from the aid of myriads of protectors; for their feet cared for their salvation more than anyone else, since they sensed that any misfortune that befell the body as a whole would fall down upon them too. And behold! I did not err in my judgment. I saved myself by trusting in my feet, in addition to God. So here I am now with you, having suffered nothing at all, as you can see.

'Yet the Barbarians' terrifying savagery remains fixed before my eyes. I am stunned by their lawless acts, horrified at the sheer audacity of their deeds.

[V.5] My master was returning through the desert to you along with the community's commander after completing their service,[151] when they were

---

151 His 'master' (τὸν … δεσπότην τὸν ἐμὸν) is identified below (VI.10) as a member of the Pharanite council, named Magadōn. Mayerson 1975, 64, considers the στρατηγὸς τῆς πολιτείας to be a 'military official' (cf. Mason 1974, 155–59). However, by the end of the

seized by the Barbarians, who took all their possessions for themselves. Then, because he tried to resist, they cut down the commander and his servants, slicing them up limb by limb. But as for my master, they led him off, trailing behind together with his son – a boy quite young, as you know.

'When the sun was low on the horizon, they pitched their tents right there where evening found them. They set out a sumptuous banquet from the spoils they had seized from us, then invited my master and his lad to the feast. They encouraged him to take heart, saying that he had absolutely nothing to fear, that he and his boy were going to make it home safe and sound – or so they pretended – since the things they had seized from them were enough ransom for their two lives.

'Only a short time passed before they seemed ready to fulfil their promise. They allowed the two captives to fetch water and collect some bread for their rations. This they did so as to make their trickery seem more plausible, so that the hope of living on provisions might make their deceit trustworthy and their ruse seem true concern, so that their barbaric cleverness in the art of treachery might go totally undetected.

[**V.6**] 'Accompanying them as escorts were two young ephebes.[152] Ostensibly they were sent to provide security on the journey, but secretly they were ordered to kill the captives when they had reached a short distance from the camp. And so they escorted them in the pre-determined manner, walking on either side.

'Before the father, they killed his son. This was meant to double the father's torment by making him watch his son's murder and experience his

---

third century, a στρατηγός simply designated an officer imposed by the Roman government to administer a provincial town or city. A century later this position had been superseded by a *defensor civitatis*, a citizen chosen from the curial class to manage revenues: see Jones 1964, 2: 727–29 and Liebeschuetz 2001, 111–13. Thus Ps.-Nilus is using classicizing terminology, perhaps simply to designate the leading official, or headman, of Pharan (cf. Obedianus in Ammonius, *Rel.* 14).

The completed 'service' (τελέσαντας τὸ λειτούργημα) to which the passage vaguely alludes would probably have been the delivery of taxes (cf. Julian, *Or.* 1.21D), usually collected and delivered by associations of leading citizens. Until 364, they had to be delivered between November 22 and December 31. Thereafter, all but the annona had to be brought before January 1 (see Karayannopulos 1958, 89, *Theodosian Code* XI.19.3). If the massacre occurred on 14 January, we may surmise that the party was returning from delivering a tax due at Elusa, the administrative capital of Third Palestine, at the start of the year.

152 In classical Athens, an ephebe was enrolled in military training before becoming a full citizen. This classicizing term is used again in VI.9, where one manuscript adds a gloss: 'Ephebes mean those who have reached the prime of life, just over 14 years old'. See Cyril Scyth., *Life of Sabas* 14, for a similar tale of desert terror.

death. Then they slew him too with many blows, while his loud cries bewailed their faithlessness and deceitful ambush. I could hear one of them sobbing for mercy while the other was screaming in pain. He shrieked at every blow: you could gauge the executioner's progress by the tone of his voice.

[**V.7**] 'And so he came to a bitter end, led astray by specious promises. He should have divined these evils from those that others had suffered beforehand. He would have realized that it was no longer possible to escape death, but only to patiently endure what long had been expected. Evils cause most anguish when they come unanticipated; but anticipation makes horror easier to bear, since it finds the mind braced for the experience. Already contemplated many times before in thought, its arrival comes as no surprise to one who is well prepared.[153]

[**V.8**] 'For, [earlier] that evening, at dinner, while they were honouring him with toasts, they proposed to play a game that was customary and dear to them, murder and human execution being their intended delight. They offered one of his slaves a drink, then killed another right in front of him. Though forced to drink, the slave could barely do so because his appetite had been squelched with fear; yet fear made him drink all the same. The way he drank made clear that he was complying under compulsion; from his choking sounds it was apparent that he was drinking against his will. For the drink did not go down his throat in silence. It washed up in his mouth until his gulping forced it back down to his stomach with great difficulty and reverberations, as if crashing through a steep, narrow gorge. It was as though his throat had become petrified and could not compress with its usual force. So the drink just swashed back and forth and did not descend.

[**V.9**] 'Finally they dispatched a young man to slay him, for it is their practice to accustom young men to cruelty from childhood by entrusting them with executions. He sets upon his cruel task in a frenzy, and you could tell that he took pleasure in the act by the way he was laughing. First he stands over the slave who was on the ground. Next he strikes the back of the slave's neck, but that makes only a slight gash because of the hardness of the bones beneath. So he draws his sword back up to the slave's mouth and sliced it from side to side, then strikes a second time below the place where he had made the first blow. Then he comes back, leaping up and down, brandishing his sword in his hand against the air.

'The slave convulsed frantically in pain, writhing in blood and howling.

---

153 Cf. Achilles Tatius I.3.3. Link notes that the idea expressed here corresponds to the Stoic notion of *praemeditatio* (cf. Marcus Aurelius, *Meditations* II.1).

Finally he brought his head to his stomach and drew in his knees as if intending to spring up from that position. He tumbled onto burning coals that lay scattered around. The pain he felt from the fire was naturally even greater, and so he began convulsing again, flapping his hands and feet like a fish, frantically trying to keep up in the air the parts of his body that were burnt. No longer able to help himself – for that capacity had left along with his blood – he was consumed by the flames. In this way he perished, tormented by the twin punishments of fire and sword at once.

[V.10] 'The day after this drama [the Barbarians] resumed the journey. It being desert, there was no direct road; they wandered, and here and there were forced to turn by rugged terrain. They circled around high mountains and passed through trackless, impenetrable ravines. Far off in the distance they saw a smooth, grassy place. From its greenness they guessed that they would find either a spot good for camping, or else some of the solitary [monastic] folk[154] dwelling nearby. So they steered their pack animals towards this goal as if to a harbour from the open sea.

'Upon reaching the spot, they found that it did not fail their expectations nor, like a mirage, had given them false hope. There was plenty of clean water, the sight of which pleased the eye with its purity even before it was tasted, but once brought to our mouths, the delight of seeing it proved lesser by far than the joy of drinking it. [V.11] There also being pasturage for animals to graze on, [the Barbarians] took off their packs and let the camels roam free, while they themselves rushed to the water. They drank it, splashed in it, and bathed in it as if they simply could not decide how to make use of its profusion.

'But as they were dancing and singing around the spring, they saw the trace of a dwelling beneath the foot of a mountain. So all ran up to it breathlessly, each striving to get there first. When they drew near, they surrounded the cave; for the dwelling consisted of some stones constructed around the mouth of a cave, built to prevent any easy access to wild beasts through a gaping hole.[155] [V.12] A few [Barbarians] ran into the cave, entering single file (there was not room for many) and brought forth a man of distinguished composure and appearance, who neither cried out nor turned pale as they trailed him along behind. They laid him down on a rock, and since no swords were at hand, they stoned him to death, laughing and singing a victory song.

---

154 Using the elipsis τινὰς τῶν μοναδικῶν, here as elsewhere studiously avoiding the common word 'monk' (μοναχός).

155 Archaeologists have found numerous hermitages of such construction on the Sinai peninsula: see Dahari 2000, *passim*.

[V.13] 'Then a short distance from that place they seized the other [resident of that cell], a youth. Pale and worn out, he bore the tracks of his discipline on his face. Him they likewise laid hands on and slew without a sword. As they did so, he raised his voice in thanksgiving and professed his gratitude to them for ending his life while he still possessed virtue. For, as he explained, he had greatly feared the uncertainty of his life's end, lest a slip in his judgment or some external force deflect him from his original commitment and, either by persuasion or compulsion, make him take care for things that were contrary to the vows he had made to God.

[V.14] 'We had not advanced far when, behold! we saw another spot that looked green – the trees in the area made it look that way. Again there was a rush of Barbarians and contest to get there fastest. When they reached it, they found a small dwelling, and in it a mere lad, whose nobility and magnanimity were such that even the Barbarians were amazed. He refused, in return for his safety, to reveal where other dwellings of solitaries were hidden, nor was he willing to leave his quarters or to take off his little tunic.[156] It would be a betrayal, he said, for him to offer information about those who were able to escape, and it would be unmanly and ignoble to submit to whatever was ordered by violent men. As he explained,

> "It is sacrilegious for those who train themselves in magnanimity to yield to fear, even if a threat appears and presents no small danger. For habit can lead to greater danger: once cowardice learns how to dictate us, it can convince us to despise even major virtues and teach us to betray piety itself. So it is, whenever fear discovers that a person's disposition has become prone to cowardice.
>
> **[V.15]** "If I were now prompt to relinquish my reasoning power's self-governance and self-determination,[157] in fear lest I might otherwise die on the spot, how would I not defect to impiety when torments are set before me with the threat of torture, having already conditioned myself to prefer what is painless to what is best?
>
> "So, since you have failed to get what you hoped, do not hesitate to do what you wish. For neither would I reveal to you the places where God's dear ones dwell – know them though I do – nor shall I, while I still

---

156 'dwellings of solitaries' translates μοναστήρια.The victims were also stripped before execution in IV.1.

157 Christian theorists believed that self-determination or 'free will' (αὐτεξουσιότης, cf. IV Macc. 2.21) was a divine gift that allowed humans to make moral choices and reap rewards of good choice: e.g. Palladius, *Dialogue on the Life of John Chrysostom* XX.330–39. On the power of self-governance (αὐτοκράτεια), see above, II.2.

have my senses and am lord of my resolve, come out past my door or take off my clothing as you command, lest someone might see me naked, and view a body that till now has been invisible even to my own eyes. **[V.16]** "Of course, once I am dead, anyone can do to my senseless body whatever he wants. Then no longer can there be reproach against me on the grounds that I failed in my resolve; I will involuntarily suffer a mere lack of sensation, once my capacity to reason has departed, along with its ability and obligation to oppose. For that which is lifeless is bereft of sensation; that which has no sensation has no sense of suffering; and that which senses nothing is assuredly free from recriminations over what it experiences, having lost the means either to suffer or not.

"Therefore I shall die here, inside and fully clothed, as I have decided. I shall do nothing against my will, like some chattel slave under a tyrant. In this, the wresting ring where I have struggled, let me also be slain. These quarters shall be my tomb. Having long received the sweat of my toil for virtue, let it now receive the blood of my gallantry."[158]

[V.17] 'The villains could not bear hearing him speak so boldly. Galled by his noble disposition, they slew him like madmen; under so many blows, his body split apart. Each wanted to vent his rage upon him. None believed the previous daggers had delivered enough retribution, unless he could relieve his vexation with his own hand by dipping his sword in the slaughter. Most of those who set upon the magnanimous [lad] were ravaging a corpse rather than a living man. After their departure they continued seething with rage, because the body they punished offered no more material for abuse.

[V.18] 'Then we met three men travelling across the desert. The encounter helped quench the wrath that still simmered within the Barbarians, for they inflicted on these men what remained of their fury against that [lad]. As wild beasts or hunting dogs become all the more frenzied when their quarry gets away, then chase it with great zeal when it falls again on their path, using the second chance to make up for their prior slackness, so too did these foul murderers rush towards those who appeared. They drew their swords before they were near and slaughtered them as soon as they came close. With such great savagery did they fall upon them that you might have thought that they again had caught that [lad] who had galled them so.

[V.19] 'While standing there with swords dripping hot, steaming blood, clutched bare in their hands, they saw two monastic cells in the direction of our travel. They were not directly in front of us, but just off our path, one

---

158 ἀνδραγαθία, perhaps 'manly virtue': see VI.6–8 below and notes *ad loc.*

on the left and one on the right, about thirty stades apart from each other,[159] but fifteen from us: each was the same distance from where we stood, like points on a circumference measured from the centre of a circle.

'And so [the Barbarians] split into two groups. Each left the booty it was carrying on the ground with the pack animals and headed off towards one of the two. I know not how the place to the south was taken, nor whom in it they killed. But the one on the northern slope sensed we were coming, hearing the rattle of arrows in their quivers as we approached. Pulling back their bows, they pierced him with multiple arrows as he started to flee. They seized him where he had fallen, face down. They did not leave him to die from the wounds he had already received – though certainly he had enough for that – but while he was still breathing and gasping for air, they rolled him onto his back and began slicing him open from the groin to the chest. As his guts gushed out through the gash and flowed out over his ribs,[160] the Barbarians churned them up with long sticks on both sides, completely disembowelling him before they departed.

[**V.20**] 'After these acts I myself ran off, as I've said already. I do not know what befell your boy who stayed behind. Though still alive when I left, he had no real hope of living, since they were whispering about his death.'

[Narrative VI: A Mother's Threnody, Embassy to Ammanes, Journey to Elusa]

[**VI.1**] When I heard what he said, a nightmare came back fresh to haunt me. You see, I had dreamt that I was reading a letter that a certain acquaintance had just delivered to me. Still unfurled, it had the following address on its outer fold: 'To my father and master after God, from the Blessed Theodulus…'[161]

Oh, how deeply stricken was my soul – if even indeed I still had a soul! I felt my heart cut up and my innards torn out; I lost all my strength, and every limb fell slack, as I heard the slave's story, and saw how it corresponded to my dream. It left no ambiguity or doubt about [Theodulus'] end. My

---

159 About 5.5 km/3 miles from each other; Ps.-Nilus is using μοναστήρια ('monastic cells') in the early sense of solitary dwellings or cells; cf. above, V.14, and Egeria, *Itin*. III.1, IV.5.

160 I follow Henrichs' suggested emendation ἀναπεδήσαντα ('gushed out'), accepted by Link, for Conca's ἀναπνεύσαντα, in which case the translation would be 'as his guts began to breathe out through the gash…' Henrichs refers to the text of Achilles Tatius III.15.4: see n. 82.

161 Dreams and the receipt of letters are commonly used as foreshadowing devices in ancient romance.

suspicions were confirmed, now made credible by the double witness [of the report and the dream].[162]

After that I did not weep or lament, but just stared at him with eyes open wide, without blinking, as if stunned by the sudden sound of clashing storm clouds.[163] **[VI.2]** For the inner power that governed my eyeballs was paralysed within me, and was utterly incapable of performing its natural function of steering those faculties of sight, leaving them motionless. Indeed, my grief was so excessive that despite their dilation they sensed no more than if they were stones. Tears were stifled deep within me too, condensed by heavy breathing that checked the progress of their moisture to my eyes.[164]

Yet, by divine Providence, I was gradually brought out of that stupor by a woman of that region whose son happened to be the lad who was slain.[165] Those who had managed to escape the calamity had reported the names of the dead. When she learned that her child had been a victim and how nobly he had struggled against his attackers, she revealed her kinship to him through her acts, proving her to be his genuine mother. **[VI.3]** For though the clothes she wore were bright, the expression she put on was brighter,[166] and with hands outstretched towards heaven she raised to her Saviour God such words as follows:

'To You, Oh Master, I commended my child, and he has been preserved for me, both now and forever. To Your hands I entrusted my lad; and he has been protected, truly safe and sound. For I do not reckon him dead, or think he has somehow been lost, but that he has escaped all temptation

162 The letter's description of Theodulus as 'blessed' (μακάριος) implied that his death was now certain (as was a divine reward for his sufferings).

163 A similar reaction is described in Achilles Tatius, III.15.5: 'I, contrary to all reason, just sat there staring. It was sheer shock: I was simply thunderstruck by the enormity of the calamity.' Trans. Winkler 1989b, 216.

164 Cf. Achilles Tatius, III.11.1–2: 'I could not weep … on occasions of overwhelming unhappiness, tears simply fail, deserting the battle and leaving the eyes alone; for as the tears arise within, they are met by grief, which checks their progress along the path to the eyes and carries them down again, condensing in a steady stream, into the soul.' Trans. Winkler 1989b, 214.

165 I.e. the magnanimous lad slain in V.17.

166 Fourth-century preachers redefined death as an occasion for celebration rather than mourning: see Alexiou 2002, 29–33, and Samellas 2002, 70–114. In his oration *In Praise of Caesarius* 15 (*Or.* VII; PG 35.773), Gregory of Nazianzus says that at his brother's funeral, his mother had put on festive dress, stifled her tears with philosophy, and replaced her sad laments with happy psalms. For Ps.-Nilus' depiction of the Pharanite mother, compare IV Macc. 14:11–17:11, 18.7–19, and Gregory of Nazianzus, *On the Maccabees and their Mother* 9 (*Or.* XV; PG 35.925C–928D).

to sin. I do not think about his body lying bludgeoned or that he suffered a bitter end, but that he brought You his soul, pure and unblemished, committing to Your hands his spirit immaculate.

[VI.4] 'I reckon those wounds to be prizes, I count the blows as victory wreaths: would that your body had had room for still more, so that more would have been your wages! With those wages, repay me for my pregnancy; with those wreaths, requite me for my birth pangs; with those prizes, honour me for nursing you!

'Share with me the trophies of your toils, for suffering was something common to us both. Yours was the struggle, and I revelled in the wounds of your struggle; Yours was the contest, and I cheered as you competed. You took your stand against the Barbarians' wrath; I made war against nature's tyranny. You scorned death – I spurned my innermost feelings; You bore with patience the pain of execution – I endured the torment of having my innards torn up. Mine were equal and no less than yours: You, through bitter pain, attained victory; I, through passage of time, will have even more. If the agony you suffered was excessive, your death came in a moment; but I will long be wrenched with anguish, even if I bear it respectably well, like a philosopher.[167]

[VI.5] 'It is not that I am insensitive to suffering: only that I have forced myself to master my pain. My anguish comes from the breaking of my visceral bonds and the ripping of the walls of my womb. Yet with sober reason I repress feelings that arise from these. For what use is manic sorrow, since nature permits no return to the departed?

'Wherefore I have not imitated mothers of fleshly offspring who ignobly make emotional displays amid such disasters. I have not emulated women who give birth to bodies and think it the only form of existence, who know nothing of the life to come, and think it something hard to be separated from ones dear to them in the present. I have not rent my gown, have not beaten bared breasts with my hands, have not torn out my hair, nor disfigured my face with my fingernails.[168] For I thoroughly believe that you are living your life unharmed in God, and that in not much time I will have you as a support for my old age there, whenever and in whatever way this clay vessel be shattered.

---

167 In ancient Christian conception, a 'philosopher' was someone whose spiritual and moral training enabled him or her to overcome physical or emotional adversity; it also became synonymous with 'monk'.

168 The foregoing lines recall Gregory of Nazianzus' *On the Maccabees and their Mother* 9 (PG 35.928AB): 'I will not tear out my hair, not tear my gown, not rip my flesh with fingernails … for these are the acts of ignoble mothers, who are only mothers of fleshly offspring…'

[VI.6] 'Blessed among mothers am I, to present such an athlete to God. Blessed and thrice blessed, for your departure now truly emboldens me to boast, when formerly I had feared for you, lest envy cause hardship for me and devise danger for your soul. But go, my child, go forth on your pleasant journey, go! For I would not concede first place to the patriarch Abraham, not if I were judged beside him, nor would I cherish taking second place after him because he, when ordered, eagerly and dispassionately offered up his son as a sacrificial victim to God. For, it is not clear that he would have remained so dispassionate after the burnt offering had been made.[169] Many have kept their resolve firm while doing a deed, but once it was done, they broke down in grief, proving the weakness of their nature by their change of heart. But I now am acting with a man's valour,[170] having changed my expression of grief to one of good cheer, whereas others have proven inferior to their suffering, overpowered by time; because the strength of their fortitude is gradually diminished by the duration [of time], as memory renews their anguish and frees them to reflect with leisure upon their grievous suffering. For it is hard, yea, exceedingly difficult to keep a correct decision completely unchanged over a great length of time, since the power of reason can be easily swayed to the opposite of what it once thought was best.

[VI.7] 'Once I bemoaned becoming a widow, and the absence of your father's guardianship made me groan as if helpless. But why need I weep now, why wallow in grief, when I have such an advocate before God? From there he can defend me in ills and provide my old age and grey hairs unstinting support: for now he has authority to tap into an everlasting flow of grace, and bathe me more gloriously than were he living here still and commanding royal treasuries. Those treasuries have limited reserves which, once spent, run dry; but when grace rains down, it gushes forth with an abundant supply that will never cease.'

[VI.8] At these words I became overwhelmed with shame at having reacted so effeminately and ignobly to my own son's suffering, and felt ashamed for appearing before bystanders to be inferior to a woman in manly valour.[171] I looked on her with admiration and on myself with scorn, receiving that

169 I.e. if Abraham had sacrificed Isaac instead of what happens in Gen. 22.

170 The Greek is genderized: ἀνδρίζομαι ('acting with a man's valour', almost 'being a man'). See VI.8 and next note.

171 ἥττων γυναικὸς εἰς ἀνδρείαν. For gender issues involved cf. Moore and Anderson 1998. For the role of women as a device for shaming men into proper behaviour, see Clark 1998.

noble woman's words like blows to the face as I compared my mania to her self-control. I had thought that the charges I had made against God for the things I had suffered had been justified, but I knew I had erred when, by the woman's example, I learned that every onslaught can be borne, however dire. For when comprehension collapses into desolation by the belief that something is unbearable, it often can be restored to affirmation by the sobriety of someone who has suffered much the same, whose calm control of suffering teaches one not to give in so easily to one's own.

[VI.9] After hearing our reports, it seemed best to the council of those who inhabited Pharan not to bear the atrocity in silence, but to make it manifest to the King of the Barbarians.[172] And so, in order to declare the violation of their treaty with him, they dispatched two swift-couriers, as they are called.[173] These are young men, slightly surpassing ephebes in age, who are just beginning to grow their beards,[174] and are often made to serve such purposes, taking with them nothing more than bows, arrows, pikes, and some flints to set fires. These would help them survive their journey: the pikes would help them kill their quarry and the flints would furnish fire to roast it. Everywhere would be kindling in abundance, since no one harvests the timbers that grow in the desert.

[VI.10] As they set off on their journey, we set off to collect the corpses. We arrived to find that the slain men, although now five days dead, had not suffered anything that corpses so old usually suffer: neither putrefaction, nor decay, nor mutilation, nor the carnage usually made by carrion birds or wild beasts. Yet it had also been noted by Magadōn's boy (Magadōn being the name of the council member[175] whom the Barbarians had murdered)

172 Ps.-Nilus uses the language of city council decrees (Ἔδοξεν οὖν τῇ βουλῇ τῶν τὴν Φαρὰν οἰκούντων ...).'King of the Barbarians' (τῷ βαρβάρων βασιλεῖ): By the early fourth century, the Greek title βασιλεύς had been adopted by leaders of Arab nomads: see Littmann 1914, 37–40 (inscription no. 41). Shahid 1989, 138, identifies this king (called 'Ammanes' below, VI.17) as the phylarch charged with keeping order among Arab tribes in Sinai and the Negev. It is notable that no bishop or other church official is mentioned as being involved in these deliberations and embassy, as would have been normal by the sixth century. This suggests that Ps.-Nilus was writing before any such officials were in Pharan (where no bishop is attested before the middle of the fifth century).

173 Literally 'day-runners' (ἡμεροδρόμοι), a classicizing term first attested in Herodotus VI.105 and frequently found in Libanius' Declamations.

174 See above, n. 152.

175 βουλευτής, 'council member': cf. above, V.5–6. Shahid 1989, 135 n. 11, suggests the name Magadōn derived from the Arabic root MJD, 'glory', and suffix -ūn (as in Arabic names such as 'Kaldūn').

that the corpses had lain there so long. There was Proclus in the region of Bēthrambē; Hypatius in Geth; Isaac in the Salaēl monastery; Macarius and Mark, both killed in the outer desert; Benjamin in the area outside Ailim; Eusebius at Thōla and Elijah at Azē.[176]

Of the two, we found the second still alive despite many wounds.[177]

[**VI.11**] After lifting him up and placing him in a cell, we turned to the burial of the other bodies. When later we returned, we reached him living no longer, but found his corpse lying beside his vessel of water. The inflammation of his wounds had made him thirsty; after taking a drink he had fallen forward on his knees, and in that position his soul left him dead.[178] So we gave him the funeral rites we had given the rest, then went back to learn what news had been brought from the Barbarian leader.

As we reached Pharan the messengers returned, delivering an answer in writing from [the Barbarian leader]. He confirmed the peace, inviting whoever had been harmed to come to him, especially any relatives of captives who might still be alive. He furthermore said that if anyone wanted to exact justice on behalf of those who had been murdered, he was ready to surrender the ones responsible for punishment; as for the booty, he agreed to give it all back to whoever had been robbed. He informed us that he did not want to dissolve the terms of the peace,[179] since he cherished the treaty he had with [the Pharanites] on account of the relief he received from them.[180] For his dealings with them brought no small profit to his people, who were helped in their want of necessities by [the Pharanites'] prosperity.

Therefore [the Pharanites] prepared gifts and selected envoys to reinstate

176 For possible identification of these sites based on modern place names, see Dahari 2000, 156–57; but there is no guarantee that ancient place names and locations are accurately preserved in modern names. Only Bēthrambē, Thōla, and Ailim are attested in other ancient texts: Bēthrambē presumably being the Gethrambē in Ammonius, *Rel.* 4 (perhaps Dayr Rabba, about 1 km/0.5 miles south-west of Mt Sinai); Thōla was where John Climacus and others lived in the early seventh century, 8 km/5 miles west of Mt Sinai. Ailim is probably the scriptural Elim (cf. Exod. 15:27), but Dahari thinks it was just another monastery near Sinai. 'In the Salaēl monastery' translates ἐν τῇ μονῇ Σαλαήλ. Nothing is known about it.

177 A wonderfully vague reference, probably to Eusebius and Elijah just mentioned, though Heussi 1917, 153 n. 5, thought it referred to Macarius and Mark.

178 To find a hermit dead in a fixed position of kneeling at prayer was a *topos* in late antique hagiography.

179 Using elevated diction, οἱ τῆς εἰρήνης θεσμοί.

180 In late Greek the word 'relief' (παραμυθία) was a euphemism for material sustenance or stipend: cf. Lampe 1961 *s.v.* Apparently it refers here to protection money or tribute paid to a local bedouin leader. For speculation concerning this treaty (an 'exceptional *foedus*'), see Shahid 1989, 498–99.

the broken peace. They sent them the next day, and we set as well – for now, you see, we had real hope.

[VI.12] The journey took twelve days in all.[181] On the eighth day, our water ran out. Driven by great thirst, we soon expected to meet the death that lurks wherever there is scarcity. But those familiar with the region said there was a spring nearby,[182] and this raised our spirits. We were wasting away, but anticipation of what was to come helped us escape the evil before us. For imaginary hope can sustain no less than truth; utter desperation may be nourished on high expectations held out by hope's hand, so as to revive energies that had completely expired.

[VI.13] Many ran eagerly ahead, hoping to find the spring before the rest arrived, so as to freely indulge in what they needed and desired. One went this way, one went that, each heading off in whichever direction hope of success led them, peering off in the distance, squinting with their eyes to make the discovery, just as we do when looking for something hidden to the eye with a lamplight.

I followed behind those who ran ahead. Someone might say that, due to feeble old age, I could not keep up with those in better health than I; but I would say that I was unwilling to offend my dignity by running around in such disorderly fashion. For I still had as much strength as I needed, since the force of compulsion is wont to mobilize a body when it has no power of its own, propelling it into motion beyond its natural capacities.

[VI.14] The spring happened to be in the direction in which I was heading, but it was obscured by a hilltop in front of me. Leaving the others here and there, I advanced up the hill, guessing I would soon discover the spring in one spot or another nearby. As soon as I got over the hill and reached the other side, I was the first to see it – but then I saw Barbarians spread out around it.

I was neither distressed nor disturbed by the surprise of falling on enemies of such savage nature. I found myself caught somewhere between fear and joy, and comforted myself by thinking that perhaps I was lucky. For, I told myself, either I would find my son living among them and gladly become enslaved with him – rejoicing at the desired sight of him, making the burden of slavery the price I paid for that joy – or else I would be

---

181 Ps.-Nilus envisions that the expedition headed north to the Negev via a central route through the Tih desert, probably the same route used by the Piacenza Pilgrim. See Mayerson 1963, 163; 1982, 46–47; and PP, *Itin.* 35–36. The 'swift couriers' travelled more rapidly: cf. IV.10–11.

182 Perhaps 'Ain Qusayma or 'Ain Qadeis in northern Sinai: thus Mayerson 1963, 163; Woolley and Lawrence 1936, 70–88.

slaughtered, and my grief would be brought to an end.

[**VI.15**] The Barbarians leapt up and raced headlong towards me, but I just stood still as if in deep concentration. They seized me and dragged me ruthlessly behind. Those who were sent to find water with me saw what was happening, but having not been seen themselves, they silently turned around and retreated undetected, scampering hastily like lizards on all fours to conceal their flight. But I was pulled in all directions and dragged on the ground. What abuse I suffered! Yet in spite of it all I did not utter a word or even take notice of what was happening to me: my mind was wholly distracted with looking for my lad. My eyes were turning, scanning, searching in every direction, frequently making me think I saw him in images they formed from the shapes that passed before them. For often our eyes seem to see things that are already impressed on our imagination, since our mind envelopes everything we see with the forms we yearn to find.

[**VI.16**] Not much time had passed in these circumstances when behold! the warriors of your forces arrived.[183] Their appearance at the top of the hill threw the Barbarians into great confusion and alarm. As soon as the warriors signalled their approach with a war cry, no one remained where he was. Suddenly the whole place appeared bare to the eyes, although just a moment ago it was teeming with bodies. Every [Barbarian] tried to save himself by taking flight: each ran off wildly, as if pursued by panic itself, leaving all else behind. So great was their fright at the sight that befell them after feeling so secure, that in their concern for capture they did not even turn back to look on their pursuers, but left them following with swords drawn ever far behind. These they believed to be wounding some, slaying many, and making the clamour that they themselves were making. Finally the distance that they gained in flight gave them liberty to catch a breath, look around, and gaze upon their pursuers. For fear tends to make us imagine what befalls us is greater in force and magnitude than it actually is, making cowardice increase beyond what circumstances really require.[184]

When they arrived, these [pursuers] found the things that those who fled had left behind. They took great delight in these provisions and remained there the rest of the day.

183 οἱ ὑμετέρας δυνάμεως μάχιμοι. Conca and Link's ὑμετέρας ('your'), though found in all the manuscripts, is odd, since in this section the narrator is no longer addressing anyone. Hence PG. 79.668 prints ἡμετερας ('our'). In any case the sudden appearance of these warriors is puzzling: either they represent a previously unmentioned escort from Pharan (cf. Ammonius, *Rel.* 33) or Roman *limitanei* from the Negev, posted near the spring.

184 Cf. John Clim., *Ladder* 21, on 'unmanly cowardice' and its origin in anticipated rather than actual dangers.

[VI.17] Another four days of travel passed before we reached the encampment.[185] Our envoys were announced and summoned to meet with Ammanes (that was the name of the Barbarian king).[186] Having brought gifts, they received a kind response. He gave them a tent next to his own and refreshed them with considerable courtesy, while an exact inquiry established clearly what had been stolen during the raid. All this was done in a short time, but all the while my heart pounded with palpitations as I awaited their report. Every sound seemed to ring with rumours regarding the one I sought. My ears were straining to hear every voice, ready to welcome as a herald any sound at all, whether it proclaimed him dead or alive. For he who has no information about something he keenly seeks will become torn with doubt, and will flit anxiously in instability from one proposition to another, until a clear exposition of the truth frees him from his fearful suspense and settles his mind, which had been made distraught because nothing was said.

[VI.18] But the envoys returned hardly bright in their faces. 'No need to speak', said I, guessing that their dark look reflected grim news. 'Your face portends misfortune in its countenance; it proclaims my suffering before you open your mouth; it foretells by its expression what you are going to say in words. I will not be fooled by specious declamations, nor be misled by sentences sophistically fashioned to sound nice and true. Perhaps you have patched together some attractive explanation to comfort me, wanting to hide sad truths for a while with seductive lies. But I will pay no attention to words that can be deceptively formed to sound plausible. I can see on your face the feelings in your soul.

---

185 Ps.-Nilus locates the 'barbarian' camp in the northern Sinai, close to the inhabited regions of the Negev (VI.19–22). This most probably would have been at 'Ain al-Qudayrat, traditional site of Cadesh Barnea (where the Israelites camped, Num. 11–20), about 40 km/25 miles (one day's travel) south-east of Nessana, which had the best perennial supply of water in the north-western Negev: see Abel 1924, 57. Since there is no evidence of Roman inhabitation, Mayerson 1987b, 242, suggests that it always remained in bedouin hands. Shahid 1989, 138, thinks a phylarch was stationed here to defend the northern Negev.

186 According to Shahid 1989, 137, the name *Ammanes* 'rings authentic as an old archaic Arab name … It could be related to the Arabic root *A-M-N* meaning "to be faithful, reliable, safe, trustworthy", and its morphological pattern is that of the intensive form in view of the double "m" in Ammanes … It is tantalizing to think that the name could be a mutilated form of Dahmān, which appears in the onomasticon of the kings of Salīh, the dominant Arab federate group in Oriens in this century.' The name *Ammayu* is attested for Nabataean priests in Sinai inscriptions found at Jaba al-Moneijah outside Pharan: Negev 1977, 222, 224. Of course, the use of a name that sounds historically authentic, regardless of whether it is or not, is typical of Greek and Jewish fiction.

'For the face is an image of the soul: its surface bears the distinct stamp of what is happening deep within. It is not natural for it to employ an artificial expression so as to project any other disposition than that which is concealed in one's soul. Our speech [on the other hand] can report even sad things brightly with ease if we want. We can wrap our utterances in graceful phrases to craft whatever impression we want, just as an ugly courtesan conceals her natural appearance through the cosmetic arts of ornamentation, transforming reality through seductive coloration. But the face cannot disguise how one's soul feels. It serves as a trusty informant on what cannot be seen; its countenance brings hidden intentions out to the open; it cannot sweeten sad news with forced smiles, any more than a mirror can make a face look rosy or bright if its expression is gloomy and dark, since that is the way it looks inside.

'Therefore, please tell the unadulterated truth, realizing that it has already been foretold by your faces, as I've just said. What advantage is there in deluding a grieving person for a short time with false encouragement, if he will become even more distressed once the bitter truth is finally disclosed?'

[**VI.19**] They assured me with many adjurations that [Theodulus] had not died, but was still alive, having been sold to someone in the city of Elusa. They advised me to set off, saying that there was where I would find my son. This allayed my grief a little, though not entirely. For, I reasoned, even if they dispelled my most dire fear – that he was dead – what good was it for him to be alive, if after being sold as a slave he would no longer be free to live with me? For compulsion hardly makes our pleasure pure; it stands in the way, impeding our impulse to pursue our preference, with someone else constraining our freedom of will. It is natural for the soul to exult in self-determination; it likes to indulge in whatever it chooses, without being forced to serve as a slave against its volition.

[**VI.20**] Nevertheless I later set out for the city they mentioned along with two guides they had given me. Down the road we met a youth who came following us, his donkeys laden with packs. He had seen me at the camp and knew all about my circumstances. Indeed, he had been in Elusa and had heard conversations about my son. Having learned how he had been taken captive by the Barbarians, he had informed [Theodulus] about my situation; having been given a letter, he had come to convey it to me as good news from him. Upon seeing me off in the distance, he had begun to approach me, smiling.

As for me, upon reflection I realized that this youngster's appearance had been foreshadowed; at a glance I could tell that he was not a complete stranger.[187] He greeted me with a bright look on his face, not like someone unknown to me. Reaching to his back with his right arm, he put his hand over his shoulder and with his fingers drew a letter out of his quiver. He gave it to me with the good news that my boy was alive.

He exhorted me to take cheer and not lower my hopes because of his enslavement. For the one who had purchased him was a celebrant of the Divine Mysteries of Christ,[188] and the boy had already been selected for initiation to the ranks of the priesthood. At present he had been entrusted with the first level of duties performed by temple-sweeps,[189] but his zeal indicated at once that he could have great expectations of advancement. In a short time he had given considerable proof of his virtues, and this had convinced everyone to approve his election, induced to do so by his goodly manners.

[VI.21] Being both penniless and homeless, I repaid [the youth] gladly with words, praying that he might enjoy great prosperity, having nothing else with which to reward his good service to me. I attributed all, however, to the God of Providence, tearfully rendering the thanksgiving due for this unexpected joy, since He had begun to resolve a calamity that had seemed so unlikely of remedy, restoring to us our former good fortune.

[VI.22] And so on my arrival in the city I first entered the holy temple in search of the one responsible for these good things, in order to pay the honours due him.[190] I filled God's sanctuary with loud lamentations and drenched the pavement with tears. From there I was guided to the house in which my child resided. Many had already gone there ahead, eager to be first to announce the happy news of my arrival. Everyone knew from advance reports that I was the much-discussed father of the one they had

187 I.e. he was the acquaintance in the dream mentioned above, VI.1. Dreams fulfilled in an unexpected manner are especially common in Achilles Tatius.

188 Here 'celebrant' (ἱερεύς) refers to a bishop: see VII.17. A bishop from Elusa signed the acts of Council of Ephesus in 431, the earliest attestation of its bishop on official record.

189 τὰς πρώτας … τῶν νεωκόρων ὑπηρεσίας. The term νεωκόρος ('temple-sweep') refers to any church attendant assigned menial tasks: the late fourth-century *Apostolic Constitutions* VIII.21.3 identifies them with subdeacons. In modern church terminology they would be sextons.

Ps.-Nilus implies that Theodulus has been freed by the bishop who purchased him; he also implies that his freedom was conditionally bound by obligations of service (see below, VII.17). Mayerson 1963, 168, believes this 'extreme measure' reflects a shortage of Christian candidates for the job at Elusa when Ps.-Nilus was writing; in any case, Ps.-Nilus provides a rare allusion to the purchase of a slave, and use of a freedman, by a church community. Canon 82 of the 'Apostolic Canons' (preserved in the *Apostolic Constitutions*, VIII.47.82) permits a slave to be ordained if he is first set free, and his master agrees. See Rapp 2005, 174–76.

190 Perhaps intentionally vague as to whether God or the bishop is meant.

purchased,[191] and all their expressions displayed visible signs of joy. Their cheerful faces expressed congratulations; each danced about as if seeing a relative for whom all hope was lost.

[VI.23] As we approached the gate, they called [Theodulus], saying I had come, and led him out to meet me. But when we saw each other, he and I, neither of us showed signs of pleasure. Instead we began to sob and lament, drenching our faces and tunics with tears. He ran towards me, not entirely recognizing me – for how could I be easily recognized, my clothes being filthy, as was the hair on my head? – nonetheless, he evidently put more trust in the report of my arrival than in the sight before his eyes, for he approached me with open arms, eager to wrap them around me. As for me, I recognized him instantly, despite the crowd surrounding him: for his face still had those same features that were etched so deeply in my memory.

No longer could I suppress my joy. All muscles in my body suddenly went limp; I fell to the ground and lay dumbstruck, so that most everyone thought I had died.[192] **[VI.24]** Indeed, my long period of grief had made me no different from a corpse, [albeit] one capable of breath and sight. But by wrapping me in his embrace, [Theodulus] gradually helped me revive from my swoon, making me realize who I was, where I was, and who it was that my eyes were now seeing. So I offered my arms to meet his, returning his embrace with my own, savouring this satisfaction of a desire that I had felt for so long.

Then I began to speak. I tried to apologize and persuade him that I was to blame for all of the evils that he had experienced. I was the one who took him from his homeland and made him dwell in a land that was constantly being ravaged: for truly it was as I've stated. While he dwelt in the country in which he was born and bred, when did he ever experience anything one might pray to avoid? There it was everywhere peaceful, and nowhere was there fear of such treachery. But let those, who think the Fates cannot be escaped, be gone! Away with those, who assert that some Necessity leads its victims to their Destinies![193]

---

191 This implies that the entire Christian community (or at least the clergy) had contributed to his purchase.

192 For a similar response to overwhelming joy, cf. Heliodorus, *Ethiopian Tale* VII.8, and Chariton, *Chaereas and Callirhoe* III.1.

193 This reminds us that theodicy is Ps.-Nilus' main theme, and that he was well aware of the conventions of ancient romance, which emphasized the influence of Fates (τὰ πεπρωμένα), Necessity (ἀνάγκη), and Destinies (τὰ εἱμαρμένα), as well as Providence (πρόνοια); e.g. Achilles Tatius, I.3.3–4. See van Steen 1998.

Finally I asked him to describe what he had endured among the Barbarians, since his trials were over and no longer would be painful to recount. For as health after illness or healing after trauma brings cheer instead of despair, so too is it pleasant to describe sad affairs once they are over; their narration may even bring as much pleasure as the original experience brought pain.

[Narrative VII: Theodulus' Story]

[**VII.1**] [Theodulus] sighed deeply as he began to speak, his eyes brimming full of tears. 'What profit is there, father, in recalling our sorrows? Memory is wont to scratch a sufferer's sores. When told for love of storytelling, its narration may charm the listener's ears, since hearing about another person's suffering can bring delight to someone else; but it does not release the one who endured it from the pain that befalls him through the retelling. For not much is needed to stir up sensations similar to those that were suffered in the past, just as pain from a wound can easily be caused by touching a scar that has not yet fully healed.

But I know that you will continue to press me until you have heard what you want to learn. For I know you intend to make my incredible salvation the theme of your doxology, as it is your habit to sing God's hymns for every benefaction that He grants you. So hear me with a manly frame of mind,[194] and let paternal sentiments not make you cry out in sympathy at the dreadful misfortunes that befell me. Do not interrupt me with sad laments. Your sobbing would hinder the telling of my story, and my words would likely be smothered by your wailing.

[**VII.2**] 'Magadōn's servant has already told you most of what happened before he escaped. To go back over those things would prolong my narrative and perhaps be tiresome to hear, eager as you are for the essentials. For hearing something over and over again is not only tedious but irksome to listeners. But since you insist, I will tell what happened after his escape.

[**VII.3**] 'The Barbarians had decided upon our sacrifice, as no doubt he told you. Everything had been made ready for the ritual since dusk: altar, dagger, libation, receptacle, incense.[195] It was avowed that death would come just before dawn – unless God intended to deter it. Then Magadōn's servant revealed his plan and made his escape. It seemed unlikely that he would be caught, considering the difficulty of a distant pursuit. For not only did the time from dusk to dawn suffice to escape under darkness, but it was

---

194 Using gendered diction, ἀνδρείῳ φρονήματι.
195 Achilles Tatius mentions all but incense in his sacrifice scene, III.15.

also unclear what route he had taken, making it anyone's guess which direction to pursue. Who could follow a trail in that desert expanse, where it is impossible to find any trace of a path? What tracker is so clever, what seer so expert in detecting invisible signs? For everywhere the desert's terrain is rough and riven with ravines, hiding any tracks left upon it.

'Meanwhile I lay prone on the ground. While keeping my head down, I lifted my mind aloft on the wings of affliction. Secretly I began to address God, focusing my thoughts so completely on prayer that I was in no way distracted by impending death.

[**VII.4**] 'For the mind, if free from fear, tends to disperse itself on frivolous affairs like trading, sailing, building, planting; betrothals, nuptials, the begetting of children; military service and procuring provisions; lawsuits, law courts, tribunal benches, high seats of state, bailiffs, magistrates; warding off enemies, convivial companies and feasting with friends; becoming tribune, governor, or procurator, and imagining this to be a royal rank.[196] But catastrophe makes it concentrate through fear of danger, dispelling all that distracted it when free and secure. Entirely consumed by the cause of its grief, it supplicates God as the only one who, with an effortless nod of assent, might effect its release from its hapless straits. And so I began:

'Master and Maker of all creation known to sight and mind,[197] You Who hold the hearts of Your creatures in Your hand; Who can turn senseless rage into acts of mercy, and can save those being sentenced to death by authority's decree whenever Your blessed judgment wishes; Who can tame the ferocity of fierce wild beasts that feed on human bodies for their food; Who can repel the surging rage of fire, or freeze flames at full blaze with a mere nod; Who keep safe and unharmed men condemned to destruction, and show with ineffable and incredible power that hair and skin have more force than fire.[198]

'Save one who has no hope for succour from anywhere else, who has not yet lost life by his enemy's decision, since he is already as good as dead. Don't let my blood become a libation for demons. Don't let sinister

---

196 A shorter but similar list of daydreams is found in Nilus of Ancyra, *On Voluntary Poverty* 22 (PG 79.997D). Such lists reflect the rhetorical practice of *enumeratio*, by which speakers described topics by their constituent parts. Here it is probably meant to charm listeners or readers with a cascade of pleasant-sounding words, chosen for their similar endings and arranged to balance their number of syllables.

197 Cf. Rom. 1:20.

198 Cf. Dan. [LXX] 3:19–27, 46–50 (three youths in the furnace) and 6:16–22 (Daniel in the lions' den).

spirits feast on the fatty smell of my flesh.[199] **[VII.5]** They are ready to make me a sacrifice to a star that takes its appellation from the passion of lust.[200] Do not let my body, kept chaste to this day, become a sacrificial offering to the demon called wantonness. No, change these savages' bestial hearts to kindness, just as You changed the wrath of Ahasuerus, King of the Medes, when it burned against Esther, and turned his rough anger to compassion and mercy.[201]

'Save a soul that seeks to become Your slave, and restore to my elderly father, who also adores You, an innocent son who is ready to revere You, God, as he has proposed. Not out of fear of danger do I now make this vow,[202] so that my promise might be thought the price of salvation; but on the basis of my freedom to reason I have already anticipated the necessity of a struggle.

[VII.6] 'Demonstrate that faith attains salvation more swiftly than flight, and that it is safer to take hope in You than in flight by our feet. For he who was to be made an offering tomorrow together with me has evaded that death and secured his salvation by running away, while I remained here, awaiting Your judgment, in my enemy's hands, trusting in Your aid. I am trusting in Your power as he did in his feet. May the expectations I placed in divinity prove more auspicious than the hope he put in his body. He was saved because he used full cover of darkness to make his escape, and well was he saved. Behold, daylight has caught me! May You now save me by Your sagacity – You, Who gave this light to the living so that they could fulfil Your commands!'

[VII.7] 'This was how the sunrise found me – sleepless, praying, and shedding bitter tears. Lifting up my head I could see the Dawn-bearer[203] glimmering on the horizon. I sat up, put my hands on my knees and pressed my tearful face upon them. Once more I cried with my heart to the Power that could whisk me away with the mighty force of its breath,[204] saying,

'Master, You Who have authority over life and death, make Your mercy towards me a thing of wonder,[205] as You wondrously have done for

199 The gods were traditionally believed to feast on the smoke and smell of roasting sacrificial meat.

200 ἄστρῳ με θυσίαν ηὐτρέπισαν ἐπωνύμῳ λαγνείας πάθει.

201 Cf. Esth. [LXX] 5:1d-e: Ahasuerus is Xerxes I, Persian King, 485–464 BCE.

202 ὁμολογία, commonly used for 'vow' in LXX, e.g. Jer. 51.44; 'agreement, compact' in classical Greek.

203 ὁ ἑωσφόρος, i.e. the Morning Star.

204 Perhaps 'spirit' (*pneuma*).

205 Cf. Ps. 17[16]:7.

holy ones[206] who have been rescued from tribulation after falling under compulsion.[207] Do this, that we might confidently call on You, encouraged that we too will be delivered from whatever disasters befall us, pondering them as a paradigm of the succour that is Yours.

[VII.8] 'For it was You Who saved Isaac from sacrifice when he lay on that altar and a sword was being whetted, diverting his father with the sound of Your voice.[208] It was You Who rescued Joseph from murderous brotherly clutches;[209] when he fell once more into ambush and unjust chains, it was You Who delivered him from prison and restored him, a king, to his father after their long sorrow.[210] You delivered Jacob, his father, from similar distress: You freed him from his father's disfavour and kept him safe from Esau's raging fury at Laban's house in the land Between the Waters,[211] where You also protected Moses[212] when he fled the Egyptians' tyranny. It was You Who, by the prophet's prayer, made two dead boys arise from their beds and return to their mothers, both widows, alive.[213] You are that same One, Unchanging Master! With that same power You can work marvels now as then. So restore me, too, to a father who hopes for Your mercy, Powerful Ruler! Release him from desperate sorrow through Your aid, and let those who do not know Your name wonder at the might of Your strength, O much-praised King of all power.'[214]

---

206 Cf. Ps. 16[15]:3.

207 Cf. Ps. 34[33]:7.

208 Cf. Gen. 22:9–13.

209 Cf. Gen. 37:26–28, where Joseph's brothers decide to sell him to a caravan of Ishmaelite traders rather than kill him.

210 Cf. Gen. 41:14, where Joseph is released by Pharaoh from the dungeon, and Gen. 45, where Jacob travels to Egypt, after learning that Joseph ruled there.

211 Cf. Gen. 27:27–43, where, after Jacob cheated his brother Esau out of their father Isaac's blessing, Esau planned to kill him. Their mother Rebecca warns him to hide in her brother Laban's house in Harran (in northern Mesopotamia). On 'Land Between the Waters' (literally, 'Land between the Rivers', i.e. Mesopotamia), see next note.

212 εἰς τὴν μέσην τῶν ποταμῶν, ἐν ᾗ καὶ Μωσῆν ἐφύλαξας. Apparently a *double entendre*, referring both to Laban's refuge in Mesopotamia in Gen. 27:27–43 and to Moses' parting and crossing of the Red Sea in Exod. 14:16–22. I have tried to capture the dual references by translating, τὴν μέσην τῶν ποταμῶν (literally, 'land between the Rivers', i.e. Tigris and Euphrates) 'Land between the Waters'. I owe this observation to Claudia Rapp.

213 1 [III] Kgs 17:22; 2 [IV] Kgs 4:34: both tell how God's prophets (Elijah in the first case, Elisha in the second) asked God to revive the sons of women (in Elijah's case, a widow) who had given them food.

214 For a similar prayer for deliverance, cf. III Macc. 6:2–15.

[VII.9] 'While I was occupied with these words, [the Barbarians] sprang up with great alarm because the moment for sacrifice had come and gone – the sun already shining down upon the earth. Unable to find the other victim, they asked me what had happened. When they learned that, since I had been with them, I could offer no intelligence about his disappearance, they fell silent, without threatening me or giving indication of annoyance.

[VII.10] 'At that point my spirit settled and I blessed God for not ignoring a humble one's prayers.[215] From then on I was filled with confidence and courage – surely because God had granted me this grace. When they bid me to eat forbidden food, I refused; when they ordered me to dally with their women, I declined.[216]

'Finally we approached the inhabited world. Then, without me knowing what they had planned, they entered a village called Subaïta,[217] and announced my sale to the people who lived there. Many times they went there and returned without selling me, since no one was willing to give more than two pieces of gold.[218] Finally they led me out and stood me in front of the village naked, as was their custom. Then they put a sword to my throat and told everyone that they would cut off my head unless someone immediately bought me. And so, spreading my arms outward like a suppliant before those who had gathered for the sale, I pleaded with them to give as much as was asked and not to haggle over the price of human blood. I said that I would soon repay whatever price they paid, would eagerly serve the buyer as a slave if he wanted, and would acknowledge as my master whoever

215 Cf. Ps. 102:17 [101:18].

216 The word μιαροφραγεῖν ('to eat forbidden food') is used repeatedly in IV Macc. (referring to Antiochus' demand that Jews eat pork) but is otherwise extremely rare. A TLG scan of Greek literature from the first to seventh centuries CE finds it only six times (excluding one citation in a dubious text). In the third century it is attested once, in Gregory Thaumaturgus' *Canonical Letter*, can. 1 (concerning Christians captured by 'barbarians' and forced to eat sacrificial meat, also concerning women raped by 'barbarians' in captivity – could this have inspired Ps.-Nilus' passage?). It is attested only five other times, all in the fourth-century texts: three times in the *Martyrdom of Pionius*, and the two others that specifically refer to IV Macc. (Athanasius, *On Endurance*, Gregory of Nazianzus, *On the Maccabees and their Mother*).

217 I.e. Sobata (modern Shivta/Isbayta). Being the southernmost Negev town (about 25 km/16 miles, or less than one day's travel, south of Elusa), this would have been a convenient frontier depot for Sinai nomads to sell flocks and other goods. By the sixth century it had some 350 houses; none of its Christian inscriptions or three churches seem to date earlier than the sixth century. See Gutwein 1981, 89–93, and Segal 1983.

218 Well below the Mediterranean average for a late antique slave, the price of which ranged between 3 to 12 *solidi* (gold coins) for a male boy: see Patlagean 1977, 396. In late sixth- or early seventh-century Nessana, six *solidi* (gold pieces) were paid for a slave boy, three for a slave girl: see *P.Colt* 89, 21–22 ('Account of a Trading Company'), translated below, p. 267.

bought my life even after I had redeemed my price. **[VII.11]** And so, since I was tearfully importuning them in this way, someone eventually took pity and bought me. To sum it up briefly: I was then sold from there to here, as you have found.

'But [concluded Theodulus], I see you shaking and on the verge of tears; I can see that you are about to disrupt your joy with a dirge. These were my sufferings, father, which by suffering I was set free. Henceforth glorify God, on account of my unexpected, incredible salvation.'

[VII.12] 'Certainly, my child', I concurred, 'you have been exposed to countless dangers and hardships, and have endured death many times over by mere anticipation, even if by God's grace you escaped actually experiencing it. For it is truly the same thing to anticipate death and to know it from experience. I dare say that to anticipate it is worse, for the cut of a knife does not cause as much pain as does anticipating it beforehand. For the longer we prolong our fear, the more intense our agony and grief become; anticipating pain over a long period of time makes us feel as though we have actually felt it.

[VII.13] 'But as for me, in your time of tribulation I opened my mouth to our Master and declared that I would assume the harsh servitude of abstinence and other austerities, if only I could see you back again alive. Then I heard a voice in a dream saying, "The Lord will abide by the words that issue from your mouth."[219] We must not break the vow we made,[220] child, or prove false to the One Who acknowledged our promise with a divine response, since our prayers have been met with such a favourable end.'

[VII.14] 'And I', he replied, 'am ready to assist in your toils and take part in what you promised, Father, since I also took part in His grace and have reaped most of its benefits.[221] For you escaped suffering, but I escaped death itself. If all has happened as God's gift of grace to you, then to claim my benefits and rewards I must give thanks to God on your behalf, even if it be necessary to suffer something terrible for that grace.

[VII.15] 'For if Jephtha's daughter willingly submitted to her own murder and offered herself as a sacrificial victim to ensure her father's good reputation after he had prayed for victory in battle, who would I be, if I did

---

219 Cf. 1 Sam. [1 Kgs] 1:23, spoken by Hannah's husband after she vowed to dedicate her newborn son, Samuel, to God.

220 For Theodulus' vow (ὁμολογία), see above, VII.5.

221 I have translated χάρις as 'gift of grace', but 'favour' (as in Mayerson 1975, 70) may be better, since Ps.-Nilus uses it to state what God offers in a two-way exchange. Cf. John Chrysostom, *Homily 18.6 on the Epistle to the Romans* (PG 60.580).

not quickly step forward to pay back what my father owes?[222] Especially since I am going to be repaying the debt to God, Who knows how to reward each repayment with a second gift of grace. When a debt is repaid, He receives it not as a debt, but as if receiving a loan. Acknowledging Himself to be indebted for our repayment of the debt, He rewards the debtor's good faith with another gift, giving it as if repaying a loan. He always pays His gifts of grace in advance; He always guarantees Himself to be indebted to those who borrow from His benefits, and reckons it a point of honour to repay them in full, in order that He might forever be the original source of gracious gifts, repaying such gifts of grace as if He actually owed them. Such is His generous and honourable nature.

'So, father, you must begin to pay back, having me as a zealous partner in your debt. Of course, God knows how much we are able to pay. He demands repayment only in proportion to our abilities; He will not take advantage of our natural weakness by exacting labours from us beyond our strength.'

[VII.16] To these words I added my own approval, saying, 'We must turn these words into deeds and realize them in our actions, my child, so that the promise we made might receive a favourable end, so that our prayer be effective, and our labours be granted their recompense. For the sign and result of every act that has God's favour is this, that efforts be confirmed with rewards and struggles be recognized with victory wreaths. For the recompense we receive somehow gives credible proof that our acts are worthy of esteem, and prizes bear undisputed testimony to the contest.'

[VII.17] God's beloved bishop of that region took great care of us and helped us recover in no small way from our previous hardship. He invited us to stay with him, courteously offering every kind of refreshment. He allowed us to do whatever seemed best in our judgment, so that he would not appear to be applying pressure on account of the price he had paid for the boy, or insisting, more like a master, on the terms of his contract.[223] On one point alone did he adamantly insist: that we assume the sacred yoke [of priesthood], even though we did not want it. [VII.18] For we anxiously considered

---

222 Cf. Jdg. 11:34–40. Like his father, Theodulus does not want to be bested by a woman.

223 The term παραμονή ('contract') can refer to a number of different kinds of labour contracts. The kind that seems relevant here was a legal proviso attached to manumission according to which a freed person was obliged to remain available (imposing *de jure* restrictions of movement) and render general services to his or her former master. See Adams 1964. On the other hand, the title παραμονάριος ('custodian', 'clerical warden') was also used to designate someone assigned by a bishop to serve as custodian of a distant church or chapel (cf. Anast., *Narr.* I.1–3, 5). Since Theodulus had been made a church attendant, Ps.-Nilus may be using the term in this sense.

the gravity of the ministry, objecting that we would be incapable of bearing its weight, were it imposed on us. Indeed, it hardly befitted even holy men, insofar as conduct was concerned. For the dignity seemed onerous to them too: when called upon [to assume it], they would avow that it surpassed them, strenuously protesting to God that they were unworthy, citing weakness as their excuse to decline ordination – although they are more fit for that work than anyone else today, since their ascetic training in goodness makes them more able to have freedom of speech in their worship of their Master.[224]

But he insisted that, in his opinion, this privilege befitted our labours, and that he was granting us the dignity as recompense for the toils of our struggle.[225] Then, when we wanted to leave and begin travelling homewards, he supplied us with exceeding generosity, furnishing ample provisions for our journey, long and distant as it would be. He also prayed that God's grace would travel with us and bring us peace thereafter, and so released us without pompously boasting about being [Theodulus'] master or flaunting his authority over a man he had purchased, as perhaps another [person] might have done. He even made light of our supposed misfortune with his many exhortations, dispelling our deluded suppositions with an appropriate and moderate outlook.

[**VII.19**] But let my words end here, where my experience of hardships also came to an end, having provided, by God's grace, after so much adversity, the beginning of a brighter life.[226]

---

224 The reluctance of monks to accept ordination because of its burdens and their unworthiness was a topos of ascetic literature.

225 The word translated here as 'dignity' (ἀξίωμα) and described as a 'privilege' (γέρας, a fine classicizing word) often simply meant 'post' or 'appointment'. This conferral of office seems to correspond to the 'rewards' promised in VII.16. In any case, Ps.-Nilus implies that the bishop ordained the father and son as honorary priests, without assigning them to any church (he lets them go home in the next sentence). Such 'ordinations at large' were more widespread than is usually thought, especially for monks who were ordained simply in recognition of their virtuous conduct. Banned in 451 by the sixth canon of the Council of Chalcedon, the earliest attestations of this practice come from fourth-century Egyptian papyri: see Wipszycka 1996b and, in general, Rapp 2005, 138–41.

From this passage seems to have arisen the tradition that Ps.-Nilus became a priest, as stated in the title of the *Narrations* in an eleventh-century manuscript. Most ancient romances end happily with marriage; Heliodorus ends his *Ethiopian Tale* with both a marriage and an ordination into a pagan priesthood. Although it has often been assumed that Ps.-Nilus and Theodulus returned to Mt Sinai, the text states that they headed homewards (οἴκαδε).

226 I.e. the experience (or 'trial', 'test', πεῖρα) provided the start to a happier life. A thirteenth- or fourteenth-century manuscript adds, 'So ends with God the story of the slaughter of the holy abbas Theodulus, Paul, and John, and of the return of the boy Theodulus. "The flow of the river Nile can bring water to the soil, but the words of the monk Nilus bring pleasure to the mind."' Cf. *Palatine Anthology* I.100.

A NINTH-CENTURY EXCERPT FROM PSEUDO-NILUS' *NARRATIONS* SECTIONS IV.11–14, VI.11–12

The following notice, drawn from Ps.-Nilus, *Narrations* IV.11–14, VI.11–12, is found appended to the Ammonius *Report* in the ninth-century MS *Vaticanus syriacus* 623, a Syriac collection of hagiography and menologia from St Catherine's. Though dated to the ninth century, its scribe elsewhere reports that he made his Syriac translation from a Greek text dated 767.[1] Thus this Syriac text indicates the earliest known witness for the *Narrations*. It also shows how it was mined in medieval times for historical information regarding the Sinai martyrs. The text is unedited, and the following translation comes courtesy of Sebastian Brock.

TRANSLATION OF THE SYRIAC TEXT

The narrative of the blessed Fathers who were killed on the holy mountain of Sinai after Epiphany.

Once the accursed Barbarians had killed these holy fathers in this desert they turned back and went on their way. When it got dark and we had the opportunity to go down and bury the bodies of these holy men, we found them dead; but we found one of the holy fathers with some life in him and still able to speak. When we had sat down in grief, devastated by what had happened to these blessed fathers, we spent the whole night in vigil. Now this holy man was comforting us, saying, 'Do not be astonished at these trials, for this is Satan's habit: to ask [permission] from God to try out and examine holy men, just as He had brought a trial on Job, and on his servants and possessions, some of which He burnt up with fire, and some He slew with the sword, while in the case of his sons/children, He caused the house to collapse and kill them. So now do not let what has happened disturb you, for God's judgements are inscrutable: He knows how to crown his chosen

---

1 For the importance of this manuscript as witness to earlier Sinai monastic sources, see Binggeli 2005, where it is noted that the translation from Greek to Syriac was probably made in the Sinai monastery.

ones – just as He gave tyrants authority over the holy martyrs, [who acted] on Satan's counsel to whom He had given permission: in this way they killed some of them by the sword, while others they burnt in the fire, while others [they subjected] to bitter tortures – and [so] God gave victory over their enemies to the resplendent who with understanding and good intention endured many afflictions on behalf of his name. And just as He showed in the case of Job, giving him double [in reward], even more than all this did He give to the holy ones, namely what the eye has not seen, the ear has not heard, and what has not entered the mind[2] of man [cf. 1 Cor 2:9] – what God has prepared for those who love Him and endure afflictions for His name's sake, giving themselves over to trials of all kinds. And thus it is right for the Giver of good gifts that are beyond understanding, [that] He prepare crowns of victory for all who have undertaken the struggle for Him; just as He has given to the martyrs that which is beyond expectation, performing an act of grace with those who fear Him that is superior to every honour in the world.' In this way he was admonishing us, and then straightaway bade us farewell, and reposed in peace, whereupon we buried him with those who had been killed.

The names of those who were killed: two of them were Paul and John; while the priest Theodulus we found in Beth Rab [*BYTRB*], and Proclus in a place called Gath, Abba Isaac in a place called Sali [*S'LY*]; Macarius and Mark we found killed in the desert, Benjamin in a place called Elim, and Eusebius in Tolah, Elia in 'Usiqta along with two others: we found them with many wounds; we carried them and laid them in a cell, because we were occupied with burying the others. Then we went back and found one of the two beside some water: once he had drunk some he found rest, because he had been parched as a result of the burning of his wounds. Once he had drunk he knelt down and prayed, and he rested.

We placed him with his companions, and stood in prayer. The repose of these holy men was after Epiphany, on the seventh day, [that is] the 14th of Kanun II.[3]

Let us, brothers, request Christ our Lord that through their prayer He may have mercy on us, amen. This quire was completed on the 12th Nisan, in the year 1197.[4]

---

2 Literally, 'heart'.
3 January.
4 April 886.

NILUS OF ANCYRA, *LETTER* IV.62,
TO HELIODORUS THE SILENTIARY[*]

INTRODUCTION AND TRANSLATION

The *Letter to Heliodorus the Silentiary*, also attributed to Nilus of Ancyra († c. 430),[1] has a plot like the *Narrations* (see above, 'Pseudo-Nilus *Narrations*: Introduction') and a puzzling history of its own. Over a thousand letters, collected in four books,[2] have passed down under the name of Nilus of Ancyra. Most of these consist of mere sentences or extracts drawn either from other works ascribed to Nilus or from works of authors such as John Chrysostom. Curiously, many of the titles of the recipients found in the letter headings did not yet exist when Nilus of Ancyra was alive, and so must have been added by a later editor, in the sixth century at earliest. Why his correspondence was treated this way, we do not know.[3]

His *Letter to Heliodorus the Silentiary*, however, was not included or transmitted in that collection. We only have it because it was read (along with a *Letter to Olympiodorus the Prefect*, also ascribed to Nilus of Ancyra and omitted from the larger letter collection) during the fourth session of the Second Council of Nicaea (1 October 787). It was cited at that council as evidence that early church fathers venerated icons. Interestingly, it had been cited to prove exactly the opposite at an earlier council (probably the iconoclast synod of 754); indeed, some believe that its reference to icons of Plato, an Ancyran martyr, is an interpolation added to support the case for icons.[4] Be that as it may, the content and attribution of this letter is otherwise regarded as genuine, largely because Nilus of Ancyra mentions the obscure

---

[*] *Silentiarii* ('men who keep silence') were established in the fourth century to serve as ushers and messengers for the emperor's court. This Heliodorus is otherwise unknown.

1 On Nilus of Ancyra, see discussion above, pp. 73–75.

2 PG 79.81–582, based on the 1660 edition by Leone Allacci (Leo Allatius). Basic studies are Heussi 1917, 31–123, and Alan Cameron 1976.

3 See Alan Cameron 1976 for engaging discussion.

4 Thümmel 1978, 19–21, based on the fact that the *Letter to Olympiodorus the Prefect* (PG 79.577C) was also interpolated at an earlier council to support the case against icons.

saint Plato in another letter.[5] The following translation is based on Mansi's 1767 edition of the acts of the Second Council of Nicaea (a new edition is under preparation by Erich Lamberz).

TRANSLATION OF THE GREEK TEXT

With every miracle that happens, where and whenever they occur,[6] our Lord invites people of little or no faith towards a firm faith, while He increases the faith and hope of His faithful all the more, and proves their resolve to be staunch and unwavering. I now want to describe to you one of the countless miracles of our trophy-winning martyr Plato,[7] who not only in our own homeland, but also in every city and countryside, most readily offers gifts of grace and shows incredible strength to those who supplicate God through him.

For on the mountain called Sina where Moses received the Law from God, dwell monks both native and foreign. One was a Galatian by birth. Together with his son, this man had embraced the monastic way of life and spent considerable time accomplishing feats of asceticism out there in the desert. One day some Barbarians who were pagan in religion[8] suddenly bore down upon the aforesaid mountain. The [God-]forsaken men seized whichever monks were readily found at hand and took them captive, including the son of the old man of Galatia. With their hands tied behind their backs, they traversed many stages in the desert,[9] driven naked and hungry, with no footwear whatsoever, trudging by force and compulsion through the most

5 Heussi 1917, 80; Alan Cameron 1976, 189; and Thümmel 1978, 20, assume its authenticity. Its existence was brought to Allacci's attention after he had finished editing the main collection. He added it to the end of the fourth book of that collection (along with the *Letter to the Prefect Olympiodorus*); hence it is commonly known as Nilus of Ancyra, *ep.* IV.62. The other letter in which Plato is mentioned is Nilus of Ancyra, *ep.* II.178 (PG 79.291ABC).

6 Allacci's older edition (PG 79.580B) repeats the word *topon* (κατὰ τόπον καὶ τόπον), in which case this phrase might be rendered 'wherever and whenever they occur'.

7 Plato was supposedly martyred at Ancyra during Maximinus Daia's persecutions (306–311). A tenth-century version of his life is found in PG 115.404–425. According to Procop., *Buildings* I.iv.27, Emperor Justinian restored a church dedicated to St Plato in Constantinople. On his cult, see Foss 1977, 34–35.

8 βάρβαροί τινες Ἕλληνες τὴν θρησκείαν: literally, 'some Barbarians who were Greeks with respect to religion'. From the mid-fourth century onwards in the term Hellene ('Greek') was the eastern equivalent of 'pagan' (a Latin term) in the West. See Bowersock 1990, 1–13.

9 πολλὰς μονὰς. Here *monai* (literally, 'staging posts') is used metaphorically for unspecified measures of distance.

desolate, dry, and dreadfully rugged terrain, though completely worn out by unimaginable fear.

Concealed alone and hidden in a cave, the old man was wasting away with sorrow, unable to bear the abduction of his God-beloved son. Through the martyr Plato, his fellow countryman, he humbly implored Christ, his Master, to be moved to mercy. Meanwhile his son, while bound in captivity, asked God through the same all-holy martyr for the same thing – to take pity on him and perform a miracle.

Both of them were heard, the father in his mountain cave and the son in his captivity. Behold, suddenly our Plato was present, appearing on horseback, and also leading another horse opportunely behind him. He revealed himself to the son, who was fully awake and recognized him because he had seen the holy one's features many times on icons.[10] [Plato] immediately urged him to rise from everyone's midst, take the horse and be seated on it. All of a sudden his bonds fell off like cobwebs. He alone was ransomed, because of the name he had invoked. With God's consent, he stood up, mounted the horse, and with courage and happiness he followed the saintly martyr directing him. Then immediately and swiftly, as if on wings, the holy Plato and the young monk both reached the dwelling where the old man was praying and crying. After restoring the longed-for son to his father, who was grieving in his heart, the triumphant martyr disappeared.

So, as you see, in every place that people call out to God through them, our renowned and celebrated athletes of our Master Christ have the strength to accomplish any miraculous and wondrous deed. I have written these things to you because you are a martyr-lover, one who never gets enough remembrance of the thrice-blessed martyrs.

---

10 Thümmel 1978, 20 n. 32, suggests this reference was interpolated by eighth-century supporters of the veneration of icons. This seems unnecessary; Gregory of Nyssa describes the icon of St Theodore at Euchaita, a city east of Ancyra, as if nothing unusual: see *On Saint Theodore* PG 46.737D. For the hagiographic *topos* of recognizing saints by their icons, see Dagron 1991, 31.

THE AMMONIUS *REPORT*:
INTRODUCTION AND TRANSLATION

The Ammonius *Relatio*, or *Report*,[1] describes two different 'barbarian' attacks that befell two different monastic groups on the same day on the Sinai peninsula: one, an attack by 'Saracens' on monks at Mount Sinai, the other an attack by 'Blemmyes' on monks at Rhaithou. It claims that the same number of monks – forty – were killed in each attack. Its purported author, Ammonius, identifies himself as a monk from Egypt who had been visiting Mount Sinai on pilgrimage when the attacks occurred. After recounting what he himself saw below Mount Sinai, he records, apparently *verbatim*, what another survivor reported had happened at Rhaithou. Its coda informs the reader that Ammonius wrote everything down upon returning to Egypt, and that another monk had later given his writings to a priest named John, who had translated them from Coptic into Greek.

The Ammonius *Report* has in fact been preserved in five different languages: Greek, Christian Palestinian Aramaic, Syriac, Arabic, and Georgian. Unlike Ps.-Nilus' *Narrations*, its original text has not been fully established, since no critical edition has yet taken all of the different language traditions into account. The following translation is made from the 1989 Greek text edited by Demetrios Tsames and K. A. Katsanes.[2] Tsames–Katsanes based their edition upon the oldest Greek exemplar, the tenth-century manuscript *Sinaiticus graecus* 519 (hereafter SGr 519); they also used the fourteenth-century manuscript *Sinaiticus graecus* 267 (hereafter SGr 267) to fill in the older manuscript's lacunae (sections 12–21 and 42).[3] Their edition represents a considerable improvement upon François Combéfis' seventeenth-century edition of the Greek text,[4] but it is not ideal, since it does not include a critical apparatus or indicate where, if at all,

---

1 The Greek title refers to it as a διήγησις (*diēgēsis*; Latin *relatio* or *narratio*).

2 Tsames–Katsanes 1989: See Bibliography.

3 Tsames–Katsanes 1989, 192. Section divisions refer to those found in the Tsames–Katsanes edition, which apparently reflect paragraph divisions in Combéfis' edition; though not original, they are convenient and are presented in brackets in the translated text.

4 Combéfis 1660, based on three fourteenth-century MSS.

SGr 267 differs from SGr 519 or other manuscripts that preserve the text.[5] This is regrettable, because it is apparent from the Christian Palestinian Aramaic, Syriac, and Arabic versions that the *Report* has been preserved in two different recensions. While it is not yet possible to describe all the differences among these versions, some provisional observations are in order here.

To this day, the most familiar version of the Ammonius *Report* has been the Christian Palestinian Aramaic (CPA) version, preserved in a palimpsest manuscript that Agnes Smith Lewis edited and translated into English in 1912. Lewis dated the manuscript on palaeographic grounds to the seventh century, making it much older and closer in time to the original than the tenth-century SGr 519.[6] Indeed, while SGr 519 is longer, more detailed, and more precise in its terminology than CPA, certain divergences suggest not only that SGr 519 and CPA represent different recensions, but also that CPA's is prior to that represented by SGr 519.[7]

In the first place, CPA and manuscripts that stem from its recension all give 28 December as the date for the death of the Sinai and Rhaithou martyrs, for their commemoration, or for both. SGr 519 and SGr 267, however, both give 14 January as the date for the death and commemoration of the Sinai and Rhaithou martyrs. Presumably this reflects Ps-Nilus' observation (*Narr.* IV.14) that certain Sinai martyrs had died much earlier than those described in the *Narrations* and were being commemorated on that date. However, Ps.-Nilus indicates that these other, earlier Sinai martyrs were being commemorated on that date only for convenience, implying that they had actually died on a different date. It therefore appears that tenth-century Greek redactors (or their predecessors) supplanted the original martyrdom date (28 December, preserved in CPA) with the by then more familiar commemoration date (14 January).[8]

Another minor yet significant divergence between SGr 519 and CPA is found in the course of the narrative. At a point corresponding to section 18

5 E.g. Tsames–Katsanes 1989, 192, mention their consultation of MS *Sinaiticus Graecus* 534 without indicating its date or relation to other Greek MSS. Mayerson 1980 reports that SGr 267 does not sufficiently differ from SGr 519 to suggest a different tradition.

6 For the MS, see Lewis 1912, ix-xi; Nau 1912; Müller–Kessler–Sokoloff 1996, 3–5. CPA was widely used in Palestinian monasteries until the eighth century: see Griffith 1997.

7 However, Gatier 1989, 510 n. 36, believes the greater length, detail, and exactitude of the Greek version (using Combéfis' edition) show its priority over CPA.

8 See *Rel.* 7 and 42, below. While the tenth-century *Synaxarion* of Constantinople commemorates both the Sinai and Rhaithou martyrs on 14 January, another tenth-century menologion commemorates them on 27 or 28 December, as do the Greek MSS behind Combéfis' edition: see Gatier 1989, 520 n. 68; Tsames–Katsanes 1989, 233.

of the Tsames–Katsanes' Greek text, CPA states that the Blemmyes who attacked Rhaithou arrived after seizing 'a boat that was on the other side' of Aila (Eilat/'Aqaba). In other words, they came from somewhere east of Aila, presumably in or towards the northern Ḥijaz. However, according to Tsames–Katsanes' text, this boat had come from Ethiopia, although it had originated in Aila. This discrepancy suggests that a later Greek redactor interpolated the reference to Ethiopia in order to clarify the narrative, for in Greek tradition, Blemmyes barbarians were normally associated with southern Egypt or Ethiopia, not the Arabian Ḥijaz. In any case, it suggests again that the CPA's tradition is prior to that of SGr 519, preserving a simpler (if less logical concerning the Blemmyes) version of the story.

Thus the SGr 519 text edited by Tsames–Katsanes represents a modification of the original *Report* in certain places. Nevertheless SGr 519 remains crucial for completing the narrative, since the CPA manuscript is missing several folios. We know that its recension is at least as old as the eighth century, as witnessed by a ninth-century Syriac manuscript (*Vaticanus syr.* 623, hereafter 'V'), which in many places comes close to SGr 519 and claims to have been translated from Greek into Syriac in the year 767. There is, however, another Syriac version, dated to 936 (British Library Add. 14645, hereafter 'L'), which comes closer to CPA.[9] These different recensions are also reflected in the Arabic tradition: one ninth-century Arabic manuscript (*Sinaiticus ar.* 542, hereafter 'Ar.1') preserves a version copied from Greek in 772 that shows links to (as well as divergences from) 'V'; another ('Ar.2') preserves a version closer to SGr 519. The Georgian tradition derives from Ar.2, and has not been consulted here.[10] Lacking an edition that reconciles all these traditions and versions, I have indicated the significant divergences between Tsames–Katsanes' Greek edition and the CPA, Syriac, and Arabic in the notes to my translation.[11] Fortunately the plot remains essentially intact.

Philological issues aside, the Ammonius *Report* is still perhaps more complex than first meets the eye. Much depends on our willingness to accept

9 Sebastian Brock informs me that M.-J. Pierre is preparing editions of both Syriac MSS; these should clarify the relation between the Syriac, Greek, and CPA versions. For the importance of V as witness to earlier Sinai monastic sources in general, see Binggeli 2005, where it is noted that the translation from Greek to Syriac was probably made in the Sinai monastery, indicating the existence of an earlier Greek MS there, now lost.

10 On MS *Sinaiticus ar.* 542, see Griffith 1985; for the Ar. 2 and Georgian versions, Gvaramia 1973.

11 The CPA translations used in the footnotes come from the Müller–Kessler–Sokoloff edition. Translations of the Syriac and Arabic versions come courtesy of Sebastian Brock.

it for what it purports to be: a simple eye-witness account of what a pilgrim saw and heard on the Sinai peninsula, apparently in the late fourth century. Modern historians have embraced it as such, believing it to be an authentic account of events and circumstances of that time.[12] Attractions for doing so are obvious. If, in fact, the Ammonius *Report* is an authentic document of the late fourth or early fifth century, then it provides extraordinary, early evidence on a wide range of subjects. As historians have long appreciated, it would provide a very early portrait, not only of Sinai's Arab inhabitants, but also of its fledgling Christian settlements, and of relations between the two.[13] It would also represent the earliest depiction of Christian pilgrimage on record, pre-dating Egeria's *Travelogue* of 383–384 CE. In addition, it would also represent one of the earliest documents to describe Christian monasticism in detail, providing a source for the study of early monastic organization and culture that has been hitherto completely neglected.

To be sure, the Ammonius *Report* contains 'no blatant anachronism' that would rule out a late fourth- or early fifth-century date.[14] Moreover, its details concerning the circumstances of Ammonius' pilgrimage (prompted by the persecution of an Alexandrian bishop named Peter, *Rel.* 1), the Saracen raid below Mount Sinai (prompted by the death of a Saracen phylarch, *Rel.* 3), and a Rhaithou monk named Moses (said to have converted many Pharan-ites to Christianity, *Rel.* 12–15), are remarkably congruent with information provided by early church historians regarding the Saracen revolt of Queen Mavia that occurred in the 370s during the persecution of the Nicene bishop, Peter of Alexandria. As discussed in the General Introduction, this late fourth-century revolt was probably based in Third Palestine, and was partly resolved by the ordination of a local monk named Moses to serve as bishop to Mavia's tribes. The *Report* would therefore seem to offer independent, contemporary testimony concerning that affair. According to one church

---

12 Mayerson 1980, 133–48; Shahid 1984, 301–29; Rubin 1990, 185–88; and Lenski 2002, 205, as opposed to Devreesse 1940, 216–20; Solzbacher 1989, 222–35; Gatier 1989, 510–17; and Flusin 1998, 133–38. Readers wishing to review all the arguments should consult these works. For a more general discussion of problems involved with interpreting hagiographical narratives, and for the chronological relationship between Ammonius and Ps.-Nilus, see General Introduction above, 'Sinai Martyr Tradition'.

13 E.g. Shahid 1984, 303: 'Pharan emerges from the [*Report*] as the main center of Arab presence in the Peninsula ... Its Arabs are settled nomads ... Its chief, 'Ubayda, converted by the holy man Moses, becomes a zealous Christian and a protector for the eremitic community of neighboring Rhaithou; he lays the foundation for the emergence of Pharan as a major Christian center in the Sinai Peninsula...'

14 Rubin 1990, 190; cf. Mayerson 1980, 139-40; see, however, below, p. 148, n. 27.

historian, the ordination of Mavia's Moses took place 'on the mountain' – perhaps a reference to Mount Sinai itself.[15]

Yet there are good reasons to be sceptical that the narrative represents either an early document or one based on actual experience. Many have suspected that its depiction of the monk Moses, reference to the Saracen phylarch's death, and other circumstantial details were derived from ecclesiastical descriptions of Mavia's revolt and added for the sake of verisimilitude.[16] Indeed, most of its other details seem more appropriate for a later date. In particular, the technical precision of its monastic terms, its reference to a single monastic superior at Mount Sinai (*Rel.* 2), as well as to 'strongholds' or 'forts' at Mount Sinai and Rhaithou (*Rel.* 3, 20, 37) and a force of 600 archers at Pharan (*Rel.* 33), all seem more appropriate to the period described by the Piacenza Pilgrim in the middle of the sixth century than to a period predating Egeria's visit in the fourth.[17] Such observations are inconclusive, however, since we cannot confirm that the details in question are anachronistic or not. The narrative form itself offers more solid ground for scepticism.

As first observed by Pierre-Louis Gatier, the portion of the narrative that describes the Saracen raid at Mount Sinai (*Rel.* 2–7) is much shorter and far less detailed than the portion that describes Rhaithou and the Blemmyes' raid there (8–39).[18] This discontinuity would be odd, if the narrative had actually been written by a contemporary who had been visiting Mount Sinai for some time, but was totally unfamiliar with Rhaithou. Had that been so, we might expect the Mount Sinai portion of his account to have been the longer and more detailed of the two, reflecting personal knowledge and experience. Also odd is the fact that the Rhaithou portion, despite its consid-

15 Socrates, *EH* IV.36, identified as Mt Sinai in Rubin 1990, 184–85 n.40.

16 Esp. Devreesse 1940a and Solzbacher 1989, 231–33. Noting the difficulties of identifying Mavia's Moses with the Rhaithou Moses of the *Report*, who seems to have died before the attack happened (*Rel.* 15), Rubin 1990, 181, proposes that the former was instead Abbot Doulas of Mt Sinai, whom 'many called Moses' (*Rel.* 3).

17 As noted by Gatier 1989, 514 n. 49, and Flusin 1998, 134, the terminology used in the *Report* (e.g. προεστώς and κυριακόν) are all standard by the late sixth century (e.g. John Climacus uses προεστώς for 'abbot' when writing to John of Rhaithou in his seventh-century 'Discourse on the Pastor') and do not indicate an early date, *pace* Mayerson 1980, 140. Rubin 1990, 181, argues that the reference to Pharanite camel-faring in Egeria, *Itin.* VI.2 provides evidence for a police force there in Egeria's day; be that as it may, the Ammonius *Report* suggests a fighting corps closer to the scale of the sixth-century Pharanite regiment described in PP, *Itin.* 40.

18 Gatier 1989, 510–17, esp. 515.

erable length, is presented as a record of someone else's words recollected *verbatim* long afterwards, once Ammonius had returned home. If the narrative were really what it purports to be, we might expect this second-hand Rhaithou report to be presented in more summary fashion, without all the vivid details, topographical descriptions, hagiographical digressions, and set speeches that we find in it.

None of those features would be odd, however, if the Ammonius *Report* was written, not by an outside visitor to Mount Sinai, but by a knowledgeable resident of Rhaithou. The brevity and banality of the Mount Sinai sections suggest that this portion of the *Report* was not based on eye-witness experience, but on some other, brief source document, and its casual reference to a 'list' [*katalogos*] of holy fathers martyred at Mount Sinai (*Rel.* 7) probably indicates the nature of that source: a liturgical record listing the date, locations, and names of monks killed in a Mount Sinai raid, according to the simple 'date–place–name' entries typical of early martyrologies.[19] In the same section (*Rel.* 7) we find a wounded Sinai monk requesting to die so as to round off the number of Mount Sinai martyrs at forty. As noted above in the General Introduction, this recalls a similar request made in the earlier and more famous legend of the Forty Martyrs of Sebaste. Such parallelism strongly supports the contention that this portion of the *Report* is an artifice, not based on actual experience.

The Rhaithou portion (*Rel.* 8–39) betrays no similar artifice, but may itself recall an event that occurred during the reign of Emperor Anastasius (491–518 CE). In that time, according to the seventh-century *Chronicle* of John of Nikiu,

> impious barbarians, who eat human flesh and drank [*sic*] blood, arose in the quarter of Arabia, and approaching the borders of the Red Sea, they seized the monks of Arâitê, and they put them to the sword or led them away captive and plundered their possessions; for they hated the saints, and were themselves like in their devices to the idolaters and the pagans. And after they had taken a large booty they returned to their own country. And when the emperor was informed of this event he had strong forts constructed as a defense to the dwelling of the monks.[20]

Scholars have surmised that 'Arâitê' is a distortion for Rhaithou.[21] If that is correct, then John's *Chronicle* might explain the events behind the Rhaithou

---

19 Solzbacher 1989, 228, explaining how Ps.-Nilus got his own Sinai martyr details.

20 John of Nikiu, *Chronicle* LXXXIX.33–34; trans. Charles 1916.125; discussed in General Introduction , pp. 37–38.

21 Solzbacher 1989, 234–35, 241, followed by Dahari 2000, 139.

martyr tradition, as well as the origin of the Rhaithou 'fort' mentioned by Ammonius (*Rel.* 20 and 37). True, John's barbarian raiders are not identified as Blemmyes. But his notice that the attack originated 'in the quarter of Arabia' may be reflected in CPA's recension of the *Report*, which refers to Blemmyes coming 'from the other side' of Aila. We might also speculate that 'Ammonius' chose to identify these raiders as 'Blemmyes' simply because this barbarian group often appears as counterparts to Saracens in late antique sources.[22]

Thus there are good narratological reasons to suspect that the Ammonius *Report* conflates two different martyr traditions (i.e. that of Mount Sinai and that of Rhaithou) within an over-arching narrative, based on the literary conceit that all had been recollected in tranquillity by a visiting pilgrim named Ammonius.[23] This would make the *Report* a forgery. In fact, the Ammonius *Report* presents numerous features which, when found in other ancient literature (both Christian and non-Christian), have been regarded as signs of forgery. These include its specification of time and place of authorship (cf. *Rel.* 1, 41); its claims to eye-witness reportage and the inclusion of detailed information from another such witness; as well as its subscription claiming later discovery by an intermediary and translation from a foreign language (*Rel.* 42).[24]

If the *Report* is a forgery, who would have crafted it, when, and for what reason? The predominance of Rhaithou – its focus on the Rhaithou raid and martyr tradition, as well as its lengthy discussion or descriptions of Rhaithou monks and Rhaithou localities (revealing accurate knowledge of prevailing winter winds there) – suggest Rhaithou authorship. Indeed, Gatier has proposed that Rhaithou monks produced the *Report* some time in the sixth century in order to enhance their monastery's prestige at a time

22 Cf. Procop., *Wars* I.19.28–36; Ps.-Zachariah of Mitylene, *Chronicle* IX.17; Hoyland 1997, 171; Gatier 1989, 517. Trimingham 1979, 252, believes the Blemmyes occupied all the deserts between the Nile and Red Sea, and that those who inhabited the Arabian Mountains in northern Egypt were confused by Roman writers with Saracens. For more specific bibliography, see Barnard 2005.

23 On this hypothesis, sections 1 and 40–42 would represent authenticating material that frame the Mt Sinai portion (sections 2–7) and Rhaithou portion (sections 8–39); Ammonius himself would also be a literary construct, as argued by Devreesse 1940a. Noting that the Sinai and Rhaithou portions differ in terminology, Mayerson concedes that, 'It may well be that the writer of the narrative took the story of the [Rhaithou] raid from another source, if in fact another hand may not have appended it to the account of the raid on Mount Sinai': Mayerson 1980, 141, 148.

24 Speyer 1971, 44–84.

when it was being overshadowed by the Mount Sinai monastery following Justinian's embellishments.[25] Alternatively, it may have been made when Emperor Justin II had Sinai martyr relics interred at Constantinople in the late sixth century,[26] or earlier, when it was decided to commemorate the Mount Sinai martyrs along with those of Ps.-Nilus' *Narrations* on 14 January. By any hypothesis, the author(s) grafted Rhaithou's tradition onto a Mount Sinai martyr record commemorating an incident that occurred on 28 December. In what year that earlier Mount Sinai incident occurred, or was first commemorated, is another matter. But it is simplest to assume that the Ammonius *Report* was set during the persecution of the Nicene bishop Peter of Alexandria because it was during that time, between 373 and 378,[27] that some Mount Sinai monks were actually killed and their deaths recorded, giving rise to a local martyr tradition.

Admittedly, such hypotheses raise as many questions as they resolve. Readers must decide whether they are cogent enough to dispel the presumption that the *Report* is a fourth-century traveller's account. But if it is in fact a later composition masquerading as an early account, then it becomes a more sophisticated and arguably more interesting document. Much may be said regarding its literary aspects (e.g. its depiction of barbarians and

25 Gatier 1989, 516 and 520, believes the Rhaithou sections were compiled from Rhaithou apophthegmata and martyr traditions, as well as from the church historians' accounts of Mavia. Interestingly, a learned monk from Rhaithou named Menas helped Cosmas Indicopleustes translate a Greek Ptolemaic inscription in sixth-century Ethiopia: see CI, *Top. christ.* II.56–57.

26 See above, p. 62.

27 All commentators have assumed that the Peter mentioned in *Rel.* 1 refers to the Nicene bishop Peter II of Alexandria (373–380), persecuted under Emperor Valens from 373 to 378. As noted above, this is largely due to perceived parallels between the *Report* and the ecclesiastical accounts of the Mavia revolt. There were, however, two other bishops of Alexandria named Peter in late antiquity. Indeed, tenth-century Byzantines dated the martyrdoms to the era of Diocletian's persecution, apparently in the belief that the Peter in question was Peter I (300–311) of Alexandria (cf. *Synaxarion* of Constantinople, col. 391). That date may be dismissed, since it is unlikely that monasticism would have developed so fully at Rhaithou, Mt Sinai, or anywhere else that early, and because many localities sought to establish links to the 'heroic age' of the Diocletianic persecution. The other candidate would be the anti-Chalcedonian bishop of Alexandria, Peter III 'Mongus' (477–489), who was persecuted under Emperor Zeno. Indeed, Ammonius' description of Peter 'hiding and fleeing from place to place' (*Rel.* 1) is similar to Ps.-Zacharias of Mitylene's description of Peter III, who 'hid himself in the city by moving about from one house to another' to escape persecution (*Chronicle* V.5; trans. Hamilton-Brooks 1899, 114, in a portion written in the late fifth-century; for context, see Haas 1997, 320–30). But this seems unlikely considering Ammonius' claim to be from Canopus (*Rel.* 1), which implies a connection with the early fifth-century Metanoia monastery, which was hostile to Mongus during his tenure. See Gatier 1989, 516 n. 53.

physical violence, or its method of narration) and devotional tone, especially in relation to Ps.-Nilus' *Narrations*. At the same time, historians can take solace that it preserves traces of an early liturgical record commemorating Mount Sinai martyrs as well as local Rhaithou traditions and concerns. In other words, it does not just represent the recollections of what some survivor saw, or heard another distressed survivor say – as would be the case were it exactly what it purports to be, a mere traveller's account.

TRANSLATION OF THE GREEK TEXT

A Report
by Ammonius, a Monk,
Concerning the Holy Fathers Slaughtered by the Barbarians
at Mount Sina and at Rhaithou[28]

[1] Once, while sitting in my humble cell near Alexandria at a place called Canobus,[29] the thought occurred to me to travel to the regions of Palestine. My primary reason was that I could not bear to see the tribulations and danger that arose daily for the faithful under the lawless tyrants,[30] and [to see] our most Holy Archbishop, Peter, hiding and fleeing from place to place,[31] unable to shepherd his sacred flock with freedom and ease. At the same time, I also desired to see the revered holy places and venerate the precious Tomb, the immaculate, life-giving [Church of the] Resurrection of our Lord Jesus

---

28 CPA: *The life of the holy fathers who were killed at Mount Sinai in Rhaithou, in the time of Peter, Pope of the city of Alexandria.* L (= British Library Add. 14645, a Syriac MS dated 936): *The history and martyrdom of the holy and blessed Fathers who were persecuted by the barbarians on the holy mountain of Sinai and at Rhaithou. It was written by the blessed Ammonios the solitary.* V (= Vaticanus syr. 623, a ninth-century Syriac MS): *Next, the fathers who were killed on the holy mountain of Sinai and at Rhaithou.*

29 Canobus (= Canopus, modern Abukir), a wealthy suburb about 20 km/12.5 miles northeast of Alexandria. Theophilus, bishop of Alexandria (385–412), founded here the monastery of Metanoia that later became known as a refuge and outpost of Chalcedonianism in Egypt.

30 CPA: *by those lawless people.* Presumably Lucius, 'Arian' bishop of Alexandria (373–378), Palladius, prefect of Alexandria, and the imperial Comes Magnus under the 'Arian' emperor Valens (364–378). For a letter by Peter II describing the persecution of the Nicene party by these three, see Theodoret, *EH* IV.19 (where Magnus is described as a 'tyrant'); also Socrates, *EH* IV.21–22 and Sozomen, *EH* VI.19.

31 Probably Peter II (373–380), who succeeded Athanasius as Nicene bishop of Alexandria but lived mostly at Rome until Valens died in 378: see Socrates, *EH* IV.37 and Sozomen, *EH* VI.39.

Christ,[32] and the rest of the revered holy places in which our Lord Jesus Christ was present and performed his incredible, awe-inspiring mysteries.

[2] Upon arriving at those revered, holy places I venerated each and every holy area and location, taking great cheer in all of God's great works and deeds. And once I had enjoyed the revered, holy places for a sufficient number of days as I desired, I decided also [to visit] the Holy Mountain called Sina, so that I might be privileged to adore it, too.[33] Having found a group of other Christ-loving men who were going there,[34] I set off through the desert. With the assistance of God who loves mankind, we reached that holy place in eighteen days.[35]

After making my prayers, I stayed on a few days to take pleasure in the spiritual holy men, visiting them frequently in their cells for my benefit. All week long they would sit in solitude, but on the evening of the Sabbath [i.e. Saturday], at the dawning of the Lord's Day [i.e. Sunday],[36] all of them would gather in the Lord's House to make the night-time prayers together and partake of the immaculate, life-giving Mysteries in the morning.[37] Then

---

32 CPA: *I desired to pray and worship at [the church called] the Holy Cross and at the Holy Sepulchre of our Lord Jesus Christ.* L: *I was extremely desirous of seeing the holy places and venerating the victorious Cross, the Saviour's tomb, the life-giving [church of the] Resurrection (and the other holy sites...).* V: *I will pray and receive blessing from the holy places of our Lord Jesus Christ, our God, (where he performed miracles...).*

The Resurrection (*Anastasis*) was a circular church built on Golgotha by Emperor Constantine to enclose Christ's tomb (*Taphos*). It was part of the church complex that also included the Basilica of Constantine that housed the Wood of the Cross: see Wilkinson 2002, 174–77, and Hunt 1982, 10–15.

33 CPA: *I intended to go also to Mount Sinai if I would be also privileged to worship at the holy place of the Almighty.* L: *I wanted also to see the holy mountain of Sinai, and He held me worthy to worship there as well.* V (but not Ar. I): *After staying a while the thought entered my mind to travel to the mountain of God, Mount Sinai.* In the sixth and seventh centuries the verb ἀσπάζομαι (lit. 'to kiss, to embrace'; here translated as 'adore') often referred to the kissing of sacred objects (e.g. altars or icons).

34 V (but not Ar. I): *I went out to see if there was anyone going to that holy place, and I discovered that there were some people all ready to set off, so I went with them by the desert road.* Evidently pilgrims going to the Sinai commonly sought out travelling companions at Jerusalem: e.g. *Life of St. Matrona of Perge* 14.

35 This conforms exactly to the total distance (18 staging-posts) recorded in the sixth-century *Itinerarium Theodosii* for the eastern route (Jerusalem–Elusa–Aila–Sinai) to Sinai. See Mayerson 1982, 53.

36 The new day began at the previous day's sunset. Ps.-Nilus, *Narr.* III.12, says that Sinai monks congregated in church only on Sundays. Cf. Palladius, *Lausiac History* 7.5.

37 CPA: *In the morning, they would receive the Holy Mysteries, the body and blood of the Lord Jesus.*

each would return to his own place. In their appearance and way of life they were angelic, for they looked exceedingly pale, and, since they had worn their bodies down with extreme abstinence, they were nearly incorporeal. They possessed absolutely nothing conducive to pleasure or luxury: no wine, no oil, no bread at all, just a few dates or nuts from which they make a light, simple diet for their bodies. But a small amount of bread is stored with the superior of the place for the guests who visit for the sake of prayer.[38]

[3] After a few days a multitude of Saracens suddenly fell upon us, because the one who was in possession of the phylarchy had died.[39] All of those whom they found in the surrounding dwellings, they killed, but those whom they did not find escaped to the stronghold as soon as they heard the uproar.[40] With them went the holy father superior. His name was Doulas [i.e. 'Slave'], since he was truly a slave of Christ: his patience and gentleness were great, like no one else's, and for this reason almost everyone used to call him Moses.[41]

[4] They killed all whom they captured at Gethrambē (these were many), as well as at Horeb, Kodar, and the rest of the places near the Holy Mountain.[42] They reached us also, and in a short time would have killed us too, since no one opposed them. But God who loves mankind, who always extends His hand to those who call on Him with their whole mind, commanded a great flame to appear at the top of the Holy Mountain summit. We saw the whole

---

38 I.e. the superior kept bread in his residence to feed Sinai pilgrims. Mayerson 1980, 140, argues that Ammonius' use of the title προεστώς, 'superior', rather than ἡγούμενος, 'leader', reflects a lack of organized monasticism on Sinai at the time of composition. But the term is commonly used to designate a leader of a coenobitic monastery in literary texts and papyri from the fifth century onwards. Indeed, Flusin 1998, 134, believes that this depiction of a superior overseeing local anchorites and pilgrim provisions reflects a greater degree of monastic organization at Sinai than what Egeria observed during her fourth-century visit; cf. PP, *Itin.* 37 and notes *ad loc.*

39 ἀποθανόντος τοῦ κρατοῦντος τὴν φυλαρχίαν. CPA: *king of the Saracens, the one who had guarded the desert.* L: *the ruler who kept guard over that region [had died].* (V omits the reason.) A phylarch was a tribal leader allied to the Romans, bound to keep peace between tribesmen and Roman citizens.

40 For this stronghold (ὀχύρωμα), see below, n. 45. CPA: *fortress;* L and V: *tower* (V adds: *where the Fathers used to pray*).

41 Gentleness and humility were Moses' cardinal virtues: see Num. 12:7 and Ps.-Nilus, *Narr.* III.16. For use of the honorific name 'second Moses' at Sinai, see Anast., *Narr.* I.12 and I.16.

42 Gethrambē (Geth Rabbi?) is presumably the Bēthrambē mentioned by Ps.-Nilus, *Narr.* VI.10 (perhaps modern Dayr Rabba); Horēb is presumably Mt Horeb (Jaba Sufsafa); Kodar is otherwise unknown. See Dahari 2000, 156–57. V (but not Ar. I): *in (the church of) the holy Mar (= St) Sergius, and on Horeb.*

mountain smoking, and fire rising up to heaven.[43] We all began to tremble and faint with fear at the sight. We threw ourselves on our faces and made obeisance to the Lord, pleading for Him to make our present straits turn out for the best. When the Barbarians saw that incredible spectacle, they all cowered and fled in an instant. Most of them even left their weapons and camels behind, unable to endure for another moment that turn of the scales.

[5] Then when we saw them flee, we thanked and glorified God, who in the end did not neglect those who had called upon Him.[44] We came down from the tower[45] and sought to learn which of the fathers had been slain, and in which place. We soon found thirty-eight persons dead with all sorts of wounds all over their bodies – but no one could tell us their manner of death, since no one had seen what had happened. Twelve of the holy men we found in the Gethrambē monastery, the rest in various other places. But Isaiah and Sabas were still breathing, although they had been deeply wounded. We took care of these wounded men as soon as we had buried the slain with great sorrow.

[6] Who could be so hard and unfeeling as not to weep or mourn bitterly at the sight of saintly, devout old men[46] strewn pitifully over the ground? One had his head hanging off his body, held on only by the skin; another was cut in half; another took such a blow to his head that his eyeballs burst out; the feet and hands of another had been cut off and were lying on the ground like dead wood.[47] Why say more? Words cannot express what we saw as we examined the bodies of the holy ones.

[7] As for the two wounded brothers, Isaiah died in the Lord when evening fell the next day, but Sabas held on to hope of recovery, since his wound was not very serious. He thanked God for the grievous things that had befallen him, but was troubled that he had not been worthy of [inclusion in] the list of the holy fathers.[48] He cried out, saying, 'Alas for the sinner, alas

43 Cf. Exod. 19:18, 20:18. Lightning storms are not unusual on the Sinai: Hobbs 1995, 55.
44 Cf. Pss. 12:2; 43:24; 73:1; and 19:76, 4–9.
45 It is not clear if this 'tower' (πύργος) is the same stronghold (ὀχύρωμα) mentioned in section 3, or a tower within it. Foundations have been found for what appears to have been a pre-Justinianic tower near the Justinianic church in the Sinai monastery: see Grossmann, 1988, 543–58, and 2001, 179–84.
46 'Old man' (geron) was a term of respect that became synonymous with 'monastic elder'.
47 CPA: *What can I say about the large number of blows with which the saints were struck without mercy, who were cut up limb by limb and were cast upon the ground?*
48 τοῦ καταλόγου τῶν ἁγίων πατέρων. This reference to a 'list' (katalogos: cf. Lampe 1961 s.v.) of martyrs indicates the probable source of Ammonius' information for this section. CPA, however, has *number*, and L: *crown*.

for me, who was unworthy of the choir of holy fathers that died for Christ's sake, who was rejected in the eleventh hour, who saw the harbour of the Kingdom, but did not enter it.'[49] Then he prayed, saying, 'Lord God, Ruler of all, who sent His only begotten Son for the salvation of the human race,[50] You who alone are good and love mankind, do not separate me from my holy fathers who died before me, but with me let the number forty of Your slaves be fulfilled.[51] Yes, Lord Jesus Christ, grant that this happen, because I have followed you since childbirth and greatly longed for you, unclean sinner though I am.' After the blessed one said these things, he also gave up his holy soul on the fourth day after the death of the holy ones.[52]

[8] While we were still mourning with grief in our souls and tears in our eyes for the holy ones, an Ishmaelite[53] came and told us that all the ascetics of the remote desert, in the place called Rhaithou, had died at the hands of the Black Ones.[54] The place was two days away from us, located on the coast of the Red Sea.[55] Here there were twelve springs and seventy palm trees according to Scripture, but now that number has increased with time.[56]

49 V (but not Ar. I) adds: *My fate is like that of the virgins who did not enter with the Bridegroom into the Bridal Chamber.* Cf. Mt. 25:10; 'Bridal Chamber' is commonly found instead of 'Marriage Feast' in references to this parable in early Syriac literature.

50 'Ruler of all … race': not in CPA.

51 In the legend of the Forty Martyrs of Sebaste (BHG 1201–1208), a Roman guard joins the number of Sebaste martyrs in order to round off the number of martyrs at forty. Cf. Basil of Caesarea, 'Homily on the Forty Martyrs of Sebaste' 6, dated 373, trans. P. Allen in Leemans–Mayer–Allen–Dhandschutter 2003, 73: 'Let the fortieth of us be crowned, Master. Let not even one person be missing from that number. It is an honorable [number], which you honored in your fast of forty days …'

52 Instead of 'of the holy ones', L has: *of that blessed man* [i.e. Isaiah], *which took place in the month of Kanun I* (i.e. December); V adds: *God thus completed the number forty for the holy men, corresponding to the number of the forty martyrs who testified in Sebaste. But the death of these holy men, that is, martyrs, took place on 28th Kanun I* [i.e. December]. *Thus they were perfected in excellent martyrdom and went to our Lord.*

53 CPA: *a Saracen*; L: *a Midianite* (i.e. a native of the region of Pharan; cf. Exod. 3:1); V: *one of the descendants of Hagar.* 'Ishmaelite' was commonly used for Saracens, i.e. nomadic Arabs.

54 CPA: *were all killed by the barbarians.* CPA and L never use *Mauroi* ('Black Ones' or 'Moors' - the Greek has Μαύροι), but V has: *Cushites, that is, Blacks.*

55 CPA: *where Moses and the people of God had camped when they went out of Egypt.* V: *after two days and a difficult journey.* On Rhaithou, see PP, *Itin.* 40; Dahari 2000, 140-45; and General Introduction above, pp. 21–22, 35–36.

56 CPA: *as described in Exodus, 'seventy palms and twelve springs'.* L: *as described in the Law.* V: *as mentioned in the Law, where Moses and the Children of Israel left the sea.* 'According to Scripture': Exod. 15:27, referring to Elim. The increase of palms is also noted in the sixth century by CI, *Top. christ.* V.14.

[9] We asked the man to describe the manner in which they had died and how many there were, but he said that he did not know; he said that he had only heard that the monks who lived there had been slain, and that this was the rumour going around. Then others came and told us the same thing. After a few days one of the monks who had lived there came to the Holy Mountain, seeking to live here, seeing that his own desert had been utterly devastated by the Blemmyes.[57] When the saintly superior Doulas found out, he warmly received him and asked him to inform him exactly what had befallen the holy fathers, how he had safely escaped the Barbarians, and with what virtuous acts those holy ones had adorned themselves.

[10] He began his narrative by saying, 'Venerable Father, I had not lived in the place many years, for my sojourn there was only about twenty years,[58] while others had been there a very long time – forty, fifty, and sixty years.[59] It is a completely flat place that stretches out in a long plain to the south, and it is about twelve miles wide. To the east the mountains are like a wall, impassable for those not familiar with the place.[60] To the west is the Red Sea that extends, they say, all the way to the ocean. Looming up over this sea is a mountain from which twelve springs issue forth,[61] watering a multitude of palm trees.

[11] 'Now, many anchorites had their dwelling on this mountain, living as the Apostle says, "in mountains and in caves and in holes in the ground".[62] Their Lord's House was not on the mountain itself, but near it.[63] Although of the earth, these men were truly heavenly, and in their souls were equal

---

57 Instead of 'Blemmyes', CPA has *barbarians*; L and V end the sentence at 'seeking to live here'. The name 'Blemmyes' was given to inhabitants of the Nile south of the first cataract (in present-day Sudan) who made raids on Roman territory from the fourth century onwards.

58 'Making oneself a foreigner' (*xeniteia*/ξενιτεία), was an important monastic ideal whereby life anywhere on earth was considered a temporary sojourn, free of worldly attachments.

59 CPA adds: *and seventy years*. L omits: 'forty, fifty, and sixty years'. V adds: *and some even longer*.

60 CPA: *The place is flat, and its plain is forty miles long, and its width is about twelve miles. On the eastern side the mountains are steep like a wall without an entrance for those who do not know the place. A road passes through there.* This seems to correspond with the site of Wadi al-Tur, the adjacent, 16-km/10-mile wide Qa' desert, and the Jabal Umm Shomer massif, as well as (in CPA's version) the Wadi Isla pass.

61 CPA adds: *those and others which flow upon them, and many other springs between them.*

62 Heb. 11:38, describing prophets 'of whom the world was not worthy'. Not in CPA.

63 κυριακόν ('Lord's house'). CPA: *there was an assembly place at the base of the mountain.* V: *They had a church where they used to gather on Sundays, close to the mountain with the springs. But let us return to what you asked of me, concerning the way of life of our fathers.*

to angels, whose conduct they achieved. By scorning their bodies as if they were alien to them, they attained not merely one virtue, but fully adorned themselves in all. Since, my dear ones, I cannot describe all the contests, struggles, and temptations that the devil raised against them, it will suffice for me to recall just one or two of their innumerable acts, so that whoever hears about them might understand that the rest were also such.

[12] 'Moses had been a monk since early age – for he was also a native of that place, having originated from Pharan.[64] He passed seventy-three years in the monastic life, living on the mountain in a cave not far from the assembly place.[65] He was truly like a second Elijah, for everything he asked God for was given to him.[66] The Lord performed a great many healings through him, having granted him dominion over unclean spirits, so that he cured many, and made Christians of nearly all the lay folk who were within the confines of the Ishmaelites and dwelled in the regions of Pharan.[67] When they saw the many prodigies and signs performed by him, they believed in the Lord and went forth to the holy, universal church to be privileged with Holy Baptism. It was said that by Christ's grace he delivered many from the sickness of unclean spirits.

[13] 'Ever since he had become a solitary, this saintly, thrice-blessed Moses had never tasted bread, though others ate it: for when the men of the place brought grain from Egypt, they would supply them with a few loaves of bread in exchange for their handicrafts.[68] But they also used to eat fruit

64 It has been argued that this is the Moses that became bishop of the Saracens at the request of their queen, Mavia, as recorded by Socrates, *EH* IV.36, Sozomen, *EH* VI.38, and Theodoret, *EH* IV.20. On her revolt, see General Introduction above, pp. 41–42.

65 οὐ μακρὰν τοῦ συνακτηρίου, i.e. the church where assemblies and services were held. CPA: *seventy-three years, on that very mountain from which springs come forth.*

66 1 [III] Kgs 19:8–9. Thus Ammonius gives Rhaithou a Moses and an Elijah, parallel to the heroes of Mt Sinai/Horeb.

67 CPA: *he dwelt in the desert, and also the inhabitants, the Pharanites, and he made them Christians.* L: *with the result that the majority of the Midianites who live in that region came to believe in our Lord and become Christians through his agency, having seen the signs and wonders which he performed.* V: *He made the people of Pharan Christians, through God's assistance and with his prayer; likewise with all the people of the region, because they saw the miracles that our Lord was performing at his hands.*

68 CPA: *The Saracens who lived there used to bring wheat from Egypt from time to time and give (it) to us. We used to give them dates from what we would gather from the place in exchange for the wheat, and we provided for our needs.* This importation of Egyptian grain recalls the report in PP, *Itin.* 40, that sixth-century Pharanite soldiers received provisions from Egypt. Being the only good harbour on the western Sinai (see Gatier 1989, 500–02), Rhaithou would have been the logical site for depositing or receiving such provisions.

from palm trees,[69] and the blessed Moses took a few dates for nourishment, along with water to drink,[70] and he made his clothes from palm fibres. He cherished tranquillity more than anyone else, and kindly received anyone who came to him with questions about their thoughts.[71] He slept only after the night-time offices,[72] spending the rest of the time keeping vigils, making prayers, and glorifying God. But during the Holy Forty[73] he did not open the door of his cell at all until the Holy, Great Thursday,[74] bringing nothing inside for nourishment except twenty dates and a beaker of water. Often he saved these until the moment he opened his door. So his attendant told me.[75]

[14] 'During the Holy Forty a man named Obedianus, the leading citizen among the pagans,[76] came under the control of an unclean spirit and was brought from Pharan to him for a cure. As he approached the old man's cell and was about a stade away,[77] that wicked, unclean spirit made him shake and howl aloud, "What violence! not even for a moment did I manage to interrupt the regimen of that evil old man!"[78] And with these words he came out of the person. The man was instantly healed and believed in Christ, as did many others. In this way they all became worthy of Holy Baptism. I could say many other things about him, but I will keep silent, since now is not the appropriate moment to tell them.[79]

69 Omitted by CPA, L and V.

70 CPA adds: *He never tasted wine.*

71 V omits: 'kindly ... thoughts', and in the next sentence: 'spending ... God'. Tranquillity or quietude (ἡσύχια) was considered an anchorite's ultimate goal, and became nearly synonymous with solitude. Whoever fully attained it was considered an expert in discerning the thoughts or temptations and passions that troubled people. Reference to such consultation is unusual in a narrative text, although it is common in the *Apophthegmata patrum* and writings of Evagrius Ponticus.

72 The night office or vigil ('Matins') of prayer was originally observed at midnight (technically the sixth hour of the morning), but later at eighth hour of the morning, i.e. before sunrise.

73 I.e. the Lenten fast, also known as the *Quadragesima* or forty-day period before Easter during which monks often imposed extreme abstinence on themselves as a form of penance.

74 Maundy Thursday, before Easter, when penitents were considered reconciled with the church. Its observance is first attested in the late fourth century.

75 Named Psoës below, sect. 15 (CPA: *Sisoes*). On such monastic attendants/apprentices, see Ps.-Nilus, *Narr.* IV.3. CPA omits: 'often ... told me'.

76 CPA: *On those fast days they used to bring a person who was being tried by an evil spirit. This was the chief of Pharan.* Shahid 1984, 301–02, believes Obedianus is a Hellenized form of the Arabic Ubayd or 'Ubayda (a diminutive of 'Abd, 'slave').

77 About 300 m/328 yards.

78 Here the Greek κακόγηρος/*kakogēros* ('evil old man') plays on a common title for a venerable monk, καλόγηρος *kalogēros* ('good old man'); cf. Anast., *Narr.* II.26.

79 CPA: *At that very moment the demon went out from him and he was healed. He was*

[15] 'This blessed Moses had a disciple by the name of Psoēs who was from the region of the Thebaïd. He had dwelled above him for forty-six years.[80] He did not make a single change to the old man's regimen, but became, so to speak, the seal and the imprint both of what he saw and what he was taught. I myself lived with him too in the beginning, but I had to leave because of his unspeakably great austerity, since I could not endure the contests, perseverance, and bodily mortification of his discipline. Later he too died in the Lord together with the rest of those who were slain.[81]

'And not only about these, but also about each one of those [who were killed] could I recall things greater and loftier than these, describing what they have done and displayed. But all the same, I'll pass over them all to describe just one holy man's work: for it would not be right to leave forgotten in silence such an awesome, incredible deed.

[16] 'A certain Joseph was born in Aila[82] and lived far from the water, about two miles on the plain,[83] where he built a dwelling with his own hands. The man was holy, saintly, discerning, and perfect in every way, having been filled with God's grace. He had been in that place for some thirty years and had a disciple, who did not dwell with him but in another dwelling nearby. One day one of the brothers visited this holy, righteous man with a question about a thought.[84] When he knocked, he got no answer. Peering in through the entrance he saw him standing entirely from head to toe like a flame of fire.[85]

---

a pagan who until then had not received the Holy Baptism. For all of the Pharanites were formerly pagans. He returned home cured. He and those who were with him thanked God. The servant of God did not open the door of his cell nor see anyone of them.' What Father Sisoes said concerning Moses is finished. L: *He returned home fully cured – while the blessed man had not been seen by anyone. I could relate many things about him, but now I will keep silent.* V: *And they asked to be baptized, and returned home thanking God and his holy servant Abba Moses, without having seen him, and he had not spoken with them. Numerous people have made known other mighty signs concerning him, but I cannot relate to you each one of them, since they are too many.*

80 CPA omits the first sentence and has: *concerning Abba Sisoes the Egyptian*; in the next sentence, instead of 'forty-six': *forty.* The section is very short in V. The Thebaïd was the area in upper Egypt around modern Luxor where monasticism thrived in late antiquity.

81 L omits this sentence – perhaps important to note, because it might mean the sentence is an interpolation. If Moses did not die in the original account, it might be argued that he lived to be bishop to Mavia's tribes.

82 Aila (Eliat/'Aqaba) was about 10 days' travel across the Sinai from Rhaithou.

83 About 3 km/1.5 miles. CPA and L have: *below the city, two miles from water.* V omits: 'on the plain ... hands'.

84 Cf. sect. 13 for consultations on *logismoi* for lay people. Instead of 'a thought', V has: *a certain matter, so that he might benefit from him and learn how to conduct himself.*

85 Cf. *Apophthegmata patrum*, alphabetical collection, Arsenius 27 (PG 65.96BC): 'A

'Filled with fear and trembling, his body went weak, and he collapsed on the ground like dead for an hour. Then he stood up again and sat down at the door. The saintly old man was still occupied with his vision and did not know what had happened. Five full hours passed before he appeared to be human once more. Then he opened the door and let the brother inside. After they sat down he said to the brother, "When did you come?" He replied to the old man, "It has been four or five hours ago since I came by, but I did not knock till now, so as not to disturb you."

'The old man realized that the brother was aware of what had happened to him, yet he said nothing about it to him. Instead he answered all the questions he was asked and cured the brother of his thought, then released him in peace. Afterwards he disappeared because he feared receiving fame among humans.

[17] 'Later his disciple, Abba Gelasius, came but could not find him. After repeatedly searching for the old man without finding him, he lived in his cell, feeling quite perturbed because of him. After six years someone knocked on the door around the eighth hour.[86] Gelasius went and saw his abba standing outside. Stunned by the vision, he thought it was a spirit. But without making an uproar, he said to him, "Say a prayer, Father." When he said a prayer, [Gelasius] received him with joy, and they embraced each other with a holy kiss.[87]

'The old man [Joseph] said, "You did well, my child, by asking for a prayer first, because the devil has many tricks." And the brother replied, "Why did you decide, Venerable Father, to separate yourself from your community, leaving me an orphan? I've been very distressed because of you." The old man said to him, "God knows the reason I did not appear. And yet, to this day I have never been away from this place, nor has a single Lord's Day passed that I have not shared with all of you in the holy, life-giving Mysteries of Christ."[88]

'And the brother was amazed that the old man had come in and out without anyone seeing him. Afterwards he asked the old man, "Why have you returned just now to your slave, Father?" The old man replied, "Because,

---

brother visited Abba Arsenius' cell at Scetis. Waiting at the door, he saw the old man as if entirely on fire: for the brother was worthy to see this. And when he knocked, the elder came out, and saw the brother as if struck dumb with wonder. He said to him, "Have you been knocking long? Did you see anything here?" The brother said "No", and left after talking with him.' Cf. Silvanus 3. CPA has the visiting brother describe in direct speech what follows in the next paragraph.

86 Two in the afternoon.

87 Cf. Rom. 16:16.

88 I.e. he did not miss a single Eucharist service.

my son, today I am migrating to the Lord from this wretched body. I have come to leave it to you, so that you might bury it as you wish and give the earth back its own."[89]

'After conversing with the brother at length about the soul and the good things to come, he spread out his hands and feet and fell asleep in peace, delivering his venerable, holy soul to the hands of the living God. Then at once Brother Gelasius ran off to assemble us all. With psalm singing and palm-leaves we went and conveyed him to the Lord's House. His face was brighter than the sun. We laid him to rest with the holy fathers who had fallen asleep before him.[90]

[18] 'As I've said before, there are many more things I could say, but I'll be content with these, since the occasion requires me to say more about the Barbarians. I can see that you want to hear about them above all.[91]

'The saintly, holy fathers were of such a kind, leading a perfect life in great poverty and freedom from possessions. Nobly did they endure tribulation and mortification for the sake of the Lord, occupying themselves with prayers and supplications alone, blameless in Christ our God. Altogether we were forty-three in number, each practising asceticism alone and aware only of God, who knows whatever is hidden.[92] While we were living this way, two men came to us with a report. They came from the opposite coast, having crossed the open sea on timbers from a foreign land, timbers found in regions of Ethiopia.[93] They said, "A multitude of Blemmyes have attacked a boat from Aila that was anchored in that place, and they captured it,[94] intending

---

89 Cf. Gen. 3:19.

90 CPA: *His face was radiant like light. We kept vigil over him the whole night. We placed him with the saints who had died there in the place* [i.e. monastery]. V: *His face was like the sun, and we were all blessed by him; and we buried him with the fathers.*

91 This paragraph is not in CPA.

92 Cf. Dan. 42, Mt. 6:6. CPA: *Those holy fathers were perfect and excelled in their discipline, in their prayer, and in their way of life. We were forty-three* [V: *forty*] *living in the place* [i.e. monastery]. *Behold, two men came from across the sea...*

93 περάσαντες τὸ πέλαγος ἐπάνω ξενικῶν ξύλων, ἅτινα ξύλα εἰσὶ τῶν μερῶν Αἰθιοπίας. CPA: *They said to us that they had crossed the sea on trunks of date palms.* V omits: 'from a foreign ... Ethiopia'.

94 τῶν Βλεμμύων πλῆθος ἐπιδραμὸν τὸ προσορμοῦν τῷ τόπῳ ἐκείνῳ πλοῖον ἀπὸ Αἰλὰ ὑπάρχον κατέσχον (following Combéfis' τὸ προσορμοῦν instead of Tsames–Katsanes' τῷ προσορμοῦντι). CPA: *many Blemmyes* [L: *barbarians*] *have suddenly come and captured a boat that was on the other side of Eilath*, which would indicate that the capture of the ship occurred east of Aila (i.e. on the coast of the Hijaz), and had sailed around to the west coast of the Sinai peninsula. V has: *Blacks have come to the harbour of the island and found there a boat from Eilat, which they took.*

to go to Clysma by sea.[95] Once they had seized control of it they said to us, 'Take us to Clysma and we will not kill any of you'. So we promised them to do this and kept watch for a day when the south wind was blowing so that we might set sail.[96] With God watching us, we were able to escape from their hands during the night.[97] Behold! we are warning you to be alert for a while and save your souls, lest when they pass by this place[98] they attack here too and kill everyone. There are about three hundred of them in number.'

[19] 'Upon hearing these things we stood on alert. We placed watchmen by the sea so that if they saw the ship coming, they could warn us in advance, and we were praying and calling on God to bring about what was good for our souls. The next day at evening the boat was seen under sail and coming towards us.

'And the lay folk, all of those who happened to be in the Place of the Pharanites,[99] also prepared themselves for war against the Blemmyes for the sake of their wives, children, and herds of camels.[100] All of them – about two hundred excluding women and small children – assembled a short distance above the palm trees, while we took refuge in our Lord's House. It was fortified with brick walls about twice the height of a man.[101]

In sect. 12 of the Greek version, 'that place' refers to Sinai, and we know that al-Tur, near the Rhaithou site, would have been the first good harbour for ships heading north to Clysma: see Gatier 1989, 500–02. However, the reference in the previous Greek sentence to the Ethiopian origin of the ship's wood suggests that the author wanted to explain 'that place' as Ethiopia. Procopius of Caesarea, *Wars* I.xix.24–25, notes that Ethiopian boats on the Red Sea were distinctive because their planks were bound together with cords and not smeared with pitch.

95 'intending ... sea' not in CPA. Clysma was important as a seaport for foreign trade and a juncture for travel between Egypt, Palestine, the Mediterranean and the Red Sea: see Egeria, *Itin.* PD,Y 5–6, PP, *Itin.* 42, and Mayerson 1982, 45–47.

96 CPA: *We were waiting until a southerly wind would blow, and we could sail as we wished.* The north-west wind prevails in the Gulf of Suez, making sailing up the west Sinai coast difficult; cf. John Mosch., *Meadow* 120 (PG 86[3].2984BC). Mayerson 1980, 145, observes that the south wind blows here mainly in winter, i.e. at exactly the time when Ammonius dates the attack: 'the least that can be said is that the narrative contains some accurate information concerning sailing conditions in the Red Sea and the Gulf of Suez'. Mayerson also proposes that al-Tur would have been the 'intended port of call before proceeding on to Clysma'.

97 L adds: *on these pieces of wood.* V adds: *on these pieces of wood. We have come to you having left them with the owners of the boat on the other side of the sea.*

98 V adds: *on their way to Clysma.*

99 An important detail, indicating that Pharan had a sizeable colony in the Rhaithou area, no doubt based there to facilitate trade and transport provisions inland. Cf. PP, *Itin.* 40.

100 'and herds of camels' not in CPA.

101 CPA: *Those Saracens and Pharanites who happened to be there prepared themselves to fight against the Blemmyes for the sake of their women and children. Two hundred men in*

'The Barbarians seized the harbour where the sailors had guided them. That night they stayed on the westward side of the mountain, a short distance away from the springs.[102] When morning came they tied up the sailors and left them in that place, but put one of them on the boat to guard it, leaving one of the Black Ones with him so that he could not sail off alone.[103]

'They came to the springs, and the natives met them to make war. The din of battle rose near the hills and springs and between the cisterns.[104] Dense volleys of arrows flew from both sides. The Black Ones, inasmuch as they were more numerous and well trained to make evil, routed our men and murdered one hundred and forty-seven of them. The rest were able to escape, some through the mountain, others by hiding among the trees, each one saving himself wherever he could. But the lawless ones took their women and children and held them near the springs.

[20] 'Next, like fierce, wild beasts they came running at us in the so-called "Fort",[105] thinking that they would find quantities of money hidden there. They circled around us, bellowing incomprehensibly and threatening us in barbaric speech. In extreme danger, we all were overcome with despair, having no idea what to do. Turning our eyes up towards God, we wept, pouring out our hearts. Some of us bore their distress with high, noble spirits, others shed tears; one gave thanks in prayer, another consoled his neighbour, while together we all exclaimed the *Kyrie Eleēson* ['Lord have mercy'].[106]

[21] 'Our most holy father, Paul, who was born in Petra,[107] stood up in the middle of the church and said,

"Fathers and Brothers, listen to me, though I be a sinner and the least

---

number, not including women and their children, gathered together on the mountain above the date palms where the springs were. We fled to our church which was fortified with bricks, and the height of its wall was three times the stature of a man [L: *about two cubits high*].

102 'westward side of the mountain' not in CPA.

103 CPA: *One of their own number ... to prevent him from taking the ship*; L: *one barbarian ... so that he could not raise the mast*; V: *One of the owners of the boat unbound* (no explanation stated).

104 'between the cisterns' not in CPA. L: *between the springs of water*. V: *over against the springs*.

105 κάστρον, the same term used to describe the Mt Sinai monastery in the seventh century (cf. John Clim., *Ladder* 7 [PG 88.812B]; Anast., *Narr.* II.8). CPA: *After these (things), quickly like wild animals they ran and attacked us at the fortress to which we had fled, because they thought ...* [CPA breaks off here, with one folio missing].

106 A famous Christian prayer first attested in the 380s. See *Apostolic Constitutions* VIII.6 and Egeria, *Itin.* XXVI.8.

107 V: *the abbot*. Probably Petra in modern Jordan, the nominal capital of Third Palestine: see General Introduction, pp. 8–9 and notes *ad loc.*

of all. Today each of you knows that we are all in this place for the sake of our Master and Lord Jesus Christ. For love of Him, we withdrew from that vain world to this harsh, rocky desert. Although we are unworthy, sinful men, we have been privileged to bear his yoke[108] by living in hunger, thirst, extreme poverty and tribulation. That is to say, we have despised all the vain and transient things of this life so that we might be privileged to become companions with Him in His kingdom.[109]

"Even now at this hour nothing will happen or befall us without Him. If He should suddenly will to free us from this vain, fleeting existence and hold us with Himself, we ought to rejoice, exult, give thanks and not grieve at this. For what could be sweeter or more delightful than to see His glory and His awesome face? Do you remember, my Brothers and Fathers, how when sitting down together we always used to speak of the blessedness of the holy men who had suffered holy martyrdom for the sake of His name, and how we used to desire that we too might be found among them? Behold, children, the time has come to fulfil our desire, so that you may live with them, as you desire, for ages upon ages in the life to come. So do not grieve or lament or cower or do anything unworthy of yourselves, but gird yourselves eagerly and confidently with power,[110] endure death nobly, and God will readily welcome you into His kingdom."[111]

[22] 'In response, all replied, "As you have spoken, Venerable Father, so shall we do. For 'how can we repay the Lord for all that He has given to us? We will take the cup of salvation and call upon the name of the Lord'".[112]

'Then that most holy father of ours turned towards the east,[113] reached out his hands to heaven and said, "Lord Jesus Christ our God, the only Holy and All-Powerful One, Hope and Help of us all, forget not Your slaves, but remember our poverty and misery. Empower us in this hour of need, and receive all of our spirits as a pleasing sacrifice with a sweet-smelling fragrance,[114] because honour and glory befits You alone, now and forever."

---

108 Cf. Mt. 11:29–30.

109 Cf. 2 Cor. 1:7; 2 Pet. 1:4.

110 Cf. Lk. 24:29.

111 V considerably differs in phraseology here and ends with the abbot quoting 1 Cor. 2:9, 'What no eye has seen, nor ear heard, nor the human heart conceived, what God has prepared for those who love him'. Cf. Ps.-Nilus, *Narr.* IV.12.

112 Ps. 116:12–13 [LXX 115:3–4].

113 'turned to the east' not in CPA. V: *went in before the holy altar and turned towards the east.*

114 Cf. Phil. 4:18.

[23] 'And when we said "Amen", we all heard a voice coming from the altar: "Come to me, all you who are weary and carry heavy burdens, and I will give you rest."[115] At the sound of this voice, fear and trembling took hold of us all. Our hearts and knees began to quake, showing that, as the Lord said, "The spirit is willing, but the flesh is weak."[116] Then we all turned our eyes to heaven, having lost hope for this life.

'Since no one was resisting or opposing them, the Barbarians brought long pieces of wood and used them to get over the wall and come inside. They opened the gates and the rest rushed in like fierce, wild beasts with unsheathed swords in their hands. The first they seized was a monk named Jeremiah who was sitting at the gate of the Lord's House. Through one of their interpreters,[117] they told him, "Show us which one is your chief." Gazing on their barbaric faces and unsheathed swords without any terror or fear, he replied, "I am not afraid of you impious enemies of God. Nor will I reveal to you him whom you seek, although he is standing nearby."

[24] 'The Barbarians were stunned by the man's high-spirited sharpness, seeing that he not only did not fear them in the least, but even had insulted them. At last they seized him, bound him hand and foot, stood him up naked before them, and shot him with so many arrows that no part of his body was left intact. Thus he contended and struggled with manly valour against the devil, and was first of all to put on the crown, struggling nobly unto death, stamping on the serpent's head,[118] to become a holy first-fruit[119] and fine exemplar for the holy ones.[120]

[25] 'When our most holy Father Paul saw this, he came right out and told them in a loud voice, "I'm the one you're looking for", pointing a finger at himself to indicate that he was the one they were seeking.[121] And the noble slave of Christ, Paul, gave himself up to the Barbarians[122] without any fear or thought for the blows and torments that the lawless ones were going to inflict on him before his death. They seized him and interrogated him, saying "Tell

---

115 Mt. 11:28. CPA is missing the folio that describes the following massacre.

116 Mt. 26:41.

117 L: *Through an interpreter, one of the sailors who was with them.* V: *There was with them one of the sailors who was interpreting the language.*

118 Cf. Gen. 3:15.

119 Rom. 11:16, 'If the first-fruits are holy, then so is the whole batch'. Jews and Christians in this period offered first fruits to God to ensure blessings for the rest of their produce.

120 Cf. the death of the magnanimous youth in Ps.-Nilus, *Narr.* V.16–17, and the death of St Stephen, the protomartyr, Acts 6:1–8:2.

121 'pointing … seeking' omitted by V.

122 V adds: *like Christ into the hands of the enemies.*

us the truth. Where have you hidden your money?" The saint replied in his usual soft tone and gentle manner, saying, "Believe me, children, my whole life I've owned nothing more than this old hair shirt you see on my body." He took his hand and clasped his cloak and showed it to them.[123]

[26] 'Beating him on his neck with stones and piercing his cheeks and his face with arrows, they kept shouting, "Bring here your money!" After torturing and mocking him for a long time without finding anything, they finally struck him in the middle of the head with a sword blade. His holy head was split in half and fell off his shoulders, one part off this side, and one part off that. After he received still more blows all over his body, he lay dead at the feet of the father who had died before him. After enduring many unimaginable tortures before his death, he became the second victor and trophy-bearer against the devil, without expressing any grief or yielding in his purpose at all.[124]

[27] 'But as for me, miserable man that I am, as I watched this bitter, inhumane death and the holy ones' venerable blood pouring out all over and their innards splattered on the ground, I searched in fear for a place where I could flee and be saved. To the left by the corner of the house[125] lay some leafy palm branches. While the Barbarians were occupied with the holy Paul,[126] I quickly fled under the palm-fronds, thinking that one of two things would happen: either I would escape without the Barbarians noticing me, or I would be caught and endure nothing more than death.[127]

[28] 'The villainous, lawless Barbarians left the two dead men outside and stampeded into the church like a herd of wild beasts, bellowing, beating the air with their swords and waving their hands as they began to make murder. Each struck this way or that, murdering whoever happened to fall in his path. One brought his sword down on a head, another drove his into a stomach up to the hilt and extracted with it all of its contents; another cast his spear through someone's back into his heart, then pulled it out, depriving that holy man of life.'

---

123 Note Paul's use of hand gestures to communicate with the Barbarians.

124 L omits this sentence. V has: *And he was glorious in his contest, vanquishing Satan, and having no fear of death.*

125 L: *of the nave.* V omits.

126 L omits; V: *While the enemies were torturing the holy men.* CPA has a lacuna here.

127 Instead of 'or I … death', CPA has: *or they would kill me.* L: *they would put me to the same death I would have been expecting had I stayed outside.* V: *I said to myself, 'Perhaps they will find me and kill me, just as the fathers were killed; perhaps I will be saved from them, and I will bury the bodies of these holy men'.*

As he related these things to us he wept bitterly, moving us all to lament and wail as well.

[29] Again he said to us, 'What can I say, or how can I express or describe, Dear Ones, exactly what my eyes have seen? There was a monk there named Adam[128] who had a relative named Sergius who was a monk and about fifteen years old. The old man had raised him from childhood and had given him monastic instruction since he was a babe, so that he was well instructed concerning warfare with the enemy.[129] When the Barbarians saw that he had a delicate face and was still young in age, they wanted to set him aside. One of the Barbarians seized the brother with his own hand and dragged him outside and held him. But when he saw that he was not being privileged to die with the other fathers, but might instead become a travelling companion for cruel and impious human beings, he began to cry, wailing bitterly. Then, since he saw that it was no use, he cast aside all fear and cowardice. His spirits rekindled, he sprang up, and with a bold, noble resolve he ran like a noble soldier[130] and grabbed a sword from one of the Barbarians and struck one of them on the shoulder, so that they might become so enraged by this that they would kill him – which is just what happened.[131] Dumbfounded, the accursed ones became greatly enraged; rolling their eyes and gnashing their teeth, they butchered him limb by limb. Meanwhile he exulted, shouting, "Blessed be the Lord our God, who did not deliver us to the hands of sinful humans!"[132] After saying this, he too died in peace. Even after he was dead he received blows and wounds all over his body – that marvellous man and slave of Christ, Sergius.[133]

[30] 'As I watched these things I was pleading to our merciful God who loves mankind that he might conceal me from the Barbarians and blind their eyes so that they would not see me and I might be saved to bury the holy ones' bodies. The entire church was filled with the blood of the fallen holy men. They had shown no fear or distress, but had rejoiced and thanked the Lord for what had befallen them. With their minds set on heaven, they had

---

128 Instead of 'Adam', SGr 267 has *Salaē*. L: *Salim*. V: *Abba Salmon*; CPA has a lacuna. In what follows, L omits: 'who had ... Sergius', making Salim the 15-year old protagonist.

129 CPA: *Father Joseph had taught this one from his youth the eremetical way of life, for from his youth he had gone out into the desert to strive with Satan through hunger and thirst.*

130 'But ... soldier' not in L or V; CPA has a lacuna here.

131 'which ... happened' not in CPA.

132 Cf. Ps.-Nilus, *Narr.* IV.3.

133 Thus martyrdom made a 'man' out of an adolescent. However, 'that ... Sergius' is not in CPA, L or V, and may have been added here as a gloss.

conducted themselves well on earth for their Master and Lord, becoming a temple of God in the Highest. They left the transient and corrupting things of this life to follow God alone. After all that they perished in diverse ways, under tribulation and sword blade.[134]

'Now that they believed they had killed everyone, the savage, ferocious Barbarians searched everywhere,[135] thinking they would find things stored away. The wretches did not realize that the martyrs, who had gained all heaven, had nothing on earth but their bodies.

[31] 'As these things happened, almost all my blood left me, the least one of all. I lay still as a corpse, sure that they would also inspect the palm branches and find me hiding. I kept peering through the palm-fronds to see when they would come to me. As the saying goes, I saw death before my eyes, and continually supplicated God Who loves mankind to save me if it pleased Him. They came right up to me, but when they saw that they were only palms, they withdrew in contempt. They went away without discovering the place I was in, since God had darkened their eyes and hearts.

[32] 'They left the holy ones piled on top of each other. Having found nothing to take, they returned to the springs, intending to resume their journey to Clysma by sea. But when they came to the beach they discovered that their boat had been smashed up.[136] For the man who stayed to guard it was a Christ-loving man; undetected by the Barbarian who had been left with him, he had cut the boat's ropes and had cast it upon the rocks. It was completely smashed. In this way he also killed the Barbarian.[137] He escaped by swimming toward the mountain, truly reaching safety with God's help.

---

134 L omits 'After … blade.' In CPA the entire paragraph is different: *They left the transient and corrupting world and adhered only to God. Thus they died by the sword and were not separated from the love of the Messiah, as it is written: 'Who will separate us from the love of the Messiah?'* [Rom. 8:35] *Neither sword nor oppression will separate us from the love of the Messiah. Thus, these saints gave over also their bodies to tribulation and to the sword. If then I call them martyrs I will not be wrong, because they suffered tribulation. They were cut completely into pieces like martyrs.*

135 Instead of 'everywhere', V has: *in the church and in the cells.*

136 CPA adds: *and their comrade killed.*

137 CPA: *he had been able secretly to escape from the barbarian who was with him on the ship, and he cut the ship's moorings. It had then all of a sudden knocked against a rock and had broken up; and he killed the barbarian who had been with him on the ship.* L: *he seized the barbarian whom the wicked men had left, and killed him; he then cut the ship's mooring ropes and let it drift, with the result that it got broken up against the shore and completely fell apart.* V (earlier omitting 'and was a Christ-loving man'): *he slew the Black Man who was with him, and cut the ropes of iron which held the boat; he brought it out on the sand and broke it up as much as he could, and left it there.*

[33] 'Bereft of hope, with no idea what to do or how to return to their country,[138] the Barbarians lost courage and became aggrieved, there being nothing they could do. Seized by great anger and fury, they first killed all the souls they had set aside, a multitude of women and children. Then they built a great fire and ruthlessly burned the palm trees so that nearly all were destroyed by fire.[139] Such was the activity that was occupying them in their rage and frustration over their homeland, when a multitude of Ishmaelite men came from Pharan, six hundred in number, all select archers. They had heard what had happened.[140] The Barbarians saw them approaching and prepared for battle.

[34] 'They met in battle as the sun rose on the plain. Both sides shot dense volleys of arrows at the other. The Pharanites, in as much as they were more numerous, killed most of the Barbarians, but since the Barbarians no longer had any hope of escape or expectation of safety, they nobly resisted and fought to hold their ground. The battle lasted until the ninth hour.[141] That day eighty-four[142] Pharanite men were killed and many others wounded, while all the Barbarians died in that very spot without turning their backs on the enemy or budging from their position.

[35] 'While they were busy with this activity – I mean, cutting down the Barbarians – I gained some confidence and came out from where I was hiding. I examined the bodies of the holy men after their slaughter. I found that all had died in the Lord except for three brothers: Domnus, Andreas, and Orion.[143] Of these three, Domnus lay in terrible agony, with a very deep blow to his side.[144] Andreas had many wounds, but not very serious, and he survived. Orion, however, received no wound at all. A Barbarian had struck him with a sword on the right side. The sword had gone through his cloak and out the left side, but its blade had passed through his hairshirt without touching his body.[145] Thinking he was dead, the Barbarian left him there and went on to another. Orion threw himself on the pile of bodies and lay like a

---

138 V adds: *or to Clysma, or to anywhere else.*

139 Instead of 'so that … fire', CPA has: *in order to destroy the place.*

140 CPA: *men came from Pharan, 600 valiant chosen men in number.* By the sixth century Pharan had a state-supported, 800- (or 80-) man garrison to protect monks: see PP, *Itin.* 40 and note *ad loc.* Presumably they were informed by the Pharanites who escaped after the battle in sect. 19.

141 Three in the afternoon.

142 L: *seventy-four.*

143 Here and elsewhere, instead of 'Domnus' and 'Orion', V has *Damianus* and *Urbanus.*

144 CPA adds: *though not mortally.*

145 Owing, no doubt, to his ascetic physique!

corpse. This Orion then got up and went around with me, scouring for the remains of the holy men and grieving and mourning greatly with me because of the terrible things that had befallen us.

[36] 'After the men from Pharan had cut down and wiped out all the Blemmyes, they returned, leaving the bodies of the Barbarians on the edge of the sea as food for birds, beasts, and winged things of the air. After collecting their own people's bodies, both those who had died earlier and the many who died later,[146] they raised for them a loud lament. They buried them at the foot of the mountain, in caves close to the springs. Then they came back to us and prepared the burial of the holy men, together with their chief, Obedianus.[147] When they entered to collect the bodies, we uttered lamentations, bitterly groaning and beating our chests, because we saw Christ's flock cast down on the ground, like sheep laid waste by wolves.[148]

'For Christ's slaves and martyrs had frightful, unbearable wounds. One had a gash from his shoulder to his navel, another was lying on the ground, cut in two; another received a blow from his forehead to his neck; another had half his guts laying in his stomach and the rest splattered on the earth. Thus they all died in this way or that, with blows on every limb of their body. To the eye they were men whose bodies were on the earth.[149] But since their minds were set on heaven, they never held a thought for their bodily tabernacles; instead, they "ever carried the death of Jesus around in their bodies",[150] so that they might have life in the world to come. All their lives they conducted themselves in a goodly manner pleasing to God, and at the end of their lives they received an additional virtue, for they were washed by their own blood and enlisted among the martyrs, since all had died for the sake of the Lord and His eternal kingdom.[151]

---

146 'both … later' not in CPA. Those who had died earlier were the 147 mentioned above, sect. 19.

147 This reference to Obedianus is not in CPA. L adds: *whom I mentioned a little earlier as the person who had been healed by the blessed Moses.* V: *whom we mentioned a little earlier as the person who had believed at the hands of the holy Abba Moses.*

148 Cf. Mt. 10:16; Lk. 10:3. Interestingly, unlike Ps.-Nilus, Ammonius does not censure such traditional funereal behaviour.

149 Instead of 'men … earth', L has: *divine people, angels on earth.*

150 2 Cor. 4:10.

151 Instead of this paragraph, CPA has: *We were in great fear, seeing the wounds which were inflicted on the bodies of the saints, the servants of the Messiah, those who during their lives were pleasing to God. At their demise they gave the blood of their necks so that they would complete their lives with the martyrs.* V: *But the servants and martyrs of Christ accepted these with joy and goodness of soul because they knew they would reach the joy that has no end, through their excellent way of life and because their ministry was a heavenly one. For this*

[37] 'Once all their remains had been gathered into one place, the Christ-loving Obedianus and the rest of the headmen of Pharan[152] brought bright, costly garments for their honour,[153] and buried the holy men. They were thirty-nine in number since Domnus, who was born a Roman, was still alive. Then all those who were there took palm-branches and went to meet the holy ones in a procession. With great joy and psalm singing we carried the remains of the holy ones and laid them down across from the Fort,[154] all except for Domnus. But when evening came, he also gave up his spirit to Christ. We carried and buried him, not with the holy men, but separately in a place close by them, so that we would not disturb the holy martyrs of Christ by opening the tomb again.[155]

[38] 'The holy martyrs of Christ died on the fourteenth of the month of January.[156] Abba Andreas and Orion remained there, trying to make up their minds whether to stay in the place or leave it.[157] But I could not bear the tribulation of the desolation of that place, nor could I cease from lamenting those who were slain. So I came to you. Often the Christ-loving Obedianus had asked me to stay in that place, promising to visit us regularly and minister happily to our needs. But I could not be persuaded, for the reasons I have already stated.

---

reason God accepted their toil and crowned them in a good martyrdom.

152 CPA: *Obedianus, the chief of the Pharanites, together with the nobles of Pharan.* The term *protoi* ('nobles', 'headmen', here πρῶτοι τῆς Φαράν) becomes commonly used for leading citizens of both cities and villages from the sixth century onwards: see Liebeschuetz 2001, 65 n. 232 and 110–12.

153 To be used as burial shrouds; cf. Anast., *Narr.* I.28. Most of the colourful textiles that survive from Byzantine Egypt come from cemeteries.

154 κάστρον; cf. *Rel.* 20 and note *ad loc.* CPA and L: *in a single place near the fortress* (L: *in the tower*). V: *in the vicinity of the fortress, to the east.*

155 CPA adds: *He was counted among them, forty martyrs for the Lord Jesus, the Messiah, the one for whom there is praise forever and ever, Amen.*

156 Clearly this represents an attempt to make the narrative reflect the commemorative date attested in Ps.-Nilus, *Narr.* IV.14. CPA has nothing here; L and V have: *These* [L adds: *forty*] *blessed men were crowned on the 28th* [L: *18th*] *of the month Kanun I* [i.e. December], *at the ninth hour* (i.e. three pm.; L adds: *in our Lord Jesus Christ, to whom be glory and honour, along with his blessed Father and living and Holy Spirit for eternal ages, amen*). According to Mayerson 1980, 141–42, the fourteenth-century Combéfis text has *the holy ones ... died around the ninth hour on the 2nd of the month of Tubi, but their memorial is celebrated on the 14th of the month of January according to the Roman* [calendar]', and SGr 267 has: *These holy, victorious [martyrs] of Christ died in the month of January on the fourteenth day around the ninth hour.* The second day of the Egyptian month of Tubi (or Tybi) would have been 28 December (cf. also below, p. 171, n. 164).

157 Instead of 'whether ... leave it', V has: *I do not know if they remain there or not.*

[39] 'Some other things befell us which I will describe to you in detail. But please tell me what went on here, since I have already given you exact information about my own circumstances.' We told him everything then and there, and we all were amazed at the incredible works of God, since all had died on the same day, both those on the Holy Mountain and those at Rhaithou, and because the number who died was the same both there and here. Once again we began to wail and mourn about the things described.

[40] Then Abba Doulas, the superior, stood up and said, 'My dear ones, those men like worthy slaves and chosen servants of Christ have been privileged with His joy and kingdom. After so many contests, tribulations, and temptations, they at last put on the crown of martyrdom, and live now in great honour and glory in heaven. As for us, Fathers and Brothers, let us remain steadfast in the things that please God. Let us ask them to represent us before Christ, so that we may have a share with them in the Kingdom of Heaven,[158] and let us unanimously thank our good God who loves mankind for sheltering us from the profane and murderous hands of [the Barbarians].' As he spoke these words the father restored us all, comforting all of us in our souls with his many words of encouragement.

[41] Then I, the humble Ammonius, with God's help[159] returned to the regions of Egypt. I wrote down everything on paper. I never went back to my original abode, the one called Canobus, but moved to a very small dwelling near Memphis in which I now live.[160] I read these notes constantly,[161] and rejoice every day in their contests and sufferings, as ever I glorify and praise Christ, our true God, to Whom is the power and the glory unto eternity, Amen.

[42] I, John the Priest,[162] found these things with God's help in the possession of a certain anchorite living near Naucratis.[163] They were written in Egyptian script, which I have translated (since I know the Egyptian language well) into Greek for the glory and praise of the holy martyrs and

158 CPA adds: *Amen.*

159 'with … help' not in CPA, L, or V.

160 L and V omit this sentence. Memphis (modern Mit Rahina, 22.5 km/14 miles south of Cairo) was the site of a military camp in late antiquity. Extensive ruins of the Monastery of Jeremias have been found on the opposite side of the Nile at Saqqara; it flourished from the late fifth to the mid-ninth centuries: see Quibell 1912, i–vii.

161 CPA: *I read all the time of the fight of the martyrs, the saints of the Messiah.*

162 'the Priest' not in CPA.

163 CPA: *in the possession of a monk Taros near Naucratis.* Naucratis (modern Kum Ga'if, Egypt) was approximately 83 km/52 miles south-east of Alexandria on the Canopic branch of the Nile.

righteous ones, with whom may the Lord give us a share in His kingdom. I ask all who encounter [this account] to pray on behalf of my worthless self, glorifying the Father, Son and Holy Spirit, now, always, and unto the ages of ages, Amen.[164]

---

164 CPA omits 'I ask … ages', and after 'Amen' has: *The life of the holy fathers who were killed at Mount Sinai and Rhaithou, in the days of Petros, the Patriarch of Alexandria, is completed. The remembrance of these saints is commemorated on the 28th of December, the month of the Romans. By their prayers may our Lord have mercy upon us and the whole world. Amen.*

Instead of section 42, L has: *Ended is the history of the blessed Ammonius, concerning the holy fathers who were persecuted by the barbarians on the holy mountain of Sinai and at Rhaithou, which is Elim.*

Instead of section 42, V has: **[a]** *These holy men were martyrs in the time of Diocletian* [i.e. 284–305 CE], *the emperor of the Greeks, who was an unbeliever, one of the godless pagans. This narrative of these resplendent men which has been translated from Greek is 474 years* [old?]; *it was translated in the month of Teshrin I, in the year 150 according to the numbering of the Arabs* [= October 767 CE], *that is, according to their years and stupid reckoning.* **[b]** *But let everyone who reads or hears the narrative of these holy men give praise to God and pray for the person who took care for and was involved in its translation, that mercy should be upon him and on all the Christian people, at the prayer of the blessed Bearer of God, our Lady Mary, and Mar Moses, the greatest of the prophets, and of everyone who has pleased God. Amen and amen.*

[c] *This volume, that is quires, belong to Mar Abba John and his brother Abba Simeon, from the district of Antioch. The sinner, truly wretched and feeblest of all Christians, whose name is Theodosi*[us], *put down in writing these narratives in the year 1197 of the years of Alexander, in the month Shbat* [i.e. February] *and* [the first] *three days of Adar* [i.e. March], *in* [the monastery of] *Mar Moses on the Mountain of God, where God spoke with Moses* [i.e. Mt Sinai]. *But let everyone who reads or copies it for our Lord's sake pray for me a sinner, amen, and for everyone who had a part in it.*

ANASTASIUS OF SINAI, *TALES OF THE SINAI FATHERS*, AND *EDIFYING TALES* (SELECTIONS):*
INTRODUCTION AND TRANSLATION

The Greek monk, priest, and author known as Anastasius of Sinai is now recognized as one of the most important witnesses to conditions in former Roman provinces soon after the Arab conquests. Probably born in the early seventh century, perhaps on Cyprus, he seems to have still been writing in 700/01.[1] Like John Moschus, he travelled widely in Palestine and Egypt, and, like Moschus, stayed for a long time (perhaps to his end) at Mount Sinai.[2] A prolific author, his works include important handbooks on orthodox faith (e.g. the *Hodēgos*, the *Questions and Responses*) and the two narrative collections translated here either in whole (Collection I, *Tales of the Sinai Fathers*) or in part (Collection II, *Edifying Tales*). All of his works are pastoral in nature, reflecting his concern to shore up Christian communities in this time of crisis.

Anastasius' stories present a different literary experience than Ps-Nilus' *Narrations* or the Ammonius *Report*. There is no over-arching narrative or obvious thematic connection between his stories, besides the holiness of the Sinai and its Christian inhabitants. On that topic, however, Anastasius adds considerable detail. His stories are minutely attuned to the daily rituals of Sinai monastic life: in them we find much on the use of incense, attendance of shrines, and care for the body. Yet they also highlight the mutable nature of that material world, describing diaphanous moments when heavenly apparitions appear on Mount Sinai, dreams transport monks to distant landscapes, or monks themselves vanish or change shape.

---

* Based on new editions of Anastasius' Collection I (*Diēgēmata paterika*) and Collection II (*Diēgēmata stēriktika*) being prepared by A. Binggeli for CNRS. These will replace the 1902 and 1903 editions of F. Nau; the numbers given to the stories by Nau are indicated in brackets beside Binggeli's new numbers. I am grateful to Dr Binggeli for providing a copy in advance of its publication. For preliminary discussion, see Binggeli 2004a.

1 Consensus has now formed over Anastasius' identity, with most agreeing that there was one author and not many writing under that name: see Haldon 1992.

2 Anastasius notes having served 'some time ago' as infirmary warden in the Mt Sinai *coenobium* (*Narr.* I.3), and mentions having lived three years as a hermit in the region of Arselaiou, and for some time at Goudda (I.14, 31).

Anastasius thus preserves the imaginative world of his Sinai contemporaries in an era of profound stress and transition. His stories are also important for their depictions of differences in ethnic and religious identity. Those of Collection I suggests that 'the pre-Islamic Arabs at Sinai seemed to have lived in relative peace with the monks and solitaries'.[3] Although in many respects they resemble John Moschus' stories (on which they may have been modelled), they often have a dreamlike or nostalgic feel, perhaps because many seem to reach back into earlier, more tranquil periods of Sinai history. Apart from some obscure allusions to sacrileges inflicted by (apparently) Arab conquerors (perhaps added to the collection at a later time?), the central event of the collection seems to have been the death of John Climacus, mentioned as a recent occurrence in *Narr.* I.16. Indeed, André Binggeli proposes that the collection was assembled c. 660–670 in order to celebrate Climacus' memory.[4] The stories in Collection II, written some thirty years later (c. 690), have a markedly different tone. The second Arab civil war had recently come to an end without any diminution of Arab dominance, and hopes that their conquests were temporary were dashed by the Arabizing and Islamicizing policies of Umayyad Caliph 'Abd al-Malik ibn Marwan (685–705), symbolized above all by his Dome of the Rock. Collection II describes some of the challenges that Jews, heretics, and Saracens – now regularly described as demons – posed for Christians in this new era.[5] However, since only two of its stories are set at Mount Sinai, they alone of that collection are translated here.

---

3 Hoyland 1997, 99.

4 Personal communication. As noted in the General Introduction, the date of Climacus' death is debated: see above, p. 24, n. 98. and notably Müller 2006, 29–32, where, in defence of an early date c. 600, it is also argued that the stories in Anastasius' collection were assembled over a long period of time and cannot be used to fix any historical date. Binggeli's edition of Anastasius, *Narr.* I.16 (= Nau 32) removes a major impediment to the later date for Climacus' death: see below, n. 65. Much will be clarified by his edition's introduction, critical apparatus, and commentary.

5 For extensive discussion of Collection II, see Flusin 1991; Hoyland 1997, 99–103; for the Christian reaction to al-Malik's policies more generally, see Hoyland 1997, 545–59; Reinink 2006.

TRANSLATION OF THE GREEK TEXT

Anastasius of Sinai, Collection I:
Diverse Narratives
Concerning the Saintly Fathers in the Desert of Mount Sina
by Anastasius,
a humble and most lowly monk

I.1 [Nau 1] Ten years ago two fathers of the Holy Mountain of Sina (one of whom is still alive in the flesh) went up at night to do reverence at the Holy Summit. When they were within two arrow shots of Holy Elijah's,[6] they noticed a certain strange fragrance, unlike fragrances of this world. The disciple suggested that the custodian[7] was making the offering of incense,[8] but the old man (who was his supervisor,[9] and is still alive) said to him, 'This is no earthly fragrance'.

As they approached the shrine, behold! they saw it blazing inside like a fiery furnace, with fire flickering out of all of its windows.[10] When the disciple saw the vision it made him shudder, but the old man reassured him, saying, 'What are you afraid of, my child? They are angelic powers, our fellow slaves.[11] Don't be a coward. In heaven, they venerate our nature,[12] not we theirs.' And so, as into a furnace, they fearlessly entered the shrine and prayed. Then they went up to the Holy Summit, since it was now morning.

When the custodian saw them, he observed that their faces were gloriously shining as the face of Moses once shined.[13] He said to them, 'What was it that you saw on your ascent?' Since they wanted to keep it secret,

---

6 Anastasius refers to a church on Mt Horeb (Jabal Sufsafa; either on Jabal al-Dayr, Jabal al-Moneijah-Musa, or in a depression in between) dedicated to Elijah: cf. Egeria, *Itin.* IV.2 and PP, *Itin.* 37. The church on the Sinai summit is also discussed in this story further below.

7 παραμονάριος/*paramonarius*, a clerical warden assigned to tend a church by a local bishop (e.g. the bishop of Pharan, if that position still existed at this time; perhaps otherwise the head of the monastery). Cf. Egeria, *Itin.* III.14.

8 For incense practices in late antiquity, see Harvey 2006, 5–98.

9 ἐπιστάτης/*epistatēs*.

10 Dan. 3:6.

11 I.e. slaves of the same master (Christ). Cf. Rev. 22:9: 'I fell down to make homage at the feet of an angel who showed these things to me, but he said to me, "You must not do that! For I am a fellow slave along with you and your brothers the prophets and those who keep the words of this book."'

12 I.e. human nature as represented by the incarnated Christ. Cf. Anastasius, *Questions and Responses* 4 (PG 89.705C).

13 Exod. 34:29.

they said, 'Nothing, Father'. Then the custodian, who was himself a slave of the Lord,[14] spoke to them once more: 'Believe me, you saw a vision, for behold! your faces are beaming with the glory of the Holy Spirit'. They made obeisance[15] before him and begged him not to tell anyone. After saying their prayers they departed in peace.

I.2 [not in Nau] Abba Misaēl the Iberian told us that, 'When I was an attendant at the Holy Summit, one night I was standing and praying inside the shrine.[16] All the doors had been shut tight, when behold! I saw three men enter without opening them. One wore an old hair shirt while the other two were wearing short-sleeved tunics made of palm-fibres.[17] When they saw me looking at them, they were surprised. They said to me, "Can we take communion, Lord Brother?" I said to them, "Yes, Fathers, if you please, I'll wake up the custodian." They said to me, "No, don't bother him."

'The door to the service area had been secured with its key and likewise the *armarium* where the Holy Communion was kept.[18] So they went and made obeisance[19] in front of the service area doors. They opened instantly and automatically, both the doors and the armarium alike. After taking communion they departed. The doors closed behind them again by themselves, and the men became invisible.'

I.3 [Nau 39] John, the most saintly *hēgoumen* of this Holy Mountain of Sina,[20] once told us that there had been a custodian on the Holy Summit years ago who had gone up one evening to throw on the incense. Suddenly

---

14   I.e. an advanced ascetic (cf. Egeria, *Itin.* III.4), and therefore possessing powers of discernment.

15   βαλόντες … αὐτῷ μετάνοιαν, literally 'Cast penance before him', i.e. lie prostrate before him. For this gesture of repentance (*metanoia*) in monastic settings, see Vivian 1999.

16   διακονητής/*diakonētēs*, an attendant who assisted the *paramonarius* in the church *diakonikon* (see below, n. 19), often by keeping lamps fuelled and trimmed (cf. Anast., *Narr.* I.6).

17   Garments (τρίχινον/*trichinon*, κολόβια/*kolobia*) designating advanced ascetics: see Patrich 1995, 217-18, and John Mosch., *Meadow* 123. These three visitors may be meant to recall Gen. 18:2 (where three supernatural beings visit Abraham's home), but cf. Anast., *Narr.* I.31, 33 and Mosch., *Meadow* 122.

18   The *diakonikon* or service area where sacred vessels were stored was usually located behind the iconostasis to the south of the church altar. An ἀρμάριον/*armarium* was a chest in which sacramental bread was stored. Cf. below, Anast., *Narr.* I.33 and John Mosch., *Meadow* 79.

19   For a similar gesture, see above, *Narr.* I.1 and note *ad loc.*

20   I.e. John Climacus, author of the *Ladder of Divine Ascent* and most famous *hēgoumen* (leader or abbot) of the Mt Sinai monastery (cf. Anast., *Narr.* I.8–12 and 26).

it began to snow heavily, so that the mountain of the Holy Summit was covered by three or four cubits of snow.[21] The custodian was cut off up there and unable to come down.

Now, in those times no one dared to sleep at all on the Holy Summit.[22] The custodian performed the office as long as he could but around dawn he grew sleepy. Transported by God, he found himself at St Peter's in Rome. The clerics were stunned to see him suddenly appear among them. Together with them he went to the pope and recounted what had happened. By God's arrangement he was found to have on his belt the door keys inscribed, 'For the Holy Summit of Mount Sina'. Therefore the most saintly pope clasped him and ordained him bishop of one of the cities under the see of Rome. But he also asked him, 'What does the monastery have need of?' Upon learning that the monastery needed an infirmary built in it, he sent money and letters and built the infirmary,[23] while also noting the month, day, and facts concerning the custodian.

In this infirmary I too was an infirmary warden, some time ago.

I.4 [Nau 38] Armenians, as everyone knows, have a custom of coming for prayer upon the Holy Mountain of Sina *en masse*.[24] Twenty years ago a large group of them came, eight hundred souls. They ascended the Holy Summit, and when they finally reached the outermost Holy Rock where Moses received the Law,[25] there occurred in that holy place and among those lay folk a vision of God, an awful work of wonder. Just as formerly at the time of the Law-Giving,[26] so now too the entire Holy Summit and lay folk appeared to be engulfed in fire. But the incredible thing was that no one saw himself being scorched or burned; instead, one person saw another, and each one saw the other [being scorched and burned]. The throng became terrified and shouted, 'Lord have mercy', for about an hour, and the fire receded again.

---

21 A cubit was an arm's length (about 50 cm/20 inches).

22 Cf. Anast., *Narr.* I.5; Egeria, *Itin.* III.5; PP, *Itin.* 37; Procop., *Buildings*. V.viii.7. The story that follows has a parallel in John Mosch., *Meadow* 127 (PG 87 [III].2988D–2992B), which tells how George, a Sinai *hēgoumen* who died in 552, miraculously appeared before the Patriarch of Jerusalem and other priests while they were performing the Eucharist; afterwards the Patriarch sent letters to the Sinai regarding him.

23 *nosokomeion*. Gregory the Great, *ep.* XI.2, presupposes that a facility called a *hierochomium* ('infirmary for Holy Ones') had already been built at the Sinai monastery by the time of his writing (1 September 600). If that facility was the same as the one mentioned here, Anastasius' story may be a remembrance or elaboration of Gregory's contributions to it.

24 Cf. Stone 1982 and 1986.

25 Cf. Exod. 33:2.

26 Cf. Exod. 19:8.

Neither a hair nor a garment among them had been harmed.[27] Instead, only their staffs had caught fire, like candles, amid the vision. After being extinguished they still bore the mark of the conflagration, having been charred at their tips as if by fire. By this form of theirs they testify even in their country, as if speaking aloud, that 'Today on the Holy Mountain of Sina the Lord was seen again in fire'.[28]

Indeed, that vision was even seen by some Saracens who were up there at that time. They did not take faith but continued to revile this holy place on account of the images and venerable crosses that are in it. But they ought rather to comprehend and say that, 'If God were blasphemed by the Christians, He would not be making in their churches such visions, which He has never made among us or among any other faith or synagogue of Jews or Arabs'.[29]

I.5 [Nau 2] Another time on the same Holy Summit, before it was polluted and defiled by the present nation,[30] a brother who was serving as the custodian's attendant contemptuously hid himself within the shrine, saying that no harm would come to one who slept there.[31] The custodian thought his disciple had gone down ahead of him, so after censing the holy place,[32] he closed the doors and went away.

At night the disciple who was hiding in the shrine rose so as to trim the oil lamps. When he came to the first lamp, the spark that he scattered instantly burned his side by divine command.[33] From that moment his whole side including a hand and a foot withered up,[34] and remained half-withered until he died.

---

27 Cf. Dan. 3:94.

28 Cf. Exod. 3:2, 19:18.

29 ὀπτασίας ... ἃς οὐδέποτε ἐποίησεν οὔτε παρ' ἡμῖν οὔτε παρ' ἄλλῃ πίστει ἢ συναγωγῇ Ἰουδαίων ἢ Ἀράβων. Here, as elsewhere, Anastasius uses πίστις/*pistis* (faith or belief) as a word for religion in general. *Synagoge* may mean a communal gathering and not a building.

30 πρὶν ἢ μολυνθῇ καὶ καταρυπωθῇ ὑπὸ τοῦ παρόντος ἔθνους. Ἔθνος/*ethnos* has the sense here of 'unbelievers' or 'pagans'; cf. *ep.* 752 in the mid-sixth-century correspondence of Barsanuphius and John of Gaza. Anastasius seems to be referring to the unspecified blasphemies mentioned in *Narr.* I.4; it is unlikely that those included the construction of a mosque: see 'Abd al-Malik 1998; Mouton 1998.

31 No doubt referring to the custom/rule noted in Anast., *Narr.* I.3.

32 I.e. lit incense in the chapel before leaving.

33 Cf. Sir. 28.12: 'If you blow on a spark, it will glow, if you spit on it, it will be put out; yet both come out of your mouth'.

34 I.e. it was paralysed; cf. 1 [III] Kgs 13:4.

I.6 [Nau 37] Five years ago another brother became an attendant on the same Holy Summit. He was an Armenian called Elisha. He used to say that not once, not twice, but almost every night he saw fire burning within the Holy Shrine of the Divine Giving of the Law. This was because he was pure and worthy.

[Nau 3] Once during a feast of Holy Pentecost, while the Holy Anaphora was being held on that Holy Summit, as the celebrant raised the triumphant hymn, all the mountains responded with an awesome cry, saying three times: 'Holy Holy Holy'.[35] The cry echoed and lingered for half an hour. This cry was not heard by everyone, but only by those who had those ears about which Christ said: 'He who has ears to hear, let him hear'.[36]

I.7 [Nau 36] Another brother – that one who has lived with the present writer since he left his mother's womb – once told me, 'Three years ago I came up from the desert to the Holy Mountain three days before the Feast of the Holy Summit.[37] At night as if in a trance I saw myself in the palace. Someone was interrogating me, saying, "Why have you come here, Lord Abba?" When I said, "I have eagerly come to venerate the Emperor", he said to me, "Very well, then, if you are going to make a request, go up to him before he receives the throng and he truly will give you as much as you ask from him."'[38] By His Glory! that is just what happened. For after he returned to himself from the vision and analysed the things seen and said, then (as he told me himself), 'I spoke to those who administered the holy place.[39] Taking a priest and everything necessary, I went up the day before the feast, held a service[40] on the Holy Summit, placed my requests before God and received what I had requested, as the course of events showed.'[41]

---

35 The 'Trisagion' was part of the *anaphora*, which invoked the presence of the Holy Spirit before a Eucharist was performed. Holy Pentecost refers either to the day of the Feast of Pentecost (on which the descent of the Holy Ghost on the disciples and the Giving of the Law to Moses were both celebrated), or to the fifty-day period after Easter that culminated with the day of Pentecost.

36 Mt. 11:15; Lk. 8:8, 14:35.

37 Binggeli proposes that this feast commemorated the dedication of the summit church.

38 Cf. Jn 11:20.

39 τοὺς τὸν ἅγιον τόπον διοικοῦντας, probably referring to clerics in charge of pilgrims: see Maraval 1985, 204–06, for those at Jerusalem. John Mosch., *Meadow* 125 (PG 87[3].2988A), suggests ascetic criticism of those at Mt Sinai.

40 σύναξις/*synaxis*, any service of formal prayer or reading; here it seems to have included a Eucharist.

41 This story seems autobiographical, with Anastasius alluding to himself in the manner of Paul, 2 Cor. 12:2 and Palladius, *Lausiac History* LXXI.1.

I.8 [Nau 4] Some years ago by the Lord's consent a deadly plague arose in our desert.[42] A saintly father – a man of virtue – died and was entombed in the place of rest.[43] The next day one of the more negligent brothers died and was entombed above the saintly man's bodily tabernacle.[44] A day later another father died. When they went to deposit his remains, they found that the saintly man had by himself tossed the sinful brother's tabernacle to the ground. At the time they thought that this had happened by accident and not through any miracle, so they picked up the brother and put him back above the father. But the next day when they came they found that the virtuous father had tossed the brother off.

When he learned this, our saintly father the *hēgoumen* came and entered the tomb. To the dead old man, who was called John, he remarked, 'Abba John, during your lifetime you were gentle and forbearing'. With his own hands he picked up the brother's remains and placed them above the old man and said to him again, 'Put up with the brother, Abba John, even if he was a sinner, just as God puts up with the sins of the world'.[45] From that day onward the old man never tossed off the brother's tabernacle.

I.9 [Nau 5] There is a desolate and very rugged place forty miles away from the Holy Mountain called Tourba.[46] Here a very wonderful old man used to reside with his disciple. In the days of our saintly father the *hēgoumen* John, two *excubitors* who were twin brothers came from Constantinople to make their renunciations on the Holy Mountain.[47] After spending two years in the monastery,[48] they went to live by themselves where that great old man resided, at Tourba.

---

42 Bubonic plague became endemic to the Near East from 542 onwards. Here Anastasius reflects a contemporary Christian understanding that all things happen because God either wills or gives consent for them to happen. The latter usually included events that, to human perspective, might appear harmful or dangerous.

43 κοιμητηρίον/*cemetery*, referring to the ossuary where bones of monks were stacked (some entire corpses can still be seen at St Catherine's). In late antiquity this cemetary was located 'near the Fort': John Clim., *Ladder* 6 (PG 88.797A).

44 σκήνωμα/*skēnōma*, 'tabernacle', i.e. corpse, as in Ammonius, *Rel.* 36. For similar stories, see Anast., *Narr.* I.9; John Mosch., *Meadow* 88; and Evagrius Schol., *EH* IV.35.

45 Cf. Jn 1:29.

46 59 km/36 miles. Site unknown.

47 John is presumably John Climacus: see above, Anast., *Narr.* I.3. *Excubitors* were an elite palace guard established by Emperor Leo I (457–474): see Jones 1964, 658.

48 I.e. after their two-year novitiate at the Mt Sinai monastery: see below, Anast., *Narr.* I.39. Two years was brief for a novitiate; in other *coenobia*, it reportedly lasted ten years. See Patrich 1995, 258–66.

After passing some time there they died. The old man and his disciple took their remains and went off and buried them, depositing them in a cave. A few days later the old man died too. His disciple went off and put his remains between the two *excubitors'* remains, in order, you see, to honour the old man. On the third day, when he went to cast incense for the old man, he discovered that the *excubitors* had tossed his remains away from between them. It upset him very much. He picked up and placed the remains between them again, but when he came back he found that they had tossed him off again.

This happened three times. Finally the disciple sat down lamenting, saying to himself, 'Did the old man commit heresy in his soul or some unforgivable sin? For behold! these novices[49] have tossed him out from between them three times.'

That night as he was tearfully pondering these things, the two *excubitors* stood before him and said, 'Believe us, sir, your old man was not a heretic, nor did he have any fault, but he too is a slave of Christ. As for you, couldn't you tell that we were born together, served the earthly king together, made our renunciations together, were entombed at the same time, and stood before Christ together? But you separated us by putting another between us.' When he saw and heard these things the brother was reassured and praised God.

I.10 [Nau 6] Abba Martyrius, who had our saintly father the *hēgoumen* tonsured,[50] remained for some years in the Gulf of Holy Antony across the Red Sea.[51] While he was residing there, some savage barbarians made a raid upon those who lived in those mountains. After laying waste to the place they murdered six fathers, among whom was Abba Conon the Cilician, a man of discernment who was endowed with the gift of prophecy. Abba Martyrius took their bodies and deposited them in a cave. He rolled a great slab over its mouth and covered it with whitewash on which he wrote the names of the holy men.

Some time later he went to inspect the tomb, lest perhaps it had been dug

---

49 ἀρχάριοι/*archarioi*.

50 John Climacus: see below, Anast., *Narr.* I.11. Tonsuring, or hair-cutting, was a basic part of the monastic initiation; probably based on ancient slave haircuts, it signified that one had become a 'slave' of God: see Patrich 1995, 169, 260. As the next story indicates, it was the-then *hēgoumen*, Anastasius, who actually tonsured John; Martyrius, his own personal spiritual supervisor, or superior, accompanied him.

51 Near the Mountain of Antony, down the western coast of the Gulf of Suez, approximately on the same latitude as Rhaithou.

up by a hyena or some other wild animal. He came and found the inscription untouched and the whole tomb intact, but when he opened it and went inside, he discovered that two of the bodies had been transported by God, where only He knows. These were the bodies of Abba Conon and another great old man.

I.11 [Nau 35] When this same Abba Martyrius tonsured our saintly father John the *hēgoumen* when he was twenty years old, he took him to the pillar of our desert, Abba John the Sabaïte, who was living in the desert of Goudda with his disciple Abba Stephen the Cappadocian.[52] When the old man – the Sabaïte – saw them, he got up, poured water into a small basin and washed the feet of the disciple[53] and kissed his hand. Yet he did not wash the feet of his supervisor, Abba Martyrius.

Abba Stephen was scandalized by this act. After Abba Martyrius had left with his disciple, Abba John could see with his discerning eye that his disciple was scandalized. He said to him: 'Why are you scandalized? Believe me, I don't know who that boy was, but I received an *hēgoumen* of Sinai and washed his feet.' And forty years later he became our *hēgoumen* in accordance with the old man's prophecy.[54]

I.12 [Nau 34] Abba John was not the only one [to make this prediction], but so too did Abba Strategius the Recluse.[55] Without even coming out of his

---

52   John the Sabaïte also appears in *Narr.* I.22, 23, and 25 below. Personally known to Climacus, he figures prominently in *Ladder* 4 (PG 88.720–21), which describes his prior experiences as a monk in Asia, Pontus, and Palestine ('Sabaïte' refers to his former membership in St Sabas' monastery in the Judaean desert). Like Anastasius, Climacus notes the Sabaïte's power of discernment (721D). Müller 2006, 38–43, however, considers Anastasius' descriptions of him as 'divine' or 'wonderful' (I.22, 23) to be evidence of a long gap of time beween Anastasius' lifetime and that of the Sabaïte. Moreover, since John Moschus associates the Sabaïte's disciple, Stephen the Cappadocian, with the Sinai *hēgoumen* George who died in 552 (*Meadow* 127), Müller reasons that the Sabaïte must have lived in the first half of the sixth century. Accordingly, since Climacus claims to have known the Sabaïte, Müller believes that Climacus must have been living and writing in the second half of the sixth century. While the implication of Moschus' anecdote for the dating of Stephen the Cappadocian, and hence for that of John the Sabaïte and John Climacus, cannot be dismissed, much nonetheless depends on the anecdote in question, and it is important to note that Moschus' text has not been edited. For Goudda, see below, Anast., *Narr.* I.31.

53   cf. Jn 13.5, where Jesus washes his disciples' feet.

54   This story is included in Daniel's *Life of John Climacus* (PG 88.608B). Cf. John Mosch., *Meadow* 139, for a similar story concerning a Red Sea hermit who washes the feet of a future bishop of Antioch and predicts his ordination.

55   ἔγκλειστος/*enkleistos*, literally 'enclosed', i.e. a hermit whose asceticism included refusing to come out of the cell.

cell he saw Abba John coming down from the Holy Summit on the day that Abba Anastasius the *hēgoumen* tonsured him. Calling to Abba Martyrius and the boy, he said to the old man, 'Tell me, Abba Martyrius, where is this boy from? Who tonsured him?' Abba Martyrius said, 'Father, he is your slave, and my disciple, and Abba Anastasius the *hēgoumen* tonsured him.' Then Abba Strategius said to him, 'Well, Abba Martyrius, who is going to tell Abba Anastasius that he has tonsured a *hēgoumen* of Sina today?'

The predictions of the saintly fathers concerning our all-saintly Father John were worthy, true and right. So 'adorned in every virtue'[56] and brilliant was he, that the fathers of the place called him a second Moses.[57]

[Nau 7] Once, for example, about six hundred strangers gathered here. While they were sitting down and eating, saintly John our father noticed a man with short-cropped hair and wearing fine linen cloth in Judaic fashion who was running around giving orders in an authoritative manner to the cooks, stewards, cellarers, and the rest of the servers. After the lay folk had left and the servants were sitting down to eat, they searched for the man who had been running around everywhere giving orders, but he was nowhere to be found. Then Christ's slave, the *hēgoumen*, said, 'Let him be. Lord Moses had done nothing strange by serving in his own place.'[58]

I.13 [Nau 33] There was also another *hēgoumen* there called Isaurus.[59] He was a man who carried the Spirit and was endowed with the gift of healing. Once when a paralytic was lying in the infirmary, our Mistress, the Holy Mother of God, appeared before him and said to him, 'Go to the *hēgoumen*. He will say a prayer for you and you will become healthy.' So the paralytic went and dragged himself to the *hēgoumen*. By God's arrangement, when he knocked there was no one to go out and open the door for him except the *hēgoumen*.[60] When he went out and opened the door for him, the paralytic clasped his feet and said, 'I will not let you go because the Mother of God sent me to you.' Compelled by his insistence, the old man took off his belt and gave it to him, saying, 'Take this and put it on.' Immediately after girding himself with it he stood up, leapt forth and walked around, bounding about and praising God.

---

56 Cf. III Macc. 6.1, describing Eleazar.

57 Also noted by Daniel of Rhaithou in his ninth-century *Life of John Climacus* (PG 88.605A and 609C).

58 I.e. at Mt Sinai.

59 Perhaps 'the Isaurian'.

60 Some monasteries had door attendants who controlled access to the *hēgoumen*: e.g. *Life of Alexander Acoemetus* 37.

I.14 [Not in Nau] Arselaiou is a place located in a ravine that is hard to reach.[61] I myself dwelled there for a period of three years. I found two Armenian fathers dwelling in this place, Abba Agathon and Abba Elijah the priest. One day Abba Elijah said to Abba Agathon, 'Prepare yourself, Brother, because in ten days you'll depart to the Lord. For today I saw you wearing new clothes [instead of] your monastic habit and departing for a royal wedding. And in truth, just when you knocked, I heard the house steward[62] say, "Welcome Abba Agathon. Make space for him and let him in."'

And so it happened: within five days Abba Agathon departed to the Lord.

I.15 [Nau 8] In this place dwelled Abba Michael the Iberian who departed to the Lord five years ago. This Michael had had a disciple named Eustathius, who is [now] in Babylon seeking treatment for his hand.[63]

When Abba Michael fell sick, Eustathius stood by his side and wept. You see, the tomb of the Fathers that is in that place has a very difficult and dangerous access down smooth rock.[64] So Abba Michael said to Abba Eustathius, 'Child, bring me [the things I need] to wash and take communion.' Once that was done, he said to him once more: 'You know, child, the descent to the tomb is dangerously slippery. If I die [here], you run the risk of having to carry me down. You might fall off the cliff and die. So come, let's instead do it together, step by step.' Once they had descended, the old man said a prayer and embraced Eustathius, saying, 'Peace be with you, child. Pray for me.' He lay down in the burial place and departed to the Lord with joy and exultation.

I.16 [Nau 32] Last year when our new second Moses, the most saintly Abba John the *hēgoumen*,[65] was about to go to the Lord, his own brother Abba George, the bishop, stood beside him and wept. He said, 'Behold, you are leaving me and going away. But I used to pray that you would lead my own funeral procession, because I am not adequate to shepherd our company

---

61 A ninth-century version of this collection identifies *ta tou Arselaiou* with Wadi Isla. Dahari 2000, 94–103, 156, and Solzbacher 1989, 403, both identify it with Wadi Rimhan off Wadi Isla and below Jabal Umm Shomer (13 km/8 miles south of Jabal Musa).

62 οἰκοδεσπότης/*oikodespotēs*, a butler in the house of a late Roman aristocrat.

63 The Egyptian Babylon (modern Cairo).

64 Evidently Arselaiou had its own tomb or ossuary in the ravine below where the hermits lived.

65 Following Binggeli, based on MS Q; Nau's edition has 'John the Sabaïte'. If correct, Binggeli's edition confirms the later date for Climacus' death, c. 659–669.

without you.'[66] Abba John said to him, 'Don't worry. Don't be distressed. If I obtain the right to address God freely,[67] I'll not let you finish a single year after me.'

And so it happened: for within ten months the bishop went in peace to the Lord, during the past winter.

I.17 [Nau 9] In the aforementioned place called Arselaiou there was also Abba George, nicknamed 'the Arselaïte'.[68] He was the famous boast of our desert. Many tell me a great many marvellous things about him, some of which I will briefly try to relate.

Once when the road from Palestine was beset by barbarians[69] a major shortage of oil arose on the Holy Mountain. So the *hēgoumen* went down to Arselaiou and asked the man of God, George, to go up to the Holy Mountain. Unable to disobey the *hēgoumen*, he went up with him. The *hēgoumen* brought him to where the oil was kept and asked him to say a prayer over the oil vats, which contained nothing at all. In jest Abba George told the *hēgoumen*, 'Let's pray only over one vat, Father. If we pray over them all, we'll soon be swimming in the oil here.' Once he had made his prayer over one of the vats, oil immediately gushed up as if from a spring. The old man said to the attendants, 'Draw off the oil and transfer it to the rest of the vats.' When all were filled, the vat stopped flowing, as happened long ago in Elisha's time.[70]

The *hēgoumen* wanted to give the vat the name 'of Abba George', but the old man said to him, 'If you do any such thing, the oil will run out – so name it after our Holy Mistress, the Mother of God.'

And so it happened: the vat is maintained to this day, and above it hangs a lamp that never goes out, burning in the name of the Holy Mother of God.

I.18 [Nau 10] This righteous George was once approached by eight Saracens who were hungry. Because he had nothing at all of this world to give them (for he ate wild capers raw, although their bitterness could kill even a camel)

66 George may have been bishop of Pharan, although the presence of the bishop of Aila at the Sinai Monastery is noted below, Anast., *Narr.* I.27.

67 Literally, 'find *parrhēsia*', the freedom given to address a superior candidly and thus possibly persuade him. On its political importance in late antiquity, see Brown 1992.

68 George the Arselaïte is also the subject of the next story. In *Ladder* 27 (PG 88.1112B) Climacus refers to him as his own former spiritual director, an expert in *hēsychia* also known to John of Rhaithou, the recipient of the *Ladder*.

69 Either the central, northern route across the desert taken by PP, *Itin.* 35–37, or the eastern route through Aila. See above, General Introduction, pp. 12–13.

70 2 [IV] Kgs 4:1–7.

and because he could see that the Saracens were starving terribly, the old man said to one of them, 'Take your bow, go up this hill and you'll find a herd of wild goats. Shoot whichever of them you want, but don't even try to shoot another.'

The Saracen went off just as the old man told him. After he had shot one and caught and killed it, he tried to shoot another as well. Immediately his bow broke. He came back with the meat and told his companions what had happened to him.[71]

I.19 [Nau 11] This thrice-blessed man revived his disciple by making the sign of the cross over him, who had been bitten by an asp and was just about to expire. Then he took hold of the asp with his hands and, as if it were a grasshopper, broke it in two, enjoining his disciple to tell no one about this until his death.[72]

I.20 [Nau 12] This great father's death (or rather, his migration through death to eternal life)[73] was as follows. When he began to grow sick in his cave, he lay on a mat and sent a Christian Saracen to Aila in order to summon someone dear to him, saying, 'Come so that I might embrace you before I depart to the Lord.' The distance of the journey was two hundred miles.[74]

Twelve days later the old man lying on the mat said to his disciple, 'Quickly, make light, for behold!, the brothers have arrived.' After the brother lit the censer, behold! the Saracen and the old man's dear one from Aila entered the cave. The old man said a prayer, embraced them both, partook of the Holy Mysteries, laid himself back down and departed to the Lord.

I.21 [Nau 13] Abba Cyriacus told me this about his supervisor Abba Stephen. 'When he lived in Malōcha' (a place in a ravine that is hard, almost impossible to access – I have been there once myself – for it is a very rough forty miles away from the Holy Mountain),[75] 'he planted,' he said, 'little green herbs for his nourishment.[76] He ate nothing else. But coneys came

---

71 Flusin 1998, 137, believes this story exemplifies the sense of 'eminent right, of supernatural origin', that monks believed they had over all who lived on the Sinai.

72 Cf. Lk. 5:14.

73 Cf. Jn 5:24.

74 I.e. ten days' travel, an accurate 'return-trip' estimation for a monk living in the Dayr Antush/Wadi Isla region; cf. above, *Narr.* I.14.

75 Dahari 2000, 111–14, identifies this site with Wadi Sigilliya or Wadi Imlaha, which ran parallel to Wadi Isla south-west of Jabal Musa.

76 κοδιμέντον/*kodimenton*, later identified as *petroselinum Macedonium*, a type of parsley.

and ate them, and laid them waste.[77] One day while the old man was sitting in distress, behold! he saw a leopard pass by. He called to it, and the beast came and sat down at his feet. The old man said to it, "Do me a favour. Don't go away from here, but protect this little garden by catching the coneys and eating them."

The leopard stayed with him for some years protecting the little greens until the old man departed, going off with joy to the Lord.'[78]

I.22 [Nau 14] In the same place, Malōcha, the divine John the Sabaïte also resided, together with the great Demetrius, [who had been] the chief imperial doctor. One day they saw a large serpent's track on the sand of the ravine.[79] Abba Demetrius said to the great John, 'Abba, let's go away from here, lest the beast harm us.' But Abba John said to him, 'Let's pray instead', and they stood in prayer. When the beast was about two stades away from them, behold! they saw it raised up on high, by divine command, up to the clouds. Then with a great crash it fell to the earth and was shattered into a thousand pieces.[80]

I.23 [Nau 15] Abba John the Roman, disciple of the aforesaid wonderful John the Sabaïte, told me that 'One day when we were at Arselaiou, behold! an adult coney brought out her nursling, a little thing, carrying it in her mouth. She placed the nursling, which was blind, at the feet of the old man. When the saint saw that it was blind, he spat on the ground to make it mud. He daubed it on the [nursling's] eyes and immediately it looked up.[81] The mother came up close and kissed the soles of the old man's feet, picked up her nursling as it was walking about, and went scurrying off.

The next day, behold! the mother brought the old man a full-grown cabbage in her mouth, dragging it with great toil. The saint gently smiled and said to her, "Where did you get that from? You must have stolen it from the fathers' gardens. I don't eat anything stolen. Take it and go and put it

77 χοιρόγρυλλοι/*choirogryllon*. Liddell and Scott translates as a coney, i.e. a type of hare (cf. Ps. 104 [103]:18, 'The high mountains are for the wild goats, the rocks are a refuge for the coneys'). But according to Dahari 2000, 6, 'the main rodents in Sinai are bushy-tailed gerbils, golden mice and Cairo-mice'. One of these is probably meant.

78 John Clim., *Ladder* 7 (88.812C) also tells of a Stephen who fed a leopard while living in the desert. Cf. Cyril Scyth., *Life of Cyriacus* 16 (where a lion protects a hermit's greens from wild goats) and Theodoret, *Religious History* IV.10, with note *ad loc*.

79 For 'track of a large serpent', cf. *History of Monks in Egypt* IX.2. Christians were specifically given power to tread on serpents in Lk. 10:19.

80 Cf. Rev. 12:9, 13. On John the Sabaïte, see above, n. 52.

81 Cf. Jn 9:6–7, where Jesus spits on the ground to make mud for a blind man's eyes.

back where you stole it from."[82] As if ashamed, the animal took the cabbage and put it back in the garden from which she had taken it.'

I.24 [Nau 16] 'Another time,' he said, 'there had been a long period in the desert without rain. A great herd of wild goats gathered and wandered all over the mountainous regions of Arselaiou searching for water to drink without finding any. It was the month of Augustus. Since the entire herd,' he said, 'was about to perish from thirst, they climbed to the highest peak of all the mountains in the desert. All those animals looked intently towards heaven and began to bleat in unison, just as if crying to the Creator. And as if in the presence of the Lord of Glory,' he said, 'they did not move from there, but rain fell down around them on that place alone. And so they drank in accordance with the prophet's utterance about God: "He gives the beasts their food, and to young ravens who call to him".'[83]

I.25 [Nau 17] This chapter is worth telling and remembering, because it shows that slander is something terrible and grievous. The same wonderful Abba John the Sabaïte told it.

'Once while I was residing,' he said, 'in the remotest part of the desert a brother from the monastery came to visit me. I asked him, "How are the Fathers?" And he said, "Doing well, thanks to your prayers." Then I asked him about a brother who had a bad reputation stuck to his name. He told me, "Believe me, father, he has not yet lost that reputation." When I heard this I said, "Humph."

'And as I said "Humph", I was carried off into a dreamlike trance and saw myself standing before Holy Golgotha as the Lord was being crucified between the two brigands.[84] I rushed forward to approach and venerate Him. When He saw this, He gave orders to the holy angels standing beside him, saying with a loud voice, "Throw him out! To me he is an Antichrist, because he has condemned his brother before I myself have judged him."[85] I was chased out, and as I went to leave by the gate through which I had come, my cowl[86] got caught on the gate as it closed. I left it there and immediately woke up. I said to the brother who was visiting me, "This is a very bad day for me." He said, "For what reason, Father?" I told him the things I had seen

---

82 Cf. Tob. 2:13.
83 Ps. 147[146]:9.
84 Mt. 27:38.
85 Cf. Mt. 7:1–2.
86 παλλίον/*pallion.* On the early monastic cowl, see Patrich 1995, 211.

and said, "Believe me, the cowl is God's shelter over me,[87] and I've lost it."

'And as in the presence of the Lord of Glory, [I swear that] from that day on I passed seven years living in the desert without tasting bread or taking shelter or talking with any human being, until I saw the Lord likewise command that I be given back my cowl.'

When we heard these things about the wonderful John, we said, 'If it is hard for the righteous to be saved, what will become of the impious, and the sinful, and the lascivious?'[88]

I.26 [Nau 18] Another wondrous offspring of our desert was Orentius. Our saintly father the *hēgoumen* and other men have told me his wondrous deeds.[89]

'This man,' said [our *hēgoumen*], 'had kindled in himself the light of the Holy Spirit to such a degree that he could quench the flames of visible fire. For he always took hot coals in his hands when offering incense.[90] Well, one day some strangers came to visit him and the old man graciously chose, under the sway of the enemy of good, to offer incense for them. As soon as the fire touched his hand, it scorched his middle finger and damaged his nerve. Since then, if ever he sent a letter to anyone, he wrote "Orentius the Scorched-Hand" as the return address.

'Yet God's favour did not abandon the old man, for later the Lord made many other signs through him, among which was this. A patrician woman once came to the Holy Mountain together with her daughter, who was possessed.[91] When she learned about the old man, she wanted to venerate him. But this the saintly one did not allow to happen; instead, he took a bunch of grapes and sent them to her. Upon seeing them, the demon inside the little girl began to shriek, "Abba Orentius, why have you come here?"[92] After making the girl convulse it departed from her.'

I.27 [Nau 19] Abba Abraham, the senior priest, also told me this story. 'When Abba Orentius was dying, I was sitting beside him, as was Abba Sergius – the bishop of Aila – and some other fathers. When he beheld the

87 Cf. Ps. 90[91]:1.

88 1 Pet. 4:18, adding 'lascivious' (πορνοβόσκος).

89 Perhaps the same Orentius described in John Mosch., *Meadow* 126.

90 Cf. Isa. 6:6 and Leontius of Neapolis, *Life of Symeon the Fool* 4, in which God enables Symeon to burn incense coals in his hand unscorched (cf. Dan. 3:19) in order to convert a heretic.

91 Cf. Gregory I, *ep*. IV.44 to Rusticiana, although there is no certainty of identifying the two.

92 Cf. Mt. 8:29.

angelic presence the old man said to the bishop, "Say a prayer, Father." After the prayer we sat down again. Then again the old man said to the bishop, "Say a prayer." After the prayer he addressed him once more: "Did you behold how many ravens came in here, my great Lord? By Christ's grace I'll take no heed of them, and none of them shall come near me."

After saying these things he departed to the Lord in peace and joy.'

I.28 [Nau 20] I was present at the death of Abba Stephen of Byzantium, the former secretary of General Maurianus.[93] So was Abba Theodosius the African, who became bishop in Babylon.[94] While we were reciting the 'blameless' psalm as is customary for those who are breathing their last,[95] the dying man suddenly cast a sharp glance and spoke harshly to someone visible to him, saying, 'Why have you come here? Get to the outer darkness![96] You have no business with me. The Lord is my portion.' Then, when we came in our recitation to the verse that says, 'The Lord is my portion',[97] Abba Stephen gave up his spirit to the Lord.

We looked around his cell for a cloak to use as his burial shroud, but we found none, even though he had once known such wealth and glory.

I.29 [Nau 21] This blessed man's companion, both in the world and in his way of life, was my Abba Epiphanius the Recluse. He migrated to the Lord two years ago. A very long description could be given about his fortitude and perseverance in asceticism and illness. He wasted away to such a degree that there was nothing left of him but breath and bones.

At the beginning of his seclusion an angel of the Lord stood beside him and said, 'If you serve Christ with perseverance, you will be privileged with the gift of the Holy Spirit.' By God's grace, that is what happened: for he received much wealth and illumination from the brilliance of the Holy Spirit. With divine light he could see the demonic spirits of darkness that would often flit about his cell. Sometimes they pestered him, and sometimes they tried to strike him. But against such as these he was protected by the armour of Christ's power; often he would openly sneer and mock them as impotent.

---

93   A Roman general who was defeated by Arabs in Armenia in 653: *PLRE* III, *s.v.* 'Marianus 2'. 'Byzantium' was the classicizing name for Constantinople.

94   The Egyptian Babylon (modern Cairo).

95   Ps. 118[119], a long and elaborate psalm that begins, 'Blessed are those whose way is blameless'.

96   Mt. 8:12, 22:13.

97   Ps. 118[119]:57.

This saint among us had the custom, one handed down to him long ago, not to meet anyone – not even his own servant – before the fourth hour,[98] unless by necessity. So when he learned from God in advance about his own departure to the Lord, the slave of Christ said in the evening to his disciple, 'Tomorrow before dawn open the gate and come to me inside, because there is a certain necessity that I want to show you.' The slave of Christ was not lying. For in the morning when the disciple opened up and came in, he found that the saint had positioned himself towards the East and had departed to the Lord. The old man's disciple is a civilian named Zacharias, who became a goldsmith in Babylon.

I.30 [Nau 22] A few years ago during the Holy Fast one of the fathers took his disciple and said to him, 'Child, during these holy days, let us observe the following conduct: let us travel around the desert, as God will surely privilege us to see one of His slaves, the anchorites, and receive a prayer from him.' While travelling around the region of Sidid,[99] they looked down a very deep ravine and saw a cell and trees bearing all kinds of fruit out of season.[100]

'Once we had descended and drawn near,' he said, 'we called out, "Blessed be you, Fathers." And they answered us, "Welcome, Fathers." But at that word, everything disappeared, both the cell and the trees. So we turned around and went back to the top of the mountain. From there we saw the cell again, and upon seeing it, went back down. We drew near and said the same thing and heard the same voice, but similarly everything disappeared again.

'Then I said to the brother, "Let's go, child, and trust God that, inasmuch as Christ's slaves said to us, 'Welcome, Fathers,' Christ will deign to welcome us with them in the life to come, thanks to their intercessions, to their supplications, and to their toil and sweat."'

I.31 [Nau 31] Goudda is a place with a garden about fifteen miles from the Holy Bush.[101] Abba Cosmas the Armenian used to reside here with me.

---

98 Ten in the morning.

99 A region also known as Siddē, described by John Clim., *Ladder* 7 (PG 88.812B) as 'the abode of anchorites … a comfortless place inaccessible to any human contact, about seventy miles [= 104 km/65 miles] from the Fort [i.e. the Mt Sinai monastery]'. Dahari 2000, 107–11, 157, locates it in Wadi Muwajed, beyond Jabal Umm Shomer south of Jabal Musa.

100 Since it was Lent, it would still be winter. Similar miracles of paradise (though that word is not used) are associated with anchorites in Anast., *Narr.* I.34–35.

101 I.e. 22 km/14 miles from the Mt Sinai monastery. Dahari 2000, 70–81, 156, locates it in the Fre'a mountains or Wadi Abū Jerus, north-west of Jabal Musa. The name may derive from the Syriac *guda*, 'company' or 'choir'.

One day each of us went out by himself to the desert in order to meditate in contemplation of God. When one had gone about two miles away from his cell, he came upon a mouth of a cave. Inside it he saw three men lying down, wearing tunics made of palm fibres. He did not know if they were alive or dead. He decided to go back to his cell and get a censer and then return to the holy fathers.[102] With great precision he marked the place by setting up cairns. Then he came to his cell, got the censer and Abba Cosmas, and went back. They searched for the place and the markers with great effort but were unable to find them. For it is the custom among the holy anchorites, both in life and after death, to reveal themselves and to conceal themselves whenever they want, by power of God.

I.32 [Nau 23] In the dreadful ravine called Sidid a holy man used to dwell alone with his disciple. One day the old man sent his disciple to Rhaithou. Three days later he was in the desert by the Crossing Point.[103] While focused on divine contemplation, he saw his disciple coming from afar. Thinking him to be a Saracen, he changed his shape into a palm tree to escape notice. When the disciple came to the place, he saw the palm tree. Bewildered, he struck it with a cup of his hand, saying, 'When did this palm tree come here?'[104]

Transported by a divine hand, the old man got back to the cave before the disciple did. He welcomed him and cheerfully said to him the next day, 'What was it that I did to you that made you box my ears yesterday?' The disciple threw himself on the ground, denying and disowning the deed. Then the old man told him the reason for the palm tree – that it had been he, and that he had instantly changed into the form of a palm tree because he had been occupied in divine contemplation and did not want to be interrupted by any human encounter.

I.33 [Nau 30] Abba Matthew told me a similar story. 'While I was dwelling at Arandoula,' he said, 'in order to distribute Holy Communion on the

---

102 The censer was used as a lamp (cf. Anast., *Narr.* I.21), but perhaps also to cover up the smell of decaying bodies.

103 ἐν τῇ ἐρήμῳ τῇ κατὰ τὴν διάβασιν. *Diabasis* ('Crossing') is used in the Septuagint for the Israelites' crossing of the Red Sea, and probably refers here to the point where that event supposedly occurred; cf. Egeria, *Itin.* PD,Y 9 and 12; CI, *Top. christ.* V.13; and PP, *Itin.* 41. Therefore the desert 'by the Crossing-Point' would probably be the 'Wilderness of Shur' north of Rhaithou and south of Clysma, described by Egeria, *Itin.* PD,Y 11; CI, *Top. christ.* V.13.

104 Cf. Jn 6:26.

Lord's Day to the prisoners of that desert,[105] I kept the Holy Communion in the Holy Church under lock and key in the *armarium*.[106] Many times I went up on Day of the Lord and found that the container[107] had been opened. Because of this I was aggrieved. So I began to count the holy portions and seal the container with wax and signet ring.[108] Then, on the following Lord's Day, I went and found the seals and locks intact.[109] But when I opened it and counted, I found three portions missing.

'I was deeply perplexed by this when, on the next Lord's Day, three monks appeared before me at night. They woke me and said, "Get up! It's time for the office." So I asked them, "Who are you, Fathers? Where are you from?" They said, "We are the captives, the ones who often come and take communion. You no longer have to worry about that." At that point I realized that the holy ones were anchorites. I thanked God for graciously bestowing such men upon our generation.'

I.34 [Nau 24] There are times when our blessed anchorites are willing to appear not only to Christians, but even to Saracens, whom they admonish to behave in orderly fashion and not molest the monks who live here.

These included the Saracen called Mundhir who lived at the gateway to the region of Arselaiou. He told us that, 'Once when I was shepherding my goats in winter, I suddenly found myself by a garden with fruits of all sorts and a small spring of water.[110] I saw an elderly man sitting at the spring and a great number of wild goats coming to drink. As I stood there astonished by the things that I saw, the old man told me, "Take as much fruit as you can carry in your sack."

'As I was gathering the fruit', he said, 'I heard the monk scolding an adult Billy goat that was butting the wild goats with his horns and not letting them drink in peace. He said to it, "Behold! how many times have I told you? Yet you have not stopped fighting with your peers. Blessed be the Lord, you

---

105 Although Solzbacher 1989, 297, believes that αἰχμάλωτοι/*aichmalōtoi* ('prisoners') is used here metaphorically for anchorites who refused to leave their place of discipline, Anastasius elsewhere uses the term to refer to Arab captives, and that is probably meant here (they are identified as ἁμαρτωλοί/*hamartōloi*, 'captives' in the next paragraph): cf. *Narr.* II.8 and 19. Arandoula is no doubt Wadi Gharandula in the north-west Sinai: see Egeria, *Itin.* PD,Y 12; PP, *Itin.* 41.

106 See above, *Narr.* I.2 and note *ad loc*.

107 σκευοφόριον/*skeuophorion*. A vessel, also called a pyx, in which communion wafers are kept or carried to the sick.

108 Cf. Dan. 14:14.

109 Cf. Dan. 14:17.

110 Cf. above, Anast., *Narr.* I.30.

shall not drink from this water one more day."[111]

'I departed, but the next day I came back to look for the place, taking my pups with me. I couldn't find the place itself, but I did find that herd of goats. When the dogs ran out, they chased the Billy goat the old man had addressed – I realized it was the same one to which he had said, "Blessed be the Lord, but you shall not drink one more day from this water".'

I.35 [Nau 25] Another Saracen said to one of the brothers here, 'Come with me and I'll show you an anchorite's garden'. So the brother followed him to the region of Metmōr.[112] When they came to the top of a mountain, the Saracen showed him a garden and cell down in a ravine. He said to him, 'Go down by yourself, lest the anchorite flee or hide because of me, since I'm not a Christian. I've never dared go down to him myself.'

As the brother went down, the Saracen fell under Satan's sway and shouted down to him, saying, 'Take your sandals, Abba. You left them here.' The brother turned around to look back[113] and said, 'I don't need them'. Then he turned his face back towards the descent – but the garden and cell had disappeared, no longer visible to the monk or the Saracen, up to this day. The monk remained distressed for a long time, saying, 'If Lot's wife suffered anything at all when she turned to look back, that's what I'm now suffering myself'.[114]

I.36 [Nau 26] A man called George the Draam[115] – who was a good Christian, but a Saracen's slave – told us this story himself.

'Once while I was grazing camels in the desert of Bilēm,[116] I found a very old man sitting in the desert with a small basket. I said to him. "Bless me, Lord." He made no sound, but set his seal on me with his right hand. I had moved four or five steps away when I thought to myself, "Believe me, I'm not going to leave until I've clasped the old man's feet and he's said a prayer for me, so that the Lord might free me from this oppression." I turned around and searched all over, looking everywhere, but no longer could I see him even though the place was bare and without trees.'

---

111 Cf. Lk. 1:68.

112 Dahari 2000, 95-103, 156, identifies Metmōr with Dayr Antush or Dayr Rimhan below Jabal Umm Shomer.

113 Cf. Gen. 19:26, where Lot's wife turns to look back and becomes a pillar of salt.

114 Cf. Gen. 19:26.

115 Perhaps from the Syriac *drm*, 'crafty, cunning'.

116 Dahari 2000, 156, identifies Bilēm with the Ailim in Ps.-Nilus, *Narr.* VI.10, and locates it close to the Mt Sinai monastery.

I.37 [Nau 27] A year ago one of the fathers confined himself in a cave for the forty-day period of the Holy Fast.[117] The devil, who always despises those who contend with him, filled his entire cave with vermin from floor to roof. They got into the water and bread and all of the monk's things, so that, in short, not a finger's length of the cave could be seen bare. But the old man endured the trial nobly and said, 'Even if I must die, I'm not going to leave until the Holy Feast'.[118]

In the third week of the Holy Fast, behold! One morning he sees an indescribable number of large ants coming into the cave to destroy the vermin. As if in a war, within six hours they had killed them all and carried them out of the cave. And so we see that perseverance under trial is good, since it surely comes to a good end.

I.38 [Nau 28] Abba Stephen the Cypriote came with me to the Holy Mountain. He was a most peaceable man and a partaker in the Holy Spirit,[119] adorned with every virtue.[120] When he was about to die, he burst out in welts such as I think no man ever saw before. He languished for many days, then died. One of those who knew his diligence and way of life became troubled, thinking to himself, 'How has such a person succumbed to such a force?' Then the blessed Stephen appeared to him in a dream and said, 'Lord Brother, even if for a little while I was made loathsome, nevertheless I've found greater freedom of speech with Christ'.

I.39 [Nau 29] Abba George the Gademite,[121] a saintly man and one of the ancient fathers on the Holy Mountain, told us how, when he was younger, 'A brother came here to make his renunciation. He told no one either his country or his name. He possessed such silence and reserve that he did not readily exchange words, many or few, with anyone unless by necessity. After he had been tonsured and had completed his two years of service in the *coenobium*,[122] he immediately departed to the Lord and was buried in

---

117 Lent.

118 Easter.

119 Cf. Heb. 6:4.

120 Cf. III Macc. 6:1.

121 I.e. a member of the Banū Judham of southern Palestine (cf. *P.Colt* 93, dated c. 685). Many members of this Arab tribe were Christian; though allied to Rome during Heraclius' Persian war, it was subsequently conquered by Arab forces and converted to Islam. See Bosworth 1986.

122 This shows that novices had to spend their first two years as monks in communal service (*diakonia*, e.g. cooking in the kitchen, serving in the refectory) in Mt Sinai's *coenobium* before becoming a full monk. Such service not only fulfilled a practical purpose; it was also considered spiritual training, in humility.

the tomb of the Fathers. The next day another of the fathers died. When we opened the tomb to bury him, we did not find the body of the brother who had previously been buried. He had been transported by God to the land of the living.'[123]

'Well, afterwards,' he said, 'when we delved more deeply into the matter, certain people were willing to tell us that he had been the son of the emperor Maurice and had been saved by his nurse when Maurice's children were slain in the hippodrome by the tyrant Phocas.[124] Amid the great uproar she was able to sneak up and made a switch, giving her own child to be slain as a substitute for the imperial child. The nurse told him the story once he had grown to manhood. For this reason,' he said, 'he decided to offer himself to God to atone for the one who had been slain in his behalf.'[125]

123 Ps. 116[114]:9.

124 Maurice was Roman Emperor from 582 to 602. The usurper Phocas had him and his sons (Maurice had six) executed at Chalcedon on 27 November 602. See Theophylact Simocatta, *History* viii.11.2–3 (c. late 620s), and *Paschal Chronicle* 602 (c. 630); in general, Michael Whitby 1988, 24–27.

125 According to Theophylact Simocatta, *History* viii.11.5 and other sources, Maurice revealed to his murderers that the nurse had made the switch, implying that this son was also executed: cf. Michael Whitby 1983. But in his tenth-century *Annals* (PG 111.1082), Eutychius records that the switch was successful and that it was Maurice's youngest son, Justinian, who escaped. (*Paschal Chronicle* 602 states that Justinian was executed but omits Maurice's son Paul from among those killed.) Stories also circulated about the survival of Maurice's eldest son, Theodosius (cf. Theophylact Simocatta, *History* viii.13.4-6, 15.8, and Sophronius of Jerusalem, *Anacreontica* 21). These were soon proved false.

Anastasius of Sinai, Collection II:[126]
Narratives
Edifying and Profitable to the Soul
That Happened in Various Places
In Our Time
by Anastasius,
a humble and lowly monk

II.5 [Nau 45] A few years ago someone here in our desert was made ill by an unclean spirit. His name was Gregory and he was an Armenian by birth. Such was the demon's sway that his constant shrieking virtually allowed none of those who dwelled nearby to sleep.

One day I and some other fathers were sitting beside the sufferer for the sake of consoling him. We had become disheartened and very distressed by his illness when he began to shriek in the Armenian language, 'Don't come here! Don't approach! You're burning me! Don't come! Don't come near me!'

We were astounded, not knowing why the demon was shouting these things, when behold! I noticed my disciple John (who by Christ's grace is now a stylite in Diospolis)[127] approaching where we were gathered beside the sufferer. When the sick man saw him, he began even more to shriek the same words and to become greatly agitated, trying to run off and flee as if he were burning with fire. Looking closely, I saw that my disciple was wearing on his neck my silver cross in which I kept a big, venerable and true piece of the holy, life-giving wood of the Cross. Then all present knew that it was because of this that the unclean spirit was agitated and was trembling and shrieking, 'Don't come here! Don't burn me!'

Taking up the same venerable cross, we were able, with great force, blows, and chains, to hang it around the sufferer's neck. From that time on he received much relief and mercy; for then at last indeed he had been released from his suffering and become healthy by Christ's grace.

II.8 [N 41] In addition, I have thought it appropriate to make clear to readers the purpose for which I have set out to write this. Many and beyond counting are the prodigies and miracles of God that have come to pass in various places among Christians, yea, even in our generation. What has been done and demonstrated in various places on land and sea merits every exposition

---

126 For date and relation to Collection I, see Anastasius Introduction above, p. 173.
127 Probably the Diospolis in west-central Palestine (modern Lud/Lydda).

and remembrance; of these, I have jotted down over thirty in my notes as a reminder. But now, because of my life's uncertainty, I am interested in collecting only those that might intensify the faith of Christians and provide great encouragement to those of our brothers who are captives, as well as to all who hear and read them with faith. Among them is the story I am now going to tell.

When by God's righteous judgment the nation of the Saracens came out of their own country, they also came here to the Holy Mountain of Sina in order to take control of the place and cause those Saracens, who were here before them and had previously been Christians, to turn away from faith in Christ.[128] When they heard this, those who had their dwellings or tents near the Fort and the Holy Bush[129] went up with their families to the Holy Summit as if to a fortified place, so as to make war upon the approaching Saracens as from on high. And that is just what they did. Nevertheless, since they could not long hold their ground against the great number of those who came, they surrendered and went over to them, embracing their faith.[130]

Among them was a Christ-lover in the extreme. When he saw the apostasy and destruction of the souls of his own race, he rushed along a dangerous, precipitous place to throw himself off and escape, having chosen to die a corporeal death rather than betray his faith in Christ and imperil his soul.

His wife saw that he had turned to flight and intended to throw himself down that frightful, dangerous place. She got up and ran after him. Firmly clutching her husband's clothes, she addressed him with a gush of tears, saying in Arabic,

'Where are you going, my good husband? Why are you abandoning the woman who has lived at your side since childhood? Why do you leave me and your orphaned children to destruction, struggling to save yourself alone? Remember that at this hour God is my witness that I've never deceived your bed – so don't let me be defiled in body and soul. Remember that I am a woman; [take care that] I don't lose my faith and children at once. But

128 On these Saracens, see the tradition preserved in Eutychius' *Annals*, below, pp. 280–82, which dates the forced conversion of the Sinai bedouin to the reign of the Umayyad Caliph 'Abd al-Malik ibn Marwan (685–705). Anastasius offers no clues as to when the episode he describes in the present narrative happened. However, the narrative comes from Anastasius Collection II, and so was probably written c. 690. Note that he views conversion something that is going on among Arab outsiders, with apparently little sense of threat to his Sinai monastic community.

129 I.e. the fortified Mt Sinai monastery and church within it.

130 Nau 1911, 45 n. 3, suggests that this was when Muslims built a mosque on the summit; cf. above, Anast., *Narr.* I.5. But as noted by 'Abd al-Malik 1998, 171, the earliest evidence for a mosque on the Sinai comes from the end of the Fatimid era (900–1171).

if you really have decided to depart, first save me and your children and then, having so saved us, save your own soul.[131] Beware lest on the day of reckoning God demand from you responsibility for my soul and your children, whom you orphaned, because you only struggled to save yourself. Therefore fear God, kill me and your children, then go on your own way with honour. Don't let us orphaned sheep fall to the hands of these wolves,[132] but imitate Abraham and offer us as a sacrifice to God in this holy place.[133] So that God might take pity on you, don't pity us: sacrifice your children to Him who gave them to you, so that by our blood God might also save you. It is good for us to be offered by you to God, and not be led astray to our destruction by lawless ones, or be punished harshly by barbarian hands. Don't go astray! I'll not release you: either you must stay with us, or slay me and your children and then go yourself.'

By saying such things as these, she persuaded her husband. He took out his sword and slew her and his children. Then he threw himself down the cliff on the southern side of the Holy Summit.[134]

By making that exit, he alone was saved from the impending destruction, since all the rest of the Saracens surrendered and apostatized from faith in Christ.[135] But whereas they went astray, he, without wandering [in faith], went 'wandering in the deserts and in the mountains and in the caves and in the holes of the earth',[136] like that prophet Elijah who saved himself from impious hands by fleeing to Horeb.[137] He lived among wild beasts,[138] having escaped wicked wild beasts; he became a wanderer who worshipped God,[139] so as not to become a wanderer who worshipped idols. From then on he never set foot in any house, city, or village, until he made the journey to the Heavenly City. Instead, for considerable years he was a hermit and at the same time a citizen of God, like Elijah, Elisha, and John.[140]

So incredible is what he dared do to his lifemate and children by his own sword, that some will probably dispute whether God would actually welcome such a sacrifice as his. As for God Who is good and loves humanity,

131 Cf. Gen. 19:20.
132 Cf. Mt. 10:16.
133 Cf. Gen. 22:1–19.
134 I.e. the highest spur of Jabal Musa.
135 Literally, 'all gave their hands and turned away from faith in Christ'.
136 Heb. 11:38.
137 Cf. 1 [III] Kgs 19:1–18.
138 Cf. Mk 1:13.
139 Cf. Job 2:9.
140 John the Baptist.

and Who wants to give assurance to all – what did He do? He revealed and foretold to His slave in the desert his transferral from this life a few days before it happened. And so he went to the Holy Bush and prayed and partook of the Holy Mysteries. As he began to grow weak in what is called the guest-house,[141] some of the saintly Fathers came beside him. Most of them are still alive and were eye witnesses to the following:

When the slave of Christ reached the very hour of his departure to God, he saw approaching him those Holy Fathers who had been slaughtered as martyrs of God in this place by the barbarians. He greeted them, embraced them, and received blessings from them as if he were seeing friends after a long time, and rejoiced and exulted with them as if in church. Some of them he even addressed by name, moving his lips to kiss them and greet them. As if invited by them all to travel with them to a feast and celebration,[142] so in this joyous and cheerful way he began his journey with the holy martyrs as fellow travellers. This he himself said and described to those who were present.

In my opinion, what he saw were angelic powers in the guise of the Holy Fathers who had fought the good fight[143] in this place and won the crown of victory.[144] They were honouring and fittingly escorting him, who had imitated their ways in these, their abodes – him, who had demonstrated to God a love and faith that exceeded the Righteous Ones of old.[145]

---

141 *xenodocheion.*

142 Possibly alluding to the Messianic Banquet: cf. Isa. 25:6, 61:3, Mt. 8:11; Lk. 13:29, 14:15.

143 Cf. 2 Tim. 4:7.

144 Cf. 2 Tim. 4:8.

145 Solzbacher 1989, 284, detects a parallel in sentiment (the language is different) between this passage and the Sinai martyr inscription (ed. Ševčenko 1966, 263). Its reference to surpassing the 'Righteous Ones of Old' is reminiscent of Ps.-Nilus, *Narr.* II.13.

APPENDIX I

Sinai Pilgrimage Accounts and Travel Documents

HYMNS 19 AND 20 ON JULIAN SABA,
ATTRIBUTED TO EPHRAIM THE SYRIAN*

To students of late antiquity, Ephraim the Syrian († 373) requires little introduction. Having spent his life on the Roman–Persia frontier, first at Nisibis (where he was made a deacon), and then after 363 at Edessa, he is considered by many to be the greatest author in Syriac literature. While works attributed to him are numerous, the authorship of some is disputed because of the difference in form and content between them and works securely attributed to him. The two Syriac *madrashe* (hymns) translated here are a case in point: they may have been written by his disciples.[1] At any rate, they were probably composed no later than the middle of the fifth century, i.e. a few generations after the death of Ephraim and of Julian Saba († 367), their subject.

An ascetic priest, Julian Saba gained renown in Ephraim's day for the spiritual seclusion he sought in a cave outside Edessa.[2] Indeed, Saba (Syriac for 'old man') is both the first Syrian anchorite we know by name and the first Sinai pilgrim we know by name. His pilgrimage to Mount Sinai probably occurred in 362. Evidently a memorable event in the communities of northern Syria, it is also noted in Theodoret of Cyrrhus' *Religious History* (below, p. 233).

The 19th and 20th hymns focus in particular on Saba's construction of a small church or chapel on the Sinai summit. This was the first Christian structure built on the summit, and perhaps the earliest Christian monument to appear on the Sinai peninsula at all.[3] Composed to celebrate Saba's

---

* Ed. Beck 1972 (see bibliography) from two MSS, Br. Lib. add. 14,592 (sixth-seventh century) and Br. Lib. add. 17,130 (dated 877 CE). Translation, introduction, and commentary courtesy of Kevin van Bladel. The texts are fragmentary and lacunae are represented here by ellipses (…).

1 For the date and related problems, see Brock 2003, 103–04; Griffith 1994, 198–203; Solzbacher 1989, 111–19. His activities at Sinai are also noted in Ps.-Ephraim, *Hymn* 14.

2 See Griffith 1994, 189–93; Sozomen, *EH* III.14.

3 See Egeria, *Itin.* III.3–5; Theodoret, *Religious History* II.13; and PP, *Itin.* 37, where it is described as a 'small oratory, more or less six feet wide by six feet long'. According to Dahari 1998 and 2000, 28–36, Justinian replaced Saba's church with one dedicated to the Theotokos.

achievement, these hymns show that contemporary Christians considered it a momentous event, like the planting of a flag on hard-fought terrain, that resulted in Mount Sinai's incorporation into Christian sacred topography. Together with Jacob of Serug's *Letter to the Monks of Mount Sinai* (translated below, pp. 242–45), the hymns help us understand the significance that late antique Christians attached to such initiatives.

The hymns follow a typical Syriac hymn structure, with coupled pairs of two-line verses (each pair consisting of two 'hemistiches', eight syllables in the first line and nine in the second, with some variations) followed by a responsorial refrain (*'ûnîtâ*, included only once in the translation) that was apparently sung by the congregation after every stanza. The parallelisms in the hymns are essential to their didactic purpose. Directions for their performances reflect those found in the manuscript; the stanza numbers are a modern addition.

TRANSLATION OF THE SYRIAC TEXTS

The 19th hymn. *[To be sung] In the same tune [as the previous hymn].*

1. O Lord, this is according to nature:
that, when people mourn their loved ones,
they put up figures over their dead
and monuments and likenesses for their departed.

Response:
Glory to you, O Son of the All-Merciful,
[You] Whose servant [i.e. Saba] is like the righteous ancients!

2. According to the victory of the one who has gone to rest,
so they make for him also a demonstration.
If … … … … … the righteous
… … … … remembered by him.

3. … he who … … … … …
… … comparison when … …
if it is fitting for that confession
of the upright and the righteous to whom they likened him.[4]

But his theory has not been verified, and Julian's chapel may have been the one still used in Anastasius of Sinai's time.

4 *kênê w-zaddîqê.*

4. But if love compares the ugly
with the beautiful and calls him [beautiful too],
then your beauty, O victorious one [i.e. Saba],
how much could it be compared with that of the beautiful!

5. If the one who has gone to rest is rich,
they remember him as one of the owners of possessions,
and if the one who has departed is a merchant,
then he is compared with [other] merchants who have departed.

6. How, then, or from where
can we make comparisons with your faith?
From the treasury of your companions
let us bring figures for your athleticism!

7. When [you are] among the penitent [i.e. anchorites] you are victorious,
and also, when among the perfect, you are superior.[5]
You are like the very best in your conduct,
and with them, too, we bring to you a comparison.

8. If a person looks at you, he sees in you
the chaste conduct of the ancient righteous.
Your behaviour is illustrated by the beautiful.
Let us bring to you the likeness of comparison with them!

9. Whoever is angry with this [comparison],
his anger is sufficient to persuade about him.
Let his wrath be like a mirror
and let his ugliness be revealed in it!

10. And whoever is pleased with this [comparison],
he is a tree bearing sweet fruit,[6]
and the fruit that comes from him testifies for him
that sweetness lives in his branches.

---

5 *abîlê* ('penitents' or 'mourners'), the standard Syriac word for 'hermit' or 'anchorite';
gmîrê ('perfect' or 'most advanced') referred to advanced Christian ascetics.
6 Cf. Mt. 7:17; Lk. 6:43.

11. In the wilderness fair Saba went to rest.
Moses, whom all the tribes mourned,[7]
the great pillar, went to rest in the wilderness,
he upon whom the hardship of the camp weighed down.

12. To you [i.e. Saba] was given on the mountain of Sinai
and for you was guarded for a thousand years
the pure cave of glory of the Father,
and then you built a church for the glory of the Son.

13. The circumcised [i.e. Jews] boast of Mount Sinai[8]
but you humiliated them down to the ground.
This proclamation is great
for now the church of the Son is on the Father's mountain.

14. [This proclamation] is against the unbelievers
who have alienated Christ from the Law.[9]
For now at Mount Sinai two testaments
are read with great love!

15. That zeal, m'Lord, is from God,[10]
for that church you built at Mount Sinai.
For all the mysteries of the tabernacle
came and were completed through the church of Christ.

16. For it is from God that he put to shame
all the [false] doctrines, together with the crucifiers,
and that he completed at Mount Sinai
both new and old [covenants].

17. His heart is of stone, he who doubts
that the holy mountains are two.
For lo! the church of the First-Born is at the Mountain of Sinai
and also at Golgotha, the Mountain of Zion.

---

7 Cf. Deut. 34:8.

8 Possibly 'boast at Mount Sinai'.

9 Probably referring to Marcionites, i.e. Christians who rejected the Old Testament.

10 The verse is addressed to Saba. To reflect the clipped Syriac form *mar(y)*, Griffith 1994,
191, translates, 'the zeal is from God, milord'.

18. For the building you built at Mount Sinai
is akin to the tabernacle
... ... as old men you were victorious ... ...[11]
that in the waste ... ...[12]

The 20th hymn. *In the same tune.*

1. ... ...
... ... [Mount] Sinai
To Moses ... ... was standing
on that construction of the tabernacle.

Response:
Glory to the Son Whose gospel
has now been proclaimed in His church also at Mount Sinai!

2. Small is the construction of Moses the great
for as for that tabernacle, its time has passed.
Great is the construction of little Saba
for he has built there the church of truth.

3. Moses set up the altar of sacrifices
and sprinkled the blood of animals on it.
Saba set up the altar of the Holy
and broke upon it there the living body [of Christ].

4. A cloud surrounded the glory
of that tabernacle that Moses made.[13]
The Holy Spirit descended there
on that medicine of life that Saba broke.

5. The one man is no greater than the other;
Moses is exalted and honoured,
but Christ is greater as the Son of the Lord
and great[er] is His covenant ... ...

11 *sabê*, perhaps referring to Saba and those who travelled with him to the Sinai.
12 It is not known how much of the hymn is lost.
13 Exod. 40:34.

6. Moses ... ... and set up
... ... that he made
... ... began ... ...
... the Church of the Holy ... ... there.

7. Moses was standing serenely
on that serene height of Mount Sinai,
and his Lord showed him likenesses
of that holy tabernacle that he made there.[14]

8. And Saba was standing in prayer
in the pure cave on Mount Sinai
and suddenly there came to his mind
a church and likenesses together with measurements.

9. Moses made the tabernacle
with the strength of many and their treasures.[15]
Saba built the Church of the Holy
with the strength of the little and of those who fast.[16]

10. Moses brought down tablets of stone
to the people who had acquired hearts of stone.[17]
The followers of Saba wrote down the truth
on the hidden tablets of their minds.

11. When Moses worshipped on the Mountain,
the people worshipped the calf below.[18]
Saba worshipped on the mountain top
where Moses also worshipped, and was resplendent.

12. At Mount Sinai Moses remembered
Abraham and Isaac by whom he would become great.
Saba in the church on Mount Sinai
remembered Moses by whom he would become great.

14 Cf. Exod. 25, where God instructs Moses in the construction of the tabernacle.

15 In Exod. 25, Moses was ordered to collect fine materials from the Israelites to build the tabernacle.

16 Probably referring to Saba's ascetic companions.

17 Cf. Exod. 31:18–32. For 'hearts of stone', Ezek. 11:19, 36:26.

18 Cf. Exod. 32.

13. Moses gave on the Mountain of Sinai
the Sabbath of rest according to its due time.
But one who wandered and gathered wood:
on account of him, clothing got tassels.[19]

14. Moses saw from Mount Sinai
that over this one nation, out of all the nations,
stretched that pillar of cloud
that withdrew its shadow from all the nations.

15. Saba stood upon Mount Sinai
and wondered about the synagogue, that it was alone
like a fleece now dry
of the dew that had moistened the whole earth.[20]

16. Saba then read out and remembered
the words that Moses had spoken there.
'They will be, in the end, a name of infamy';[21]
indeed this is what now, today, they wear.[22]

17. There he recalled the word of the High One:
'Let me blot them out.
I will give you a people greater and more excellent than they',[23]
this [people] with whom the universe is [now] full.

18. Moses fixed a serpent in the wilderness
and whoever beheld it was cured.[24]
Saba fixed a cross on the mountain
and the soul was restrained by it from error.

---

19 Cf. Num. 15:32–41, where the use of tassels is ordained as reminders of God's command-ments after a man gathered wood on the Sabbath (and was stoned to death for working on that day).

20 Jdg. 6:40.

21 Quoting Exod. 32:25 from the Syriac Old Testament (*Pshittah*).

22 Perhaps referring to the tassels mentioned in stanza 13.

23 Cf. Exod. 32:10.

24 Cf. Num. 21:9.

19. Do not hear, O bitter one,
[these] pure words according to your own wishes.
For each one who goes astray does so by this:
that he has heard the truth as he wishes.

20. Words of truth in the mind of truth!
Let us hear them like discerning people.
For the listener should
seek the meaning of the speaker in his words.

21. Do not twist according to your will
the words that I have spoken according to my will.
Let my intentions not taste like
the bitterness that springs from your will.

End of the 20th hymn on Julian Saba.

EGERIA, *TRAVELOGUE* I–IX
(WITH ABRIDGEMENTS BY PETER THE DEACON)

Written in the late fourth century, Egeria's *Travelogue* provides our earliest narrative account of Christian developments and imperial security concerns in the late antique Sinai region.[1] Probably originating from Spain, Egeria was one of many western Christians to tour the eastern provinces after another Spaniard, Emperor Theodosius I (c. 346–395), established his court in Constantinople in 379. This new court, stridently Christian in ideology and image, made Holy Land pilgrimage and patronage more fashionable than ever before.[2] Egeria visited the Sinai during a month-long expedition (December 383 to January 384) that started in Jerusalem and included an excursion to the 'Land of Jesse' (Goshen/Gessen), i.e. the region between the Egyptian Nile Delta and modern Suez Canal. This was her third journey since arriving at Jerusalem in 381. Before going to Sinai she had already travelled to the Galilee, and on another trip had visited Alexandria and the monks of Upper Egypt.[3]

Addressed to 'sisters' (perhaps nuns) back home, her *Travelogue* has not survived in full. Its sole, eleventh-century manuscript begins with the description of her approach to Mount Sinai (starting below, *Itin.* I.1). Fortunately, much of what she wrote about the earlier stages of her Sinai journey can be retrieved from later authors who read her *Travelogue* intact. Especially important are the twelfth-century abridgements made by a librarian of Monte Cassino named Peter the Deacon, who used her text to compile his own guide, *On the Holy Places*.[4] His method was to copy her geographical descriptions but to delete any remark concerning herself or people she met *en route*. Thus, apart from those deletions, we may assume

---

1 For the text, see Maraval 1997, 120–64; for Egeria, her work, and its dates, Maraval 1997, 15–55. For a translation of her entire *Travelogue*, see Wilkinson 1999.

2 See Matthews 1975, 109–45, and Hunt 1982.

3 See Maraval 1997, 57–117, and Wilkinson 1999, 35–44.

4 Petrus Diaconus, *De locis sanctis*, ed. Geyer 1965. The section of Peter's work based on Egeria's *Itin.* is designated as section 'Y'; hence the use of the abbreviation **PD,Y** in the translation below.

that his abridgements (marked **PD,Y** below in brackets) closely represent what Egeria herself originally wrote.[5] In addition, an observation of hers concerning inhabitants of Pharan has been preserved in a ninth-century manuscript in Madrid,[6] and further details may be gleaned from a letter written in the seventh century (c. 680) by the Spanish monk Valerius of Bierzo.[7]

TRANSLATION OF THE LATIN TEXTS

ABRIDGEMENTS OF PETER THE DEACON, *On The Holy Places*, **4–17:** From Jerusalem to the 'Graves of Craving', near Mount Sinai

[**PD,Y 4**] From Jerusalem to the Holy Mountain of Sina there are twenty-two staging-posts. Pelusium is the capital of the province of Augustamnica, and the province of Augustamnica is in Egypt. From Pelusium to Mount Sina there are twelve staging-posts.[8]

[**PD,Y 5**] Before you arrive at the Holy Mountain of Sina, Fort Clysma appears right by the Red Sea, where the Children of Israel crossed the sea with dry feet. The tracks of Pharaoh's chariot are visible for all eternity in the middle of the sand. His wheels had much more space between them than do the chariots of our own time which are now made in the Roman Empire; for his have a span of twenty-four feet or more from wheel to wheel, the ruts of which are two feet wide. The tracks of Pharaoh's chariot run straight down to where he entered the sea when he tried to capture the Children of

---

5 For Peter's method, see Solzbacher 1989, 122. He also rendered Egeria's scriptural allusions into more current Latin, substituting 'Vulgate' translations for her 'Vetus' translations of the Old Testament. Egeria had used the Vetus, which became out-dated after Jerome completed his Vulgate translation in the early fifth century. Based on the Greek Septuagint (LXX), the Vetus included names and phrases not found in the Hebrew Scriptures or Jerome's translation of them. Hence PD and Egeria give different names for certain sites: e.g. *sepulchra concupiscentiae* (PD,Y 17, 'Graves of Craving') instead of *memoriae concupiscentiae* (Egeria, *Itin.* I.1, 'Tombs of Craving').

6 *Excerpta Matritensia* frg. 1, ed. De Bruyne 1909, 483; see also Geyer 1965, 90.

7 *Epistula Beatissime Egerie*, ed. Díaz y Díaz in Maraval 1997, 337–48, sections 2–3 of which vaguely describes Egeria's Sinai visit. For full translation, see Wilkinson 1999, 200–04.

8 Pelusium (Tall al-Farama, approx. 41 km/26 miles south-east of Port Said) was the *metropolis* (administrative-judicial centre) of *Augustamnica prima*, a province in the diocese of Egypt. The term 'staging-post' (*mansio*) referred not only to a rest-house or inn built along Roman highways, but also to a distance of about 32 km/20 miles or 'one day's travel' between such houses. Egeria's Mediterranean route by the *via maris* may be seen on the Peutinger Map; portions of it are also described by PP, *Itin.* 32–33.

Israel. In the place where the Children of Israel entered the sea – I mean, the place where Pharaoh's tracks are visible today – there are two markers, one on the right and the other on the left, made like small columns. This place is not far from the fort – I mean, from Clysma.[9]

[**PD,Y 6**] Clysma is on the shore – I mean, right by the sea. The harbour there is enclosed, so that the sea enters inside the fort. This harbour sends ships to India or receives those coming from India; for nowhere else but there do ships from India have access to Roman soil. The ships are numerous and immense. After all, the harbour is famous for the merchants who come there from India. Also the official called a 'logothete' (I mean, the emissary who goes to India each year at the order of the Roman emperor) has his residence there, and for this reason his ships are stationed there.[10] This is the place where the Children of Israel arrived when they set out from Egypt while fleeing from Pharaoh. The fort was later put there to maintain defence and authority, in case of a raid by Saracens.[11]

[**PD,Y 7**] This place is all desert, I mean fields of sand, except for a sole mountain that looms over the sea. On the back of this mountain, porphyry marble is quarried. It is said that the 'Red Sea' gets its name from the fact that this mountain lies for a huge stretch over along the Red Sea and has reddish or purplish stone, so that the mountain itself has a kind of reddish

9 Cf. Exod. 14 and 15. Clysma (Kum al-Qulzum, north of Suez) was founded by the Roman Emperor Trajan (98–117 CE) to replace the Ptolemaic city of Arsinoë, built at the eastern terminus of the Ptolemaic canal connecting the Red Sea to the Nile. The Roman fort (*castrum*) was built to protect the canal after Trajan had rebuilt it; the text has *castrum Clysma*, as if that were its name. See Bruyère 1966 and Mayerson 1996a.

The visibility of Pharaoh's chariot tracks is also noted by Orosius, *Historia adversus paganos* I.10.17; CI, *Top. christ.* V.8; and PP, *Itin.* 41. Wilkinson 1999, 102 n. 1, suggests that such references were inspired by ancient tracks used to drag boats onto shore for work on their hulls, and that the markers Egeria observes were meant to help align the boats.

10 The *logothete* was an auditor (Latin: *discussor*) in charge of collecting duties and other fees; this is the only reference to one being annually sent on an embassy to India. Clysma was well known as a port for ships from India, but Egeria is mistaken in saying that Clysma was the only place they could enter Roman territory: Pliny the Elder (*Natural History* VI.103) and Epiphanius (*Panarion* 66) both refer to Berenice (al-Bander al-Kabir/Madinat al-Haras) on the Red Sea, and PP, *Itin.* 40, refers to Aila (Eilat/'Aqaba). Egeria (and the others) may have meant India in a broader sense, for in ancient times it was regularly used to refer to Ethiopic Eritrea and the Axumite port of Adoulis: see Dihle 1964.

11 *pro defensione et disciplina pro incursione Saracenorum*. In *Itin.* VII.6 below, Egeria indicates that the region of *Augustamnica secunda* south of Pelusium and east of the Nile Delta was considered part of 'Saracen territory'. In *Itin.* IX.3 she notes that she had a military escort in this area 'on behalf of the Roman authority while we were travelling through dangerous places'. Such references may allude to problems arising from the Mavia revolt five years earlier.

colour. Now, this mountain was on the right of the Children of Israel when they were escaping from Egypt, at least where they began to approach the sea; for this mountain is on the right-hand side of those coming from Egypt. It is very steep and high, and it looks so much like a wall that you might think it had been cut by a human hand. The mountain is totally dry, such that it has not even a shrub on it.[12]

[PD,Y 8] Upon leaving Ramesses,[13] the Children of Israel at first wandered amid the sands; but as they approached the Red Sea, this mountain became visible and up close on their right. By cleaving to the mountain they reached the sea. They kept the flank of that high mountain on their right and the sea on their left. Then, as they continued, there suddenly appeared to them a place where the mountain met the sea – or rather, went into it, making a promontory.[14]

[PD,Y 9] That field in which the Children of Israel camped with Moses that night is vast – an immense, level plain.[15] The place where the mountain looms over the sea is 500 paces from the fort at Clysma. Half-way between the fort and mountain is the place near the mountain promontory where the Children of Israel entered the sea with Pharaoh following after them. The crossing point, where they crossed the Red Sea with dry feet, is eight miles wide.[16]

[PD,Y 10] The sea does not take its name 'Red' from the fact that its water is red or turbid. On the contrary, it is crystal clear, and cold as the Ocean. Its shell-fish are especially tasty and sweet.[17] Every kind of fish in

---

12 I.e. the Jabal 'Ataqa range of the eastern Egyptian desert, which appears on the right-hand side if looking south from Clysma/Suez. Having already been to the Egyptian Thebaïd (see below, IX.6 and Maraval 1997, 79–80), Egeria knew it included Mons Porphyritēs (Jabal Abū Dukhan) and Mons Claudianus (Dayr Wadi Umm Husayn), major sources of porphyry marble in ancient times.

13 Cf. Exod. 12:37; on Ramesses (modern Qantir), see below, *Itin.* VIII.1–5. Egeria is describing how the Israelites arrived at the Gulf of Heroopolis/Suez through their wanderings, detailed further below, *Itin.* VII.2–3. Exod. 13:18 mentions a 'roundabout way through the wilderness to the Sea of Reeds'; Egeria's tradition may reflect an attempt to identify that Sea of Reeds (probably originally one of the marshy lakes north of Clysma/Suez) with the Red Sea.

14 Ras 'Adabuya.

15 Egeria identifies the plain between Clysma/Suez and Jabal 'Ataqa with the Beelsephon of Exod. 14:2. See also below, Egeria, *Itin.* VII.4.

16 I.e. heading south-east across the water, from Ras 'Adabiya to the Sinai Peninsula. For this 'crossing point' (*transitus*) cf. CI, *Top. christ.* V.7; PP, *Itin.* 41; and Anast., *Narr.* I.32.

17 Wilkinson 1999, 104, translates Egeria's *elecess[a]e*, otherwise unknown, as 'fish', assuming it derives from the Latin word *alac*; I follow his alternative suggestion that it derives from the Greek word *helikos* ('with a spiral'), referring to shell-fish or snails.

that sea has as much taste as the fish of the Italian Sea.[18] Furthermore, they have in abundance everything that people usually want to eat from the sea. There are conches and oysters of different kinds, mollusks and a variety of immense shells: on its shores lie things of various sorts, but bigger and more beautiful than in any other sea. And the coral on this shore is most plentiful. The Red Sea is part of the Ocean.[19]

[**PD,Y 11**] The wilderness of Shur is a desert of boundless size, as far as anyone can see, and the amount of sand in this wasteland is beyond telling. Here they travelled for three days without water.[20] From the Shur wilderness to Marah is one staging-post along the seashore. In Marah there are palm trees, but very few; there are also the two springs that Holy Moses made sweet.[21]

[**PD,Y 12**] From there on the left is a vast wilderness for three days until the place named Arandara. Arandara was the place called Elim. A stream runs there; even if it sometimes dries up, water can be found in its bed or beside its bank.[22] There is also plenty of grass there, and the palm trees are especially numerous. From [region of] the Red Sea crossing point (I mean, from Shur), there is no place so pleasant, with so much water, of such quality and in such abundance. Next from there is the midway staging-post, beside the sea.[23]

[**PD,Y 13**] Eventually two very high mountains appear; but before you come to the mountains there is the place on your left where the Lord rained manna on the Children of Israel.[24] As for the mountains, they are high and very steep. On the other side of the mountains the valley is quite flat and like a portico: it is 200 paces wide, and the mountains on either side of the

18 I.e. the Mediterranean sea.

19 I.e. the Ocean that was supposed to encircle the earth. The abundance of coral reefs along the Sinai coast prevents large ships from coming close: see Meistermann 1909, 168.

20 Exod. 15:22 and Num. 33:8, referring to the Israelites.

21 Cf. Exod. 15:23–25 and Num. 33:8 (neither the LXX/Vetus nor the Hebrew version specifies two springs). Two oases have been identified with this Marah: 'Ain Musa (ancient Phoinikon) and 'Ain Abū Mereir. The former is approx. 10 km/6 miles south-east of Clysma/ Suez (and so rejected as being too near to Clysma by Solzbacher), the latter 58 km/36 miles, or one long day from Wadi Gharandula. But the location identified with this site, as with many other Old Testament sites, may have shifted over time. See Mayerson 1981 and Solzbacher 1989, 160.

22 Cf. Exod. 15:27. This must be Wadi Gharandula, approx. 85 km/53 miles from Clysma/ Suez: it is the only wadi in the area that would have had a reliable source of water. PP, *Itin.* 41, appears to refer to the same site.

23 *media mansio iusta mare est.* Probably Ras Abū Zunayma, a promontory along the al-Markha plane. Cf. Num. 33:10. and Mayerson 1982, 54.

24 Cf. Exod. 16:1–36, in the 'wilderness of Sin'.

valley are high and steep.[25] Where the mountains open up the valley is six miles wide and much greater in length.[26]

[**PD,Y 14**] The mountains have been carved out all around their sides. These vaults have been made in such a way that if you wanted to hang a curtain, they would make most beautiful bedchambers; and each bedchamber has been decorated with Hebrew letters.[27] There are also good and plentiful supplies of water at the end of the valley, but not of the quality found at Elim. This place is called the Pharan desert; it was from here that Moses sent out scouts to reconnoitre the land.[28] It is protected on either side by mountains, but has no fields or vineyards. Nothing else is there but water and palm trees.

[**PD,Y 15**] Near the town of Pharan[29] – about 1500 paces away – the mountains converge so that the valley there is barely 30 paces wide. That is the place called Rephidim; it is where Amalek met the Children of Israel,[30] where the people grumbled for water,[31] and where Moses was met by his father-in-law, Jethro.[32]

The place where Moses prayed when Joshua fought Amalek is a high and very steep mountain looming over Pharan. A church has now been built where Moses prayed.[33] Today you can see the place where he sat down and had the stones placed under his elbow.[34] There Moses also built an altar to

25 The mountains seem to hang over the traveller, providing shelter: hence the comparison to a portico: see next section.

26 Heading east from Ras Abū Zunayma, Egeria enters either Wadi Mukattab or Wadi Shallal, through Naqb Budrah: see next note.

27 The vaulted chambers are rock grooves or overhangs (Wilkinson notes that Paran ['Pharan' in LXX] means 'Full of Caves'), and the Hebrew letters are Nabataean: see CI, *Top. christ.* V.53–54 with notes *ad loc.* It is usually supposed that Egeria passed through Wadi Mukattab, the 'Valley with Writing' (thus Maraval 1997, 114, and Wilkinson 1999, 105 n. 3), but Solzbacher 1989, 125, prefers Wadi Shallal, which not only has inscriptions like Wadi Mukattab, but also has a source of water at its end.

28 Num. 12:16, 13:1–33.

29 *ad vicum Faram.* In *Itin.* VII.7 below, Egeria uses *vicus* for 'a huge village' or 'town'. For a sixth-century description of Pharan (modern Feiran), see PP, *Itin.* 40.

30 Exod. 17:8–16.

31 Exod. 17:1–7; Num. 33:14.

32 Exod. 18:1–9; not explicitly connected in Scripture to Rephidim.

33 Egeria refers to Jabal Tahuna on Pharan's north side. The chapel is probably the basilica whose ruins may be seen today; it was later converted to a mosque. See Dahari 2000, 134–35. Section 3 of Valerius' letter (see above, p. 212, n. 7) indicates that Egeria took communion there.

34 Cf. Exod. 17:12, which describes how Moses was propped up with rocks to keep him praying for victory over the Amalekites. Dahari 2000, 135, notes that 'Moses raising his hands in prayer is a motif incised on several capitals and lintels in and around Pharan'. See also PP, *Itin.* 40.

the Lord once Amalek had been defeated.[35] For 500 paces the place is so steep that it is like climbing up a wall.

[PD,Y 16] From Pharan to the mountain of Holy Sina is thirty-five miles.[36] Out at Hazeroth you can still see how stony the valley was where the Children of Israel dwelled when they returned from the Mountain of God.[37] There are also three thrones made of stone in a slightly higher spot, one for Moses and the others for Aaron and Jethro. And the cell where Moses' sister Miriam was separated for seven days is still visible today, two feet above ground.[38]

[PD,Y 17] From Hazeroth to the Holy Mountain of Sina, along the valley, between the mountains on the right and left, it is all full of monuments.[39] Near the Holy Mountain, in the place called the 'Graves of Craving',[40] it is all full of graves.

EGERIA, *TRAVELOGUE* I–VI: From 'Tombs of Craving' to Mount Sinai and back to Clysma

[I.1] … were pointed out, following the Scriptures.[41] Meanwhile, as we walked on we arrived at a place where the mountains that we were going through opened up, making a vast valley: immense, completely flat, and very beautiful. Across the valley appeared the Holy Mountain of God, Sina. This place where the mountains opened up is near the place where the Tombs

---

Egeria met monks at Pharan or Rephidim who escorted her to Mt Sinai (see below, *Itin.* I.2; V.11–12). The Madrid fragments include an observation that she seems to have made about them: 'With such concord they live among themselves, like true monks, not at all like Amalekites. Indeed, they so hate the name Amalekite that they have an oath, "May my body not lie among the Amalekites".' (Cf. Exod. 17:16, 'The Lord will have war with Amalek from generation to generation'.) Solzbacher 1989, 129, suggests that no monastic graves have been found in the Pharan valley because monks associated it with the Amalekite dead.

35 Exod. 17:14.
36 About 51 km/32 miles, an accurate figure.
37 Cf. Num. 14:2 and 33:17. Egeria passes through Wadi Sholaf, then through Naqb al-Hawa to Wadi al-Raha. The dwellings, thrones, and other monuments she sees along the way (I.1 and V.5-10) were either boulders or the remains of *nawāmīs*, i.e. circular prehistoric structures found all over the southern peninsula: see Goren 1980 and Bar Yosef 1977.
38 Cf. Num. 12:14–15.
39 Described below in Egeria, *Itin.*V.5–10.
40 *sepulchra concupiscentiae*, i.e. Kibroth Hataavah, where the Israelites were buried who craved meat and died of plague after eating Sinai pigeons: cf. Num. 11:33–34. Following her Vetus translation, Egeria called them *memoriae concupiscentiae*: 'Tombs of Craving' below, *Itin.* I.1, V.10.
41 Referring to sites mentioned in PD,Y 16. Here begins Egeria's unabridged text.

of Craving are.[42] **[I.2]** Upon coming to this place, as our escorts (the holy men who were with us) informed us, 'it is customary for whoever comes to make a prayer here, since it is from this place that the Mountain of God is first seen'. And so we did too. It was about four miles in all from this place to the Mountain of God through that valley which, as I said, was immense.

[II.1] The valley really is immense. Lying below the flank of the Mountain of God, it is about – as much as we could guess by looking, or as they told us – sixteen miles long, and they said it was four miles wide.[43] We had to cross the valley to get to the Mountain.

[II.2] This is that immense and perfectly flat valley in which the Children of Israel dwelled in the days when Holy Moses 'went up the mountain' of the Lord and 'was there forty days and forty nights'.[44] This is that valley in which the calf was made, the location of which is shown still today, for a great boulder stands there, fixed in the spot.[45] This is that valley at the end of which is the place where Holy Moses, while 'grazing the flock of his father-in-law'[46] – God spoke to him again from a bush on fire.[47]

[II.3] Our route was as follows: first we would ascend the Mountain of God, because the ascent was better from the direction of our approach.[48] Then we would descend from there to the end of the valley (I mean, where the Bush is) because the descent from the Mountain of God was better from there. And so it was decided that, once we had seen all that we desired to see, after making the descent from the Mountain of God, we would go where the Bush is; and from there we would go the whole way back through the centre of the valley that extended at length, returning to our route with the men of God, who would point out to us each place in the valley that was mentioned in Scripture. And so it was done. **[II.4]** Accordingly, as we went from the place where we had made our prayer after coming from Pharan, our route

42 Egeria has passed from Wadi Sholaf through Naqb al-Hawa into Wadi al-Raha ('Valley of Repose'), from which Jabal Sufsafa (but not Jabal Musa) is visible. See appendix, Map 5. On the Tombs of Craving, see above, p. 217, n. 40.

43 This statement has puzzled scholars. Egeria may have combined the lengths of Wadi Sholaf, Wadi al-Raha and Wadi al-Dayr (which she reaches below, *Itin.* IV.6), or she may have calculated 16 miles from her guides' reference to the valley's width: i.e. to her, the valley seemed to be about four times as long as its width.

44 Cf. Exod. 24:18.

45 Exod. 32:4, 32:8, 32:20.

46 Exod. 3:1–2.

47 Exod. 3:4. The Latin sentence is awkwardly broken up by the insertion of the scriptural reference.

48 From the west. See next note.

was such that we passed through the middle of the valley to its end, and then turned towards the Mountain of God.[49]

[II.5] The mountain from its outskirts looks like one; but once you enter, there are many. The whole thing is called the Mountain of God, but the particular one, at the top of which is the place where, as it is written, 'God's majesty descended',[50] is in the centre of them all. **[II.6]** And though all the ones on its outskirts were as high as I think I had ever seen, nonetheless that centre one, the one on which 'God's majesty descended', is higher than them all – so much so that after we had climbed it, those mountains that had seemed high were all so far below us, that they were like tiny little hills.[51] **[II.7]** What is really quite miraculous – and I do not think it would be without God's grace – is that, although the one in the centre that is properly called Sina – I mean, the one on which 'God's majesty descended' – is higher than all the others, nonetheless it cannot be seen unless you come to its very base, just before you climb it. Yet afterwards when you descend it with your desires fulfilled, you can see it right in front of you – which is not possible to do before you climb up. But I had already known that from conversations with the brothers before we arrived at the Mountain of God. And once we arrived there, I saw it was so.

[III.1] We entered the mountain range on the evening of the Sabbath,[52] and arrived at some monastic cells. The monks who dwelt there received us there very hospitably, offering us every hospitality. There was also a church with a priest.[53]

And so we stayed there that night, and early on the morning of the Lord's Day,[54] together with the priest and monks living there, began to climb the

49 I.e. proceeding first through the Wadi Leja/al-Arba'in (on the west side of Jabal Musa), then turning sharply north to face Jabal Musa; then, after climbing Jabal Musa, descending to Wadi al-Dayr, then back west through Wadi al-Raha, Naqb al-Hawa, and Wadi Sholaf, returning to Pharan. See Map 5, below.

50 Exod. 24:16.

51 Egeria exaggerates: Jabal Musa's peak is visibly lower than Jabal Katharina to the south. Its identification with Mt Sinai may have been based on its apparent centralized location.

52 Saturday, 16 December 383.

53 Probably located where the Monastery of the Forty Martyrs (Dayr al-Arba'in) now stands in Wadi Leja (a.k.a. Wadi al-Arba'in). Some believe Egeria's reference to a church and community here indicates that martyrs were already being commemorated there at the time. However, Egeria does not call the church a *martyrium* (a word she uses elsewhere), and the first explicit identification of the site with martyrs does not appear until the fifteenth century. Solzbacher 1989, 132, believes the church was there simply for the convenience of the local hermits. Later tradition placed the 'Cave of Onophrius' nearby: see Dahari 2000, 66.

54 Sunday, 17 December 383.

mountains, one by one. These mountains were climbed with endless toil, since you do not go up them gradually around and around – in a spiral, as we say – but you go all the way straight up, as if up a wall. Then it is necessary to go straight down each and every one of those mountains, until you arrive at the base of the one in centre, which is Sina proper. **[III.2]** And so in this way, by the will of Christ our God, supported by the prayers of the holy men in our company – in this way, with great toil (since I had to make the ascent on foot, since it was utterly impossible to ascend on saddleback),[55] yet without noticing that toil (since by God's will I saw the desire I had being fulfilled, and therefore did not notice the toil), in the fourth hour[56] we reached the summit of the Mountain of God, Holy Sina, where the Law was given – that very place where 'the majesty of the Lord descended', on the day when the mountain was smoking.[57]

[**III.3**] There is now a church in that place. It is not huge, since this place (I mean, the mountain's summit) is not exactly huge. Nevertheless the church has a huge charm of its own.[58] **[III.4]** And so by God's will, after we had climbed all the way up to the summit and reached the gate of the church, behold!, a priest came out of his monk's cell to meet us. He was assigned to that church,[59] an elder in good health, a monk from his early life, and, as they say here, an 'ascetic'.[60] What more to say? He was such as was worthy to be in that place. Some other priests also met us, as did all the monks who were dwelling there near the mountain (I mean, those not prevented by age or infirmity).

[**III.5**] But in fact no one dwells on the summit of this central mountain,[61] for there is nothing there except for the church and the cave where Holy Moses was.[62]

55 Cf. Egeria's more prosaic description of her ascent up Mt Nebo in *Itin.* XI.4: 'And so we came to the base of Mt Nebo, which was very high, but most of it is such that it can be ascended while sitting on donkeys. There were also a steeper part where you have to ascend with some effort by foot, and so we did.'

56 Ten in the morning.

57 Exod. 19:18, 20:18.

58 Probably the church built by Julian Saba: see Ephraim, *Hymns* 19 and 20; Theodoret, *Religious History* II.13; and PP, *Itin.* 37; also Anast., *Narr.* I.1–7 and 12. The present chapel dates to 1934.

59 Such a chapel custodian was officially called a *paramonarius*, and would have been appointed by a local bishop (from the fifth century onwards, the bishop of Pharan): cf. Anast., *Narr.* I.1.

60 *ascitis*. The Greek term, ἀσκητής, seems to have been unfamiliar to Egeria, who uses it here and in *Itin.* X.9 to designate an advanced monk.

61 Cf. Procop., *Buildings* V.viii.7; PP, *Itin.* 37; and Anast., *Narr.* I.3.

62 Cf. Exod. 33:22. The cave is now beneath a mosque.

[III.6] Once every passage had been read from the book of Moses and an offering had been made in due order, then, after we had taken communion and just as we were leaving the church, the priests gave us *eulogiai* from that place – I mean, some of the fruit that grows on the Mountain.[63] For although the Holy Mountain of Sina is so completely rocky that it has not even a shrub, nonetheless down at the base of these mountains (I mean, around the base of the central mountain and of those on its outskirts) are some small patches of earth. The holy monks keep themselves constantly busy planting small orchards or establishing fruit trees and tilled plots, next to which they put their cells.[64] It is as if they pluck fruits from the earth of the very mountain, even if they seem to have laboured over them with their hands.[65]

[III.7] After we had taken communion and those holy men had given us *eulogiai* and we had gone outside the church gate, then I proceeded to ask them to show us each and every place. So then those holy men promptly deigned to show us each and every one. For they showed us that cave where Holy Moses had been when he went up to the Mountain of God a second time to receive tablets again, after he had shattered the earlier ones because his people sinned.[66] They also deigned to show us other places, whichever we desired or they knew well. **[III.8]** But what I want you to know, my Venerable Lady Sisters, is that, from the place where we were standing (I mean, around the walls of the church – I mean, from the summit of that central mountain), those mountains which we at first had climbed with difficulty now seemed far below us next to the central one on which we were standing, like little hills. Because even though they were so vast that I wouldn't think I had ever seen any higher, nevertheless the one in the centre far surpassed them. From there we could see Egypt, Palestine, the Red Sea and the Virgin's Sea that extends to Alexandria,[67] as well as the unbounded

---

63 A 'blessing' (Greek *eulogia*, Latin *benedictio*) was a gift that was believed to embody the generous spirit of God's own blessing: cf. 2 Cor. 9:5; also Stuiber 1966 and Caner 2006. Egeria's use of the Greek word suggests that she regarded it a technical term.

64 On the textual emendation *arationes*, 'tilled plots', for *orationes*, 'oratories', see Maraval 1997, 135 n. 3. Wilkinson 1999, 110, translates it as 'vegetable beds'.

65 Solzbacher 1989, 142, suggests that the availability of ample water for such pursuits may explain why Jabal Musa was identified with Mt Sinai instead of the higher Jabal Katharina.

66 Exod. 32:19 and 34:1–4.

67 *Mare Parthenicum*, the 'Virgin's Sea', also known as the *Mare Isiacum*, 'Sea of Isis', was the easternmost part of the Mediterranean, between Egypt and Cyprus: cf. Gregory Nazianzus, *Or.* XVIII; Ammianus Marcellinus, XIV.8.10. Since it is not visible from Jabal Musa, Egeria may have been looking at the Gulf of Heroopolis/Suez.

bounds of the Saracens.[68] These were so far below us it was hard to believe. Yet those holy men showed us each and every one.

[IV.1] And so, having fulfilled every desire for which we had hastened to ascend, we then started to descend from the summit of the Mountain of God we had ascended, down to the other mountain that adjoined it, a place called 'On Horeb'. There is a church there.[69] **[IV.2]** Here is that place, Horeb, where Holy Elijah the prophet was when he fled from the face of Ahab the King,[70] and where God spoke to him, saying, 'Why are you here, Elijah?', as is written in the Books of Kings.[71] Even today they show the cave where Holy Elijah hid, in front of the gate of the church that is there; they also show the stone altar which Holy Elijah set up there in order to make an offering to God:[72] thus those holy men deigned to show us each and every one. **[IV.3]** So there too we made the offering and a most earnest prayer, and read the passage from the Book of Kings – for this was something I always very much desired for us, that we would always read a passage from a book wherever we went.

[IV.4] Once we had made the offering there too, we came to another place not far from there which the priests and the monks pointed out – I mean, that place where Holy Aaron had stood with the seventy elders when Holy Moses received the Law from the Lord for the Children of Israel.[73] And so in that place, even though there is no structure, nevertheless there is an immense, round rock with a flat surface on top. Those holy men are said to have stood on it, and in the centre there is a kind of altar made of stones. And so there too we read a passage from the book of Moses and said a psalm appropriate for the place; then with our prayer done we descended from there.

[IV.5] Behold! already it was getting to be about the eighth hour,[74] and we still had three miles to go before we came out of the mountains that we had entered the previous evening.[75] But we could not exit from the direction

---

68 *fines Saracenorum infinitos*, apparently all the land south-east of the places previously mentioned.

69 Exod. 17:6. 'On Horeb' derives from LXX's *en Chōrēb*, preserved in Egeria's Vetus translation of Exodus. The church was probably on Jabal Sufsafa's plateau, where the chapel of Elijah is today.

70 1 [III] Kgs 12:2 and 19:8–18.

71 1 [III] Kgs 19:9.

72 Not mentioned in 1 [III] Kgs 19.

73 Exod. 24:9–14.

74 Two in the afternoon.

75 PP, *Itin.* 37 gives the same distance between Mt Horeb to Wadi al-Dayr; but it is inaccurate, and so 'three miles' may simply mean 'very far'.

in which we had entered, as I said above, since we had to visit all the holy places and see the monastic cells which were there, and then exit at the end of the valley mentioned above – I mean, the valley which lay beneath the Mountain of God.[76] **[IV.6]** But we had to exit from the end of that valley because there are a very great number of monastic cells of holy men there and a church in the place where the Bush stands. The Bush is alive to this day and sends out green shoots.

[IV.7] So we climbed all the way down from the Mountain of God and arrived at the Bush, at about the tenth hour.[77] This is the Bush that I already mentioned, from which the Lord spoke to Moses in fire. It is in a place at the end of that valley where there are very many monastic cells, and a church. In front of the church is a most charming garden with plenty of very good water.[78] In the garden is the Bush itself. **[IV.8]** Also shown nearby is the place where Holy Moses was standing when God said to him, 'Loosen the strap of your sandal', etc.[79] When we arrived in that place it was already the tenth hour, and since it was already evening, for this reason we were unable to make the offering. But we made a prayer in the church as well as in the garden by the Bush, and a passage from the book of Moses was also read, following our routine. Then, since it was evening, we ate there in the garden in front of the Bush together with those holy men, and then camped there.

Upon waking early in the morning the next day,[80] we asked the priests to make an offering there, and so it was done.

[V.1] Since this was our route, we went through the central valley that stretched out far – I mean that valley which I mentioned above,[81] where the Children of Israel had settled while Moses ascended and descended the Mountain of God. And again, the holy men made each and every place clear to us as we went through the whole valley. **[V.2]** At the farthest end of the valley where we had stopped and seen the Bush from which God spoke to Holy Moses in fire, we had also seen the place where Holy Moses had stood in front of the Bush when God said to him, 'Loosen the strap of your sandal, for the place where you are standing is holy ground.'[82] **[V.3]** Likewise they

76 Wadi al-Dayr. Egeria was now heading north-west, back towards Pharan. 'Monastic cells' translates *monasteria*.

77 Four in the afternoon, in Wadi al-Dayr.

78 Cf. PP, *Itin.* 37.

79 Exod. 3:5, etc.

80 Monday, 18 December 383.

81 Wadi al-Raha, mentioned above, I.1–II.2.

82 Exod. 3:5.

began to point out the rest of the places as we proceeded from the Bush:[83]

They indicated that place where the camps of the Children of Israel were during the days when Moses was on the mountain.[84]

They also indicated that place were the calf was made – here a large stone stands fixed to this day.[85] **[V.4]** As we went, we also could see the summit of the Mountain right in front of us. It overlooked the entire valley. From it Holy Moses saw the Children of Israel dancing on the days they had made the calf.[86]

They also showed the immense rock in that place where Holy Moses had descended with Joshua the son of Nun – the rock on which 'he angrily smashed the tablets' he was carrying.[87] **[V.5]** They also showed how throughout the valley each of them had their dwellings, the foundations of which are still visible today, since they were made with rounded stone.

They also showed that place where Holy Moses had commanded the Children of Israel to run 'from door to door' after he returned to the mountain.[88]

[V.6] Next they showed us that place were the calf which Aaron had made for them was burned at Holy Moses' direction.[89]

Next they showed that stream from which Holy Moses 'made the Children of Israel drink', as is written in Exodus.[90]

[V.7] They also showed us the place where the seventy men received the spirit of Moses.[91]

Next they showed that place where the Children of Israel craved food.[92]

They also showed us that place too which has been named 'The Burning' because 'a certain part of the camp burned'; then while Holy Moses prayed, 'the fire abated'.[93]

[V.8] They also showed that place where it rained manna and quails for them.[94]

---

83 The following list is based on Exod. 32 and Num. 11; for the monuments, probably *nawāmīs*, see above, p. 217, n. 37.

84 Cf. Exod. 19:2.

85 Cf. Exod. 32:4, referring to the 'Mould of the Calf'.

86 Cf. Exod. 32:19.

87 Exod. 32:19.

88 Cf. Exod. 32:27 and 30–31.

89 Cf. Exod. 32:20.

90 Cf. Exod. 17:6.

91 Cf. Num. 11:25.

92 Num. 11:4.

93 Cf. Num. 11.2–3, referring to Taberah.

94 Cf. Num. 11:7–9, 31–32. Exod. 16:13–15 places the manna incident near Elim: hence the reference to it in PD,Y 13.

And so in that way each and every thing was shown to us that the holy books of Moses record had been done in this place, I mean, in the valley which I said lies below the Mountain of God – I mean, Holy Sina. It was enough to write them all down one by one, because it would be impossible to remember so many. But when you, my Beloved, read the holy books of Moses, you may examine more carefully all the things that were done there.

[V.9] This is the valley where Passover was celebrated upon the completion of the year of the departure of the Children of Israel from the land of Egypt, because in the valley the Children of Israel dwelt for a long time, I mean, while Holy Moses ascended and descended the Mountain of God the first and second times, then staying again long enough for the tabernacle and each of those things shown on God's Mountain to be made.[95] They also showed us the place where Moses first constructed the tabernacle, and where each thing was carried out that God on the mountain had commanded Moses to do.[96]

[V.10] At the farthest end of the valley we saw the Tombs of Craving. But this was the place where we returned again to our route – that is, where we exited that great valley and rejoined the road by which we had come, between the mountains I mentioned above.[97] That day we also visited the rest of the very holy monks, who on account of age or infirmity were unable to meet us on God's Mountain to make the offering. They nonetheless deigned to welcome us very hospitably when we came to their cells.

[V.11] So then, once we had seen all the holy places that we desired to see, as well as all the places that the Children of Israel had trod while going to and coming from the Mountain of God, and once we had also seen the holy men who dwelt there, we went back to Pharan in the name of God.[98] **[V.12]** And though I ever ought to thank God for all things (I pass over how many great things He has deigned to grant me – unworthy and undeserving as I am – so that I visited all those places, none of which I deserved), nevertheless I cannot sufficiently thank all those holy men who deigned to kindly welcome my little self into their monastic cells, and even to escort us through all the places I kept asking about, as found in the Holy Scriptures. Still, a great many of the holy men who dwelt on or around the Mountain of God deigned to escort us up to Pharan – those, at any rate, who were physically strong enough.

---

95 Cf. Exod. 25:40.
96 Cf. Exod. 40:15–32.
97 Cf. above, *Itin.* I.1 and PD,Y 17.
98 19 December 383.

[**VI.1**] And so, when we reached Pharan, which is thirty-five miles from the Mountain of God,[99] we had to stay there two days to rest. On the third day, we rose early and came once more to our staging-post, I mean, in the Pharan desert where we had camped on our approach, as stated above.[100] Then the next day[101] after getting water we went a little distance still farther between the mountains until we reached the staging-post that was on the sea, I mean at the place where one exits from the mountains,[102] and starts to travel once more the whole way beside the sea. But 'beside the sea' means this: at one moment the waves are lapping your animals' feet, but at the next you are 100, 200, and sometimes even 500 feet or more away from the sea, travelling through desert – for there is no road there at all, but it is entirely a desert of sand.

[**VI.2**] But the Pharanites, who are wont to travel there with camels, put markers for themselves here and there and direct themselves to these when travelling by day. But at night the camels head towards the markers. What more to say? By this practice the Pharanites are able to travel in that place more carefully and safely at night than some people travel in places where the road is open to view.

[**VI.3**] And so on our return we left the mountains in the same place that we had entered them, and thus finally went on our way back to the sea. The Children of Israel, when they returned from the Mountain of God, Sina, also returned by the route they had taken to go there – I mean, by that place where we left the mountains and finally rejoined the Red Sea. From there we retraced the route by which we had come; the Children of Israel made their route from the same place, as is written in the books of Holy Moses. And so we returned to Clysma by the same route and staging-posts by which we had come.[103] When we came to Clysma,[104] we again had to rest there for two days again, since our desert route had been very sandy.

---

99 As noted above, PD,Y 15.

100 Presumably in the section that was abridged as PD,Y 14. Third day: 23 December 383.

101 24 December 383.

102 See above, PD,Y 12.

103 Cf. Num 10:12, 33:16–49; see above, PD,Y 9–12.

104 On Clysma, see above, PD,Y 5–8.

[From Clysma to the Land of Goshen and Jerusalem]

[VII.1] While it is true that I had already come to know the land of Jesse[105] when I was first in Egypt,[106] nevertheless, in order that I might see all the places that the Children of Israel had trodden after leaving Ramesses[107] till they reached the Red Sea at the place that is now known as Clysma because of the fort there, accordingly it was my wish to set out from Clysma to the land of Jesse – I mean, to the city called Arabia. This city is in the land of Jesse, and so the countryside gets its name – I mean 'the land of Arabia' is 'the land of Jesse'.[108] Though part of Egypt, it is really much 'better' than all the rest of Egypt.[109]

[VII.2] From Clysma (I mean, from the Red Sea) to the city of Arabia there are four staging-posts through desert. And as it is through desert, at every staging-post there were outposts with soldiers and officers who would always escort us from fort to fort.[110]

---

105 Cf. Gen. 45–47 and 50. Following her Vetus translation of the LXX, Egeria identifies 'the land of Jesse', or 'Gessen' ([LXX] Gen. 46:34; i.e. Goshen) with the 20th Egyptian nome called Arabia, which, starting from the eastern (Pelusiac) branch of the Nile Delta, extended north-east to Pelusium and south-east to the Sinai peninsula and Red Sea. It lay in the province of *Augustamnica prima*.

106 Egeria travelled through this region in 381–383; for fragments of her travelogue pertaining to that trip, see Wilkinson 1999, 93–95.

107 On the city of Ramesses (modern Qantir), see Exod. 12:37, Num 33:3, and below, *Itin.* VIII.1–5.

108 Cf. [LXX] Gen. 46:34. LXX was originally made in Egypt and adds a number of Ptolemaic place names (e.g. Arabia, the name for this region since Hellenistic times) not found in the Hebrew text.

Egeria is travelling north-west. The 'City of Arabia' to which she repeatedly refers has not been securely identified, but was probably Phakussa (modern Faqūs), which Ptolemy identifies as the capital of the Arabian nome, about 4 km/2.5 miles south of modern Qantir (Ramesses). For other possibilities, see Maraval 1997, 158 n. 1.

109 Cf. [LXX] Gen. 47.11 and 47:6, quoted below, *Itin.* VII.9, where it is called the 'best land of Egypt', which is probably why here Egeria calls it 'better' than the rest of Egypt.

110 For 'outposts', the manuscript has *manasteria*. Most assume this to be a corrupt form of *monasteria*, making it the only attested non-religious use of that term. However, Mary Whitby has suggested to me that *manasteria* may derive from the verb *maneo*, 'to stay' or 'remain'. Wilkinson 1999, 115, translates it 'quarters'.

As noted above, p. 213, n. 11, the military presence described here may relate to the Mavia revolt of 377/8, which, according to Sozomen, *EH* VI.38, resulted in attacks on 'the regions of Egypt lying to the left of those sailing up the Nile, generally called Arabia'. This must refer to the area described here by Egeria. Rubin 1990, 180–81, argues that Saracen problems had ceased after the Mavia revolt five years earlier, but Lenski 2002, 207, suggests otherwise. In any case as Rubin and Isaac 1984, 200, observe, the main problem in this area were bandits (whether Saracen or not) who preyed on caravans headed from Clysma into Egypt.

On this route the holy men who were with us – I mean, the clerics and monks – would point out to us each place that I, following the Scriptures, was constantly asking about. Some were on the left of our route, others on the right; some far off the road, others nearby. **[VII.3]** And I want you, my Beloved, to believe me that, as far as I could see, the Children of Israel travelled in such a way, that to whatever degree they went to the right, by so much did they return to the left, and however far they went in one direction, by so much did they go back in the other; and so they made their journey, until they reached the Red Sea.[111]

[VII.4] Epauleum was pointed out, opposite to us, when we were at Magdalum.[112] For there is a fort there now with an officer and soldiers who govern there on behalf of the Roman authority. Following procedure, they escorted us from there to the next fort.[113] We were shown Belsephon – indeed, we were at the place itself. It is a field on the Red Sea beside the flank of that mountain which I mentioned above.[114] Here the Children of Israel cried out when they saw the Egyptians coming after them.[115] **[VII.5]** We also were shown Oton (which is 'on the edge of the wilderness', according to Scripture) as well as Soccoth.[116] Soccoth is a modest knoll in the centre of a valley; near this little hill the Children of Israel pitched their camp, and here they received the Law of Passover.[117]

[VII.6] On this route we were also shown Pithom, a city built by the Children of Israel. Now at this point we were entering the bounds of Egypt and leaving the territories of the Saracens.[118] Pithom is now also a fort.[119]

[VII.7] Heroum city – which it was in those days when Joseph went

111 Cf. above, PD,Y 8.

112 Cf. Exod. 14:2; Num. 33:7. Egeria is listing sites outside Clysma where the Egyptians and Israelites camped near the Red Sea. The Vetus, following LXX, has Epauleum (Greek for 'encampment') for Pi-hahiroth (Hebrew for 'encampment'). Magdalum (from Migdol, 'fortress') was perhaps the outpost whose remains are seen today at Tall Abū Hassan.

113 See above, p. 227, n.110.

114 Beelsephon and Jabal 'Ataqa, described above, PD,Y 7–9. Cf. Exod. 14:2.

115 Cf. Exod. 14:2, 9–10 and Num 33:7.

116 Cf. Exod. 12.37, 13:20 and Num 33:5–7. After leaving Ramesses, the Hebrews made their first camp at Soccoth, their second at Oton (Etham). These sites probably were located near the Bitter Lakes, near which ruins of ancient fortresses have been found. See Servin 1948–49 and Bourdon 1924.

117 Cf. Exod. 12:37, 13:20; Num 33:5–6. Passover celebrates the Israelites' release from bondage in Egypt (Exod. 12:1–13:16).

118 *terras Saracenorum*: see above, p. 222, n. 68, and General Introduction, p. 43.

119 Pithom (modern Abū Suwayr) had a Roman fort guarding the Ptolemaic-Trajanic canal (Wadi Tumilat). For the scriptural reference cf. Exod. 1:11.

there 'to meet his father Jacob', as is written in the Book of Genesis – is now a *kōmē* [village], but a huge one – what we would call a *vicus* [town].[120] This town has a church, martyrs' shrines, and a very great many monastic cells of holy monks. It was necessary for us to go down to see each one in keeping with our routine. **[VII.8]** This town is now called Heroum; it is at the sixteenth milestone from the land of Jesse, and within the bounds of Egypt. The place is quite charming, as part of the Nile river runs through it.[121]

[VII.9] So after leaving Heroum we reached the city called Arabia, the city in the land of Jesse, of which it is written that Pharaoh said unto Joseph, 'Settle your father and brothers in the best land of Egypt, in the land of Jesse, the land of Arabia'.[122]

[VIII.1] From the city of Arabia it is four miles to Ramesses, which we passed through to get to the staging-post at Arabia. The city of Ramesses is now just a field without a single dwelling-place. You can see that it was once huge in circumference and had many buildings: for today its ruins, though fallen, appear vast. **[VIII.2]** Now there is nothing there but a single, immense Theban stone on which are two immense, carved statues. These are said to be of the holy men Moses and Aaron; they say that the Children of Israel put them up in their honour.[123] **[VIII.3]** In addition there is a sycamore tree that is said to have been planted by the Patriarchs. It is now extremely old (and so very small), yet it still bears fruit. If anyone has an ailment they go there and pick its twigs, and it helps them. **[VIII.4]** We learned this from the information given by the holy bishop of Arabia.[124] He told us the tree's name in Greek, *Dendros Alethias* [Tree of Truth], which we would call *Arbor Veritatis* [Tree of Truth].[125]

120 *Hero[or]um civitas* is Latin for *Heroöpolis*, a town mentioned in the LXX/Vetus version of Gen. 46:29 but not in the original Hebrew. Egeria uses *kōmē*, a Greek administrative term designating a large village; she had apparently used the word *vicus* to describe Pharan: see above, PD,Y 15. Heroöpolis lay beside the Ptolemaic-Trajanic canal (Wadi Tumilat), and has been identified with Tall al-Makhuta.

121 I.e. through Wadi Tumilat, a canal first built by Pharaoh Necho (609–594 BCE) and later reconstructed by Trajan. Egeria had passed into Egypt's eighth nome, called 'Heroopolitēs', and was less than one day's travel from Arabia/'Gessen' (see next section).

122 Cf. [LXX] Gen. 47:6. On the 'City of Arabia', probably Phakussa (modern Faqūs), see above, p. 227, n.108.

123 Probably red granite statues of Pharaoh Ramesses II and his god Atmu, like those still seen in Upper Egypt near the Valley of the Kings. In Exod. 1:11, Ramesses (modern Qantir) is called a supply city, indicating its size and importance in earlier times.

124 I.e. of the City of Arabia (bishops being identified with cities, not provinces).

125 According to Maraval, the sycamore tree had long been sacred in this region and

This holy bishop deigned to meet us at Ramesses. He is an old man, really quite pious, and a former monk. He is friendly and very welcoming towards pilgrims; he is also very learned in God's Scriptures. **[VIII.5]** Since he had deigned to take the trouble to meet us there, he pointed out each place and told us about those statues I mentioned as well as about that sycamore tree. The holy bishop also told us that when Pharaoh saw that the Children of Israel had got away from him, then, before pursuing them, he went with his whole army into Ramesses and set it all on fire – that vast city – and subsequently went after the Children of Israel.[126]

[IX.1] To our good fortune, the day on which we came to our stop at Arabia happened to be the day before the most blessed day of Epiphany;[127] and on this very day a vigil was to be held in the church. So the holy bishop had us there for two days. Truly he is a holy man of God, one well known to me from the time that I was at the Thebaïd. **[IX.2]** This bishop is a former monk, reared in a monastic cell from childhood, which is why he is so learned in the Scriptures and so correct in his whole way of life, as I said above.[128]

[IX.3] We now dismissed the soldiers who had provided us with military support on behalf of the Roman authority while we were travelling through dangerous places.[129] It was no longer necessary to trouble the soldiers, since there was a state highway through Egypt that passed through the city of Arabia – the one that goes from the Thebaïd to Pelusium.

[IX.4] And so from there we set out and made our way through the entire land of Gessen,[130] always among vineyards for wine and vineyards for balsam, as well as orchards and well-tilled fields and first-rate gardens. All along the Nile bank our route passed by very fertile farm land that once had been the estates of the Children of Israel. What more to say? I think I have never seen a more beautiful countryside than the land of Jesse.

[IX.5] After travelling two days from the city of Arabia all the way through the land of Gessen we came to the city of Tatnis in which holy

---

dedicated to the goddess Hathor; Pliny, *Natural History* XXIII.134–40 calls it the 'Egyptian mulberry' and also notes its medicinal properties.

126 This account is otherwise unknown.

127 I.e. Egeria arrived on 5 January 384; the next day was Epiphany. She describes its celebration at Jerusalem in *Itin.* XXV.

128 Egeria, *Itin.* VIII.4.

129 Cf. above, Egeria, *Itin.* VII.2 and notes *ad loc.*

130 'Gessen' was the LXX/Vetus word for Goshen, or 'land of Jesse': see above, p. 227, n. 109.

Moses was born. This city, Tatnis, was once Pharaoh's capital.[131] **[IX.6]** And though these places were already known to me from when I had been at Alexandria and the Thebaïd, as I said above,[132] yet I still wanted to learn as much as possible about the places where the Children of Israel had travelled when they went from Ramesses to the Mountain of God, Holy Sina. It was therefore necessary to return to the land of Gessen and go from there to Tatnis. After setting out from Tatnis, I travelled by the familiar route and came to Pelusium.

[IX.7] After setting out again from there and passing through each of the staging-posts in Egypt passed on our previous route, I arrived at the bounds of Palestine. And from there, in the name of Christ our God, after several more staging-posts, I returned through Palestine to Aelia – I mean, to Jerusalem.[133]

131 Cf. Ps. 77:12, although Moses' birth at Tanis (Tatnis) is not scriptural. Tanis was the Hyksos capital of Egypt. It has been identified with modern Tall Defenneh and modern Sam al-Hagar, both south-west of Pelusium.

132 Egeria, *Itin.* VII.1, referring to her trip in 381–383. See Wilkinson 1999, 93–95; Maraval 1997, 79–80.

133 Jerusalem had been officially renamed *Aelia Capitolina* by Emperor Hadrian (a.k.a. *Publius Aelius Hadrianus*) after the Bar Chocba revolt of 132–135 CE. Egeria arrived there after travelling along the Mediterranean coast from Pelusium to Rhinocorura/Al-Arish and on through Ascalon.

THEODORET OF CYRRHUS, *RELIGIOUS HISTORY* II.13 (LIFE OF JULIAN SABA), VI.7–13 (LIFE OF SYMEON THE ELDER)*

The *Religious History* of Theodoret, bishop (393–466) of Cyrrhus (Nebi Ouri, Syria), celebrates the achievements of exemplary monks who lived in northern Syria-Mesopotamia in the fourth and early fifth centuries. An important source for early Syrian monastic tradition, it includes descriptions of two journeys by monks to Mount Sinai in the fourth century: one by Julian Saba († 367) from the region of Edessa, another by Symeon the Elder († c. 375–380) from outside Antioch.[1] As noted in the introductions to the hymns on Julian Saba, his is the earliest of any known pilgrimage to the Sinai.

Theodoret wrote about these journeys c. 444, long after they took place. No doubt his account includes later suppositions and inventions. However, he says that he was informed about Julian from Acacius of Beroea (a follower of one of Julian's disciples), and he no doubt learned much about Symeon from his mother, who used to visit the holy man for blessings and cures.[2] Stylistically and intellectually, Theodoret was a Hellenist: of all the authors in this volume, he comes closest to Ps.-Nilus and Nilus of Ancyra with his stilted, classicizing diction (e.g. his use of *palaistra*, 'wrestling school', for monastery, *philosophia* for ascetic practice), and in his assumption that desire (*eros*) for tranquillity (*hēsychia*) was the main reason that such monks went to the Sinai.[3]

---

* Ed. Canivet and Leroy-Molinghen 1977, vol. 1, 222–24, 354–62.

1 For Theodoret's depiction of Syrian monasticism, see Canivet 1977 and Urbainczyk 2002.
2 See Solzbacher 1989, 111–14.
3 On Theodoret's Hellenism, see Millar 2007.

TRANSLATION OF THE GREEK TEXT

RELIGIOUS HISTORY II.13, ON JULIAN SABA

II. 13 Once [Julian Saba] became known to everyone, his fame attracted to him lovers of good things. To escape this fame, he finally set out for Mount Sinai with a few of his very close associates.[4] In no city or village did they set foot, but put down their tracks in untracked desert. On their shoulders they carried essential foodstuffs – I refer to bread and salt – as well as a wooden cup and sponge tied to a string, so that, if ever they found water in a deep down spot, they might soak it up with the sponge, squeeze it into the cup and drink it up.

Eventually after many days of travel they reached the mountain of their yearning. After venerating their Master, they remained there for a long time because they considered the land's desertedness and the tranquillity it afforded the soul to be the greatest luxury. And on that rock, hidden by which Moses, the pinnacle of the prophets, was privileged to see God – in as much as it was possible to see Him – he built a church and consecrated a divine altar which is there even now.[5] Then he returned to his own wresting ground.

RELIGIOUS HISTORY VI.7–13, ON SYMEON THE ELDER

VI.7 But since [Symeon the Elder] desired tranquillity once more, he set his heart on visiting Mount Sinai. When many of the best men who pursued the same philosophy learned of this, they hurriedly assembled, yearning to take part in this expedition with him.

After many days of travel, when they were in the desert of Sodom,[6] they saw in the distance a man's hands stretching up high from below. At first they supposed it to be a demon's deception, but after they had prayed more earnestly and still saw the same thing, they hastened towards the spot and saw a shallow ditch such as foxes are wont to make when they make hideouts. Yet they saw no one visible there, because the one who had

---

4 One of Julian's companion was Adelphius, a monk later identified as the founder of the 'Messalian' heresy after his return from Sinai in the 380s or 390s. The monks are said to have met many Egyptian holy men and to have had many visions: see Philoxenus of Mabbug (c. 440–523), *Letter to Patricius* 108; ed. R. Levant (PO 30.850) and Fitschen 1998, 92–95.

5 On Julian's church, see above, p. 203.

6 The desert south of the Dead Sea; this suggests that Symeon took the eastern route to Mt Sinai, via Aila.

stretched out his hands had heard their footsteps and hidden in his hideout.

VI.8 The Elder peered in and implored the man many times to show himself – if in fact he were a human being in nature, and not some deceiving demon that had taken such a form:

'For we too,' he said, 'pursue the ascetic life and desire tranquillity. We are wandering in this desert with our hearts set on venerating the God of the Universe on Mount Sinai, where He made Himself manifest to His servant Moses and gave him the tablets of His legislation. It is not that we believe the divine is circumscribed in space,[7] for we hear him who says, "Do I not fill heaven and earth? saith the Lord",[8] and, "He holds the circle of the earth and those who live on it like grasshoppers".[9] Rather, it is because, for those who burn with love, not only are the people they love objects of excessive yearning, but also are the places beloved that received their presence and intercourse.'

VI.9 While the Elder was saying this and other such things, the man who was hidden revealed himself from his hideout. He looked savage, with his hair matted, his face shrivelled up, and all the limbs of his body reduced to a skeleton. He was wrapped up in filthy rags stitched together from palm fibres.

After greeting them and giving them the salutation of peace, he inquired who they were, where they had come from, and where they were going. [Symeon the Elder] answered his questions and asked in turn where he had came from and why in the world he had chosen this way of life. 'I too had the same desire,' he said, 'that set you on your way. I had taken as a companion for the journey a close associate who shared my views and had the same goal as me. We had persuaded each other under oath not to sever our union, even in death. As it turned out, during the journey he met the end of his life in this place here. And so I, bound by my oath, dug down as much as I could, and committed his body to the grave. Then I dug another grave for myself beside his barrow. So here I await my life's end and offer my Master the customary liturgy. For food I have the dates that a certain brother has been assigned to bring me by my protector.'[10]

VI.10 Just as he said this, a lion appeared in the distance. The Elder's companions became greatly distressed. When the man who was sitting in

---

7 For this sentiment cf. Theodoret, *Religious History* IX.1; Gregory of Nyssa, *ep*. II; and Augustine, *Confessions*, I.3.3, VII.1.2; also Bitton-Ashkelony 2005, 177–78.

8 Jer. 23:24.

9 Isa. 40:22.

10 Probably referring to the lion who appears in the next section, or to God.

the hideout noticed this he stood up and gestured to the lion to pass on the other side. It immediately obeyed him and drew near, carrying a cluster of dates. Then it turned around and went away again. It lay down far from the men and fell asleep.

And so, after distributing the dates to everyone and joining them in prayer and psalm-singing, he embraced them at the end of the liturgy and sent them off early in the morning. They were completely awed by the novel spectacle.[11]

VI.11 If there is anyone who does not believe what has been said, let him recall the famous Elijah's mode of life and the crows that ministered to him by continuously bringing him bread in the early morning and meat in the late afternoon.[12] It is quite easy for the Creator of the Universe to find all sorts of ways to care for His own: thus He sheltered Jonah in the belly of a whale for three days and nights;[13] He arranged for lions to be awestruck by Daniel in the den,[14] and made inanimate fire act as if it were intelligent, illuminating those within while burning those without.[15] But it is superfluous for me to offer proofs of divine power.

VI.12 They say that, once they had reached the mountain for which they had yearned, that wondrous old man, in that very spot where Moses was privileged to see God (as much as it was possible for human nature to see [Him]), bent his knees and did not stand up again until he had heard a divine voice revealing to him his Master's favour. When he had been crouching this way for the full span of a week without taking even a bit of food, the voice came, and ordered him to take what was set in front of him and to eat it happily. He stretched out his hand and found three apples. After he had consumed them as instructed by their giver, he regained full strength and embraced his companions with high spirits, as might be expected. Then he came down with glad rejoicing, since he had both heard a divine voice and refreshed himself in turn on food given by God.

VI.13 Upon coming down he constructed two philosophical retreats,[16] one on the ridge of the mountain of which I have spoken before, and the

11 The obedience of wild animals to desert hermits was a common hagiographical motif, indicating that the area had been restored to paradise: see Anast., *Narr* I.21 and Rapp 2006, 101–02.

12 Cf. 1 [III] Kgs 17:6.

13 Cf. Jon. 2.1

14 Cf. Dan. 6:22.

15 Cf. Dan. 3:22–23.

16 φροντιστήριον, common for 'monastery' among classicizing authors who viewed monks as philosophers.

other down at the very edge of the mountain's foot.[17] In each of these he gathered athletes of virtue and became trainer and coach for them both, teaching them the throws of their enemy and adversary, assuring them of the benevolence of the Master of the Contest,[18] enjoining them to have courage, filling them with resolve, bidding them to show moderation towards their fellow men, while urging them to be magnanimous towards the enemy.

17 Probably referring to Jabal Sufsafa/Horeb (see note to Egeria, *Itin.* IV.1) and Wadi al-Dayr/Bush or Wadi Leja/al-Arba'in, where Egeria saw monastic cells (III.1). Archaeology indicates that the Jabal Sufsafa plateau had the highest concentration of monastic cells on the late antique Sinai: see Dahari 2000, 39–47.

18 A common description of God among authors who used wrestling motifs to describe a monk's spiritual struggle; e.g. Ps.-Nilus, *Narr.* IV.12.

EMPEROR MARCIAN, *LETTER TO BISHOP MACARIUS AND THE MONKS OF SINAI* (453)[*]

The Council of Chalcedon sat throughout October 451, and issued on 25 October its famous Definition of the Faith, defining that the Godhead and manhood of Christ constitute 'two natures', that is, two distinct and countable realities, and condemning (though not by name) the archimandrite Eutyches, who had firmly rejected the doctrine.

Opposition was immediate, particularly in Constantinople, Egypt, and Palestine. The Palestinian bishops had opposed the issuing of such a definition in the early stages of the council, but then capitulated. Even before they had returned to Palestine, opposition had become vocal and organized. When Bishop Juvenal of Jerusalem returned to his see and refused to denounce the council, his opponents stormed the city; while he fled to Constantinople, they elected the monk Theodosius in his place. Many of the other sees in Palestine were taken over by opponents of the council, and Bishop Severianus of Scythopolis (the metropolitan of the province of Palestine II) was murdered. For twenty months the opponents of Chalcedon, who enjoyed the patronage of Empress Eudocia, widow of Theodosius II (408–450), controlled the province, and only in 453 did Dorotheus, the military commander in Palestine, crush the revolt and reinstate Juvenal.

Theodosius fled to the Sinai peninsula. In the letter translated here, Emperor Marcian urges the monks there to hand him over to the proper authorities. In another letter sent soon afterwards to a synod held somewhere (location unknown) in Palestine, the emperor referred to this Sinai letter and repeated its message, urging the bishops at the synod to make sure that Theodosius did not return to Jerusalem.[1] After travelling in Egypt and Syria

* Ed. E. Schwartz, *ACO* II.I.3, pp. 490–91 (no. 29; no Latin copy extant). I thank R. M. Price for kindly providing translation, introduction, and commentary for this letter.

1 Schwartz, *ACO* II.I.3, pp. 492–93 (no. 30; no Latin copy extant), which comes immediately after the Sinai letter in the conciliar collection; it is important because it presents a different list of recipients for the Sinai letter than is found in the heading of the letter itself. See below, n. 3.

in disguise, Theodosius was eventually captured at Antioch and spent his last years as a prisoner in Constantinople, dying in 457.[2]

TRANSLATION OF THE GREEK TEXT

Copy of the divine letter sent by the same to Macarius bishop and archimandrite and the other devout monks on the holy mountain of Sinai.[3]

The dangerous innovations against the pure religion and the Roman way of life in which Theodosius, for whose deeds one would not be able to find a worthy penalty, has been detected have escaped no one, and the greatness of his offences has certainly come to your devoutness. For anticipating the awaited coming of the Antichrist, according to the pronouncements of the divine scriptures, or to speak more truly, when sent by him to wage war on the holy and orthodox faith, he thought himself to be doing nothing wrong if he imitated the impiety of Eutyches.[4] He rose up against the pious religion

---

2 See Solzbacher 1989, 184–90 and Fliche–Martin 1937, 276–78. The principal source is Ps.-Zachariah of Mitylene, *Chronicle* III.3–9; trans. Hamilton-Brooks, 1899, 49–56.

3 Μακαρίῳ ἐπισκόπει καὶ ἀρχιμανδρίτῃ καὶ λοιποῖς τοῖς ἐν τῷ ἁγίῳ ὄρει Σινᾶ εὐλαβέσι μοναχοῖς. A different list of recipients is found in a letter (hereafter designated **B** to distinguish it from the Sinai letter, hereafter **A**) that the emperor sent to bishops at a Palestinian synod: 'to Macarius, the most pious Bishop, and to all the archimandrites and monks on the aforesaid [i.e. Sinai] mountain' (*ACO* II.I.3.493, lines 8–9: πρὸς Μακάριον τὸν εὐλαβέστατον ἐπίσκοπον καὶ τοὺς ἐν τῷ προλεχθέντι ὄρει ἀρχιμανδρίτας τε καὶ μοναχοὺς πάντας). This list is embedded in **B**'s text, which is important, because that means it would have made it less susceptible to scribal error than had it been a separate contents of a letter heading. Indeed, it would be easier to assume that a hasty scribe misread and miscopied the original list of recipients in **A** (e.g. by mistaking what would have been a Greek iota-sigma dative plural of 'archimandrites' for a iota-side script or subscript) than to explain why, in **B**, one would have first turned the single 'archimandrite' into a plural set of archimandrites, then separated them grammatically from the bishop and grouped them grammatically with the mountain's monks. The former error would have been the result of a simple misreading, while the latter would have involved both a misreading and a creative, new grammatical and conceptual construction. For this reason – in addition to the fact that no abbot-bishop is otherwise attested on the Sinai until the medieval period, after Pharan disappears – we may conclude that **B** more likely reflects the original Sinai letter's heading than does **A**. Accordingly, this imperial letter represents the first official document to refer to a Sinai bishop, but not a bishop who is also an archimandrite or *hēgoumen*. See also Solzbacher 1989, 189, and Flusin 1998, 136.

4 According to Ps.-Zachariah of Mitylene, *Chronicle* III.9, Theodosius when a prisoner at Constantinople actually attacked the teaching of Eutyches, which was likewise criticized by Dioscorus of Alexandria after his deposition, despite his support of Eutyches prior to Chalcedon: see Price and Gaddis 2005, vol. 1, 116, n. 8. Eutyches' rejection of 'two natures' had won him widespread support, but his rejection of Christ's consubstantiality with human beings was a major embarrassment for his supporters.

of the orthodox, emulating Photinus the stranger to the truth, and eager to be an imitator of the doctrine, opposed to God, of Apollinarius, Valentinus, and Nestorius;[5] he presented himself openly as a false accuser of the most holy council that was recently convened in the city of Chalcedon at our command out of ardour for the faith and which confirmed the creed of the 318 holy fathers for the upholding of the faith, making no change by addition or subtraction from the teaching of the same sacred fathers, and pronouncing that Eutyches, for opposing the truth and intending to undermine the faith, cannot share the name of the orthodox.[6]

Imitating Eutyches' wicked and reckless audacity, Theodosius made his way to the region of the Palestines[7] and deceived the ignorant by concocting the fiction that certain things rather than others were decreed by the holy council; for he asserted that the said most holy council decreed that two sons and two Christs and two persons ought to be worshipped and that it interpreted the faith in contradiction to the creed of the holy fathers.[8] Having by these means attracted to himself a multitude of the deceived and acquired as an ally the ignorance, so to say, of the simple-minded, he hastened to the city of Aelia,[9] where he committed arson, murders of devout men, and the release of people convicted on charges of the utmost gravity. Seeking through these actions to win a reputation as a devout person, he perilously usurped power, breaking open the prisons with the intention, once those accountable had been freed from justice, as far as he could ensure, that he might confer on virtually everybody ease to offend without accountability. Aiming at treason itself and transgressing the laws of our divinity, he closed the city's gates and attempted to arrogate permanently to himself the title of episcopacy, against all the canons, even though the most sacred Juvenal is still alive and is bishop of the city, desecrating and violating rights both divine and

---

5 A standard list of heretics, with no special application to Theodosius.

6 The Chalcedonian Definition condemned the teaching of Eutyches, though without naming him. Eutyches' condemnation, decreed at the Home Synod of Constantinople of 448 but annulled at the Second Council of Ephesus of 449, was taken for granted from the moment of Marcian's accession in 450.

7 Palestine was divided into three provinces by this date. See General Introduction, p. 8.

8 The Definition defined Christ as 'acknowledged in two natures … coming together into one person and one hypostasis' (Price and Gaddis 2005, vol. 2, 204). Since the terms 'nature' (*physis*) and 'hypostasis' had hitherto been used as virtually equivalent, the opponents of the council argued from the 'two natures' formula that the council implied two hypostases. The formula 'two persons' was used by Nestorius (who also acknowledged, however, 'one person of union'), whose errors were attributed by the anti-Chalcedonians to the council itself.

9 *Aelia Capitolina,* i.e. Jerusalem.

human alike. Then proceeding on his way to yet worse deeds, he subjected to even greater evils the most holy churches and cities throughout Palestine, contriving the murder of the most devout bishops[10] and consecrating in their sees those whom he wished; for with maniacal effrontery he ordered those who had formerly become bishops of the cities by just vote according to the divine canons to be stripped, according to his pleasure, of the priest-hood, and to be driven from the sees to which they had been appointed. He made war on the most sacred bishop Juvenal, seeking his murder by sending in a multitude from every side; for he thought by this means to take permanent possession of the bishopric to which he had no right and to bring his endeavours to complete realization. The Holy Trinity and (as the event showed) courage in the faith saved the most sacred bishop Juvenal, but in his stead Severianus of devout memory, bishop of Scythopolis,[11] was impiously murdered along with others, as a by-product of Theodosius' madness.

When Theodosius had committed these misdeeds and ones still worse, and after everything about him had been made known to our rule, orders were given for him to be hunted down everywhere, together with his henchmen and the partners in his crimes. He fled from the region of the Palestines, which he had treated in this way, revealing by his very deeds that he was a minister and forerunner of the Antichrist.[12] He moved from place to place, disrupting the most holy churches and making the more simple-minded about the faith hold opinions contrary to the truth and worship the deity impiously. He, as we have learnt, made his way to Mount Sinai, the abode of piety and the haunt of holy men, where are situated your monastic cells,[13] dear to the Almighty and worthy of all honour from us. In this way, hiding there, he is still plotting against orthodoxy and waiting for an opportunity to come to him. But of him there is no single reckoning, since one could not find an appropriate limit for the punishment of the offences of him and his henchmen. Yet even though our rule has every confidence that the wicked purpose of Theodosius, opposed to God, will in no way be able to shake the faith that is truly and firmly rooted in you, all the same, lest some work

10 The plural may refer simply to Severianus of Scythopolis, for whose murder see the end of the paragraph, where likewise the reference to the deaths of several bishops may be a mere rhetorical flourish based on a single case.

11 Severianus' name was included in the list of the signatories to the Chalcedonian Defini-tion, but it remains unlikely that he attended the council in person (Price and Gaddis 2005, vol. 3, 195).

12 Theodosius is also called 'the forerunner of the Antichrist' in Cyril Scyth., *Life of Euthymius* 41, trans. Price 1991, 38.

13 *monastēria*: cf. Egeria, *Itin.* IV.5.

of the demon he serves might be able to prevail over your resolve and that of our rule, in this divine letter we urge your devoutness to hand him over (he is so unholy, estranged from the orthodox faith, and the enemy of the most holy churches, and has been hunted down everywhere together with his accomplices) to the governor of the province,[14] to be taken to the most great lawcourt of the most glorious general of the east, consular and patrician[15] – not so much that he may pay the penalty, but so that for the future at least he may cease from ensnaring devout souls that are somewhat simple-minded about the deity, as a result of his peregrinations for the destruction of whatever places he visits.

Your devoutness should know that we, descended from ancestors of the orthodox faith and taught by the sacred scriptures to worship the Holy Trinity, embrace the creed of the 318 fathers of sacred memory. Walking accordingly and believing correspondingly, we reject the impiety of Photinus, Apollinarius, Valentinus, Nestorius, Eutyches and all the others who have resolved to hold opinions contrary to the creed, and we believe that our Lord and Saviour Jesus Christ was born from the Holy Spirit and Mary the Virgin the Mother of God. Confessing one and the same Son Jesus, the same perfect God and perfect man, the same truly God and truly man, in no way divided or separated or changed, we worship Christ the Saviour, praying to remain always steadfast in this faith, and openly anathematizing those who say that there are two sons or two Christs or two persons, or who have said or written it or who dare to say it. This aforesaid most holy faith, which is true and orthodox, the most holy council recently convened at Chalcedon confirmed, by applying a concordant understanding to the pure and orthodox religion, and by condemning the heresy of Eutyches alone by a unanimous vote of the holy fathers.

---

14 Third Palestine.
15 Ardabur, *magister utriusque militiae per Orientem* 453–66; cf. *PLRE* II.135–37.

JACOB OF SERUG, *LETTER* VII,
TO THE MONKS OF SINAI *

Born on the Euphrates, educated in Edessa, Jacob († 521) became bishop of Serug (*Srûg*, south-west of Edessa) in 519. His fame as a Syriac author comes primarily from his innovative metrical sermons, but he also wrote many homilies and letters. The following letter comes from a manuscript dated to 603 CE, copied a mere eighty-two years after Jacob's death.[1]

Its outward purpose is to praise Sinai monks and ask for their prayers. Jacob also takes the opportunity, however, to express his understanding of their mission at Mount Sinai. According to him, the monks are representatives of the covenant that God had made with Moses, which pre-figured the later covenant God made through his son Jesus. God's presence (*skîntâ*) at that event at Mount Sinai was the counterpart to his appearance through the Son at the crucifixion, these being the two great moments of God's appearance on earth. Jacob also wrote a *mêmrâ* (metrical sermon) on Julian Saba,[2] and his knowledge of Sinai monastic settlements and their traditions may have come partly through traditions about Julian Saba such as those found in the Ephraimic hymns included in this volume. In particular, the 19th hymn attributed to Ephraim offers close thematic parallels.

TRANSLATION OF THE SYRIAC TEXT

To the holy and elect and God-loving blessed fathers living at Mount Sinai, [from] Jacob, the imperfect and wretched, in need of God's mercy and the assistance of your prayers. In Jesus, the light and the life and God Who is from God, Who is the hope of your salvation: Greetings.

---

* Ed. Olinder (see bibliography). Translation, introduction and commentary come courtesy of Kevin van Bladel.

1 Br. Lib. add. 14,587, designated 'A' in Olinder's edition; for discussion of the text, see Olinder 1938, whose edition page numbers are noted with brackets in the translation for clarity. To my knowledge, this text has not been discussed by previous scholars.

2 Unedited and unpublished: see Griffith 1994, 185–86.

God the Word appeared in our world through His birth from a virgin, and He did good works through His manifestation in the flesh for the whole human race. For He became poor for our sake and made us rich through His mercies; He became a son of man, and made us sons for God; He brought us up from the lowliness of slaves and established us in the rank of beloved sons; He became dead by His own will and handed us over to undying life so that death might never rule over us again; He illuminated the world that was darkness and trod out the way of salvation to men so that we might go unto His glorious Father.

Now, you, O elect and holy ones, He has roused you for His glory by the sufferings of His crucifixion, for you have realized that God was crucified for your sake. Trembling has fallen upon you **[p. 35]** so that you might despise the world and abandon country and family, brothers and fathers, transient possessions and temporal leisure. Carrying His Cross, you will follow Him in order to enter the glorious bridal chamber with Him. It is good for you, O you wise in God, that in that great country of the tabernacle of the Father you will be witnesses and disciples of God's gospel. For Moses, the greatest of the prophets, saw there the Son in the lap of His Father.[3] Indeed, from that place he petitioned the Father to send the Son for the salvation of the world. For Moses had perceived and knew in prophecy that the only-begotten of the Father would be sent for the salvation of creation. Because of this, he petitioned the glorious Father, saying, 'I beseech my Lord, send a message by means of the messenger that You are sending'.[4] And the anger of the Lord flared up against Moses[5] because he was asking Him to reveal a mystery at the incorrect time.

But when the Cross appeared in the world, what was hidden came into the open and all of creation was illuminated by it. Only the crucifying Jews, haters of light and lovers of darkness, did not want to be illuminated by it. For this reason they are reproved when they say 'We are disciples of Moses',[6] for if they were disciples of Moses, they would not have crucified the Lord of Moses. But *you* are the disciples of Moses and the ministers of the Old [Covenant]. In you Moses takes pride, for his mysteries have come into the open through you. In you the beauty of his prophethood appears. For you have drunk water and blood from the mountain of Golgotha and

---

3 Literally 'Begetter', *yālôdâ*.

4 Exod. 4:13, quoted here from the Syriac *Pishitta* translation of the Hebrew Scriptures. Jacob evidently thinks the messenger it mentions to be Jesus.

5 Exod. 4:14.

6 Cf. Jn 9:28.

have become drunk on love of the Crucified One.[7] The mystery has led you to go and be witnesses to the prophethood of Moses. In all of its abodes, [his prophethood] was [pre-]figuring the Son. For on Mount Sinai the Law[8] was given, and from Golgotha the Sun of Righteousness arose. You have become loyal ambassadors for the Christ on Golgotha and on Sinai, for you have perceived with your souls, which are near to God, that by the **[p. 36]** Only-Begotten both mountains have become celebrated, one by the written Law and one by the all-accomplishing Cross. For He who went down to Mount Sinai with His Father was crucified on Golgotha for the sake of the salvation of the world.

Because the two covenants, old and new, belong to the Son, because of this, two mountains have become celebrated through Him. Your residence at Sinai is testimony that the two mountains are fellows of one another. For if the disciples of the Cross were to live on Golgotha alone, and the disciples of Moses [i.e. the Jews] were to live today on Mount Sinai the place of Moses, there would be an opportunity for them [i.e. the two mountains] to speak against each other, and those who were at Mount Sinai would be thought to be followers of Moses, and those who were at Golgotha to be followers of Jesus.

But the Only-Begotten of the Father, to whom both mountains belong, has driven the crucifiers from both of them, and has established you to be heirs for Golgotha and Sinai, and for you to love and cherish the glorious presence[9] of the Father and the Cross of the Son. You have not left anywhere for the sole of the foot of the crucifiers to rest, because they have been driven from Golgotha and do not go into Mount Sinai. Now the beauty of your solitary life[10] is visible in the wilderness of Pharan and on the mount of Jebus![11] Through you the localities are mixed with one another so that you will say openly, 'The whole earth is the Lord's!'[12] For it is neither good for the crucifying Jew to enter the place of God's presence[13] nor to read from the Law of Moses. For how can he who hung the Lord of Mysteries on the Cross proclaim the mysteries and expose himself as a murderer?

7 Or, 'love of the Cross'.

8 *nāmôsâ*.

9 *škîntâ* is often used to refer to God's divine presence, such as was manifest at God's appearance at the Burning Bush.

10 *îhîdāyûtkôn*.

11 I.e. Jerusalem.

12 Ps. 24:1. This sentence evidently refers to the variety of ethnic backgrounds and origins of the monks at Sinai.

13 God's presence is *škîntâ* again. See above, n. 9.

But through you, O lovers of God, who are the ministers of the mystery, now Sinai is rich through you like Eden through the trees of paradise![14] Horeb exults in you like the Garden of Eden with the tree of life. The sounds of your services are heard from your residences **[p. 37]** like the praise of the holy angels from their ranks. Every day you eat the sweet fruits from the tree of life, but there is no cherub, no turning lance of fire,[15] no serpent speaking deception, no Eve plucking fruits, eating, and offering to you so that you eat and come to shame. But you have donned the Son of the Holy Virgin and have virginally taken up his yoke. You realized in your God-worthy souls that He who was begotten virginally from the womb of the virgin was crucified on Golgotha in order to give the world life, and now it is glad and exults with sweet fruits made by His crucifixion on Golgotha. Now Sinai delights in you by day and by night, seeing what heirs are in it, crying out and saying, 'Praise the Lord with a new praise-hymn! Praise the Lord, the whole earth!'[16] while the mountain is proud that the crucifiers of its Lord have not inherited it. And the place of the presence[17] of the Father exults because the Cross of His beloved Son is honoured in it. You are made the cause of glory for the Cross and the cause of shame for the crucifiers. You have a great blessing that was spoken by the mouth of the true one: 'Blessed is the servant because of whom the name of his Lord shall be praised.'[18]

But I am an imperfect wretch. I ask you, O elect ones, to mention me in your elect prayers that are accepted, and to pray about my imperfection that I may be worthy to be the footstool under the soles of your holy feet, and so that I may be saved from the evil world to the glory of Jesus to whom be praises and blessings together with His Father and His Spirit, now and always and forever, Amen.

---

14 For the notion of Sinai as paradise regained, see Theodoret of Cyrrhus, *Religious History* VI.10, above, p. 235.

15 Cf. Gen. 3:24, where cherubim guard the gates of Eden with fiery lances, preventing Adam and Eve from returning.

16 Cf. Ps. 96:1.

17 *škîntâ*. See n. 9 above.

18 Cf. 2 Thess. 1:12.

COSMAS INDICOPLEUSTES, *CHRISTIAN TOPOGRAPHY* V: SELECT PASSAGES, CLYSMA TO PHARAN

An Alexandrian merchant, Cosmas Indicopleustes (meaning 'Sailor to India') travelled the length of the Red Sea and possibly beyond. He was also an amateur theologian, whose *Christian Topography*, written in the late 540s, is famous for maintaining that the earth is flat and the sky vaulted over it like a dome, theories he deduced from biblical descriptions of the tabernacle, following an interpretative method associated with the fifth-century 'Nestorian' theologian, Theodore of Mopsuestia. At the same time he was an empiricist who sought to ground scriptural events in observable phenomena, believing that God had filled the world with signs to educate humans about spiritual and historical truths.[1]

The following passages come from the fifth book of his *Christian Topography*.[2] Here, like Egeria, Cosmas strives to relate certain features of Sinai topography to events described in Exodus and Numbers. He claims to be working from first-hand knowledge: while discussing (V.53–54) the origin of human writing, he explains that he himself knew about Hebrew letters written on Sinai rocks because he had been there himself, 'on foot'. This remark, together with his references to Clysma, Phoinikon, and Rhaithou (which, like Ammonius, *Rel.* I.8, he identifies with Elim), demonstrates that Cosmas was at least somewhat familiar with the west coast of the Sinai peninsula, as we might expect of someone who had sailed the Red Sea.

All the more puzzling, then, is his apparent identification of Mount Horeb with a mountain just outside Pharan: 'Horeb, the mountain, that is, in the Sinai that is near Pharan, about six miles away' (V.16). This has generally

---

1 Cf. his digression (*Top. christ.* II.54–65) on the biblical information to be found in Ptolemaic and Axumite inscriptions at Adulis (near modern Zula in Eritrea), which Cosmas himself had seen. His world-view, which shows many affinities to Syrian cosmologies of the day, was formulated against the heliocentric cosmology propounded by another Alexandrian, the Christian philosopher John Philoponus: see Wolska-Conus 1962.

2 *Top. christ.* V.7, 9, 13, 14, 19, and 53–54, ed. Wolska-Conus 1970, 21, 25–35, 85–87. Cosmas illustrated his descriptions with schematic drawings; though preserved (to some degree) in the MSS, they are not reproduced here.

been interpreted to mean that Cosmas was placing Mount Sinai/Horeb just outside Pharan, and that he was referring to Jabal Serbal, a high mountain about 9.5 km/6.5 miles south of modern Feiran. Attempts to explain his remark by supposing his text originally included further geographical details now lost, or has somehow been corrupted (e.g. through interpolation), have not won acceptance.[3] Should we therefore suppose his text bears witness to an alternative, 'competing' tradition regarding the identity of God's Mountain, Mount Sinai/Horeb, in the sixth century?

Some have proposed that Cosmas was following a 'Nestorian' tradition about the location, derived from sources now lost.[4] That is somewhat unsatisfactory, however, since no trace of such an alternative, sectarian tradition has otherwise been found (though some have interpreted the extensive monastic ruins on Jabal Serbal as evidence of special devotion to that mountain). Therefore another possibility warrants consideration.

Stephan Schiwietz long ago observed that the phrasing of the passage in question is sufficiently vague as to leave unclear whether Cosmas had meant to identify Mount Horeb with Mount Sinai itself, or rather (as Schiwietz proposed) with the Sinai region in general.[5] Schiwietz's proposal has not held ground, since we have no other instance in antiquity where the phrase 'the Sinai' is used, as it is today, to refer to the entire peninsula. It is notable, however, that Cosmas' attempt to identify Sinai biblical localities with contemporary sites ends at Pharan (V.16). This suggests that he himself never actually travelled past Pharan – where he may have gone not as a pilgrim, but as a merchant, like other Egyptian merchants who supplied Pharan and Rhaithou with foodstuffs.[6] If that is so, then his knowledge of Sinai terrain may be more general and less trustworthy than previously assumed.

Indeed, the most likely explanation for Cosmas' belief that Mount Horeb was to be found in the vicinity of Rephidim/Pharan is, in my view, simply because of Exod. 17:6: 'I will be there in front of you, on the rock at Horeb'.

3 For this 'lacuna' theory, see Schiwietz 1908, 26–28. Wolska-Conus 1970, 36 n. 2, rejects it on the grounds that the drawing accompanying *Top. christ.* V.19 has no detail that might have come from a lost description. Elsewhere the text does show signs of interpolation (see Wolska-Conus 1968, 62–86), but not here.

4 See Solzbacher 1989, 162. Cosmas' apparent links to the 'Nestorian School' of Persia are discussed in Wolska-Conus 1968, 39–40.

5 Schiwietz 1908, 25 n. 3. See further discussion below, n. 20.

6 Cf. Ammonius, *Rel.* 13; PP, *Itin.* 40. Cosmas was accompanied on his voyage to Ethiopia by another learned Alexandrian merchant named Menas who became a monk at Rhaithou and died there (*Top. christ.* II.56, 1968, 369). This led to the erroneous belief that he himself was a Sinai monk who had once been a merchant: see Anastos 1946.

This prophecy was later fulfilled at Rephidim, the site where the Israelites defeated the Amalekites, near Pharan. We might speculate that Cosmas' interest in Sinai's Hebrew (i.e. Nabataean) inscriptions led him to ask if any were concentrated on a mountain in the vicinity of Rephidim. Had he done so, he surely would have been referred to Jabal al-Moneijah, about 5.5 km/3.5 miles south of Wadi Feiran. While not as imposing as Jabal Serbal, it is in the same vicinity, and is the only mountain on the Sinai that features ancient inscriptions, having once been a major Nabataean cult centre.[7] Perhaps having heard about these inscriptions (which he would have thought were Hebrew) he assumed – without verifying on foot – that the mountain corresponded to a significant mountain of the Hebrews' experience.

TRANSLATION OF THE GREEK TEXT

V.7 [*following a summary of the events of Exod. 14:2 and 9*] When all the Egyptians with their chariots reached the middle of the sea in pursuit of the Israelites, the waters turned back over them in accordance with divinely ordained wrath, and they perished by drowning. The actual place is at Clysma, as it is called, on the right if you are travelling towards the Mountain.[8] Here you can see even the tracks of the actual chariot wheels. These are visible for a considerable distance down to the sea.[9] They are preserved to the present day as a sign for unbelievers, not for believers.

V.13 [*following a discussion of prophecies regarding Christ's nativity*] The Israelites crossed to the opposite side at the place called Phoinikon.[10] They began to go through the Shur Desert.[11] During the day God sent a cloud over them for shelter from the heat of the sun and led them within it; at night He appeared in a pillar of fire, guiding them all the way through the desert. As it is written, 'He spread a cloud to shelter them and fire to give them light by night.'[12] This can also be sketched out in such as way as follows: [*Here Cosmas presents a schematic drawing of the Israelites travelling beneath a cloud and past a pillar crowned with fire.*]

---

7 On the inscriptions and cult centre, see Negev 1977 and Solzbacher 1989, 53.

8 True, once you had passed Clysma and were headed down the Sinai coast by land.

9 Cf. Egeria, *Itin.* PD,Y 5 and notes *ad loc.*

10 Presumably 'Ain Musa, 10 km/6 miles south-east of Clysma. Agatharchides of Cnidos also referred to this site as Phoinikon ('Palm Groves') in his early second-century BCE treatise, *On the Red Sea*.

11 Exod. 15:22 and Num. 33.8; cf. Egeria, *Itin.* PD,Y 11; Anast., *Narr.* I.32.

12 Ps. 105[104]:39.

V.14 Next, setting out from Marah,[13] they came to Elim, which we now call Rhaithou. Here were the twelve springs and seventy palm trees.[14] The springs are preserved to the present day, but the palm trees have become much more numerous.[15]

Up to here the Israelites had had the sea on their right side and the desert on their left. From this point they travelled on the road up toward the Mountain, leaving the sea behind them and heading out into desert. Here the manna came down on them, when they were between Elim and Mount Sinai;[16] here too for the first time they observed the Sabbath, following the unwritten commandments that God had given to Moses at Marah.[17] These things can also be illustrated thus: [*Here Cosmas presents a schematic drawing of the events described in V.13–14. Section V.15 recapitulates those descriptions, and may be an interpolation.*]

V.16 Next they camped at Rephidim, at the place now called Pharan.[18] Since they were thirsty, Moses, by God's command, went with the elders, staff in his hand, to Horeb,[19] the mountain, that is, on the Sinai that is near Pharan, about six miles away.[20] There he struck the rock, much water flowed

---

13 Cf. Exod. 15:23–25.

14 Exod. 15:27.

15 οἱ δὲ φοίνικες πολὺ πλείους ἐγένοντο. For a similar observation, see Ammonius, *Rel.* I.8. Wilkinson 2002, 199, translates, 'but at one time there were many more palm-trees there', which seems less likely, as then one might expect the adverb *pote* and an imperfect tense. In identifying Elim with Rhaithou, Cosmas and Ammonius differ from Egeria, *Itin.* PD,Y 12, and PP, *Itin.* 41, who identify it with Wadi Gharandula, much farther north.

16 Cf. Exod. 16:1-36 and Egeria, *Itin.* PD,Y 13.

17 Cf. Exod. 15:26 and 16:28–30.

18 See Egeria, *Itin.* PD,Y 15 and notes *ad loc.*

19 Cf. Exod. 17:5–6, 'take some of the elders of Israel with you; take in your hand the staff with which you struck the Nile, and go. I will be standing there in front of you at the rock on Horeb'.

20 εἰς Χωρὴβ τὸ ὄρος, τουτέστιν ἐν τῷ Σιναίῳ ἐγγὺς ὄντι τῆς Φαρὰν ὡς ἀπὸ μιλίων ἕξ. As noted above, this phrase, 'the mountain ... six miles away', has caused scholars to believe that Cosmas identified Mt Horeb and Mt Sinai with Jabal Serbal, 10 km/6 miles southeast of Feiran. Wilkinson 2002, 123, translates to Mount Horeb, which is near Sinai, about six miles from Pharan', but that does not make grammatical sense (the dative participle form of the verb 'to be', ὄντι, must modify 'Sinai', which is in the dative case, not 'Horeb', which is in the accusative). Since the phrase seems garbled, it is tempting to explain the entire portion from τὸ ὄρος to the end of the sentence as a later interpolation, added as a gloss on 'Horeb'. Yet all MSS include it, and a TLG search shows that the locution τουτέστιν and word order of the phrase are used throughout the work. However, this is the only place in which Cosmas refers to 'the Sinai' without calling it 'Mt Sinai' (cf. II.35; III.7 and 12; V.14, 53 and 114; XII.4). I am therefore inclined to agree with Schiwietz 1908, 25 n. 3, that Cosmas is referring to the

out, and the people drank. As David exclaims in the *Book of Psalms*, 'He split open a rock in the desert and gave them drink as from a great depth', and 'He split open a rock and water gushed out; it flowed through the desert like a river', and 'He brought water out of a rock and caused waters to flow down like rivers'.[21]

V.18 *[Following an exegesis of the Davidic passages in V.17]* Again it was here [Rephidim] that they fought against and vanquished the Amalek;[22] here again that Jethro came to meet Moses, his son-in-law, with his two sons and his wife.[23] For Moses had turned out his wife and children, after he saw the vision of the angel in the desert and it weakened him.[24] In this place also Sepphora circumcised his second son, since he was uncircumcised.[25] These things can also be illustrated as follows: *[Here Cosmas presents a schematic drawing of the events described in V.16–18.]*

V.19 In the third month they came to Mount Sinai. God variously spoke to Moses in a pillar of cloud. Later, so that the people might also be stunned with great awe, He showed them that awesome vision of the mountain in flames and the smoke going up as if from a furnace, along with darkness, shadows, squalls, and the sound of resounding trumpets.[26] Here too God led up the great one, Moses, and hid him in the cloud for forty days without any food.[27] Then He showed him in visions how He set about creating the universe: He prolonged the act of creation for six days, and rested on the seventh. And so he gave the written Law. The following is an illustration of what has just been described: *[Here Cosmas presents a schematic drawing of these events. The next sections (V.20–52) explain the symbolism of the Tabernacle (20–44), the clothing of a Jewish priest (45–49), and God's feeding of the Israelites in the desert (50–52).]*

V.53 When they received the Law from God in writing and were taught letters for the first time, God used the desert like a quiet school, allowing them to hew the letters on stone for forty years. For that reason one can see, at all the stopping-places in that desert (I mean, the [desert] of Mount Sinai), that all the rocks of the area that have broken off from the mountains

---

Sinai region as a whole rather than Mt Sinai. This means he is not identifying Horeb with Mt Sinai or the 'Mountain of God'.

21 Ps. 78[77]:15; 105[104]:41; 78[77]:16.

22 Cf. Exod. 17:12 and Egeria, *Itin.* PD,Y 15; PP, *Itin.* 40.

23 Cf. Exod. 18:1–9 and Egeria, *Itin.* PD,Y 15.

24 Cf. Exod. 3:3–20.

25 Cf. Exod. 3:24; Sepphora [Zipporah] was Moses' wife and Jethro's daughter.

26 Cf. Exod. 19:16–19.

27 Cf. Exod. 20:21, 24:15–18.

have been inscribed with carved Hebrew letters. I can attest this myself, having travelled in those places on foot.[28] This was also what certain Jews who had read them told us, saying that what was written went thus: 'Departure of so-and-so, from the tribe of so-and-so, in the year such-and-such, in the month such-and-such', just as some of us also often write in lodging places.[29]

V.54 But as for the Israelites themselves, once they had acquired letters for the first time, they constantly put them to use with prolific writing, so that all those places are still full of carved Hebrew letters, preserved to the present day for the sake of unbelievers, I think. Whoever wishes can go and look in those places, or may ask and learn that we have told the truth.

The Hebrews were the very first to be instructed by God. After receiving letters through those stone tablets and studying them for forty years in the desert, they passed them on, around that time, to their neighbours, the Phoenicians, and first to Cadmus, King of the Tyrians. From him the Greeks received them, and thereafter all the nations in succession.[30]

---

28 Cf. Egeria, *Itin*. PD,Y 14.

29 This is the formula of many of Nabataean graffiti inscriptions found in western Sinai. These graffiti, dated from the first to third centuries CE and concentrated in Wadi Mukattab and elsewhere near Wadi Feiran, were probably written by Nabataean miners when Pharan was under Nabataean control: see Solzbacher 1989, 53–60. Some Hebrew inscriptions have been found in Wadi Umm Shidir, but they are very rare: see Rothenberg 1970, 19–20. Nabataean was similar to Hebrew in vocabulary, structure, and script. Probably that similarity, as well as strong imaginations, misled Cosmas and his translator.

30 Cadmus was the mythical founder of Thebes who came to Greece in search of his sister Europa. The tradition that Moses first learned the art of writing and passed it on to the Hebrews, Phoenicians, and Greeks was very old by Cosmas' day: see Clement of Alexandria, *Stromata* I.23.153.

PIACENZA PILGRIM, *TRAVELOGUE* 33–42: JERUSALEM TO MOUNT SINAI AND CLYSMA

The only late antique travelogue to rival Egeria's in breadth or detail is the one that reflects a pilgrimage undertaken c. 551–570 (most probably early in the 550s) by a man from Placentia (modern Piacenza) in northern Italy.[1] Like Egeria, this 'Piacenza Pilgrim' (his real name is unknown) travelled to Holy Land sites from Constantinople and Syria to Mesopotamia and Egypt, but his focus differs from hers, in that he shows less interest in the scriptural background of the sites he visits than in the physical marvels and exotic peoples to be found in those regions,[2] including those of the Negev and Sinai, described here. These interests make his account, after Egeria's, the most illuminating and congenial document regarding the Sinai to survive from late antiquity.

His journey was part of a longer pilgrimage from Jerusalem to Egypt, approaching Mount Sinai ('Sina') by the so-called 'central pilgrimage route', i.e. through the Negev and al-Tih desert. Accompanied by at least one other companion, he set out in late winter or early spring, after celebrating Epiphany in the Jordan and touring Jerusalem and environs beforehand. He seems to have ascended Mount Sinai with a larger group, which broke

---

1 The traditional ascription of this *Travelogue* (*Itinerarium*, *Itin. Plac.*) to 'Antoninus Placentinus' (also 'Antoninus Martyr', 'the Antonine Pilgrim') is due to the invocation of a local martyr named Antoninus in its first sentence, mistaken to be a reference to the author himself. Most scholars refer to him as the Anonymous of Placenta or the 'Piacenza Pilgrim' (hereafter, 'PP'). For detailed discussion, see Milani 1977; Mian 1972, 267–301; and Solzbacher 1989, 143–53. A date of c. 570 is often assigned to PP's journey. This is based on the assumption that PP's reference in *Itin.* 1 to the destruction of Beirut by an earthquake 'in the time of Emperor Justinian' (*tempore Iustiniani imperatoris*) meant that he was writing after Justinian had died (i.e. after 565), and that his excursion to Mesopotamia (mentioned in *Itin.* 46) would have occurred before war was renewed with Persia in 572. However, in *Itin* 1, PP says legal education had existed at Beirut *nuper* ('recently'), until an earthquake had destroyed it; hence Solzbacher 1989, 144, prefers to date it closer to 551, the probable date of the earthquake that destroyed Beirut (another is recorded in 554).

2 See Leyerle 1996; Krueger 2005.

up soon afterwards.[3] His account, written after he returned to Placentia, survives in two recensions. The longer recension, dating to the ninth century, is considered to be more faithful, and is translated here.[4]

TRANSLATION OF THE LATIN TEXT

[33] We came to Ascalon. The Well of Peace is there.[5] Its width is very great, and it is built like a theatre: you go down to the water by steps. Three brothers – Egyptian martyrs – rest there. They have names of their own, but are commonly called 'the Egyptians'.[6]

At the next milestone is the city of Sarafia and nearby, the city Maiuma of Ascalon. From there we came to the city Maiuma of Gaza, where the martyr, Holy Victor, is resting. From Maiuma to Gaza is one milestone.[7] Gaza is a splendid, delightful city. Its people are decent and outstanding in every generosity – real lovers of pilgrims. At the second milestone from Gaza the holy father, Hilarion, is resting.[8]

3 For the season of the journey, cf. PP, *Itin.* 11 (not translated here) and Solzbacher 1989, 337 n. 111. Springtime is preferable, since it would conform to our information about the Saracen festival calendar (see below, n. 17), and would have also been when water was most available on the central Sinai route.

4 Ed. Geyer 1965, 129–53. On the priority of the longer recension (Recension I) over the shorter (Recension II), see Mian 1972, 271–73. Geyer is responsible for the divisions, with 47 sections in all; 33–42 are translated here. For a translation of the entire account, see Wilkinson 2002, 129–51.

5 Ascalon (modern Ashkelon) was an episcopal see on the Palestinian coast. In the third century, Origen noted its 'wonderful wells ... which are worth mentioning on account of their strange and extraordinary style of construction in comparison to other wells' (*contra Celsum* IV.44, trans. H. Chadwick). PP's 'Well of Peace' (*puteus pacis*) may be the dilapidated Roman theatre later identified as the 'Well of Abraham' and also celebrated for its stepped descent. The tradition probably derived from Gen. 26:22, where Isaac dug a well in Gerar (south of Gaza) that provoked no quarrel with the Philistines.

6 The Egyptian Ares, Promus, and Elijah were martyred in Ascalon in 309 CE: Eusebius, *Martyrs of Palestine* X.1. A fragment of the sixth-century Madaba Map mosaic locates a tomb 'of the Egyptians' outside the city.

7 Maiuma-Ascalonitēs (modern Barnea) and Maiuma-Gaza (also known as Maiuma Constantia, i.e. modern Al Minha) were both seaports for their associated cities; *maiuma* may be Phoenician for 'coastal' or 'maritime'. Maiuma of Gaza became recognized as a *polis* and received its other name, Constantia, when its citizens elected to adopt Christianity under Constantine: see Sozomen, *EH* II.5, V.3. Sarafia (modern Khirbat al-Sharaf) was officially known as Diocletianopolis. Mian 1972, 275, suggests that Christians preferred to use its Hebrew name, Sarafia, instead of one associated with the notorious persecutor, Diocletian.

8 Probably modern Umm al-'Amr in the Gaza strip: see Elter and Hassoune 2005. For

[34] From there we came to the city of Elusa, at the head of the desert that leads to Sina. Here, as we were told by its bishop, there had been a noble girl by the name of Mary. She had just been married, when on the very night of her wedding her bridegroom died. She bore it calmly, and within a week had freed all his family slaves [...] and made distributions to beggars and monasteries. On the seventh day she was still at home – but that night her husband's clothing was taken, and she could not be found.[9] It is said that she is in the desert across the Jordan, roaming among the reeds and palm trees in the region of Segor along the Salt Sea.[10]

We found in those parts a monastery of about 16 or 17 girls in a place in the desert. Christians supplied them with grain, and they had a small ass that turned a grindstone for them. They also kept a lion, tame since a cub, but huge and frightening to see. As soon as we drew near to their cells, its roar made all of our animals piss, and some fell to the ground. They were saying that the lion would guide the little ass to pasture.[11]

That most Christian man who was with me had me offer them 100 *solidi*, but they refused to accept [it].[12] Nevertheless he sent to Jerusalem and procured for them thirty tunics, beans for their storehouse, and oil for their lamps. They also told us about the marvels of Mary who was roaming the desert. For two days my companion roamed in search of her. He declined to tell us whether he found her or not, but as for the tunics, dates, and baskets of roast chick-peas that he had carried with him, and the lupine – none of these did he bring back with him. All our reasoning was unable to console his sorrow and grief. He just kept saying, 'Alas, how wretched I am! What right do I have to call myself a Christian?'

[35] Setting out from the city of Elusa we entered the desert. At the twentieth milestone there is a fort, in which there is a guest-house of Saint

---

Hilarion († 371), see Jerome, *Life of Hilarion.*

9 I.e. she departed on the eighth day (with day beginning at nightfall), immediately after her week of mourning was over.

10 The story of this Mary of Segor (Zoora on the Madaba Map, modern Zoara/Ghor es-Safi south of the Dead Sea) seems to be a version of the Mary of Egypt story, for which see Sophronius of Jerusalem, *Life of Mary of Egypt* (PG 87:3697–3726), trans. Kouli 1996.

11 The same story was told at the Lavra of Gerasimus near the Jordan regarding an ass and lion owned by the monastery's founders: John Mosch., *Meadow* 107.

12 *quibus per me centum solidos offerebat ille christianissimus.* Others have interpreted this as an offer to purchase the animals from the female monks. But the intended antecedent of *quibus* is more likely to have been the women themselves, not the animals: as the rest of the passage shows, PP's point is to describe his companion's eagerness to support the local saints. (This may also explain PP's use of the superlative, *christianissimus*, to describe his companion, although Solzbacher believes it means he was a priest.)

George, in which travellers have, as it were, a refuge, and hermits receive rations.[13]

From here we entered the inner desert and came to the region about which it is said, 'A land transformed into a salty waste because of the wickedness of those who dwell in it'.[14] Here we saw a few people with camels, who fled from us. We had also seen some in Jerusalem. They were people from the land of Ethiopia, who had pierced noses, pierced ears, leather boots and rings on the toes of their feet. When asked why they did this, they said, 'Trajan the Roman Emperor set this mark on us.'[15]

[**36**] For five or six days we walked through the desert. Camels carried water for us; we received a pint per person, once in the morning and once

13 Candidates for this *castrum in quo est xenodochius sancti Georgi* include Nessana (about 32 km/21 miles from Elusa), Sobata (about 54 km/32 miles from Elusa) and Mizpe Shivta/ Khirbat al-Mushrayfa (about 42 km/26 miles from Elusa). Abel 1935, 10, identified it with Sobata, which has produced an inscription referring to a church of St George. But Sobata is farther from Elusa than the distance given here. Mizpe Shivta (ancient name unknown) overlooking Sobata, features a small church, a four-roomed central building within a circle of low fortress walls, and numerous cells or storage rooms with arched entryways, on one of which is painted an (unpublished) invocation to the 'Lord of St George' to protect its author, his family, and servants. It has therefore been identified with PP's site by Baumgarten 1993 and Figueras 1995, 420–23 (with pl. 8); cf. Woolley and Lawrence 1936, 50, 108–07. However, this site would have been remote from the valley road, and unequipped to receive an unpredictable number of pilgrims. Until it is more thoroughly excavated and the inscription published, Nessana remains the preferable candidate. Besides having a *kastron* ('fort') that we know was in use in PP's time, it also had a caravanserai, visible till the late nineteenth century; furthermore, a copy of the *Acts of St. George* was found among the Nessana papyri (*P.Colt* 6). See Kraemer 1958, 27–29; Mayerson 1963, 170–71.

Stipendia is standard for monastic rations (cf. John Cassian, *Institutes* IV.5; PL 49.159), but may refer here to a subsidy similar to the *annona*: see Caner 2006, 374–77.

14 Cf. Ps. 106[107]:34, a verse meant to refer to Sodom and the Dead Sea. Salt plains are common in northern Sinai, and Mayerson 1963, 171, suggests that PP was inspired by one that lay towards 'Ain Qusayma, about a day's walk south of Nessana. From there he would have entered the Tih desert. Solzbacher 1989, 157, believes that PP would have then proceeded to Jabal al-Egma, near Naqb Seyala. From there he could reach Wadi al-Shaykh and the Watija Pass, and so on to Mt Sinai.

15 The mark (*signum*) presumably refers to the body piercings displayed by this group. Such piercings were a traditional mark of slavery (cf. Exod. 21:5) but the reference is otherwise unclear. Wilkinson 2003, 145 n. 45, suggests that the nomads in question were Nabataeans, not Ethiopians, which might explain the reference to Trajan, who annexed the Nabataean kingdom in 106 CE. But it is doubtful that PP would consider Nabataeans so distinct from other Arabs of the area, many of whom would have been Nabataean descendants. Another possibility (though it does not explain the reference to Trajan) is that they were Nubians (i.e. 'Blemmyes'). *P.Colt* 96 records a prayer at Nessana otherwise only attested in Nubia. Whoever they were, they were probably following the Darb e-Shawi trail that crosses northern Sinai from Egypt to Aila.

in the evening. When the water in the skins turned bitter like gall, we would put sand in it and it became sweet.[16]

A group of female slaves belonging to Saracens (or else they were their wives) came from the desert and sat by the road in tears. They put a sheet in front of themselves and kept pleading for loaves of bread from travellers. Their husbands also came; they brought skins of cool water from a more remote part of the desert and gave them, taking bread for themselves. They also brought out garlic and radishes, whose sweet odour surpassed any spice. They charged nothing for these, since they consider it anathema [to do so] while they were celebrating their festival days.[17] The people who would enter through that major desert region number twelve thousand.[18]

[37] We walked through the desert and on the eighteenth day came to the place where Moses drew water out of a rock.[19] From there the next day

16 A *sextarius* (translated here as 'pint') was about half a litre.

17 According to Nonnosus, Justinian's ambassador to the Ethiopians, c. 530, 'most of the Saracens – those who live in Phoinikon as well as those who live beyond Phoinikon and the Taurenian mountains – have a sacred meeting-place consecrated to one of their gods where they assemble twice a year. One of these meetings lasts a whole month, almost to the middle of spring, when the sun enters Taurus; the other lasts two months, and is held after the summer solstice. During these meetings complete peace prevails, not only amongst themselves, but also with all the natives; even animals are at peace, both with themselves and with human beings.' Nonnosus, *Historia*, frg. in Photius, *Bibliotheca* I.3; ed. Müller 1975; trans. Freese 1920. Cf. Procop., *Wars* II.xvi.18: 'at this season [of the vernal equinox] the Saracens always dedicated about two months to their god, and during this time never undertook any inroad into the land of others'. Cf. Hoyland 2001, 161–62.

Nonnosus' Phoinikon ('Palm Grove', as oases often were called) seems to have been located outside the Sinai peninsula, in the northern Hijaz (so Shahid 1995, 125; cf. Diodorus Siculus III.42; Procop., *Wars* I.19.7–11). Nevertheless his information about the festival and related truce may have applied to the Sinai too. Until recently, local bedouin celebrated a spring festival at Jabal Harounja, a small hill at the entrance of Wadi al-Dayr: see Ubach 1933.

18 Geyer's text has 12,600, but the oldest MS ('G') has 12,000. That figure seems preferable, since, as Solzbacher 1989, 146, notes, it probably derives from Num. 31:5 (Moses' mustering of 12,000 troops against the Midianites). Mayerson 1963, 186, and Shahid 1984, 320, have regarded it as an attempt to estimate Sinai's bedouin population at the time. But the use of the imperfect tense (*ingrediebatur*) suggests temporary travellers, and may refer to the number of Saracens who came for the festival.

19 Exod. 17:1–7 (i.e. Rephidim); Egeria, *Itin.* PD,Y 15 places the miracle nearer Pharan; PP, approaching from a north-eastern direction, locates it to the north-east. Apparently PP did not approach Horeb through Wadi al-Raha, but from the north-east through Wadi al-Shaykh (see Map 3). Recension II has 'eighth day' instead of 'eighteenth day'; the former is adopted by Mayerson 1981 and Wilkinson 1999 because it would be more appropriate for a period of travel to reach Mt Sinai from the Negev; however, Recension I's 'eighteenth day' might refer to the time elapsed since PP's departure from Jerusalem, once the two-day search for Mary of

we 'came to Horeb, the Mountain of God'.[20] As we headed on from there to ascend Sina, behold!, a great number of monks and hermits beyond counting came out to meet us, carrying crosses and singing psalms.[21] They lay down on the ground and made obeisance to us, and we did likewise, weeping.

They led us into the valley between Horeb and Sina.[22] At the foot of the mountain is that spring where Moses saw the sign of the burning bush and at which he gave water to his sheep. The spring is enclosed within a monastery, and the monastery is surrounded by fortified walls.[23] In it are three elders who are learned in [several] languages – I mean Latin and Greek, Syriac, Egyptian, and Bessan[24] – as well as many translators of individual languages. In it are the monks' provisions.[25]

Segor is included: thus Solzbacher 1989, 157; Mian 1972, 271.

20 Exod. 3:1; PP refers either to Jabal al-Dayr (2065 m/6,775 feet) or Jabal al-Moneijah-Musa (1864 m/6,116 feet); cf. Solzbacher 1989, 337 n. 116.

21 PP distinguishes between coenobites and anchorites ('monks and hermits'; cf. 'monasteries and hermitages' below, PP, *Itin.* 40), a distinction also found in Anastasius' narratives. For a similar monastic welcome, cf. the early fifth-century *History of Monks in Egypt* VIII.48.

22 Wadi al-Dayr.

23 While others have focused on PP's failure to mention Justinian's church (see below, n. 25), it is equally striking that he fails to mention any 'bush' – only a spring, on which cf. Egeria, *Itin.* IV.7. It is now the well that is located to the north of the basilica.

24 I follow Solzbacher 1989, 148, in interpreting *abbates* as 'elders' rather than 'abbots', since there is no evidence for multiple *hēgoumens* at the Sinai monastery. Regarding the languages listed here, 'Egyptian' refers to Coptic, but the meaning of 'Bessan' (*linguas ... bessas*) remains uncertain. Several 'Bessan' monasteries existed in Jordan and Palestine at this time: see Cyril Scyth., *Life of Saba* 86; John Mosch., *Meadow* 157; and Theodore of Petra, *Life of Theodosius*, ed. Usener p. 45, 13–16. Mian 1972, 291, and Flusin 1992 vol. 2, 38 n. 130, believe PP was referring to Ge'ez, the language spoken by Ethiopians (*Ḥabash* in Arabic, and so arguably 'Bessan'; cf. 'Abyssinian'). However, no inscription on Sinai has been identified in Ge'ez, and Solzbacher 1989, 337 n. 119, argues that if PP had meant that he would have used something like *aethiopas*. Following Devreesse 1940, 214 n. 5 *et al.*, he assumes that 'Bessan' refers to the language spoken by a Thracian tribe which Herodotus calls 'the Bessi'. But that solution is hardly satisfying. I prefer Georgian or Abkhazian since, as noted in *Brill's New Pauly*, *s.v.* 'Bessi, Bessoi', there is evidence that the name 'Bessan' eventually came to be applied to northern tribes in general, and early Georgian pilgrim graffiti have been found at St Catherine's (Ševčenko 1966, 257). Others have proposed Persian (i.e. Farsi), even Arabic (see Shahid 1984, 320 n. 143).

25 PP's description (*monasterium circumdatum muris munitis ... in quo sunt condita monachorum*) corresponds to the picture sketched by archaeologists, who believe that the fortifications initially contained little more than chambers or cells built as casements around the inner circumference of the defensive walls (Grossmann 1988 and Dahari 2000, 57–59); it would also conform to the early phase of the monastic fort at Wadi al-Tur (Kawatoko 1995, 51–53). PP makes no reference here to Justinian's impressive basilica within the walls, but in section 41 does note seeing the church and guest houses within the *castellum* at Surandala. It

Going three miles straight up the mountain we came to the place at a cave where Elijah hid when he fled from Jezebel.[26] In front of the cave rises a spring that waters the mountain. From there we climbed three miles straight up to the highest peak of the mountain. Here there is a small oratory, more or less six feet wide and six feet long. No one presumes to live in it, but at the beginning of each day the monks climb up and make God's service.[27] At this place everyone shaves off their beards and hair and casts it away as a devotional act.[28] Here I cut off my beard too.

[38] Mount Sina is rocky and scarcely has any soil. All around it there are many cells of slaves of God, and similarly on Horeb. They say Horeb is clean ground.[29]

And on this mountain, on a part of the mountain, the Saracens have set up their own idol, made of marble white as snow. Here also their priest resides, dressed in a dalmatic and a linen cloak.[30] When the time of their festival arrives with the new moon, before the moon has risen on the day of their feast, the marble begins to change colour; as soon as the moon appears, when they begin to worship, the marble turns black as pitch. When the time of the festival is over, it returns to its original colour. We were totally amazed by this.[31]

---

therefore seems safe to conclude that Justinian's basilica had not yet been built at the time of his visit.

Others have assumed that *condita monachorum* refers to a structure (e.g. an ossuary, or hermits' cells). However, John Climacus locates the monks' cemetery 'near' (i.e. outside) 'the Fort' (*Ladder* 6, PG 88.797A), and *condita* in *Theodosian Code* VII.4.3 refers to 'provisions in storage'. Elsewhere in late Latin, *conditum* more specifically meant 'seasoned wine'. Since it is specifically used to refer to a beverage given to pilgrims as hospitality in section 39 below, that may be its precise meaning here.

26 1 [III] Kgs 19:1–9. PP ascended in the opposite direction from Egeria, taking the 3,000-step path (the modern 'Stair of Repentance') behind the monastery.

27 *faciunt opus dei*. Cf. Ps.-Nilus, *Narr.* IV.1.

28 *pro devotione*: perhaps, 'for the sake of a vow'. This custom may have originated in an Arab traveller's custom: see Ps.-Lucian, *De Dea Syria* 61 and Kötting 1980, 75 n. 381, 312–30. It was also a Sinai monastic initiation rite: see Anast., *Narr.* I.10–12 and 39.

29 I.e. 'land purified' (*terra munda*) by God or monks (thus Mian 1972, 295, and Solzbacher 1989, 338 n. 126), but perhaps simply 'good soil'. Solzbacher believes this refers to a wadi below Horeb, perhaps identical to the fertile areas described in Egeria, *Itin.* III.6.

30 The *dalmatic* (a long-sleeved tunic that went down to the knees and was usually made of white linen) and *pallium* (an ornamental wrap that was pinned over it at the shoulder) were formerly items of late Roman aristocratic dress; by PP's day it had become part of the uniform worn by church clerics in the West.

31 An example of the traditional Arab worship of aniconic stones, or *baetyls*; this particular stone may correspond to the numerous *welis* found near Jabal Musa: see Marx 1977. For other references to 'Saracen' cult and priesthoods see Hoyland 2001, 157–60 and above, n. 17.

[39] Between Sina and Horeb is a valley in which dew sometimes comes down from heaven, which they call manna. It solidifies and becomes like crystals of gum; it is collected, and they keep jars full of it in the monastery from which they give out small flasks as a blessing. And they gave us five pints of it too; they also drink this as a liqueur, and they gave it to us, and we drank.[32]

Also in those mountains there is a lion, and a panther, and wild asses, and gazelles, as well as goats and mules that graze in the mountains. They all feed together and none is molested by the lion because of the vastness of the desert.

But since the days of the Saracen festival were now coming to an end,[33] a herald went out: as a result, since it would not be good to return via the desert through which we had come in, some returned to the Holy City through Egypt, others through Arabia.[34]

[40] From Mount Sina to the city in Arabia called Aila there are eight staging-posts.[35] Ships come down to Aila from India with various spices.[36] But it seemed best for us to return via Egypt, and we came to the city of Pharan. Here Moses fought with Amalek; there is an oratory, the altar of which is placed on those rocks that they placed under Moses when he was praying.[37] In this place the city is fortified by walls on its sides. It is an

---

32 Cf. Exod. 16:1–36. PP seems to refer here to the Raha valley; in Egeria's day, the manna miracle was located on the coast (cf. Egeria, *Itin.* PD,Y 13). Such 'manna' was probably the secretion from the insects that infest tamarisk trees (*tamarix mannifera*) on the Sinai peninsula; it is still harvested and sold today to pilgrims to Sinai and Mecca: see Hobbs 1995, 48–49. For this sort of 'blessing' (*benedictio*) given out in small flasks (*ampullae*), see Kötting 1980, 403–13, and Egeria, *Itin.* III.6, with references. Elsewhere *conditum* means 'seasoned wine'; here some such beverage or liqueur is meant (cf. above, p. 258, n. 25). Skrobucha 1966, 92, notes that St Catherine's once had a distillery to produce and sell raki made from grapes.

33 See above, p. 256, n. 17.

34 *ut … non subsisteret*: in late Latin, *subsistere* can mean 'to hold as good'. Does PP mean it was dangerous to return the way he came because of a Saracen threat? So readers have often interpreted it, due in part to the implication of Nonnosus' report (above, p. 256, n. 17) that peaceful conditions did not hold after the end of a Saracen festival. Mary Whitby has proposed that *non subsisteret* might also refer to an unavailability of provisions on the way back through the desert, due to the festival's end (see above, PP, *Itin.* 36). In any case, the *ut* clause indicates that the choice of routes was contingent on the herald (*praeco*)'s proclamation. For the Sinai routes, see General Introduction, pp. 12–13.

35 PP may have read this on a map; only here does he uses the word *mansiones*. Aila (Eilat/'Aqaba) was the main port of Third Palestine.

36 Cf. Egeria, *Itin.* PD,Y 6 and note *ad loc.*

37 Cf. Exod. 17:12. Probably this was the church that Egeria visited on Jabal Tahuna on Pharan's north side: see Egeria, *Itin.* PD,Y 15 and note *ad loc.*

extremely barren place, apart from water and palm trees. There is a bishop in this city. Women with babies came out to meet us carrying palms in their hands and flasks of radish oil. Stooping at our feet, they anointed the soles of our feet and our heads, while singing antiphonal psalms in Egyptian: 'Blessed be you with the Lord and blessed be your arrival: Hosanna in the highest.'[38]

This is the land of Midian, and it is said that the city's inhabitants descend from the family of Jethro, Moses' father-in-law.[39] Eighty garrison men serve the state with their wives, receiving state-issued supplies and uniforms from Egypt.[40] They have no work, since there is nowhere to go, because everywhere is sand. However, everyday they patrol the desert, each on a Saracen horse (for which they receive straw and barley as fodder from the state) as a guard for the monasteries and hermits, on account of attacks by Saracens. But the Saracens do not tremble in fear of them.[41] When they go out from the city, they lock the gates and take the keys with them, as do those inside as well, on account of attacks by Saracens, since there is nowhere for them to go to outside – just sky and sand.

---

38 Cf. Ps. 118:26 and Mt. 21:9. The population's use of Coptic indicates affinities with Egypt. Shahid 1984, 322, contends the PP confused Arabic with Coptic, but it seems likely that Pharan's population at this time would have spoken Coptic as well as Greek and Arabic, since it received supplies and visitors from Egypt, coming up from Rhaithou's harbour (*Rel.* 13, 19; CI, *Top. christ.* V.14–16).

39 Cf. Exod. 2:15–22.

40 On the garrison (*condomas militantes in publico*), see Shahid 1984, 323. Geyer's text has 800 (*octingentas condomas*), but MS 'G' gives 80 (*octoginta condomas*), which most scholars have followed, apparently on the assumption that it seems more plausible. According to Kraemer 1958, 21, however, a *numerus* could include from 200 to 900 soldiers; furthermore, Ammonius, *Rel.* 33 describes a band of 600 archers coming from Pharan; indeed, PP's comment regarding the difficulty of finding work in the desert may indicate that most male Pharanites served as *limitanei* for the state. In any case the receipt of government provisions from Egypt (*annonas et vestes de publico ... de Aegypto*) indicates that this was managed by the Roman duke of Alexandria (which makes sense, as it would have been much faster and cheaper to transport supplies across the Gulf of Suez to Rhaithou than overland from Aila). We know that Justinian installed a garrison on the Sinai: see Procop., *Buildings* V.viii.9. Saracens were known to ride 'swift horses' as well as camels: Ammianus Marcellinus, XIV.4.3.

41 *ante quorum timorem non exagitantur Saraceni.* Wilkinson 2002, 88, translates, 'But they [viz. monasteries and hermits] are not specially worried or afraid about them [i.e. Saracens]', omitting *Saraceni* as a later gloss. I follow Solzbacher 1989, 151–52, in retaining *Saraceni* as the subject. It seems improbable that PP meant that local monks had no fear of the Saracens, which would not only go against the Sinai martyr tradition, but also suggest no need for such a garrison (see also the precautions described in the next sentence).

[41] [From there we went to Succoth, and from there down to Migdol][42] and also to the place of the 72 palms and 12 springs, where we happily stopped for two days after so much toil and desert wasteland. In this place there is a modest fortress, which is called Surandala. It has nothing inside except a church with a priest and two guest-houses for travellers. In this place I saw a pepper tree and gathered [fruit] from it.[43]

From there we came to a place where the sons of Israel set up camp after crossing the sea. Here similarly there is a modest fortress with a guest-house in it.[44] From there we came to the place on the shore where the sons of Israel crossed: where they came out of the sea there is an oratory of Elijah, and passing over to the place where they entered the sea there is an oratory of Moses. There is also a small city here called Clysma where ships from India come as well.[45]

At that part of the sea where they made their crossing, a gulf issues from the main sea and extends many miles inland with a tide that rises and falls. When the tide recedes, all the shapes cast by the weapons of Pharaoh and the tracks of his chariot are laid bare, but the weapons have all turned into marble.[46] There we got plump green nuts, which come from India. People think they come from paradise, the reason being this, that however few you eat, you feel full.

[42] Eleven miles out to sea there is a small island of living rock, from which hang fingers that are soft as flesh, like dates. These excrete a viscous fluid called rock oil,[47] which they take as a great blessing. If the vessel in

---

42 These references may be out of place in the manuscripts, since all other references to Succoth and Magdalum locate them in Egypt, north of Clysma, an area through which PP later passes (*Itin.* 43): cf. Exod. 12:37, 14:2, and Egeria, *Itin.* VII.4–5. But Wilkinson 2002, 148, and Solzbacher 1989, 152, propose their placement here reflects how the identity of Old Testament sites shifted over time.

43 Surandala probably refers to Wadi Gharandula, which Egeria, *Itin.* PD,Y 12 also identifies as Elim; Solzbacher 1989, 340 n. 146, suggests that 'Surandala', otherwise unattested, derived from a misunderstanding and contraction of a hypothetical Greek phrase, *eis Arandala* (i.e. 'Into/at [Gh]arandala').

44 Cf. Exod. 14:22–29. Probably Marah or the Phoinikon near Clysma: cf. Egeria, *Itin.* PD,Y 11; CI, *Top. christ.* V.13.

45 On Clysma and its Indian shipping, see Egeria, *Itin.* PD,Y 5 and notes *ad loc.*

46 Exod. 14:23; see Egeria, *Itin.* PD,Y 5. 'all the shapes cast by [the weapons and tracks] are laid bare' renders PP's obscure *omnis praefiguratio ... parent*; Wilkinson 2002, 148, translates, 'you can see the shapes of' the weapons and tracks.

47 *oleum petrinum*, i.e. 'petroleum'. Solzbacher 1989, 275, suggests this island may be the same one in the Gulf of Suez called *Petrolaia* in Slavic MSS of John Mosch., *Meadow* 122. However, that island seems to have been further south (the story describes trouble returning to

which it is carried has been filled and you want to go back to get more, it will no longer receive or hold any. All the sick people who manage to reach this place are cured, especially demoniacs. But those who take it away as a blessing are not allowed to take it beyond Clysma undiluted, but it is mixed with oil. If it were not diluted, I think it would always work that miracle. The liquid from that fluid extends continuously for two miles[48] and has a sulphuric smell. However stormy the sea may be, it nonetheless stands still as a lake below that liquid.

In the church below the city of Clysma itself we saw more than eighteen wooden caskets of holy fathers, the hermits.[49]

Rhaithou due to winds). In the eighth century, Epiphanius the Monk, *Itin.* VII.2–3, observed that 'rock oil [*petroleum*] flows near' the stone where Moses had stood while parting the waters.

48 I.e. an oil slick on the surface of the water.

49 MS 'G' gives 13 hermits, perhaps anchorites whose early fifth-century presence at Clysma is recorded in several apophthegmata. Solzbacher 1989, 341 n. 150, suggests the church was the one Justinian reportedly built for 'St Athanasius' at Clysma in Eutychius, *Annals* (below, p. 280). PP continued from Clysma to the Nile and Alexandria before returning to Jerusalem.

GREGORY THE GREAT
LETTER IV.44, TO RUSTICIANA
LETTER XI.2, TO JOHN, ABBOT OF MOUNT SINA

The following letters are preserved in the fourteen-book *Register*, or collection, of letters of Pope Gregory I (590–604).[1] The first is addressed to a Roman aristocrat in Constantinople whom Gregory probably met while serving there as the papal representative from 579–586. The second is addressed to John, 'Abbot of Mount Sina'. It is tempting to identify this John with the Mount Sinai monastery's most famous *hēgoumen*, John Climacus, and this identification has recently been defended. However, that would require dating him much earlier than is generally accepted[2] (see above, Anastasius of Sinai, *Narr.* I.3, 11, 16 and notes *ad loc.*).

On the same date Gregory also wrote a letter to a priest at Mount Sinai named Palladius, otherwise unknown, sending a tunic and cowl and requesting his prayers.[3] Because of its length and because it is mainly hortatory in content, it has not been included here.

TRANSLATION OF THE LATIN TEXTS

LETTER IV.44 (August 594)

Gregory to Rusticiana, Patrician[4]

Upon receiving what your Excellency wrote, I learned with joy that you had reached Mount Sinai. Believe me, I would have liked to have gone

---

1 Ed. Norberg 1982. For a translation of Gregory's entire *Registrum epistularum*, see Martin 2004.

2 Müller 2006, 51–52. For the problem, see General Introduction, p. 24 n. 98.

3 Gregory the Great, *ep.* IX.1. For translation, see Martin 2004, vol. 3, 735–36.

4 Rusticiana was a member of the *familia Anicia*, one of the most illustrious late Roman families; the philosopher Boethius was her grandfather. She and Gregory remained friends long after his return to Rome; other letters he sent to her are *ep.* II.27 (dated 592, where he encourages her to set out on pilgrimage), VIII.22 (dated 598), XI.26 (601), and XIII.24 (603). A poem has survived that she may have given him before his departure to Rome: see Averil Cameron 1979 and *PLRE* III, *s.v.* 'Rusticiana 2'.

with you, but certainly not to have returned with you. Yet it is very hard for me to believe that you have been to the holy places, and have seen many Fathers. For I think that if you had, you would not have been able to return so quickly to the city of Constantinople. But inasmuch as the love of such a city has by no means left your heart, I suspect that your Excellency hardly took to your heart the holy things you saw in the flesh. But may Almighty God illuminate your mind with the grace of His compassion, and may He grant that you be wise, and consider how transitory all temporal things are. Even as we say these things, time is running out, the Judge approaches, and behold! it is already almost time for us to leave, against our will, the world that we would not wish [to leave] of our own accord.

I ask that Lord Appion, Lady Eusebia and their daughters be greeted on my behalf.[5] As for the lady, my nurse,[6] whom you commended to me in your letter, I am very fond of her, and in no way want her to be weighed down. But we are pressed by such straitened circumstances that we cannot relieve even ourselves from government impositions and burdens at this time.

LETTER XI.2 (1 September 600)

Gregory to John, Abbot of Mount Sina

Your Humility's letter attests the sanctity of your way of life; hence we greatly thank Almighty God for the knowledge that there still exist those who are fit to supplicate for the sake of our sins. For we, under the veneer of church governance, are being buffeted by the waves of this world. Often they overwhelm us, but we are raised up from the depths by the protecting hand of heavenly grace. And so you, who lead a tranquil life in such quiet serenity and stand, as it were, securely on the shore, extend to us the hand of your prayer as we sail, or rather, risk shipwreck. With as many prayers as you can, help those who are trying to reach the 'land of the living',[7] so that you might hold forever a reward not only for your way of life, but also for our rescue.

May the Holy Trinity shelter your beloved self with the right hand of His protection, and grant that you might graze the flock entrusted to you

---

5 Rusticiana's daughter, Eusebia, was married to the patrician and honorary consul Flavius Apion III, scion of the great 'house of Apion' known from Oxyrhyncus papyri: *PLRE* III, *s.v.* 'Eusebia 2', 'Apion 4'.

6 Or, 'As for Domna, that nurse of mine'.

7 Ps. 116[114]:9.

correctly in His sight, through prayer, admonition, and examples of good work, so that you might reach the pastures of eternal life with the flock that you graze. For indeed it is written, 'My sheep will come and find pastures'.[8] Those pastures we will only discover once we have been freed from the winter of this present life, and become sated upon eternal life as upon the greenness of a new spring.[9]

We have learned from a message from our son, Simplicius,[10] that there is a lack of beds and bedding in the infirmary for Holy Ones built there by a certain Isaurus.[11] For this reason we have sent fifteen sheets, thirty blankets, and fifteen beds; we also have given a sum for the purchase of mattresses and for the cost of transporting them. We ask that your Beloved receive them without indignation, and put them in the place for which they have been sent.

---

8 Jn 10:9, 27.

9 Reading *viriditate* ('greenness') of MS 'M' for Norberg's *veritate* ('truth'): see Martin 2004 vol.3, 737.

10 Also mentioned in *ep.* XI.1; perhaps a monk Gregory knew from Rome.

11 Anastasius of Sinai refers to the healing powers of a Sinai abbot named Isaurus in *Narr.* I.13, and to the building of a monastery infirmary (*nosokomeion*) by a 'Bishop of Rome' in *Narr.* I.3. Gregory's term, *hierochomium* ('infirmary for Holy Ones'), is a *hapax legomenon*, probably inspired by the Greek word *gerokomeion* ('infirmary for the aged'). A *gerokomeion* for aged monks is attested in Theodosius' famous sixth-century *coenobium*: see Theodore of Petra, *Life of Theodosius*, ed. Usener, pp. 40–41.

THREE PAPYRI FROM NESSANA:
P.COLT 89, 72, AND 73

The following documents were among the papyri discovered by the Colt expedition in the ruins of Nessana (Nitzana/Auja al-Hafir) in the Negev in 1935. Dated to the sixth and seventh centuries and written in Greek, they attest the close connections between Mount Sinai and the people of that Third Palestine desert town even after the Arab conquests.[1]

The first document, *P.Colt* 89, lists the purchases and receipts of a trading company or caravan that operated between Nessana, Mount Sinai, and elsewhere. Reflecting at least two different journeys, including one to Mount Sinai (section 'B'), it shows the careful preparations the traders made before undertaking the journey there and back, and preserves illuminating financial data, especially regarding relative values (e.g. a camel costs as much as a female slave), the sums left at Mount Sinai as donations, and the extraordinary sum (over 270 *solidi*) handed over to the traders by the Mount Sinai monastery (as it appears) for purposes unknown. Its editor, Caspar Kraemer, proposed a late sixth- or early seventh-century date based on its reference (line 23) to an 'Abba Martyrius' at the Mount Sinai monastery; he believed this might be the same Martyrius mentioned by Anastasius in *Narr.* I.6, 35, and 36.[2] The traders, identified as Sergius, Abraham, and Zunayn in line 3, and the Nessana group or individuals who commissioned them (lines 3, 24–25) are otherwise unknown. The total size of the papyrus was 48 x 32.5 cm in all; the text is scribbled in minute letters in compact lines of wildly uneven length. It survives in thirteen fragments, with four major pieces or sections (A,B,C,D).[3] Since section A and the beginning of B (lines 1–19) are highly fragmentary, they are not included here.

P.Colt 72 and *P.Colt* 73 are both small letters (21 x 16.5, 26.5 x 16.3 cm), written apparently by the same hand, requesting guides to Mount Sinai. Both were issued by a provincial governor named Abū Rashid (otherwise

---

1 All three ed. and trans. Kraemer 1958, 205–08, 251–60; his translations are reproduced here with some alterations, but his annotations are not.

2 Kraemer 1958, 252.

3 See Kraemer 1958, pl. 7.

unknown) to a Nessana administrator named George, known from other papyri.[4] Both refer to the 'twelfth indiction', suggesting a date of 683/684, fifty years after the Muslim conquest (669 and 699 are also possible for the twelfth indiction). Although the religion of the pilgrims involved is not identified, both letters provide evidence for continued pilgrimage to Mount Sinai at that time, and reinforce the impression that Nessana was the last important stopping point for pilgrims before they entered the al-Tih desert. A photograph of *P.Colt* 72 is presented on the frontispiece to this volume, with its wax seal visible.

TRANSLATION OF THE GREEK TEXTS

1. *P.Colt* 89: Trading Company Account (Late Sixth–Early Seventh Century)

[Section B, a journey to Mount Sinai]
[line 20] The two of us smelted it [at the order?][5] of his holiness Abba Mantheas, 1½ lbs [of iron?],[6] 5 1/3 sol.[7]
[line 21] Paid as price for slave girl, 3 sol., plus camel worth 6 1/3[8] Total: 9 1/3. As price for slave boy, 6 sol., plus camel worth 4 1/3
[line 22] Total (including fee of man who drew up bill of sale): 10 1/3. Paid to the Saracen escort who took us[9] to

---

4 *P.Colt.* 68, 70, and 74 concern his duties as a tax collector. Although George was a common name in Nessana, Kraemer 1958, 5–6, suggests that this particular George was the scion of a prominent family that had provided abbots, priests, nuns, and patrons for the town since the middle of the sixth century. The Nessana papyri preserve a considerable number of this family's documents, dubbed the 'archive of George Son of Patrick'; Kraemer 1958, 6, believes George collected and discarded them shortly before 700. His position as administrator and tax collector shows how members of such old families would be selected to represent and run the town by the new Arab government.

5 About nine spaces missing.

6 About four spaces missing.

7 sol. = *solidus*, the basic currency standard of the day.

8 This document contains some of our few references to the price of camels in Byzantine times. See lines 29–31, 35, 42. The average price is 6–7 *solidi*.

9 δοθ(έντα) τῷ Σαρακαινῷ τῷ σικοφαντέσαντι ἐμᾶς ἰς τὸ ἅγιον ὄρος (thus the Greek). *Sycophanteō* in this phrase must be derogatory (*pace* Christides 1972, 332) and although Kraemer translated it simply as 'escort' (hence its definition in LSJ suppl.), he notes that it probably was meant to indicate contempt for the Saracen in question. But that would be a very mild use of the word, and there is no other attestation of *sycophanteō* to refer to a guide. Moreover, Kraemer notes that the price paid was steep, more than half as much again as that

[line 23] the Holy Mountain, 3½ sol. Turned over to us by Abba Martyrius, 270½ sol.[10] We went for prayer

[line 24] at the Holy Mountain and gave a blessing,[11] 1 sol. Expenditures for you, also purchase of fish and almonds, 1 sol.[12]

[line 25] Donation to the Holy Mountain on behalf of the group from your town:[13] 10 sol., and on behalf of [.....sos]: 7 sol. Total: 17 sol.

[line 26] Paid to Egyptus when Stephen abandoned [?] the first ... and the big camel ran away ...

[line 27][14] ... 20 modii of wheat by the unhurt camel of the Arabs and because of this he received ...

[line 28] ... Bishop Stephen received ... wool [?] ... 160 folles.

[line 29] ... they gave for an ass [?] – it died – 2 1/3 He received ... the large camel, 15 [sol.]

[Section C, recording sundry purchases made on another journey]

[line 30] Account of purchases and receipts of ... the caravan in the month of Dius.[15] Purchased: female camel, 7 sol.

[line 31] also purchased: camel, 5 1/3 sol. female ass, 2 1/3 sol. Given for [...........................?[16]] [...]

---

of a camel. Mayerson 1989, 285, therefore proposes to translate this line, 'Paid to the Saracen who extorted [3½ *solidi*] from us [en route] to the Holy Mountain', explaining, 'The likelihood is that the Saracen was not a passing nomad but the sheikh of a tribe who demanded the money so that the caravan would travel under his protection and be free from harassment, or worse, by his tribesmen.'

10 On this large sum, see above, General Introduction, p. 31.

11 In some late antique texts, 'for prayer' means 'to fulfil a vow'. A 'blessing' (*eulogia*) was a type of gift: see Egeria, *Itin.*, III.5 and note *ad loc.*

12 Kraemer suggests that the fish and almonds refer to meals (purchased?) at the monastery, and 'your expenditure' (ἀνάλωμα) refers to relics purchased at the monastery.

13 ὑπὲρ τῆς κυνότετος τοῦ χορίου ὑμῶν (thus the Greek). Kraemer prefers to translate the presumed word κυνότετος (i.e. κοινότης) as 'group' or 'commission' (viz. of leading citizens of Nessana) rather than as 'community' (i.e. of monks of Nessana), for which he thinks κοινωνία would have been more likely. But in line 33, *koinonia* refers to the trading company, itself an unusual use of that word.

14 Lines 27–29 are highly fragmentary. Kraemer 1958, 252, explains, 'one Stephen seems to have done something as the result of which a big camel ran away and it became necessary to use an Arab camel to carry wheat. There was bakshish for this, some money paid to a bishop, the death of a donkey and perhaps the recapture of the big camel, but the data given are insufficient to tie all the events together.'

15 17 November–16 December, according to the Seleucid calendar.

16 Kraemer suggests: 'people in the cities and villages'.

[line 32] Out of the price of the unmarked stolen ...[17]

[line 33] For the month of Apellaeus[18] there was assigned to our partnership (Sergius,[19] Abraham, and myself Zunayn), 16 sol.

[line 34] Given as price of a female ass (it died) for [the trip to] Nessana, 5 1/3 sol.

[line 35] We recovered as the price of the camel which the Saracens Sons al-Udayyid took,[20] 4 [sol.]

[line 36] [...] 10. We spent when we went to Emazen,[21] to the wife of the guardsman,[22] 1 sol.

[line 37–38, after about 19 spaces] ... everything in every way, 10 sol. Received, as the price of a mare, 3 sol. Received, as the price of a foal, 1 sol. Received, as the price of ... 1 sol. Received, as my share, 1 sol. Received, as the price of wool and oil, 2 sol. Total: 18 sol.

[line 39, after about 18 spaces] ... which we gave you and Martyrius as expenses of God,[23] for the price of a linen curtain, 2 sol.

[line 40, after about 16 spaces] ... given to the Saracen [named] 'Adi,[24] the money we borrowed for the price of wool, 1 1/6 sol.

[lines 41–43, after about 16 spaces] ... of Stephen son of Mioi[...] and John son of Lar[...h, 3 sol. We have recovered from him ... modii of barley ... Given for the price of a camel, 6 sol. Also as the price of a large camel, 6 sol. Also purchased for you – wine, 1 sol. ...] for the 10 measures of ... which Theodore received from him, 7 sol.

[Three lines missing, followed by section D, a closing prayer and addendum]

[lines 44–45 after about 16 spaces] ... and by the intercession of our Lady [Mary], Mother of God and Ever-Virgin, [and of the holy,] glorious John the

---

17 Kraemer leaves this line untranslated, being uncertain about the reading 'stolen...'

18 17 December–16 January, according to the Seleucid Calendar.

19 Perhaps named for St Sergius, who had a shrine at Nessana.

20 οἱ Σαρακενοὶ ὑοὶ Ειαλωδεειδ. Kraemer: 'which the Arabs, the bani al-Udayyid [*sic*], took'. This tribe, the Banū Udayyid, is unknown, but Avni 1996, 78, conjectures that the name refers to a small well or waterhole.

21 Unknown; Kraemer suggests this is a clipped form of Sykomazon (cf. Egeria, *Itin.* VII.8 and note *ad loc.*), a village (modern Khirbat Suq Mazon) south of Gaza.

22 πρὸς τὲ γυνêκαν τοῦ σπαθαρίου (thus the Greek), perhaps 'to the woman of the Guardsman', i.e. a keeper of an inn or brothel.

23 ἀναλόματα θ[ε]ο[ῦ], perhaps referring to church altar coverings.

24 Kraemer: 'to the Arab 'Adī'.

Forerunner and Baptist, and of all the holy [m]a[rtyrs ...[25]
[line 46] For price of the camel bag, 200 folles.[26]

2. *P.Colt* 72: Order from the Governor for a Guide, March, 684?

[Lines 1–2] In the n[ame] of Al[mighty] God! Abū Rashid, Governor,[27] to George of Nessana
[Red Wax Seal]
[Lines 3–9] Thanks be to God. When Abū l-Mughira, *mawla* of 'Urwa ibn Abi Sufyan,[28] comes to you, be kind enough to furnish him a man from Nessana bound to guide him on the road to the Holy Mount.[29] Also furnish the man's pay. Written in the month of March, twelfth indiction, by hand of Theodore.

3. *P.Colt* 73: Order from the Governor for a Guide, December, 683?

[Lines 1–2] In the n[ame] of Al[mighty God! Abū] Rashid, [Governor], to the people of Nessana
[Lines 3–8] Thanks be to God. When my wife Ubayya comes to you, furnish her a man bound to direct her on the road to Mt Sina.[30] Also furnish the man's pay.
[Line 9] Written 5 December, twelfth indiction.

---

25 Kraemer translates the last word as 'saints', but conjectures 'martyrs' on the basis of the spacing around the letter alpha. This seems to be a closing prayer for the entire list of accounts.

26 Kraemer considers this entry to be an overlooked item added as postscript. *Folles* were bronze coins; 180 *folles* equalled one *solidus*.

27 σύμβου[λος], Greek for the Arabic *amīr*.

28 μαυλε, for Arabic *mawlā*, a freed slave who remained the client of his liberator (as here, 'Urwa ibn Abi Sufyan). Cf. Ps.-Nilus, *Narr*.VII.17 and note *ad loc*.

29 τὴν στρᾶταν τοῦ ἁγίου ὄρους. These words may be read at the end of line 7 and the beginning of line 8 of the text in this book's frontispiece photograph.

30 Τυρσινα, *Tur Sina*, Arabic for Mt Sinai.

APPENDIX II

Sinai Defences

PROCOPIUS OF CAESAREA, ON BUILDINGS V.viii.1–9*

The great sixth-century historian of Emperor Justinian's reign, Procopius of Caesarea, author of *The Wars* and the notorious *Secret History*, also wrote a panegyrical account of Justinian's building projects, called *Buildings*. Completed either in 554/55, 559/60, or 560/61,[1] its fifth book surveys the Roman East and concludes with the following section, which describes Justinian's constructions at Mount Sinai.

Anyone who visits Mount Sinai with Procopius in hand will find that his description is slightly misleading: Jabal Musa is not exactly 'close to the Red Sea' (*Buildings* V.viii.1), and Justinian's basilica church was built within the fortress walls at its base; Procopius' description does not put the two together.[2] Also notable is his implication that these walls were not built for the protection of Sinai monks; indeed, Procopius' description of these monks as living in their desert 'without fear' would suggest they had no need of them. Although it is generally assumed that Procopius had a good understanding of Justinian's motives (he had served as secretary to Justinian's generalissimo, Belisarius), such inconcinnities have caused some to doubt his accuracy regarding Justinian's motives for building the Sinai fortress: did the emperor intend it to protect distant Palestine from Saracen raids as Procopius says, or to protect the local Sinai monks, as we read in the

---

* Translation reprinted by permission of the publishers and the Trustees of the Loeb Classical Library from *Procopius: Volume VII*, Loeb Classical Library Volume 343, translated by H. B. Dewing, pp. 255, 257 (Cambridge, MA: Harvard University Press). Copyright © 1940 by the President and Fellows of Harvard College. The Loeb Classical Library ® is a registered trademark of the President and Fellows of Harvard College.

1 There is no consensus, and the evidence is too complex to be reviewed here. Averil Cameron 1985, 84–112, and Greatrex 1994 argue for c. 554, while Whitby 1985, Evans 1996, and Roques 2000, 43, argue for c. 560 (Kaldellis 2004, 46: 'probably … the middle years of that decade' (550s)'). On other aspects of the work, see also Carrié, Duval and Roueché 2000.

2 Dahari 2000, 28–36 and 1998a, following Mayerson 1978 and Eutychius' description, maintains that Procopius is wrong, and that Justinian, besides building the monastery basilica (which Dahari identifies as the Church of the Transfiguration), also built a chapel dedicated to the Theotokos on Jabal Musa's summit.

tenth-century account by the Alexandrian Patriarch Eutychius (translated in the next section below)?[3]

No doubt some of these problems are explained by the fact that Procopius was writing in far-off Constantinople for audiences little concerned about descriptive precision; he may have written this passage before all the Sinai structures had been built, and in any case probably based it upon information from imperial archives.[4] There is no strong reason to think his account of Justinian's strategic objectives was mistaken, since the Roman government had used towns and caravanserais as military outposts 'within Saracen lands' since at least the late fourth century (cf. Egeria PD/Y 6, *Itin.* VII.5). However, Procopius may have emphasized the strategic aspect of those defences to the neglect of more local purposes. Note his very similar explanation of the fortifications that Justinian built for some monasteries in North African Cyrene (modern Libya):

> The greatest part of this land of Libya chances to have been desert, which was in general neglected. Yet our Emperor takes thought for this land also with watchful care, so that it might not have the ill fortune to suffer anything from inroads of the Moors [Black Ones] who inhabit the adjoining country. And to this end … on the extreme boundaries of the Pentapolis which faces south, he constructed fortresses [or 'strongholds', ὀχρώματα] in two monasteries … these stand as bulwarks against barbarians of that region, so that they might not come down stealthily into Roman territory and suddenly fall upon it.[5]

Here, too, Procopius emphasizes imperial security over monastic safety. This should come as no surprise. Procopius wrote his panegyric to celebrate and advertise the fact that Justinian had taken concern for his Empire as a

---

3 Mayerson 1978, 33–38. For Eutychius' version, see below, pp. 280–82.

4 So Averil Cameron 1985, 96–97, contra Mayerson 1978. Visiting about the time of Procopius' work, PP, *Itin.* 37 notes only the existence of the fortress walls and a small chapel (probably built by Julian Saba) on the summit.

5 *Buildings* VI.ii.1–2, 7–8, trans. Dewing, 365–67; cf. VI.v.11 on Carthage, where Justinian 'built a monastery … and by surrounding it with very strong defences (ἐρύματί … ἐχυρωτάτῳ), he made it a most impregnable fortress' (φρούριον ἀνανταγώνιστον, text and trans. Dewing, 380–81). The construction of a church or monastery-within-a-fort was so common in border regions during Justinian's reign that it has been likened to the creation of 'a new type of city': thus Liebeschuetz 2001, 80–83, describing Justinian's foundations in Thrace and the southern Balkans. There may be truth to the speculation of Armstrong 1969, 23: 'A church, as often as not dedicated to the Virgin Mary, was [considered by Justinian to be] essential for the defense of the Empire against the barbarians, for sacraments and relics represented a power greater than human armies'. It would be nice to see a study that examined in depth the perceived role of religion and prayer in late Roman frontier defence.

whole, not for just a few monks living on its peripheries.[6] For a more local – though not necessarily accurate – explanation of the Sinai constructions and their historical origins, we must refer to the later account by Eutychius.

TRANSLATION OF THE GREEK TEXT

[**V.viii.1.**] In what was formerly called Arabia and is now known as 'Third Palestine', a barren land extends for a great distance, unwatered and producing neither crops nor any useful thing. A precipitous and terribly wild mountain, Sina by name, rears its height close to the Red Sea, as it is called. **2.** There is no need at this point in my account to write a description of that region because everything has been set forth in my books *On the Wars*, where I gave a full description of the Red Sea and what is called the Arabian Gulf, as well as of the Ethiopians and Auxomitae and the tribes of the Homerite Saracens.[7] At that point I showed also in what manner the Emperor Justinian added the Palm Groves to Roman rule.[8] **3.** Therefore I omit further mention of these things, that I may not acquire a reputation for vulgar excess.

4. On this Mount Sina dwell monks whose life is a kind of 'careful study of death',[9] and they enjoy without fear the solitude which is very precious to them. **5.** Since these monks have nothing to crave – for they are superior to all human desires and have no interest in possessing anything or in caring for their bodies, nor do they seek pleasure in any other thing whatsoever – the Emperor Justinian built them a church which he dedicated to the Mother of God,[10] so that they might be enabled to pass their lives therein praying and

---

6 Averil Cameron 1985, 96 n. 97, notes that Procopius' description of Sinai monks is 'highly intellectualised', suggesting he was not particularly knowledgeable about the monks themselves.

7 Cf. *Wars* I.xix.3–7, 14–26. The 'Arabian gulf' is the ancient 'Gulf of Aila' and modern Gulf of Eilat/'Aqaba. For late Roman interests in the Axumite kingdom of Ethiopia and the Himyarite ('Homerite') kingdom of southern Arabia/Yemen, see Fowden 1993, 109–16.

8 Cf. *Wars* I.xix.8–13. This Palm Groves ('Phoinikon') was probably a site in the northern Ḥijaz, perhaps identical to the Bedouin camp described in the fifth-sixth century *Life of Paul the Bishop and John the Priest*. It was 'given' to Justinian c. 528 by a Ghassanid sheikh, Abū Karib, in return for the phylarchy of Palestine: see Shahid 1995, 124–30.

9 ἠκριβωμένη τις μελέτη θανάτου, literally 'an exacting study of death', from Plato, *Phaedo* 81a, where Socrates notes that individuals who free themselves from bodily concerns and contemplate their end will enter into divine company after death. Cf. Climacus, *Ladder* 6 (PG 88.797c).

10 *Theotokos*.

holding services. **6.** He built this church, not on the mountain's summit, but much lower down.[11] **7.** For it is impossible for a human to spend a night on the peak, since constant crashes of thunder and other terrifying manifestations of divine power are heard at night, striking terror into a man's body and soul.[12] **8.** It was in that place, they say, that Moses received the laws from God and made them known.[13]

9. And at the base of the mountain this Emperor built a very strong fortress and established there a considerable garrison of troops,[14] in order that the Saracen barbarians might not be able from that region which, as I have said, is uninhabited, to make inroads with complete secrecy into the lands of Palestine.[15]

11 See above, n. 3.

12 Cf. Egeria, *Itin*. III.5; PP, *Itin*. 37; Anast., *Narr.* I.3. This shows that stories or rumours regarding Mt Sinai's divine portents were known in distant Constantinople.

13 Exod. 24:9–14.

14 φρούριον ἐχυρώτατον ... φυλακτήριόν τε στρατιωτῶν ἀξιολογώτατον. Perhaps 'most select' or 'elite' for ἀξιολογώτατον.

15 As noted above, this account of Justinian's motive for establishing security in the Sinai has been disputed: see Mayerson 1978; Averil Cameron 1985, 96–97. Procopius does not specify where the garrison was located. Most probably it was based in Pharan (see PP, *Itin*. 40), although its camp may have been located east of the Justinianic complex. One might question, however, whether the garrison Procopius attributes to Justinian was actually first created by him and not by his predecessor Anastasius († 518). John of Nikiou (*Chronicle*, LXXXIX.33–34) claims that the latter had already provided defences along the Rhaithou coast. Several projects that Procopius attributed to Justinian have since been found to have been built or begun by earlier emperors.

EUTYCHIUS OF ALEXANDRIA (SA'ĪD IBN BATRĪQ), *ANNALS*: ON JUSTINIAN'S CONSTRUCTIONS AT MOUNT SINAI*

Sa'īd ibn Batrīq (877–940), better known by his Greek patriarchal name Eutychius (the Greek equivalent of Sa'īd), is one the most important medieval Christian authors who wrote in Arabic. Elected Melkite (i.e. Chalcedonian) Patriarch of Alexandria in 933 (possibly 935), he authored several books, including the first (apparently) Christian universal history to have been written in Arabic. Entitled the *Chronicle Compiled by Way of Verification and Affirmation* and usually called the *Annals* (*Annales ecclesiastici*), it survives in as many as thirty manuscripts, indicating its wide popularity and dissemination during the Middle Ages. One of these is preserved in the library at St Catherine's.[1]

The account translated here describes and explains Justinian's constructions at Mount Sinai. Not extant in any other source, it differs from Procopius' account of Justinian's activities in some basic respects. For example, whereas Procopius states that Justinian built his church 'not on the mountain's summit, but much lower down' (*Buildings* V.viii.6), Eutychius claims that it was built on the summit itself. And whereas Procopius states that Justinian's new church was dedicated to the Theotokos, Eutychius claims that a Theotokos church already existed in a tower beside the Burning Bush, before Justinian built his new church on the summit. Eutychius also claims that Justinian built both the Mount Sinai and the Rhaithou monasteries, and markedly differs from Procopius in his representation of Justinian's motivation: here it is monastic security, not imperial security, that moves the emperor to build.

Some believe that Eutychius' account makes more sense than Procopius' account, and that his details (e.g. its reference to a tower pre-existing

---

* Trans. courtesy of Kevin van Bladel, from the Arabic edition of Breydy 1985, 107–09; also ed. Cheikho 1905, 202–04. For a Latin translation of Eutychius' entire Arabic text, see PG 111.903A–1156A; for the Sinai account, see cols.1071A–1072D.

1 *Sinaiticus Arab.* 580. Breydy based his new edition upon this MS in the belief that it was written by Eutychius himself. Its tradition is problematic, but fortunately in the portion translated here there are no significant variants between Breydy's text (B) and Cheikho' text (Ch). For more on Eutychius and this work, see Micheau 1995.

Justinian's fortifications below Mount Sinai) can be substantiated by archae-ology.[2] In addition, Eutychius' account of a monastic embassy approaching a Roman Emperor to provide defence is not unparalleled. According to Cyril of Scythopolis' sixth-century *Life of Abraamius*, the Syrian monk Abraam and his *hēgoumen* were prompted by a Saracen attack on their Judaean monastery to seek aid from Constantinople during Emperor Anastasius' reign. Indeed, as noted in the General Introduction, a monastic anecdote, presumably of fifth-century date, refers to ten Mount Sinai monks being sent to the imperial court, obviously on a matter of importance.[3] But the best-known example of a monastic embassy is that which Cyril describes in his sixth-century *Life of Sabas*. According to Cyril, the Palestinian *hēgoumen* Sabas approached Justinian in 531 after Saracens had devastated several Judaean monasteries during the Samaritan revolt in the previous year. When asked what he wanted, Sabas reportedly replied, 'On account of the inroads of the Saracens, we beg Your Serenity to order the most glorious Summus to build at public expense a fort in the desert at the foot of the monas-teries'. Sabas is said to have promised the restoration of the entire western Roman Empire in return for this and other favours; and so Justinian ordered Summus, the duke of Palestine, to spend 1,000 *solidi* from his treasury 'for the construction of a fort and a military guard to protect his monasteries, supported from public funds'.[4]

Those arrangements sound similar to what Procopius attributes to Justinian on the Sinai. Should we therefore trust that Eutychius' account otherwise represents Justinian's motives with informed accuracy? Perhaps, but there are good grounds for being sceptical about its historicity. Besides the fact that Procopius had much better access to contemporary documents or Justinianic informants than Eutychius, it is notable that Eutychius' account comes directly after a passage in the *Annals* that actually describes Sabas' embassy to Justinian. Although Eutychius does not mention Sabas' request for a monastery fortress, it is reasonable to suspect that he (or his

2 See Grossmann 1988 for remains of a tower, which Grossmann interprets partly on the basis of this text; for the accuracy of the description in general, see Mayerson 1978 and Dahari 1998a and 2000, 30–37. Dahari maintains that Justinian built two churches, one on top of the Sinai and one by the Burning Bush below. Interestingly, Eutychius' account does not mention the latter.

3 See above, General Introduction, p. 57; on Abraam's embassy, see Cyril Scyth., *Life of Abraamius* 1.

4 Cyril Scyth., *Life of Sabas* 72–73, ed. Schwartz 175, 17–19, 178.6–9; trans. Price, 184, 187. For the date, see *PLRE* II, *s.v.* 'Summus'. After Sabas' death, the money was diverted and the fortress never built.

source) shaped his Sinai account along the lines of Cyril's description of Sabas' embassy. In fact, Eutychius' reference to Justinian's execution of an architect for mishandling the building of the Mount Sinai monastery comes only a little after his description of Justinian's execution of an architect for misbuilding a church at Bethlehem. Such parallelism, especially for events of such dubious historicity, casts doubt on the entire account.[5]

Noting that the Melkite See of Alexandria had close ties to Mount Sinai's monastery in the tenth century (Eutychius' patriarchal successor, Isaac, resided there several years), Richard Solzbacher proposes that the monastery itself was the source of this account. He notes that much of its circumstantial information – e.g. its reference to an early *hēgoumen* named Doulas, to a defensive tower, to a Bedouin attack – could have been obtained from the Ammonius *Report* or similar sources.[6] Indeed, there are signs that a number of sources were behind the account. In particular, its references to Justinian's construction, to a *hēgoumen* named Doulas, and to a construction date some time early in Justinian's reign (it is more or less synchronized with the Saba embassy of the early 530s) recall the (evidently late) Arabic-Greek foundation inscription that may be seen today in the walls of St Catherine's.[7]

Thus what we seem to have here is a local tradition handed down by Mount Sinai monks to explain their monastery's history and connect it with other significant churches and monasteries on the peninsula, resulting in a conveniently simplified and unified account of Christian foundations on the Sinai.

5 Cf. PG 111.1070D–1071A. Hence Solzbacher 1989, 254, rejects Eutychius' account.

6 Solzbacher 1989, 255.

7 Although the passage immediately follows a reference to Justinian's rebuilding of Hagia Sophia in Constantinople in 537, that reference is clearly inserted as an addendum to the effects of the Sabas embassy, which occurred in 531/32. The inscription in question is Sinai Inscription no. 17, translated in the General Introduction above, pp. 28–29. Dismissed as an eighteenth-century fabrication by Ševčenko 1966, 255–56, it may nonetheless derive from an earlier monastic source (of course, that source may have been Eutychius). It dates Justinian's foundation to the thirtieth year of his reign (557).

TRANSLATION OF THE ARABIC TEXT

When the Monks of Mount Sinai heard of the good will of King Justinian[8] and his love for building churches and populating monasteries,[9] they came to him and complained that the Bedouin Arab Ishmaelites were harming them and eating their food and laying their places to waste, entering their monastic cells and seizing everything in them, entering the churches[10] and then eating the offering. Justinian said to them, 'Then what do you want?' They said to him, 'We ask you, O King, to build a monastery for us so that we can be protected in it.'

Previously at Mount Sinai there was not a monastery in which the monks could gather. Rather they were dispersed in the mountains and the *wadi*s around the Bush[11] from which God – Exalted be His name[12] – spoke to Moses. Above the Bush they had[13] constructed a large tower which is standing to this day, in which was the church of Lady Mary.[14] Whenever something befell the monks that they feared, they used to gather and take protection in that tower.

So the king sent a messenger along with them and supplied him with a lot of money. He wrote to his governor in Egypt to pay the messenger whatever money he wanted, to assist him with men, and to bring provisions from Egypt to him. He ordered the messenger to build a church at Clysma,[15] to build the monastery of Rhaithou,[16] and to build the monastery of Mount Sinai, to fortify it so that there be no monastery in the world more secure than it, and to be sure that there be no place in the monastery in which one would fear harm against the monastery or the monks.

When that messenger came to Clysma, he built at Clysma the Church of Mar Athanasius and built the Monastery of Rhaithou. He came to the mountain of Mount Sinai and came upon the Bush in a pass between two

8 This refers to the building activities that Justinian had commenced in Palestine after listening to the monk Saba.

9 B has 'his love for building churches and monasteries'.

10 B does not have 'entering the churches'.

11 Here B first transliterates the Greek *batos* into Arabic, then provides an Arabic gloss; Ch does not include the Greek word.

12 Not in B.

13 B: *near the bush there was.*

14 The Arabic letters, *mrt mrym*, represent the Syriac words 'Lady Mary' (*Mārat Maryam*), probably indicating the linguistic background of some of the monks inhabiting the area. On possible remains of this tower, see Grossmann 1988.

15 The Arabic has al-Qulzum. This is possibly the church mentioned in PP, *Itin.* 42.

16 *Raya.*

mountains and the tower built over it. He approached the Bush and the springs of water that issue forth near the Bush and the monks who were dispersed in the *wadis*. He was concerned to build the monastery on top of the mountain, abandoning the site of the tower and the Bush, but he decided against it for the sake of the water, because there was no water on top of the mountain. So he built the monastery over the Bush on the site of the tower with the tower inside the monastery, the monastery being between the two mountains, in the pass. If a person went up on the peak of the northern mountain and threw a rock, it could fall in the middle of the monastery and harm the monks, but he built the monastery on that pass only for the sake of the Bush, the distinguished antiquities, and the water. He built the church on the mountain top above where Moses took the Law. The name of the head of the monastery was Doulas.[17]

When the messenger returned to King Justinian, he informed him about the churches and monasteries he built and described for him how he built the monastery of Mount Sinai. The king said to him, 'You have erred, you have harmed the monks, and you have given the enemies power over them. Why did you not build the monastery on top of the mountain peak?'[18] The messenger said to him, 'It is over the Bush and near water that I built the monastery. If I had built the monastery on top of the mountain peak, then the monks would be left without water, and if an enemy were to besiege them and prevent them from getting water, they would die from thirst. The Bush would also be far from them.' The king said to him, 'Then you should have demolished the northern mountain that overlooks the monastery down to the ground so that the monks receive no harm from it.' The messenger said to him, 'If we were to spend the wealth of Rome, Egypt, and Syria, it would not be feasible for us to overtake that mountain.'[19] The king became angry at him and ordered him to be beheaded.

Then he sent another messenger and dispatched a hundred men from among the Roman slaves along with him, together with their wives and children, and ordered him to take from Egypt another hundred men from among the slaves, together with their wives and children. He built houses for them outside Mount Sinai for them to live in there, to guard the monastery

17 Arabic: *Dula*. Cf. Ammonius, *Rel.* 3, 9, 40, and Sinai Inscription no.17, discussed and translated above, General Introduction, pp. 28–29.

18 Forsyth 1973, 6, also observes that the situation of the Justinianic complex is peculiar, since it is vulnerable to attacks from the slopes. However, its situation may be explained by the need to enclose the site of the Bush and the basilica within its walls.

19 'to overtake the mountain' not in B.

and the monks, to provide them [i.e. the monks] with sustenance, and to bring the provisions they needed from Egypt to them and to the monastery. When the messenger arrived at Mount Sinai he built many residences outside the monastery to its east and fortified them, and put the slaves in residence in them. They would guard and defend the monastery. The place is called up to the present time 'The Slaves' Monastery'.[20]

When they had begotten children together and multiplied and much time had passed, and Islam appeared [there] – that happened in the caliphate of 'Abd al-Malik ibn Marwan[21] – they attacked one other and killed one other. Some of them were killed, some of them fled, and some converted to Islam. Their descendants in the monasteries, until the present time, are Muslims.[22] They are called the Banū Sālih, and they are dubbed 'servants of the monastery' up to today.[23] The Lakhmids are from them.[24] The monks destroyed the homes of the slaves after they converted to Islam so that no one could live in them. They are in ruins until today.[25]

20 *Dayr al-Abīd* (B has *Dār al-Abīd*, 'The Slaves' residence'). The phrase, 'outside the monastery to its east', would locate this structure (or encampment) near Jabal Muneijah-Musa at the east end of Wadi al-Dayr. According to Dahari 2000, 54, no Byzantine remains have been found there, but Müller 2006, 78, reports a recent discovery. The slaves in question probably are a later development (cf. Anast., *Narr.* II.8) that should not be confused with the imperial garrison mentioned in Procop., *Buildings* V.viii.9. For some reason Nandris 1990 and others seem to think these slaves came from Wallachia. There is no evidence for that in the text, unless it is a misunderstanding of the otherwise strange reference to Lakhmids, discussed below.

21 Umayyad caliph 685–705 CE, whose building of the Dome of the Rock and minting of aniconic currency reflect early efforts to Arabize or Islamicize regions conquered by his predecessors.

22 Cf. Anast., *Narr.* II.8 (perhaps not written until c. 690).

23 *ǧilmān ad-dayr*. This reference is odd. Having settled in Third Palestine by c. 400, the Banū Sālih were Rome's main ally in the region for the next hundred years, but their subsequent history is unknown: Shahid 1995b. On Mt Sinai's modern 'Jabaliyah' ('Mountain Tribe') and their relations with St Catherine's, see Bailey 1985; Hobbs 1995.

24 The reference is bizarre. Both B and Ch have *al-Lakhmīyīn*, indicating in their notes that the form might be slightly corrupt. Dr van Bladel tells me that the form is unusual: one might expect instead the form 'Banū Lakhm'. The Lakhmids were a pre-Islamic Arab dynasty centred in Iraq whose tribe, the Lakhm, was absorbed into the Judham tribe after the Arab Conquests: see Shahid 1986.

25 Robert Hoyland observes (personal communication), 'There is evidently something wrong with the last paragraph. Eutychius says that the descendants of the slaves living in the monasteries are Muslims "until the present time", but then says that "the monks destroyed the homes of the slaves after they converted to Islam so that no one could live in them". From the incompatibility of all the "until the present times" and "to this days" one may infer that Eutychius is using more than one source here, one (probably Greek) much earlier than the other (probably Arabic), and this may explain the confusion.'

THEOPHANES, *CHRONOGRAPHIA* AM 6123, 6124 (630/1 CE, 631/2 CE)*

The early ninth-century *Chronicle* compiled by the monk Theophanes the Confessor († 818) is our major source for Roman-Byzantine history of the seventh and eighth centuries. The following passages describe the initial Arab invasion of the Roman Empire through Third Palestine c. 630–632. Much of both entries derive from a Greek translation of a lost Syriac source, the so-called *Chronicle of 750*. Those portions are printed in a different typeface.[1]

TRANSLATION OF THE GREEK TEXT

Anno Mundi 6123 [630/1 CE]
Herakleios, [emperor of the Romans] 22nd year
Aboubacharus, leader of the Arabs (3 years), 1st year
Sergius [bishop of Constantinople (29 years)], 23rd year
Modestus, bishop of Jerusalem, (2 years),[2] 1st year
George, [bishop of Alexandria], 13th year

In this year the Persians rose up one against the other and fought in an internecine war. At the same time the King of India sent gratulatory gifts to Heraclius on the occasion of his victory over Persia, namely pearls and a considerable number of precious stones.[3]

---

* Trans. C. Mango and R. Scott, *The Chronicle of Theophanes Confessor: Byzantine and Near Eastern History AD 284–813* (Oxford, 1997), pp. 466–68, by permission of Oxford University Press. The original Greek text is edited by de Boor 1963, vol. 1, 335–36.

1 For introduction to Theophanes, see Mango–Scott 1997, lxxxii–lxxxiv and Conrad 1990. Conrad argues that some of the information in these passages also derived from a lost Arabic source. For earlier chronicles dealing with this period and its events, see Palmer 1993.

2 Other sources give Modestus one year or less as patriarch.

3 The defeat of the Persian Shah Chosroes II in 627 by the Roman emperor Heraclius (575–641) was facilitated by internecine strife, and soon gave rise to civil war in the Persian Empire.

Mouamed, who had died earlier, had appointed four emirs to fight those members of the Arab nation who were Christian,[4] and they came in front of a village called Mouchea,[5] in which was stationed the *vicarius* Theodore,[6] intending to fall upon the Arabs on the day when they were sacrificing to their idols.[7] The *vicarius*, on learning this from a certain Koraishite[8] called Koutabas[9] who was in his pay, gathered all the soldiers of the desert guard[10] and, after ascertaining from the Saracen the day and hour when they were intending to attack, himself attacked them at a village called Mothous, and killed three emirs and the bulk of their army. One emir, called Chaled, whom they call God's Sword,[11] escaped. Now some of the neighbouring Arabs were receiving small payments from the emperors for guarding the approaches to the desert. At that time a certain eunuch arrived to distribute the wages of the soldiers, and when the Arabs came to receive their wages according to custom, the eunuch drove them away, saying, 'The emperor can hardly pay his soldiers their wages, much less these dogs!' Distressed by this, the Arabs went over to their fellow-tribesmen, and it was they that led them to the rich country of Gaza, which is the gateway to the desert in the direction of Mount Sinai.[12]

4 Here Theophanes begins using his eastern source to describe the so-called battle of Mu'ta, dated 629 by Muslim sources (and so well before Muhammad's death). Mu'ta was a plain located south-east of the Dead Sea. For this event, see Kaegi 1992, 44, 71–78; Conrad 1990, 21–26.

5 Probably modern Al-Minha, overlooking the Mu'ta plain: thus Kaegi 1992, 72; for alternatives, see Mango–Scott 1997, 467 n. 3.

6 A *vicarius* was a deputy of the Praetorian Prefect: see Jones 1964, 373–75.

7 κατὰ τῶν Ἀράβων τῇ ἡμέρᾳ τῆς εἰδωλοθυσίας αὐτῶν. Mango–Scott 1997, 467 n. 4, believe this refers to Arab idolatry (cf. Anast., *Narr.* II.11, referring to Arab sacrifices before their 'stone'). But the passage seems to describe a plot against a Christian group. Conrad 1990, 23–26, argues that Theophanes was sloppy when transferring to his text an Arab account of a Christian festival, in which case the reference to 'idolatry' here would refer to the Christian use of icons, a practice that the Arab conquerors maligned (cf. Anast., *Narr.* I.4 and II.2).

8 *Korasēnos*, i.e. 'Qurayshite'. The Quraysh tribe controlled Mecca and other parts of the Hijaz; Muhammad came from one of its clans. See Watt 1986.

9 Presumably Qutba.

10 τοὺς στρατιώτας τῶν παραφυλάκων τῆς ἐρήμου. Kaegi 1992, 72, describes these as local Arab irregulars. However, the phrasing is similar to that used by Cyril of Scythopolis to describe the garrison that Justinian ordered to protect Sabas' monastery (*Life of Sabas* 72, ed. Schwartz, 178.8–10), and the guards here may be remnant *limitanei* like the camel corps posted at Nessana (see General Introduction, pp. 11–12; also PP, *Itin.* 40). Mayerson 1986, 40, cites this passage as an example of the Roman strategy of mustering a reserve force against (what were perceived to be minor) Saracen incursions.

11 Khālid ibn al-Walīd (584–642), largely responsible for the Muslim capture of Damascus in 635 and victory at Yarmuk in 636.

12 ἐπὶ τὴν χώραν Γάζης στομίου οὔσης τῆς ἐρήμου κατὰ τὸ Σιναῖον ὄρος, i.e. the Negev. A different account is found in the later *Short History* of Nicephorus, patriarch of

Anno Mundi 6124 [631/2 CE]
Year of the divine Incarnation, 624
Heraclius, emperor of the Romans (31 years), 23rd year
Aboubacharus, leader of the Arabs (3 years), 2nd year
Sergius, bishop of Constantinople (29 years), 24th year
Modestus, bishop of Jerusalem, (2 years), 2nd year
George, bishop of Alexandria (14 years), 14th year

In this year Aboubacharos sent four generals who were conducted, as I said earlier, by the Arabs and so came and took Hera and the whole territory of Gaza.[13] At length, Sergius arrived with some difficulty with a few soldiers from Caesarea in Palestine.[14] He gave battle and was first to be killed along with his soldiers, who were 300.[15] Taking many captives and much booty, the Arabs returned home after their brilliant victory.

At the same time an earthquake occurred in Palestine; and there appeared a sign in the heavens called *dokites* in the direction of the south, foreboding the Arab conquest. It remained for thirty days, moving from south to north, and was sword-shaped.[16]

Constantinople (*Short History* 20, trans. Mango 1990, 69): 'Now Sergius *kata Niketan* died in the following manner. The Saracens, having flayed a camel, enclosed him in the hide and sewed it up. As the skin hardened, the man who was left inside also withered and so perished in a painful manner. The charge against him was that he had persuaded Herakleios not to allow the Saracens to trade from the Roman country and send out of the Roman state the 30 lbs. of gold which they normally received by way of commercial gain; and for this reason they began to lay waste the Roman land.'

On this *candidatus* Sergius (perhaps different from the one mentioned in the next entry), see *PLRE* III, *s.v.* 'Sergius 43'; Mango 1990, 187; Kaegi 1992, 88–89, 93.

13 ἔλαβον τὴν Ἥραν καὶ τὴν χώραν Γάζης. Mayerson 1964, 161–66, argues that the 'Hēra' here refers to Pharan on the Sinai peninsula, and is 'a garbled or clipped form of the Arabic name of the same site, Fārān Hārūn (Ahrūn)'. But Conrad 1990, 30, and Kaegi 1992, 55, 90–92, believe it refers to a 'camp' (from the Arabic *hīra*, used here in the Greek accusative) of Arabs posted as guards outside Gaza (as near Syrian cities, e.g. Beroea, Emesa, Chalkis).

On the four Arab commanders, see Donner 1981, 113–19. Abū Bakr died in 634, the traditional date for this invasion. Gaza did not fall until 637. We have a Latin account of a 60-man garrison that died in the siege: see *Passio sanctorum sexaginta martyrum* in Bibliography.

14 Caesarea (modern Qesaria, Israel) was the headquarters of the Roman military commander in Palestine, about 125 km/75 miles north of Gaza.

15 The Battle of Dāthin, February 634. See Kaegi 1992, 93–95.

16 A *dokitēs* was a meteor that appeared long in shape.

SINAI PLANS AND MAPS

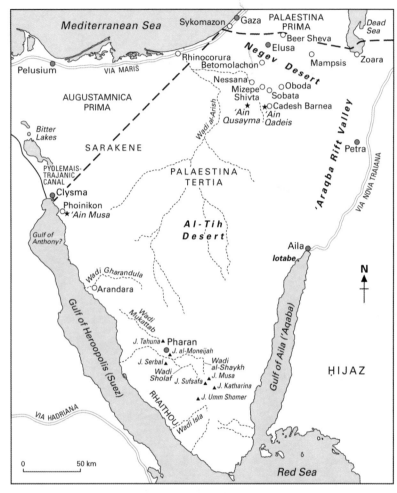

Map 2: Late Antique Sinai Peninsula and Negev Desert

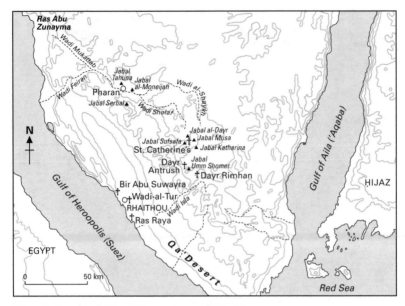

Map 3: Southern Sinai Mountains and Rhaithou

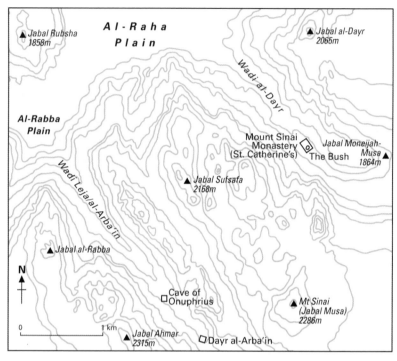

Map 4: Mount Sinai-Horeb (Jabal Musa-Susafa) Topography

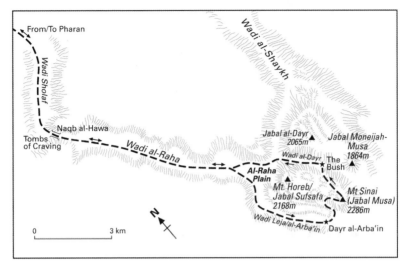

Map 5: Egeria's Mount Sinai Pilgrimage Route

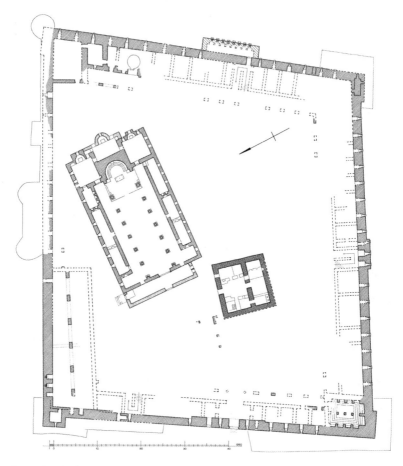

Plan 1: Justinian's Mount Sinai Fort and Church Complex (St Catherine's)
Courtesy of Peter Grossmann

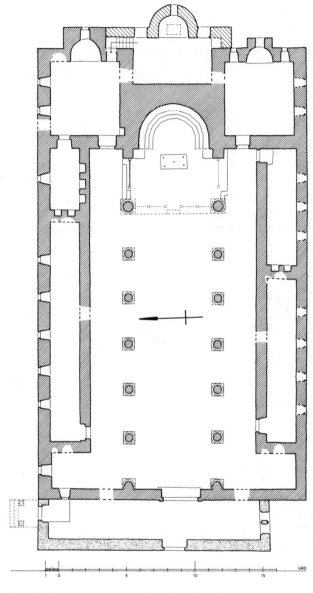

Plan 2: Justinian's Mount Sinai Basilica Church
Courtesy of Peter Grossmann

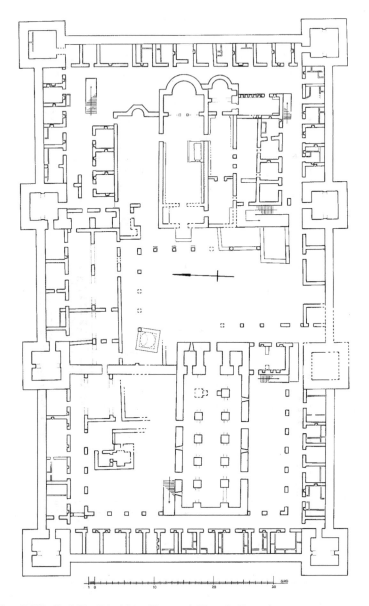

Plan 3: Wadi al-Tur/Rhaithou Fort and Church Complex
Courtesy of Peter Grossmann 2002, pl. 188

BIBLIOGRAPHY

SOURCE EDITIONS AND TRANSLATIONS

Achilles Tatius, *Leucippe and Clitophon*. Ed. E. Vilborg, 2 vols. (Stockholm, 1955–62). English trans. Winkler 1989b.

Acta Conciliorum Oecumenicorum, Tome II.I.3: *Concilium universale Chalcedonense*. Ed. E. Schwartz (Berlin and Leipzig, 1935).

Ammianus Marcellinus, *Res gestae*. Ed. W. Seyfarth. (Leipzig, 1978). English trans. J. C. Rolfe, *Ammianus Marcellinus: Roman History*, 3 vols., LCL 300, 315, 331 (Cambridge, MA, and London, 1936–39).

Ammonius, *Report on the Slaughter of the Monks of Sinai and Rhaithou (Relatio a Ammonio de monachis in Sina et Raithu interemptis)*. Arabic ('Ar.2') and Georgian version, ed. R. G. Gvaramia, *Amoniosis 'Sina-Raithis cmida mamatha mosrvis' arabul-k'art'uli versiebi* (Tbilisi, 1973). Christian Palestinian-Aramaic version ('CPA'), ed. with English trans. C. Müller-Kessler and M. Sokoloff, *A Corpus of Christian Palestinian Aramaic III: The Forty Martyrs of the Sinai Desert, Eulogios, the Stone-Cutter, and Anastasia* (Gröningen, 1996), 9–69; also ed. with English trans. A. S. Lewis, 'The Forty Martyrs of the Sinai Desert', *Horae Semiticae* 9 (1912), 1–24. Greek version ('SGr 519' and 'SGr 267'), ed. with modern Greek trans. D. G. Tsames and K. G. Katsanes, in *To Martyrologion tou Sina: periechei keimena kai metaphraseis peri tōn agōnōn, palaismatōn kai martyriōn tōn anairethentōn hagiōn paterōn en tōi theovadistōi orei Sina kai tēi sinaitikēi erēmōi hina mimēsamenei tēn aretēn tōn martyrōn toutōn kakei tōn stephanōn dynēthōmen autois koinōnēsai* (Thessaloniki, 1989), 194–234; also ed. F. Combéfis, *Illustrium Christi Martyrum Lecti Triumphi* (Paris, 1660), 88–132. Syriac versions ('V' and 'L') edn. forthcoming, M-J. Pierre.

Anastasius of Sinai, Collection I: *Tales of the Sinai Fathers (Diēgēmata paterika)*. Ed. A. Binggeli, forthcoming, CNRS; also ed. F. Nau, 'Le texte grec des récit du moine Anastase sur les saints pères du Sinaï', *Oriens Christianus* 2 (1902), 58–89. French trans. F. Nau, 'Les Récits inédits du moine Anastase: Contribution à l'Histoire du Sinaï au commencement du VIIe siècle', *Revue de l'Institut Catholique de Paris* 1–2 (1902), 1–70.

——, Collection II: *Edifying Tales (Diēgēmata stēriktika)*. Ed. A. Binggeli, forthcoming, CNRS; also ed. F. Nau, 'Le texte grec des récits utiles à l'âme d'Anastase (le Sinaïte)', *Oriens Christianus* 3 (1903), 56–75, 87–89.

Antony of Choziba, *Life of George of Choziba*. 'S. Georgii Chozebitae vita', *Analecta Bollandiana* 7 (1888), 95–144, 336–59. English trans. T. Vivian, *Journeying into God: Seven Early Monastic Lives* (Minneapolis, MI, 1996), 53–105.

Apophthegmata patrum, Greek alphabetical collection. PG 65.71–442.

——, Latin anonymous collection *(verba seniorum)*. PL 73.855A–1022A.

——, Syriac collection. Trans. E. W. Budge, *The Paradise of the Holy Fathers*, 2 vols. (London 1904, repr. New York, 1972).

Bardaisan of Edessa, *The Book of the Laws of Countries: Dialogue on Fate of Bardaisan of Edessa*. Ed. H. J. W. Drijvers (Assen, 1965).

Barsanuphius and John of Gaza, *Letters*. Ed. with French trans. F. Neyt and P. de Angeli-Noah, *Barsanuphe et Jean de Gaza: Correspondance*, 4 vols., SC 426, 427, 450, 451 (Paris, 1997–2002). English trans. J. Chryssavgis, *Barsanuphius and John: Letters*, 2 vols. (Washington, DC, 2006).

Chalcedon, Council of, *Acta*. See *Acta Conciliorum Oecumenicorum*, II. English trans. R. M. Price and M. Gaddis, *The Acts of the Council of Chalcedon*, 3 vols., TTH 45 (Liverpool, 2005).

Choricius of Gaza, *In Praise of Aratus and Stephanus*. Ed. R. Foerster and E. Richtsteig, *Choricii Gazae opera* (Stuttgart, 1972), 48–69.

Claudius Ptolemaius, *Geographia*. Ed. C. F. A. Nobbe (Hildesheim, 1966).

Cosmas Indicopleustes, *Topographia christiana*. Ed. W. Wolska-Conus, *Cosmas Indicopleustès: Topographie Chrétienne*, 3 vols., SC 141, 159, 197 (Paris, 1968–73).

Cyril of Scythopolis. Ed. E. Schwartz, *Kyrillos von Skythopolis*, TU 49 (Leipzig, 1939). English trans. R. M. Price, *Cyril of Scythopolis: The Lives of the Monks of Palestine*, CS 114 (Kalamazoo, MI, 1991).

Daniel of Rhaithou, *Life of John Climacus*. PG 88.596A–609B. English trans. L. Moore, *St John Climacus: The Ladder of Divine Ascent* (London, 1959), 35–39.

Egeria, *Travelogue (Itinerarium)*. Ed. with French trans. P. Maraval, *Égérie: Journal de Voyage (Itinéraire)*, SC 296 (Paris, 1997). English trans. Wilkinson 1999. Abridgements by Petrus Deaconus: see Peter the Deacon.

Ephraim, *Hymns on Julian Saba 19* and *20*. Ed. E. Beck, *Des heiligen Ephraem des Syrers Hymnen auf Abraham Kidunaya und Julianos Saba*, CSCO 322, Script. Syri 140 (Louvain, 1972), 71–76. German trans. E. Beck, *Des heiligen Ephraem des Syrers Hymnen auf Abraham Kidunaya und Julianos Saba*, CSCO 323, Script. Syri 141 (Louvain, 1972), 75–79.

Eusebius of Caesarea, *Ecclesiastical History [EH]*. Ed. with French trans. G. Bardy, *Eusèbe de Césarée: Histoire ecclésiastique*, 4 vols., SC 31, 41, 55, 73 (Paris, 1952–60).

Eutychius (Sa'īd ibn Batrīq), *Annals (Annales Ecclesiastici)*. Ed. with German trans. M. Breydy, *Das Annalenwerk des Eutychios von Alexandrien; ausgewählte Geschichten und Legenden kompiliert von Said ibn Batriq um 935 AD*, CSCO 417/472, Script. Arabici 44 (Louvain, 1985); also ed. L. Cheikho, B. Carra de Vaux, and H. Zayyat, *Eutychii Patriarchae Alexandrini Annales*, CSCO 50/51; Script. Arabici 3:6–7 (Paris, 1906–09). Latin trans. PG 111.903A–1156A.

Evagrius Ponticus, *Eight Thoughts* and *On Thoughts*. English trans. R. E. Sinkewicz, *Evagrius of Pontus: The Greek Ascetic Corpus* (Oxford, 2003), 66–90, 236–82.

Evagrius Scholasticus, *Ecclesiastical History [EH]*. English trans. Michael Whitby, *The Ecclesiastical History of Evagrius Scholasticus*, TTH 33 (Liverpool, 2000).

Gregory the Great, *Letters IV.44* ('To Rusticiana') and *XI.2* ('To John, Abbot of Mt. Sinai'). Ed. D. Norberg (Turnhout, 1982), 264–65, 857–59. English trans. J. C. R. Martin, *The Letters of Gregory the Great*, 3 vols. (Toronto, 2004).

Jacob of Serug, *Letter VII* ('To the Monks of Sinai'). Ed. G. Olinder, *Iacobi Sarugensis Epistulae quotquot supersunt*, CSCO 110, Script. Syri 57 (Louvain, 1937, 1952), 34–37.

Jerome, *Life of Hilarion*. PL 23.29–60. English trans. C. White, *Early Christian Lives* (London and New York, 1998), 87–115.

John Cassian, *Conferences*. Ed. M. Petschenig and G. Kreutz, *Cassiani Collationes I–XIII*, CSEL 13.2 (Vienna, 2004). English trans. B. Ramsay, *John Cassian: The Conferences*, ACW 57 (Mahwah, NJ, 1997).

John Climacus, *Ladder of Divine Ascent*, PG 88.632A–1164D. English trans. C. Luibheid and N. Russell, *John Climacus: The Ladder of Divine Ascent* (Mahwah, NJ, 1982).

John Moschus, *Spiritual Meadow [Meadow; Pratum spirtuale]*. PG 87[3].2851–3112. French trans. M.-J. de Journel, *Jean Moschus: Le Pré Spirituel*, SC 12 (Paris, 1946). English trans. J. Wortley, *The Spiritual*

Meadow of John Moschus, CS 139 (Kalamazoo, MI, 1992).

John of Nikiu, *Chronicle*. English trans. R. H. Charles (London, 1916).

John Rufus of Maïouma, *Plerophoriae*. Ed. with French trans. F. Nau, PO 8.1–208 (Paris, 1912).

Justinian, *Novels*. Ed. R. Schoell and W. Kroll, *Corpus iuris civilis*, vol. 3 (6th edn, Berlin, 1954).

Life of Abramius: see Cyril of Scythopolis.

Life of Barṣawma: see Nau 1913.

Life of Cyriacus: see Cyril of Scythopolis.

Life of Euthymius: see Cyril of Scythopolis.

Life of George of Choziba: see Antony of Choziba.

Life of Hilarion: see Jerome.

Life of James. Ed. and trans. E. W. Brooks in *John of Ephesus, The Lives of the Eastern Saints*, Appendix: 'The Spurious Life of James', PO 19.228–68.

Life of John Climacus: see Daniel of Rhaithou.

Life of Mary of Egypt: see Kouli 1996.

Life of John the Hesychast: see Cyril of Scythopolis.

Life of Paul the Bishop and John the Priest. Greek version, ed. A. Papadopoulos-Kerameus, *Analekta Hiersolymitikēs stachylogias* 5 (1898), 368–83. Syriac version, edn forthcoming, H. Arneson, C. Luckritz-Marquis and K. Smith.

Life of Sabas: see Cyril of Scythopolis.

Life of Theodosius: see Cyril of Scythopolis.

Life of Theognius: see Paul of Elusa.

Nessana papyri: see Casson and Hettich 1950; Kraemer 1958.

Nicephorus, *Short History*. English trans. Mango 1990.

Nilus of Ancyra, *Letter IV.64* ('To Heliodorus the Silentiary'). Ed. J. D. Mansi, *Sacrorum conciliorum nova et amplissima collectio* 13 (Florence, 1767; Paris 1901), 32C–33C; also ed. L. Allacci, PG 79.580B–581B.

Nilus, Pseudo, *Narrationes* (= *Narrations*, BHG 1301–1307). Ed. F. Conca, *Nilus Ancyranus Narratio* (Leipzig, 1983) (= Conca 1983a); also ed. with German trans. M. Link, *Die Erzählung des Pseudo-Neilos - ein spätantiker Märtyrerroman* (Leipzig, 2005); also ed. with Latin trans. P. Poussines, *Narrationes VII de caedibus monachorum montis Sinae et captivitate Theoduli filii eius* (Paris 1639; PG 79.589–693), repr. with modern Greek trans. in D. G. Tsames and K. G. Katsanes, *To Martyrologion tou Sina: periechei keimena kai metaphraseis peri tōn agōnōn, palaismatōn kai martyriōn tōn anairethentōn hagiōn paterōn en tōi theovadistōi orei Sina kai tēi sinaitikēi erēmōi hina mimēsamenei tēn aretēn tōn martyrōn toutōn kakei tōn stephanōn dynēthōmen autois koinōnēsai* (Thessaloniki, 1989), 256–356.

Nonnosus, *Historia,* fragments. Ed. C. Müller, *Fragmenta Historicorum Graecorum* 4 (Frankfurt am Main, 1975), 179–80. English trans. J. H. Freese, *The Library of Photius* (London, 1920), 18–19.

Passio sanctorum sexaginta martyrum. Ed. H. Delehaye, *Analecta Bollandiana* 23 (1904), 289–307.

Paul of Elusa, *Life of Theognis.* English trans. T. Vivian, *Journeying into God: Seven Early Monastic Lives* (Minneapolis, MI, 1996), 134–65.

Peter the Deacon, *De locis sanctis*, section Y (= Egeria abbridgements). Ed. P. Geyer, *Itineraria et alia Geographica,* CCSL 175 (Turnhout, 1965), 100–03.

Piacenza Pilgrim, *Travelogue (Itinerarium).* Ed. P. Geyer in *Itineraria et alia geographica*, CCSL 175 (Turnhout, 1965), 129–53 (= Recension I), 158–74 (= Recension II).

Procopius of Caesarea. *On Buildings [de Aedificibus].* Ed. J. Haury, *Procopii Caesariensis opera omnia* III.2 (Leipzig, 1905). Rev. with English trans. H. B. Dewing, *Procopius: Buildings*, LCL 343 (Cambridge, MA, and London, 1940, 1954).

——. *Wars.* Ed. J. Haury, *Procopii Caesariensis opera omnia*, vols. I–III (Leipzig, 1913). Rev. with English trans. H. B. Dewing, *Procopius: Wars*, LCL 48, 81, 107, 173, 217 (Cambridge, MA, and London 1914–28, 1954).

Severus of Anioch, *Homily 18* ('On the Holy Martyrs'). English trans. P. Allen and C. T. R. Hayward, *Severus of Antioch* (London and New York, 2004), 118–26.

Socrates, *Ecclesiastical History [EH].* Ed. G. C. Hansen and M. Sirinjan, *Sokrates Kirchengeschichte*, GCS n.F. 1 (Berlin, 1995).

Sozomen, *Ecclesiastical History [EH].* Ed. J. Bidez and G. C. Hansen, *Sozomenus Kirchengeschichte*, GCS n.F. 4 (Berlin, 1995).

Sulpicius Severus, *Dialogus.* Ed. C. Halm, *Sulpitii Severi libri qui supersunt*, CSEL 1 (Vienna, 1866).

Synaxarium Ecclesiae Constantinopolitanae e codice Sirmondiano (= Propylaeum ad AS Novembris). Ed. H. Delehaye (Brussels, 1902).

Theodoret of Cyrrhus, *Ecclesiastical History [EH].* Ed. L. Parmentier and G. C. Hansen, *Theodoret Kirchengeschichte [EH]*, GCS n.F. 5 (Berlin, 1998).

——. *Religious History [Historia religiosa].* Ed. with French trans. P.

Canivet and A. Leroy-Molinghen, *Théodoret de Cyr: Histoire des moines de Syrie*, 2 vols., SC 234, 257 (Paris, 1977–79). English trans. R. M. Price, *Theodoret of Cyrrhus: A History of the Monks of Syria* (Kalamazoo, MI, 1985).

Theodosius, *On the Situation of the Holy Land* (*De situ terrae sanctae*). Ed. P. Geyer, *Itineraria et alia geographica*, CCSL 175 (Turnhout, 1965), 115–24.

Theophanes Confessor, *Chronographia*. Ed. C. de Boor, *Theophanis Chronographia* (Hildesheim, 1963). English trans. C. Mango and R. Scott, *The Chronicle of Theophanes Confessor: Byzantine and Near Eastern History AD 284–813* (Oxford, 1997).

Valerius of Bierzo, *Epistula Beatissime Egerie*. Ed. with French trans. M. C. Díaz y Díaz in P. Maraval, *Égérie: Journal de Voyage* (*Itinéraire*), SC 296 (Paris, 1997), 337–48.

Zacharias of Mitylene, Pseudo, *Chronicle*. English trans. F. J. Hamilton and E. W. Brooks, *The Ecclesiastical History of Ps.-Zachariah of Mitylene* (London, 1899).

SECONDARY WORKS

'Abd al-Malik, S. S. 1998. 'Les mosqués du Sinaï au Moyen Âge'. In Bonnet and Valbelle 1998: 171–76.

Abel, F. M. 1924. 'Une mention byzantine de Sbaïta', *Byzantion* 1: 41–58.

——. 1933. *Géographie de la Palestine I: Géographie physique et historique* (3rd edn, Paris).

——. 1935. 'Note sur Subaïta', *Journal of the Palestine Oriental Society* 15: 7–11.

Adams, B. 1964. *Paramoné und verwandte Texte: Studien zum Dienstvertrag im Rechte der Papyri* (Berlin).

Aharoni, Y. 1954. 'The Roman Road to Aila (Elath)', *IEJ* 4: 9–16.

Alexiou, M. 2002. *The Ritual Lament in Greek Tradition* (2nd edn, ed. D. Yatromanolakis and P. Roilos, New York and Oxford).

Alt, A. 1921. 'Die griechischen Inschriften der Palaestina Tertia westlich in der 'Araba'. In *Wissenschaftliche Veröffentlichungen des deutsch-türkischen Denkmalschutz-Kommandos*, ed. Th. Wiegand (Berlin and Leipzig).

Anastos, M. V. 1946. 'The Alexandrian Origin of the Christian Topography of Cosmas Indicopleustes', *DOP* 3: 73–80.

Andreopoulos, A. 2002. 'The Mosaic of the Transfiguration in St Cathe-rine's Monastery on Mount Sinai: A Discussion of its Origins', *Byzantion* 72: 9–41.

Armstrong, G. 1969. 'Fifth and Sixth-Century Church Building in the Holy Land', *Greek Orthodox Theological Review* 14: 17–30.

Avi-Yonah, M. 1953. 'The Economics of Byzantine Palestine', *IEJ* 8: 39–51.

Avni, G. 1996. *Nomads, Farmers, and Town Dwellers: Pastoralist-Seden-tist Interaction in the Negev Highlands, Sixth-Eighth Centuries CE* (Jerusalem).

Bailey, C. 1985. 'Dating the Arrival of the Bedouin Tribes in Sinai and the Negev', *JESHO* 28: 20–49.

Banning, E. B. 1986. 'Peasants, Pastoralists and *Pax Romana*: Mutualism in the Southern Highlands of Jordan', *BASOR* 261: 25–50.

Bar Yosef, O. 1977. 'The Nawamis near 'Ein Huderah (Eastern Sinai)', *IEJ* 27: 65–88.

Barker, G. 2002. 'A Tale of Two Deserts: Contrasting Desertification Histo-ries on Rome's Desert Frontiers', *World Archaeology* 33: 488–507.

Barnard, H. 2005. 'Sire, il n'y a pas de Blemmyes: A Re-Evaluation of Historical and Archaeological Data'. In *People of the Red Sea: Proceed-ings of the Red Sea Project II*, ed. J. C. M. Starkey (Oxford), 23–40.

Barth, F. 1961. *Nomads of South Persia: The Basseri Tribe of the Khamseh Confederacy* (Boston).

Baumgarten, J. 1993. 'Mizpe Shivta'. In *New Encyclopaedia of Archaeo-logical Excavation in the Holy Land*, vol. 3, ed. E. Stern, A. Lewinson-Gilboa, and J. Aviram (New York), 1059–61.

Beaton, R. 2003. 'The Byzantine Revival of the Ancient Novel'. In *The Novel in the Ancient World*, ed. G. Schmeling (Boston and Leiden), 713–33.

Beaux, N., and Boutros, R. 1998. 'Ermitages chrétiens autour du mont Moïse'. In Bonnet and Valbelle 1998: 139–43.

Beneševic, V. 1924. 'Sur la date de la mosaïque de la Transfiguration au Mont Sinaï', *Byzantion* 1: 145–72.

Binggeli, A. 2001. 'Anastase le Sinaïte, Récits sur le Sinaï et Récits utiles à l'âme: édition, traduction, commentaire', 2 vols. (unpublished PhD thesis, University of Paris).

——. 2004. 'Un nouveau témoin des Narrationes d'Anastase le Sinaïte dans les membra disjecta d'un manuscrit sinaïtique (*Sinaiticus MG 6 + MG 21*)', *Revue des Études Byzantines* 62: 261–68.

——. 2005. 'La version syriaque des Récits d'Anastase le Sinaïte et l'activité des moines syriaques au Mont Sinaï aux VIIIe-IXe siècles'. In

Patrimoine syriaque. Actes du Colloque IX. Les Syriaques transmetteurs de civilisations: l'expérience du Bilâd el-Shâm à l'époque umayyade (Antelais), 165–77.

Birchall, J. 1996. 'Lament as a Rhetorical Feature in the Greek Novel', *Gröningen Colloquia on the Novel* 7: 1–17.

Bitton-Ashkelony, B. 2005. *Encountering the Sacred: The Debate on Christian Pilgrimage in Late Antiquity* (Transformation of the Classical Heritage 37; Berkeley and Los Angeles).

Bonnet, Ch., and Valbelle, D. 1998. *Le Sinaï durant l'antiquité et le Moyen Age: 4000 ans d'histoire pour un désert: acts du colloque 'Sinaï' ui s'est tenu à l'UNSECO du 19 au 21 septembre 1997* (Paris).

Bordreuil, P. 1998. 'L'image du Sinai dans l'Ancien Testament'. In Bonnet and Valbelle 1998: 116–18.

Bourdon, C. 1924. 'La route de l'Exode, de la terre de Gesse à Mara'. *Revue Biblique* 41: 225–42.

Bosworth, C. E. 1986. 'Djudham'. In *The Encyclopaedia of Islam*, vol. 2, ed. C. E. Bosworth, E. van Donzel, B. Lewis, and Ch. Pellat (2nd edn, Leiden), 253.

Bowersock, G. W. 1980. 'Mavia, Queen of the Saracens'. In *Studien zur Antiken Sozialgeschichte. Festschrift Friedrich Vittinghoff*, ed. W. Eck, H. Galsterer, and H. Wolff (Cologne), 477–95.

——. 1983. *Roman Arabia* (Cambridge, MA).

——. 1987. 'Arabs and Saracens in the Historia Augusta'. In *Bonner Historia-Augusta Colloquium: 1984/85*, ed. W. Ameling and J. Straub (Bonn), 71–80.

——. 1990. *Hellenism in Late Antiquity* (Ann Arbor, MI).

Braun, J. M. 1973. 'St. Catherine's Monastery Church, Mount Sinai: Literary Sources from the Fourth through the Nineteenth Centuries' (unpublished PhD thesis., University of Michigan, Ann Arbor).

Brock, S. 2003. 'Syriac on Sinai: The Main Connections'. In *Eukosmia: Studi miscellanei per il 75o di Vincenzo Poggi S.J.*, ed. V. Ruggieri and L. Pieralli (Soveria Mannelli), 103–17.

Brown, P. 1988. *The Body and Society: Men, Women, and Sexual Renunciation in Early Christianity* (New York).

——. 1992. *Power and Persuasion in Late Antiquity: Towards a Christian Empire* (Madison, WI).

——. 1999. '*Gloriosus Obitus*: The End of the Ancient Other World'. In *The Limits of Ancient Christianity: Essays on Late Antique Thought and Culture in Honor of R.A. Markus*, ed. W. E. Klingshirn and M. Vessey (Ann Arbor, MI), 289–314.

Brünnow, R.-E., and von Domaszewski, A. 1904–1909. *Die Provincia Arabia*, 3 vols. (Strasbourg).

Bruyère, B. 1966. *Fouilles de Clysma-Qolzoum (Suez) 1930–1932* (Cairo).

Cameron, Alan. 1976. 'The Authenticity of the Letters of St. Nilus of Ancyra', *Greek, Roman, and Byzantine Studies* 17: 181–96. Repr. with additional notes in idem, *Literature and Society in the Early Byzantine World* (London, 1985), VI.

Cameron, Averil. 1979. 'A Nativity Poem of the Sixth Century A.D.', *Classical Philology* 74: 222–32.

——. 1985. *Procopius and the Sixth Century* (Transformation of the Classical Heritage 10; Berkeley).

——. 1991. *Christianity and the Rhetoric of Empire: The Development of Christian Discourse* (Berkeley and Los Angeles).

Caner, D. 2004. 'Sinai Pilgrimage and Ascetic Romance: Pseudo-Nilus' *Narrationes* in Context'. In *Travel, Communication and Geography in Late Antiquity: Sacred and Profane,* ed. L. Ellis and F. Kidner (Aldershot), 135–48.

——. 2006. 'Towards a Miraculous Economy: Christian Gifts and Material Blessings in Late Antiquity', *JECS* 14: 329–77.

Canivet, P. 1977. *Le monachisme syrien selon Théodoret de Cyr* (Théologie historique 42; Paris).

Carrié, J.-M., Duval, N., and Roueché, C. 2000. *De Aedificiis: Le texte de Procope et les réalités* (Antiquité tardive 8; Turnhout).

Casson, L., and Hettich, E. L. 1950. *Excavations at Nessana*, vol. 2: *Literary Papyri* (Princeton).

Chitty, D. 1966. *The Desert A City: An Introduction to the Study of Egyptian and Palestinian Monasticism under the Christian Empire* (Oxford).

Christides, V. 1972. 'The Names *ARABES, SARAKHNOI* etc. and their False Byzantine Etymologies', *BZ* 65: 329–33.

——. 1973. 'Once again the 'Narrations' of Nilus Sinaiticus', *Byzantion* 43: 39–50.

Chryssavgis, J. 2004. *John Climacus: From the Egyptian Desert to the Sinaite Mountain* (Aldershot).

Clark, E., 1998. 'The Lady Vanishes: Dilemmas of a Feminist Historian after the "Linguistic Turn"', *Church History* 67: 1–31.

Colt, H. D., ed. 1962. *Excavations at Nessana (Auja Hafir, Palestine)*, vol. 1 (London).

Conca, F. 1982. 'Osservazioni sullo stile di Nilo Ancirano', *XVI. Internationaler Byzantinistenkongreß* 2.3: 217–25 (Vienna).

——. 1983a. *Nilus Ancyranus Narratio* (Leipzig).

——. 1983b. 'Le Narrationes di Nilo e il romanzo greco'. In *Studi bizantini e neogreci. Atti del IV congresso nazionale di studi bizantini: Lecce 21-23 aprile 1980* (Galatina), 343–54.

Conrad, L. 1990. 'Theophanes and the Arabic Historical Tradition: Some Indications of Intercultural Transmission', *Byzantinische Forschungen* 15: 1–44.

Constas, N. 2000. '"To Sleep, Perchance to Dream": The Middle State of Souls in Patristic and Byzantine Literature', *DOP* 55: 91–125.

Dagron, G. 1991. 'Holy Images and Likeness', *DOP* 45: 23–33.

Dahari, U. 1993. 'Remote Monasteries in Southern Sinai and their Economic Base'. In *Ancient Churches Revealed*, ed. Y. Tsafrir (Jerusalem), 341–50.

——. 1998a. 'Les constructions de Justinien au Gebel Mousa'. In Bonnet and Valbelle 1998: 151–56.

——. 1998b. 'Les lointains monastères du sud du Sinaï'. In Bonnet and Valbelle 1998: 144–50.

——. 2000. *Monastic Settlements in South Sinai in the Byzantine Period: The Archaeological Remains* (Israel Antiquities Authority Reports 9; Jerusalem).

Dan, Y. 1982. 'Palaestina Salutaris (Tertia) and its Capital', *Israel Exploration Journal* 32: 134–37.

De Bruyne, D. 1909. 'Nouveaux fragments de l'Itinerarium Eucheriae', *Revue Bénédictine* 26: 481–87.

Devos, P. 1967. 'La date du voyage d'Égérie', *Analecta Bollandiana* 85: 165–94.

Devreesse, R. 1940a. 'Le christianisme dans la péninsule sinaïtique des origines à l'arrivée des Musulmans', *Revue Biblique* 49: 205–23.

——. 1940b. 'Le christianisme dans le Sud Palestinien (Négeb)', *Revue des sciences religieuses* 20: 235–51.

Di Segni, L. 2004. 'The Beer Sheva Edict Reconsidered', *Scripta Classica Israelica* 23: 131–58.

Dihle, A. 1964. 'The Conception of India in Hellenistic and Roman Literature', *Proceedings of the Cambridge Philological Society* 190: 15–23.

Donahue, C. 1959. 'The ΑΓΑΡΗ of the Hermits of Scete', *Studia Monastica* 1: 97–114.

Donner, F. M. 1989. 'The role of nomads in the Near East in Late Antiquity (400-800)'. In *Tradition and Innovation in Late Antiquity,* ed. F. M. Clover and R. S. Humphreys (Madison, WI), 73–85.

Ducène, J.-C. 2002. 'Une description arabe du 4ème/10ème siècle du mont

Sinai', *Acta Orientalia Academiae Scientiarum Hungaricae* 55: 319–26.

Duffy, J. 1999. 'Embellishing the Steps: Elements of Presentation and Style in *The Heavenly Ladder*', *DOP* 53: 1–17.

Eckenstein. L. 1921. *A History of Sinai* (New York).

Elert, E. 1951. 'Theodore von Pharan und Theodor von Raithu', *Theologische Literaturzeitung* 76: 67–76.

Elsner, J. 1995. *Art and the Roman Viewer: The Transformation of Art from Pagan World to Christianity* (Cambridge).

Elter, R., and Hassoune, A. 2005. 'Le monastère de saint Hilarion: les vestiges archéologiques du site de Umm el-'Amr'. In *Gaza dans l'Antiquité tardive: Archéologie, rhétorique et histoire. Actes du colloque international de Poitiers* (6-7 mai 2004), ed. C. Saliou (Salerno), 13–40.

Erickson-Gini, T. 2004. 'Crisis and Renewal – Settlement in the Central Negev in the Third and Fourth Centuries CE with an Emphasis on the Finds from Recent Excavations in Mampsis, Oboda and Mezad 'En Hazeva' (unpublished PhD thesis, The Hebrew University of Jerusalem; Jerusalem).

Evans, J. A .S. 1996. 'The Date of Procopius' Works: A Recapitulation of the Evidence', *Greek, Roman and Byzantine Studies* 37: 301–13.

Evenari, M., Shanan, L., and Tadmor, N. 1982. *The Negev: The Challenge of a Desert* (Cambridge, MA).

Évieux, P. 1995. *Isidore de Péluse* (Théologie historique 99; Paris).

Fabian, P. 1995. 'The Late Roman Military Camp at Beer Sheba'. In *The Roman and Byzantine Near East: Some Recent Archaeological Research*, ed. J. H. Humphrey (Journal of Roman Archaeology, Supplementary Series 14; Ann Arbor, MI), 235–40.

Fahd, T. 1968. *Le panthéon de l'Arabie centrale à la veille de l'Hégire* (Paris).

Feissel, D. 2000. 'Les édifices de Justinien au témoignage de Procope et de l'épigraphie'. In Carrié, Duval, and Roueché 2000: 81-104.

Figueras, P. 1981. 'The Christian History of the Negev and Northern Sinai'. In *Christianity in the Holy Land*, ed. D. A. Jaeger (Studia Oecumenica Hierosolymitana 1; Jerusalem), 147–68.

——. 1982. 'Beersheva in the Roman-Byzantine Period', *Boletín de la Asociación Española de Orientalistas* 16: 135–62.

——. 1985. *Byzantine inscriptions from Beer-Sheva and the Negev* (Beer-Sheva).

——. 1995. 'Monks and Monasteries in the Negev Desert', *Liber Annus* 45: 401–50.

———. 2000. *From Gaza to Pelusium: Materials for the Historical Geography of North Sinai and South-West Palestine 332 BCE-640 CE* (Beer Sheva).

Finkelstein, I. 1981. 'Byzantine Prayer Niches in Southern Sinai', *IEJ* 31: 81–91.

———. 1995. *Living on the Fringe: The Archaeology and History of the Negev, Sinai, and Neigbouring Regions in the Bronze and Iron Ages* (Sheffield).

Fitschen, K. 1998. *Messalianismus und Antimessalianismus: ein Beispiel der ostkirchliche Ketzergeschichte* (Forschungen zur Kirchen- und Dogmengeschichte 71; Göttingen).

Fliche, A. and Martin, V. 1937. *Histoire de l'Église, vol. 4: De la mort de Théodose à l'élection de Grégoire le Grand* (Paris).

Flinders Petrie, W. M. 1906. *Researches in Sinai* (London).

Flusin, B. 1991. 'Démons et sarrasins', *Travaux et Memoirs* 11: 381–409.

———. 1992. *Saint Anastase le Perse et l'histoire de la Palestine au début du VIIe siècle*, 2 vols. (Paris).

———. 1998. 'Ermitages et monastére. Le monachisme au mont Sinaï à la période protobyzantine'. In Bonnet and Valbelle 1998: 133–38.

———. 2006. 'Le monachisme du Sinaï à l'époque de Jean Climaque', *Contacts: Revue française de l'Orthodoxie* 214: 190–217.

Forsyth, G .H. 1968. 'The Monastery of St. Catherine at Mount Sinai: The Church and the Fortress of Justinian', *DOP* 22: 3–19.

———. 1985. 'The Monastery of St. Catherine at Mount Sinai: The Church and Fortress of Justinian'. In J. Galey, *Sinai and the Monastery of S. Catherine* (Cairo), 49–64.

———, and Weitzmann, K. 1973. *The Monastery of St. Catherine at Mount Sinai: The Church and Fortress of Justinian* (Ann Arbor, MI).

Foss, C. 1977. 'Late Antique and Byzantine Ankara', *DOP* 31: 29–87.

———. 1995. 'The Near Eastern Countryside in Late Antiquity: A Review Article'. In *The Roman and Byzantine Near East: Some Recent Archaeological Research,* ed. J. H. Humphrey (Journal of Roman Archaeology Supplemental Series 14; Ann Arbor, MI), 213–34.

Fowden, G. 1993. *Empire to Commonwealth: Consequences of Monotheism in Late Antiquity* (Princeton).

Frank, G. 2000. *The Memory of the Eyes. Pilgrims to Living Saints in Christian Late Antiquity* (Transformation of the Classical Heritage 30; Berkeley and Los Angeles).

Gatier, P.-L. 1989. 'Les Traditions et l'histoire du Sinaï du IVe au VIIe siècle'. In *L'Arabie préislamique et son environnement historique et culturel. Actes du Colloque de Strasbourg 24–27 juin 1987*, ed. T.

Fahd (Travaux du Centre de Recherche sur le Proche-Orient et la Grèce Antiques 10; Leiden), 499–533.

Géhin, P. 1998. 'La bibliothèque de Sainte-Catherine du Sinaï. Fonds ancien et nouvelles découvertes'. In Bonnet and Valbelle 1998: 157–64.

Gerster, G. 1962. *Sinaï, Terre de la Révélation* (Paris).

Glucker, C. A. M. 1987. *The City of Gaza in the Roman and Byzantine Periods* (Oxford).

Gould, G. 1993. *The Desert Fathers on Monastic Community* (Oxford).

Graf, D. 1978. 'The Saracens and the Defense of the Arabian Frontier', *BASOR* 229: 1–26.

——. 1989. 'Rome and the Saracens: Reassessing the Nomadic Menace'. In *L'Arabie préislamique et son environnement historique et culturel. Actes du Colloque de Strasbourg 24–27 juin 1987*, ed. T. Fahd (Travaux du Centre de Recherche sur le Proche-Orient et la Grèce Antiques 10; Leiden), 341–400.

——. 2000. 'Map 76: Sinai, Introduction'. On CD-Rom in Talbert 2000.

——. and O'Connor, M. 1977. 'The Origin of the Term Saracen and the Rawwāfā Inscriptions', *Byzantine Studies/Études Byzantines* 4: 52–66.

Granić, B. 1929. 'Die rechtliche Stellung und Organisation der griechischen Klöster nach dem justinianischen Recht', *BZ* 29: 6–34.

Greatrex, G. 1994. 'The Dates of Procopius' Works', *Byzantine and Modern Greek Studies* 18: 101–14.

Greenwood, N. H. 1997. *The Sinai: A Physical Geography* (Austin, TX).

Gribomont, J. 1969. 'La tradition manuscrite de saint Nil. 1. La correspondence', *Studia Monastica* 11: 231–67.

Griffith, S. 1985. 'The Arabic Account of 'Abd al-Masīh an-Nagrani al-Ghassani', *Le Muséon* 98: 337–42.

——. 1987. 'Anastasios of Sinai, the Hodegos and the Muslims', *Greek Orthodox Historical Review* 32: 341–58.

——. 1994. 'Julian Saba, "Father of the Monks" of Syria', *JECS* 2: 185–216.

——. 1997. 'From Aramaic to Arabic. The Languages of the Monasteries of Palestine in the Byzantine and Early Islamic Periods', *DOP* 51: 11–31.

Grossmann, P. 1988. 'Neue baugeschichtliche Untersuchungen im Katharinenkloster im Sinai', *Archäologischer Anzeiger* 3: 543–58.

——. 1991. 'Keep'. In *The Coptic Encyclopedia*, vol. 5, ed. A. S. Atiya (New York), 1395–96.

——. 1996. 'Report on the Season in Firan-Sinai (February-March 1992)', *Byzantinsche Zeitschrift* 89: 11–36.

——. 1999. 'Besuche und Überfälle in der vorjustinianischen Laura am

Mosesberg: Zur Glaubwürdigkeit der diesbezüglichen Quellentexte im Hinblick auf die mitgeteilten topographischen Gegebenheiten', *BZ* 92: 455–65.

——. 1999–2000. 'Wadi Fayran/Sinai. Report on the seasons in March and April 1985 and 1986 with an appendix on the church at Mount Moses', *Annales du service des antiquités de l'Égypte* 75: 153–65.

——. 2001. 'Early Monks at Mount Moses and Justinian's Monastery', *Pegaso: rivista annuale di cultura mediterranea* 1: 177–201.

——. 2002. *Christliche Architektur in Ägypten* (Handbook of Oriental Studies 1; Leiden).

Guidi, I. 1906. 'Une description arabe du Sinaï', *Revue Biblique* 3: 433–42.

Guillou, A. 1955. 'Le monastère de la Théotokos au Sinaï', *Mélanges d' archéologie et d'histoire* 67: 217–58.

Gutwein, K. C. 1981. *Third Palestine: A Regional Study in Byzantine Urbanization* (Washington, DC).

Haas, C. 1997. *Alexandria in Late Antiquity: Topography and Social Conflict* (Baltimore and London).

Haiman, M. 1995. 'Agriculture and Nomad-State Relations in the Negev Desert in the Byzantine and Early Islamic Periods', *BASOR* 297: 29–53.

Haldon, J. 1992. 'The Works of Anastasius of Sinai: A Key Source for the History of Seventh-Century Mediterranean Society and Belief'. In *The Byzantine and Early Islamic Near East I: Problems in the Literary Source Material (Papers of the first Workshop on Late Antiquity and Early Islam)*, ed. Averil Cameron and L. I. Conrad (Princeton), 107–47.

Halkin, F. 1984. 'Les moins martyrs du Sinaï dans le ménologe impérial'. In *Mémorial André-Jean Festugière: Antiquité païenne et chrétienne*, ed. E. Lucchesi and H. D. Safrey (Geneva), 267–73.

Harmless, W. 2004. *Desert Christians: An Introduction to the Literature of Early Monasticism* (Oxford).

Harvey, S. A. 2006. *Sensing Salvation: Ancient Christianity and the Olfactory Imagination* (Transformation of the Classical Heritage 42; Berkeley and Los Angeles).

Harper, R. P. 1995. *Upper Zohar, an early Byzantine Fort in Palaestina Tertia. Final Report of Excavations in 1985–1986* (Oxford).

Heather, P. 2006. *The Fall of the Roman Empire: A New History of Rome and the Barbarians* (Oxford).

Henninger, J. 1955. 'Ist der sogenannte Nilus-Bericht eine brauchbare religionsgeschichtliche Quelle?', *Anthropos* 50: 81–148.

——. 1958. 'Menschenopfer bei den Araben', *Anthropos* 53: 721–805.

Henrichs, A. 1972. *Die Phoinikika des Lollianos. Fragmente eines neuen griechischen Romans* (Bonn).

Hershkovitz, I. 1988. 'The Tell Mahrad Population in Southern Sinai in the Byzantine Era', *IEJ* 38: 47–58.

Heussi, K. 1916. 'Nilus der Asket und der Überfall der Mönche am Sinai', *Neue Jahrbücher für das klassische Altertum* 37: 107–21.

——. 1917. *Untersuchungen zu Nilus dem Asketen* (Texte und Untersuchungen zur Geschichte der altchristlichen Literatur 42; Leipzig).

Hirschfeld, Y. 1997. 'Farms and Villages in Byzantine Palestine', *DOP* 51: 33–72.

——. 2003. 'Social Aspects of the Late Antique Village of Shivta', *Journal of Roman Archaeology* 16: 395–408.

Hobbs, J. J. 1995. *Mount Sinai* (Austin, TX).

Hobsbawm, E. J., and Ranger, T. O. 1983. *The Invention of Tradition* (Cambridge).

Hoyland, R. G. 1997. *Seeing Islam as Others Saw It: A Survey and Evaluation of Christian, Jewish, and Zoroastrian Writings on Early Islam* (Studies in Late Antiquity and Early Islam 13; Princeton).

——. 2001. *Arabia and the Arabs: From the Bronze Age to the Coming of Islam* (London and New York).

Hunt, E. D. 1982. *Holy Land Pilgrimage in the Late Roman Empire, AD 312–460* (Oxford).

Isaac, B. 1984. 'Bandits in Judaea and Arabia', *Harvard Studies in Classical Philology* 88: 171–203.

——. 1988. 'The Meaning of Limes and Limitanei in Ancient Sources', *JRS* 78: 125–47.

——. 1990. *The Limits of Empire: The Roman Army in the East* (Oxford).

——. 1995. 'The Army in the Late Roman East: the Persian Wars and the Defence of the Byzantine Provinces'. In *The Byzantine and Early Islamic Near East III: States, Resources and Armies* (Papers of the Third Workshop on Late Antiquity and Early Islam), ed. Averil Cameron (Princeton), 125–51.

——. 1998. 'Postscript to "Bandits in Judaea and Arabia"'. In idem, *The Near East Under Roman Rule: Selected Papers* (Leiden and New York), 152–58.

——. 2000. 'Map 70 Pelusium-Ierusalem, Introduction'. On CD-Rom in Talbert 2000.

Jacobs, A. S. 2004. *Remains of the Jews: The Holy Land and Christian Empire in Late Antiquity* (Stanford, CA).

Jeffreys, E. M. 1986. 'The Image of the Arabs in Byzantine Literature'.

In *International Congress of Byzantine Studies* (New Rochelle, NY), 305–23.

Johnsén, H. R. 2007. *Reading John Climacus: Rhetorical Argumentation, Literary Convention, and the Tradition of Monastic Formation* (Lund).

Jones, A. H. M. 1964. *The Later Roman Empire, 284–602 A.D.*, 2 vols. (Norman, OK).

Kaegi, W. E. 1992. *Byzantium and the Early Islamic Conquests* (Cambridge).

Kaldellis, A. 2004. *Procopius of Caesarea: Tyranny, History, and Philosophy at the End of Antiquity* (Philadelphia).

Kamil, M. 1970. *Catalogue of All Manuscripts in the Monastery of St. Catherine on Mount Sinai* (Wiesbaden).

Karayannopulos, J. 1958. *Das Finanzwesen des frühbyzantinischen Staates* (Munich).

Kawatoko, M. 1998. *A Port City Site on the Sinai Penninsula: al-Tur. The Eleventh Expedition in 1996 (A Summary Report)* (Middle Eastern Culture Center in Japan).

——. 2004. 'Archaeological Survey in the Raya/al-Tur Area, South Sinai', *Al-'Usur Al-Wusta: The Bulletin of Middle East Medievalists* 16: 26–30.

——. 2005. 'Multi-disciplinary approaches to the Islamic period in Egypt and the Red Sea Coast', *Antiquity* 79: 844–57.

Kirk, G. E., and Welles, C. B. 1962. 'The Inscriptions'. In Colt 1962: 131–97.

Knauf, E. A. 1982. 'Vier thamudische Inschriften vom Sinai', *Zeitschrift des Deutschen Palästina-Vereins* 98: 170–73.

Kötting, B. 1980. *Peregrinatio Religiosa. Wallfahrten in der Antike und das Pilgerwesen in der alten Kirche* (2nd edn, Münster).

Kotsifou, Ch. 2007. 'Books and Book Production in the Monastic Communities of Byzantine Egypt'. In *The Early Christian Book*, ed. W. E. Klingshern and L. Safran (Washington, DC), 48–67.

Kouli, M. 1996. 'Life of Mary of Egypt'. In *Holy Women of Byzantium: Ten Saints' Lives in English Translation*, ed. A.-M. Talbot (Byzantine Lives in Translation 1; Washington, DC), 70–93.

Kraemer, C. J. 1958. *Excavations at Nessana*, vol. 3: *Non-Literary Papyri* (Princeton).

Krueger, D. 2005. 'Christian Piety and Practice in the Sixth Century'. In *The Cambridge Companion to the Age of Justinian*, ed. M. Maas (Cambridge), 291–315.

Lagrange, M.-J. 1899. 'Le Sinaï biblique', *Revue Biblique* 8: 369–92.

Lampe, G. W. H. 1961. *A Patristic Greek Dictionary* (Oxford).

Lane, B. C. 1995. 'The Sinai Image in the Apophatic Tradition', *St. Vladi-*

mir's Theological Quarterly 39: 47–69.

Lee, A. D. 1993. *Information and Frontiers: Roman Foreign Relations in Late Antiquity* (Cambridge).

Leemans, W., Mayer, W., Allen, P., and Dehandschutter, B. 2003. *'Let Us Die That We May Live: Greek Homilies on Christian Martyrs from Asia Minor, Palestine and Syria (c. A.D. 350–450)* (London and New York).

Leitzmann, D. H., and Aland, D. H. 1956. *Zeitrechnung der römischen, Kaiserzeit, des Mittelalters, und der Neuzeit für die Jahre 1–2000 nach Christus* (Berlin).

Lenski, N. 2002. *Failure of Empire: Valens and the Roman State in the Fourth Century A.D.* (Transformation of the Classical Heritage 34; Berkeley and Los Angeles).

Lewin, A. 1989. 'Roman Urban Defences in the East in Antiquity: the Case of the Negev'. In *The Eastern Frontier of the Roman empire: Proceedings of a Colloquium held at Ankara in September 1988,* ed. D. H. French and C. S. Lightfoot (Oxford), 295–309.

——. 2002. 'Il Negev dall'età nabatea all'epoca tardoantica', *Mediteranneo antico* 5: 319–75.

Lewis, N. 1987. *Nomads and settlers in Syria and Jordan, 1880–1980* (Cambridge).

Leyerle, B. 1996. 'Landscape as Cartography in Early Christian Pilgrimage', *Journal of the American Academy of Religion* 64: 119–43.

Liebeschuetz, J. W. H. G. 2001. *The Decline and Fall of the Roman City* (Oxford).

Lifshitz, B. 1971. 'Inscriptions de Sinaï et de Palestine', *ZPE* 7: 151–63.

Link, M. 2005. See Source Editions and Translations: Nilus, Pseudo, *Narrationes.*

Littmann, E. 1914. *Nabataean Inscriptions from the Southern Hauran* (Leiden).

Longo, A. 1965–1966. 'La Narrazione degli Abati Giovanni e Sofronio', *Rivista di studi bizantini e neoellenici* n.s. 2–3: 246–67.

MacDonald, M. C. A. 1995. 'Quelques réflexions sur les Saracènes, l'inscription de Rawwāfā et l'armée romaine'. In *Présence arabe dans le croissant fertile avant l'hégire,* ed. H. Lozachmeur (Paris), 93–101.

McCormack, S. 1990. 'Loca Sancta: The Organization of Sacred Topography in Late Antiquity'. In *The Blessings of Pilgrimage,* ed. R. Ousterhout (Urbana, IL, and Chicago), 7–40.

McLynn, N. 1995. 'Paulinus the Impenitent: A Study of the Eucharisticos', *JECS* 3: 461–86.

Magness, J. 2003. *The Archaeology of the Early Islamic Settlement in Palestine* (Winnona Lake, IN).

Mango, C. 1990. *Nikephoros, Patriarch of Constantinople: Short History* (Dumbarton Oaks Texts 10; Washington DC)

———, and Scott, R. 1997. *The Chronicle of Theophanes Confessor: Byzantine and Near Eastern History AD 284–813* (Oxford).

Maraval, P. 1985. *Lieux saints et pèlerinages d'Orient* (Paris).

———. 1997. See Source Editions and Translations: Egeria.

Markus, R. A. 1994. 'How on Earth Could Places Become Holy? Origins of the Christian Idea of Holy Places', *JECS* 2: 257–71.

Martindale, J. R. 1980. *The Prosopography of the Later Roman Empire, vol. 2 (A.D. 395–527)* (Cambridge).

———. 1992. *The Prosopography of the Later Roman Empire, vols. 3A–B (A.D. 527–641)* (Cambridge).

Marx, E. 1977. 'Communal and Individual Pilgrimage: The Region of Saints' Tombs in South Sinai'. In *Regional Cults*, ed. R. P. Webner (London), 29–51.

Mason, H. J. 1974. *Greek Terms for Roman Institutions* (Toronto).

Matthews, J. 1975. *Western Aristocracies and Imperial Court, A.D.364–425* (Oxford).

Mayerson, P. 1962. 'The Ancient Agricultural Regime of Nessana and the Central Negev'. In Colt 1962: 211-69 (repr. in Mayerson 1994a: 1–21).

———. 1963. 'The Desert of Southern Palestine according to Byzantine Sources', *Proceedings of the American Philosophical Society* 107: 160–72 (repr. in Mayerson 1994a: 40–52).

———. 1964. 'The First Muslim Attacks on Southern Palestine (A.D. 633–634)', *Transactions and Proceedings of the American Philological Association* 95: 155–99 (repr. in Mayerson 1994a: 53–98).

———. 1975. 'Observations on the "Nilus" Narrationes: Evidence for an Unknown Christian Sect?', *Journal of the American Research Center in Egypt* 12: 51–74 (repr. in Mayerson 1994a: 105–28).

———. 1976. 'An Inscription in the Monastery of St. Catherine and the Martyr Tradition in Sinai', *DOP* 30: 375–79 (repr. in Mayerson 1994a: 129–33).

———. 1978. 'Procopius or Eutychius on the Construction of the Monastery at Mount Sinai: Which is the More Reliable Source?', *BASOR* 230: 33–38 (repr. in Mayerson 1994a: 134–39).

———. 1980. 'The Ammonius Narrative: Bedouin and Blemmye Attacks in Sinai'. In *The Bible World: Essays in Honor of Cyrus H. Gordon*, ed. G. Rendsburg, R. Adler, M. Arfa, and N. H. Winter (New York), 133–48 (repr. in Mayerson 1994a: 148–63).

——. 1981. 'The Clysma-Phara-Haila Road on the Peutinger Table'. In *Coins, Culture, and History of the Ancient World: Numismatic and Other Studies in Honor of Bluma L. Trell*, ed. L. Casson and M. Price (Detroit), 167–76 (repr. in Mayerson 1994a: 173–82).

——. 1982. 'The Pilgrim Routes to Mount Sinai and the Armenians', *IEJ* 32: 44–57 (repr. in Mayerson 1994a: 183–96).

——. 1983. 'P. Oxy 3574: "Eleutheropolis of the New Arabia"', *ZPE* 53: 247–53 (repr. in Mayerson 1994a: 204–11).

——. 1985. 'The Wine and Vineyards of Gaza in the Byzantine Period', *BASOR* 257: 75–80 (repr. in Mayerson 1994a: 250–55).

——. 1986. 'The Saracens and the Limes', *BASOR* 262: 35–47 (repr. in Mayerson 1994a: 271–83).

——. 1987a. '"Palaestina" vs "Arabaia" in the Byzantine Sources', *ZPE* 56: 228–30 (repr. in Mayerson 1994a: 229–31).

——. 1987b. 'Urbanization in Palaestina Tertia: Pilgrims and Paradoxes', *Cathedra* 45: 19–40 (in Hebrew; in English in Mayerson 1994a: 232–49).

——. 1987c. 'Libanius and the Administration of Palestine', *ZPE* 69: 251–60 (repr. in Mayerson 1994a: 284–93).

——. 1988. 'Justinian's Novel 103 and the Reorganization of Palestine', *BASOR* 269: 65–71 (repr. in Mayerson 1994a: 294–300).

——. 1989a. 'The Meaning of the Word Limes (λίματον) in the Papyri', *ZPE* 77: 287–91 (repr. in Mayerson 1994a: 308–12).

——. 1989b. 'Saracens and Romans: Micro-Macro Relationships', *BASOR* 274: 71–79 (repr. in Mayerson 1994a: 313–21).

——. 1989c. 'The Word Saracen (Σαρακηνός) in the Papyri', *ZPE* 79: 283–87 (repr. in Mayerson 1994a: 322–26).

——. 1990. 'Towards a Comparative Study of a Frontier', *IEJ* 40: 267–97 (repr. in Mayerson 1994a: 342–46).

——. 1994a. *Monks, Martyrs, Soldiers and Saracens: Papers on the Near East in Late Antiquity (1962–1993)* (Jerusalem).

——. 1994b. 'Urbanization in Palaestina Tertia'. In Mayerson 1994a: 232–49.

——. 1996a. 'The Port of Clysma (Suez) in Transition from Roman to Arab Rule', *Journal of Near Eastern Studies* 55: 119–26.

——. 1996b. 'Some Observations on the Negev Archaeological Survey', *IEJ* 46: 100–05.

Meimaris, Y. E. 1986. *Sacred Names, Saints, Martyrs and Church Officials in the Greek Inscriptions and Papyri Pertaining to the Christian Church of Palestine* (Athens).

Meistermann, B. 1909. *Guide du Nil au Jourdain par le Sinaï et Petra* (Paris).

Mian, F. 1970. '"Caput vallis" al Sinai in Eteria', *Liber Annuus* 20: 209–23.

——. 1972. 'L'Anonimo Piacentino al Sinai', *Vetera Christianorum* 9: 267–301.

Micheau, F. 1995. 'Saʿīd b. al-Bitriq'. In *Encyclopaedia of Islam*, vol. 8, ed. C. E. Bosworth, E. van Donzel, W. P. Heinrichs, and G. Lecomte (2nd edn, Leiden), 853–56.

Milani, C. 1977. *Itinerarium Antonini Placentini: Un viaggio in Terra Sancta del 560-570 d.c.* (Milan).

Millar, F. 1981. 'The World of the Golden Ass', *JRS* 72: 63–75.

——. 1993. *The Roman Near East, 31 BC–AD 337* (Cambridge, MA).

——. 2007. 'Theodoret of Cyrrhus: A Syrian in Greek Dress?' In *From Rome to Constantinople: Studies in Honour of Averil Cameron*, ed. H. Amirav and B. ter Haar Romeny (Leiden).

Mohammed, A. 1978. 'The nomadic and the sedentary: polar complimentaries - not polar opposites'. In *The Desert and the Sown: Nomads in the Wider Society*, ed. C. Nelson (Berkeley), 97–112.

Moore, S. D., and Anderson, J. C. 1998. 'Taking it Like a Man: Masculinity in IV Maccabees', *Journal of Biblical Literature* 117: 249–73.

Morgan, J. R. 1993. 'Make-believe and Make Believe: The Fictionality of the Greek Novels'. In *Lies and Fiction in the Ancient World*, ed. C. Gill and T. P. Wiseman (Austin, TX), 175–229.

Moritz, B. 1916. 'Der Sinaikult in heidnischer Zeit'. *Abhandlungen der königlichen Gesellschaft der Wissenschaften zu Göttingen* (Philologisch-historische Klasse, n.F. 16.2; Berlin), 3–64.

Mouton, J-M. 1998. 'Les Musulmans à Sainte-Catherine au Moyen Âge'. In Bonnet and Valbelle 1998: 177–82.

Müller, A. 2002. 'Die Vita Johannes des Sinaiten von Daniel von Raithou: Ein Beitrag zur byzantinischen Hagiographie', *Byzantinische Zeitung* 95: 585–601.

——. 2006. *Das Konzept des geistlichen Gehorsams bei Johannes Sinaites: Zur Entwicklungsgeschichte eines Elements orthodoxer Konfessionskultur* (Tübingen).

Nau, F. 1902. 'Les Récits inédits du moine Anastase: Contribution à l'Histoire du Sinaï au commencement du VIIe siècle', *Revue de l'Institut Catholique de Paris* 1–2: 1–70.

——. 1912. Review of Agnes Smith Lewis, 'The Forty Martyrs of the Sinai Desert', *Revue de l'Orient Chretien* 17: 445–46.

——. 1913. 'Résumé de monographies syriaques', *Revue de l'Orient chretien* 8: 270–76, 378–89.

Nandris, J. G. 1990. 'The Jebaliyeh of Mount Sinai, and the Land of Vlah', *Quaderni di studi arabi* 8: 45–90.

Negev, A. 1969. 'The Chronology of the Middle Nabataean Period', *PEQ* 101: 5–14.

———. 1974. 'The Churches of the Central Negev: An Archaeological Survey', *Revue Biblique* 81: 397–420.

———. 1975. 'Elusa (Halutza)', *Revue Biblique* 85: 109–13.

———. 1976. 'The Early Beginnings of the Nabataean Realm', *PEQ* 108: 125–33.

———. 1977a. *The Inscriptions of the Wadi Haggag, Sinai* (Qedem 6; Jerusalem).

———. 1977b. 'A Nabatean Sanctuary at Jebel Moneijah, Southern Sinai', *IEJ* 27: 219–31.

———. 1981. *The Greek Inscriptions from the Negev* (Studium Biblicum Franciscanum 25; Jerusalem).

———. 1982. 'Christen und Christentum in der Wüste Negev', *Antike Welt* 13: 3–33.

Nevo, Y. D. 1991. *Pagans and Herders: A Re-examination of the Negev Runoff Cultivation Systems in the Byzantine and Early Arab Periods* (Midreshet Ben-Gurion, Negev).

Olinder, G. 1938. 'The Letters of Jacob of Serug: Comments on an Edition'. In *Lunds Universitets Årsskrift*, n.F. 34: 1–141.

Palmer, A. 1993. *The Seventh Century in the West-Syrian Chronicles* (TTH 15; Liverpool).

Parker, S. T. 1986. *Romans and Saracens: A History of the Arabian Frontier* (Winona Lake, IN).

———. 1987. 'Peasants, Pastoralists, and Pax Romana: A Different View', *BASOR* 265: 35–51.

———. 1989. 'The Fourth-Century Garrison of Arabia: Strategic Implications for the South-Eastern Frontier'. In *The Eastern Frontier of the Roman Empire: Proceedings of a Colloquium Held at Ankara in September 1988*, ed. D. H. French and C. S. Lightfoot (Oxford), 355–66.

———. 1997. 'Geography and Strategy on the Southeastern Frontier in the Late Roman Period'. In *Roman Frontier Studies, 1995: Proceedings of the XVIth International Congress of Roman Frontier Studies*, ed. W. Groenman-van Waateringe, B. L.van Beek, W. J. H. Willems, and S. L. Wynia (Oxford), 115–22.

———. 2000. 'The Defense of Palestine and Transjordan from Diocletian to Heraclius.' In *The Archaeology of Jordan and Beyond: Essays in Honor of James A. Sauber*, ed. L. E. Stager, J. A. Greene, and M. D. Coogan (Winona Lake, IN), 367–88.

Patlagean, E. 1977. *Pauvreté économique et pauvreté sociale à Byzance 4e-7e siècles* (Paris).

Patrich, J. 1995. *Sabas, Leader of Palestinian Monasticism: A Comparative Study in Eastern Monasticism, Fourth to Seventh Centuries* (Dumbarton Oaks Studies 32; Washington, DC).

Perevolotsky, A. 1981. 'Orchard Cultivation in the High Mountain Region of Southern Sinai', *Human Ecology* 9: 331–57.

Plepelits, K. 1996. 'Achilles Tatius'. In *The Novel in the Ancient World*, ed. G. Schmeling (Boston and Leiden), 387–416.

Price, R. M., and Gaddis, M. 2005. *The Acts of the Council of Chalcedon*, 3 vols. (TTH 45; Liverpool).

Quibell, J. E. 1912. *Excavations at Saqqara (1908-9,1909-10): The Monastery of Apa Jeremias* (Cairo).

Rabino, H. L. 1935. *Le monastère de Sainte-Catherine (Mont-Sinaï). Souvenirs épigraphiques des anciens pèlerins* (Cairo).

Rajak, T. 1997. 'Dying for the Law: The Martyr's Portrait in Jewish-Greek Literature'. In *Portraits: Biographical Representation in the Greek and Latin Literature of the Roman Empire*, ed. M. J. Edwards and S. Swain (Oxford), 39–68.

Rapp, C. 1998. 'Storytelling as Spiritual Communication in Early Greek Hagiography: The Use of Diegesis', *JECS* 6: 431–48.

——. 2005. *Holy Bishops in Late Antiquity: The Nature of Christian Leadership in an Age of Transition* (Transformation of the Classical Heritage 37; Berkeley and Los Angeles).

——. 2006. 'Desert, City, and Countryside in the Early Christian Imagination'. In *The Encroaching Desert: Egyptian Hagiography and the Medieval West*, ed. J. Dijkstra and M. van Dijk (Leiden), 93–110.

——. 2007. 'Holy Texts, Holy Men, and Holy Scribes: Aspects of Scriptural Holiness in Late Antiquity'. In *The Early Christian Book*, ed. W. E. Klingshern and L. Safran (Washington, DC), 194–222.

Rassart-Debergh, M. 1999. 'Sinai'. In *Late Antiquity: A Guide to the Postclassical World*, ed. G. W. Bowersock, P. Brown and O. Grabar (Cambridge, MA, and London), 697–98.

Reinink, G. J. 2006. 'Following the Doctrine of the Demons: Early Christian Fear of Conversion to Islam'. In *Cultures of Conversions*, ed. W. J. van Bekkum, J. N. Bremmer, and A. L. Molendijk (Louvain), 127–38.

Reizenstein, R. 1916. *Historia Monachorum und Historia Lausiaca. Eine*

Studie zur Geschichte des Mönchtums und der frühchristlichen Begriffe Gnostiker und Pneumatiker (Göttingen).

Ringshausen, H. 1967. 'Zur Verfasserschaft und Chronologie der dem Nilus Ancyranus zugeschriebenen Werke' (unpublished inaugural dissertation, Goethe-Universität zu Frankfurt am Main, Frankfurt).

Robin, C.J. 1999. 'Himyar'. In *Late Antiquity: A Guide to the Postclassical World*, ed. G. W. Bowersock, P. Brown, O. Grabar (Cambridge, MA, and London), 492–93.

Robins, W. 2000. 'Romance and Renunciation at the Turn of the Fifth Century', *JECS* 8: 531–57.

Roques, D. 2000. 'Les Constructions de Justinien de Procope de Césarée'. In *De Aedificiis: Le texte de Procope et les réalités*, ed. J.-M. Carrié, N. Duval, and C. Roueché (Antiquité tardive 8; Turnhout), 31–43.

Rosen, S. A. 1987. 'Byzantine Nomadism in the Negev: Results from the Emergency Survey', *Journal of Field Archaeology* 14: 28–41.

Rothenberg, B. 1970. 'An Archaeological Survey of South Sinai', *PEQ* 102: 4–29.

Rowton, M. 1974. 'Enclosed Nomadism', *JESHO* 17: 2–9.

Rubin, R. 1996. 'Urbanization, Settlement and Agriculture in the Negev desert – The Impact of the Roman-Byzantine empire on the Frontier', *Zeitschrift des Deutschen Palästina-Vereins* 112: 49–60.

——. 1989. 'The Debate over Climatic Changes in the Negev, Fourth-Seventh Centuries', *PEQ* 121: 71–78.

Rubin, Z. 1989. 'Byzantium and Southern Arabia – the Policy of Anastasius'. In *The Eastern Frontier of the Roman Empire: Proceedings of a Colloquium held at Ankara in September 1988*, ed. D. H. French and C. S. Lightfoot (Oxford), 383–420.

——. 1990. 'Sinai in the Itinerarium Egeriae'. In *Atti del Convegno internazionale sulla Peregrinatio Egeriae 1987 nel centenario della pubblicazione del Codex Aretinus 405 (già Aretinus VI, 3), Arrezo 23-25 ottobre 1987* (Arezzo), 177–91.

Rutgers, L. V. 1998. 'The Importance of Scripture in the Conflict between Jews and Christians: The Example of Antioch'. In *The Use of Sacred Books in the Ancient World*, ed. L. V. Rutgers, P. W. van der Horst, H. W. Havelaar, and L. Teugels (Louvain), 287–303.

Sahas, D. J. 1998. 'Saracens and the Syrians in the Byzantine Anti-Islamic Literature and Before'. In *Symposium Syriacum VII*, ed. R. Lavenant (Rome), 387–408.

Samellas, A. 2002. *Death in the Eastern Mediterranean (50–600 A.D.). The*

Christianization of the East: An Interpretation (Tübingen).

Schaefer, J. 1979. 'The Ecology of Empire: An Archaeological Approach to the Byzantine Communities of the Negev Desert' (unpublished PhD thesis, University of Arizona).

Schatkin, M. 1974. 'The Maccabean Martyrs', *Vigiliae Christianae* 28: 97–113.

Schiwietz, St. 1908. 'Die altchristliche Tradition über den Berg Sinai und Kosmas Indikopleustes', *Der Katholik* (4th series) 38: 9–30.

Segal, A. 1983. *The Byzantine City of Shivta (Esbeita), Negev Desert, Israel* (BAR International Series 179; Oxford).

——. 1988. *Architectural Decoration in Byzantine Shivta, Negev Desert, Israel* (BAR International Series 420; Oxford).

Segal, J. B. 1984. 'Arabs in Syriac Literature Before the Rise of Islam', *Jerusalem Studies in Arabic and Islam* 4: 89–124.

Servin, A. 1948–49. 'La tradition judéo-chrétienne de l'Exode', *Bulletin de l'Institut d'Egypte* 31: 315–55.

Ševčenko, I. 1966. 'The Early Periods of the Sinai Monastery in the Light of its Inscriptions', *DOP* 20: 255–64.

Shahid, I. 1984. *Byzantium and the Arabs in the Fourth Century* (Washington, DC).

——. 1986. 'Lakhm', 'Lakhmids'. In *The Encyclopaedia of Islam*, vol. 5, ed. C. E. Bosworth, E. van Donzel, B. Lewis, and Ch. Pellat (2nd edn, Leiden), 632–34.

——. 1989. *Byzantium and the Arabs in the Fifth Century* (Washington, DC).

——. 1995a. *Byzantium and the Arabs in the Sixth Century*, vol. 2 (Washington, DC).

——. 1995b. 'Salih'. In *The Encyclopaedia of Islam*, vol. 8, ed. C. E. Bosworth, E. van Donzel, B. Lewis, and Ch. Pellat (2nd edn, Leiden), 981-82.

Shaw, B. 1982–1983. '"Eaters of Flesh, Drinkers of Milk": The Ancient Mediterranean Ideology of the Pastoral Nomad', *Ancient Society* 13–14: 5–31.

——. 1996. 'Body/Power/Identity: Passions of the Martyrs', *JECS* 4: 269–312.

Shereshevski, J. 1991. *Byzantine Urban Settlements in the Negev Desert* (Beer Sheva).

Shick, R. 1995. *The Christian Communities of Palestine from Byzantine to Islamic Rule: A Historical and Archaeological Study* (Studies in Late Antiquity and Early Islam 2; Princeton).

Sivan, H. 1990. 'Pilgrimage, Monasticism, and the Emergence of Christian Palestine in the 4th Century'. In *The Blessings of Pilgrimage*, ed. R. Ousterhout (Urbana, IL, and Chicago), 54–65.

——. 2008. *Palestine in Late Antiquity* (Oxford and New York).

Skrobucha, H. 1966. *Sinai* (London).

Solzbacher, R. 1989. *Mönche, Pilger und Sarazenen. Studien zum Frühchristentum auf der südlichen Sinaihalbinsel – Von den Anfängen bis zum Beginn islamischer Herrschaft* (Münsteraner Theologische Abhandlungen 3; Altenberge).

Speyer, W. 1971. *Die literarische Falschüng im heidnischen und christlichen Altertum: eine Versuch ihrer Deutung* (Munich).

Stewart, Z. 1984. 'Greek Crowns and Christian Martyrs'. In *Mémorial André-Jean Festugière: Antiquité païenne et chrétienne*, ed. E. Lucchesi and H. D. Saffrey (Geneva), 119–24.

Stone, M. E. 1982. *The Armenian Inscriptions from the Sinai* (Cambridge, MA).

——. 1986. 'Holy Land Pilgrimage of Armenians before the Arab Conquest', *Revue Biblique* 93: 93–110.

Stuiber, A. 1966. 'Eulogia'. *Reallexikon für Antike und Christentum* 6, ed. Th. Klauster (Stuttgart), 900–28.

Talbert, R. J. A. 2000. *The Barrington Atlas of the Greek and Roman World* (Princeton and Oxford).

Talbot, A.-M. 2001. 'Les saintes montagnes à Byzance'. In *Le sacré et son inscription dans l'espace à Byzance et en occident*, ed. M. Kaplan (Paris), 263–75.

Teixidor, J. 1998. 'Les Nabatéens du Sinaï'. In Bonnet and Valbelle 1998: 83–87.

Thomas, J. P. 1987. *Private Religious Foundations in the Byzantine Empire* (Dumbarton Oaks Studies 24; Washington, DC).

Torp, H. 1964. 'Murs d'enceinte des monastères coptes primitifs et couvents-forteresses', *École française de Rome. Mélanges d'archéologie et d'histoire* 76: 173–200.

Trimingham, J. S. 1979. *Christianity among the Arabs in Pre-Islamic Times* (London and New York).

Tsafrir, Y. 1971. 'Monasticism at Mount Sinai', *Ariel* 28: 65–78.

——. 1978. 'St. Catherine's Monastery in Sinai: Drawings by I. Dunayevsky', *Israel Exploration Journal* 28: 218–29.

——. 1986. 'The Transfer of the Negev, Sinai and Southern Transjordan from Arabia to Palaestina', *Israel Exploration Journal* 36: 77–79.

——. 1993. 'Monks and Monasteries in Southern Sinai'. In *Ancient Churches Revealed*, ed. Y. Tsafrir (Jerusalem), 315–33.

Tsames, D. G., and Katsanes, K. G. 1989. *To Martyrologion tou Sina: periechei keimena kai metaphraseis peri tōn agōnōn, palaismatōn kai martyriōn tōn anairethentōn hagiōn paterōn en tōi theovadistōi orei Sina kai tēi sinaitikēi erēmōi hina mimēsamenei tēn aretēn tōn martyrōn toutōn kakei tōn stephanōn dynēthōmen autois koinōnēsai* (Thessaloniki).

Ubach, B. 1933. 'Le sacrifice de Néby Haroun au Sinaï', *Revue Biblique* 30: 79–81.

Urbainczyk, T. 2002. *Theodoret of Cyrrhus: The Bishop and the Holy Man* (Ann Arbor, MI).

Van de Vorst, Ch. 1920. Review of Heussi, *Untersuchungen zu Nilus dem Asketen*, *Analecta Bollandiana* 38: 419–23.

Van den Ven, P. 1908. 'Un opuscule inédit attribué à S. Nil'. In *Mélanges Godefroy Kurth*, vol. 2 (Paris), 73–81.

van Henten, J. W. 1997. *The Maccabean Martyrs as Saviours of the Jewish People: A Study of 2 and 4 Maccabees* (Leiden).

van Parys, M. 1988. 'Abba Silvain et ses disciples', *Irénikon* 61: 315–30.

van Steen, G. 1998. 'Destined to be? Tyche in Chariton's Chaereas and Callirhoe and the Byzantine Romance of Kallimachos and Chrysorroi', *L'Antiquité classique* 67: 203–22.

Vivian, T. 1999. 'Monks, Middle Egypt, and Metanoia: The Life of Phib by Papohe the Steward (Translation and Introduction)', *JECS* 7: 547–71.

Ward, W. D. 2009, 'From Provincia Arabia to Palaestina Tertia: The Impact of Geography, Economy, and Religion on the Sedentary and Nomadic Communities in the Later Roman Province of Third Palestine' (unpublished PhD thesis, University of California, Los Angeles).

Ware, K. 1982. 'Introduction'. In C. Luibheid and N. Russell, *John Climacus: The Ladder of Divine Ascent* (Mahwah, NJ), 1–70.

Watt, W.M. 1986. 'Kuraysh'. In *The Encyclopaedia of Islam*, vol. 5, ed. C. E. Bosworth, E. van Donzel, B. Lewis, and Ch. Pellat (2nd edn, Leiden), 434–35.

Weill, R. 1908. *La presqu'île du Sinaï: étude géographique et d'histoire* (Paris).

Weingarten, S. 2005. *The Saint's Saints: Hagiography and Geography in Jerome* (Leiden).

Weitzmann, K. 1982. *Studies in the Arts at Sinai* (Princeton).

Whitby, Michael. 1983. 'Theophanes' Chronicle Source for the Reigns of Justin II, Tiberius and Maurice (A.D. 565–602)', *Byzantion* 53: 312–45.

——. 1985. 'The Sangrius bridge and Procopius', *Journal of Hellenic Studies* 105: 124–48.

——. 1988. *The Emperor Maurice and His Historian: Theophylact Simocatta on Persian and Balkan Warfare* (Oxford).

Whittow, M. 1996. *The Making of Byzantium, 600–1025* (Berkeley and Los Angeles).

Wilken, R. L. 1992. *The Land Called Holy: Palestine in Christian History and Thought* (New Haven, CT).

Wilkinson, J. 1999. *Egeria's Travels* (3rd edn, Warminster).

——. 2002. *Jerusalem Pilgrims Before the Crusades* (2nd edn, Warminster).

Winkler, J. J. 1989a. 'Introduction to Achilles Tatius, Leucippe and Clitophon'. In *Collected Ancient Greek Novels*, ed. B. R. Reardon (Berkeley),170–75.

——. 1989b. Achilles Tatius, 'Leukippe and Kleitophon' (Translation). In *Collected Ancient Greek Novels*, ed. B. R. Reardon (Berkeley), 175–284.

Wipszycka, E. 1996a. 'Les aspects économiques de la vie de la communauté des Kellia'. In eadem, *Études sur le christianisme dans l'Égypte de l'antiquité tardive* (Rome), 337–62.

——. 1996b. 'Les clercs dans les communautés monastiques d'Égypte', *The Journal of Juristic Papyrology* 26: 135–66.

Wolska-Conus, W. 1962. *La Topographie chrétienne de Cosmas Indicopleustès: Théologie et science au VIe siècle* (Paris).

Woolley, C. L., and Lawrence, T. E. 1936. *The Wilderness of Zin* (New York).

Young, R. D. 1991. 'The "Woman with the Soul of Abraham": Traditions about the Mother of the Maccabean Martyrs'. In *"Women Like This": New Perspectives on Jewish Women in the Greco-Roman World,* ed. A.-J. Levine (Atlanta, GA), 67–81.

Youtie, H. C. 1936. 'Ostraca from Sbeita', *American Journal of Archaeology* 40: 452–57.

Zayadine, F. 1990. 'The Pantheon of the Nabataean Inscriptions in Egypt and Sinai', *Aram* 2: 151–74.

INDEX

Index Note: n indicates footnotes; nn indicates footnotes over a range of pages. Titles are abbreviated in sub-headings as follows: *Narrations* refers to Ps.-Nilus, *On the Slaughter of the Monks of Sinai and the Captivity of Theodulus*; *Report* refers to *Report Concerning the Slaughter of the Monks of Sinai and Rhaithou* (Ammonius